Springer Series on Cultural Computing

More information about this series at http://www.springer.com/series/10481

Arnold Vermeeren · Licia Calvi
Amalia Sabiescu
Editors

Museum Experience Design

Crowds, Ecosystems and Novel Technologies

Springer

Editors
Arnold Vermeeren
Delft University of Technology
Delft
The Netherlands

Amalia Sabiescu
Loughborough University London
London
UK

Licia Calvi
NHTV Breda University of Applied Sciences
Breda
The Netherlands

Additional material to this book can be downloaded from http://extras.springer.com.

ISSN 2195-9056 ISSN 2195-9064 (electronic)
Springer Series on Cultural Computing
ISBN 978-3-319-58549-9 ISBN 978-3-319-58550-5 (eBook)
https://doi.org/10.1007/978-3-319-58550-5

Library of Congress Control Number: 2017961738

Printed on acid-free paper

This Springer imprint is published by Springer Nature
The registered company is Springer International Publishing AG
The registered company address is: Gewerbestrasse 11, 6330 Cham, Switzerland

Arnold Vermeeren · Licia Calvi
Amalia Sabiescu
Editors

Museum Experience Design

Crowds, Ecosystems and Novel Technologies

Springer

Editors
Arnold Vermeeren
Delft University of Technology
Delft
The Netherlands

Amalia Sabiescu
Loughborough University London
London
UK

Licia Calvi
NHTV Breda University of Applied Sciences
Breda
The Netherlands

Additional material to this book can be downloaded from http://extras.springer.com.

ISSN 2195-9056 ISSN 2195-9064 (electronic)
Springer Series on Cultural Computing
ISBN 978-3-319-58549-9 ISBN 978-3-319-58550-5 (eBook)
https://doi.org/10.1007/978-3-319-58550-5

Library of Congress Control Number: 2017961738

Printed on acid-free paper

This Springer imprint is published by Springer Nature
The registered company is Springer International Publishing AG
The registered company address is: Gewerbestrasse 11, 6330 Cham, Switzerland

Foreword: Are We Ready to Listen to These Truths? Are We Ready to Act on Them?

What is common to the studies in this book is their user-centered design approach. As articulated by Vermeeren et al. (Chap. 15), it entails focusing on an audience, identifying a need through audience research (which often entails segmenting "The Crowd"), brainstorming design ideas that might fill that need, focusing on one or two solutions to prototype in simple form, testing and evaluating the results, and then adjusting and iterating. (Participatory and agile design processes, as detailed by Sabiescu in Chap. 13, are variations on this process, as is Design Thinking).

This is precisely what most museums fail to do.

How many museums prototype the exhibitions they put in their galleries? How many interview members of their community about future exhibitions in advance? We are not simply referring here to marketing campaigns. How many do so to help shape their interpretative strategy, which should ideally be a blend of analog and digital components? How many museums set experience goals that correspond to their community's own expectations and stated desires? How many then evaluate to what degree their exhibition met those goals, and then adjust and iterate accordingly?

Museums have so much to learn from Human–Computer Interaction (HCI), and the enormous scientific literature that has developed around User experience (UX), if we are only willing to do so.

Conversely, designers have to learn not to be intimidated by their museums as clients, but to hold our feet to the fire and force us to sacrifice some of our shibboleths, if only on a test or "pilot" basis, so we can dare find out what we don't know.

I have to state my fear. Reading the essays gathered in this volume, which is devoted to the potentially beneficial impact of human–centered design approaches to the museum field, these questions come to mind:

1. Are designers actually empowered to conceive of the most far-reaching visitor-centered changes to which they aspire, in order to ensure the continued vitality and relevance of the museum field?

2. Do they run the risk of not being bold enough—of being co-opted by their museum clients' entrenched power hierarchies and legacy systems?
3. Are we in museums ready to avail ourselves of human-centered design processes and really listen to the new truths that emerge from them—even if those insights force us to change some of our long-held traditions and cherished beliefs?

Too often, I have seen user-centered design practices stop short of the "ground-zero" of museum experience: the gallery door. Museums and galleries (the latter in the European sense of the term) often do hire audience research and marketing firms to create new strategic plans, glossy identity packages, and promotional partnerships that, at least superficially, acknowledge the four Key Themes of this book: engaging the public, cultivating diverse audiences, availing ourselves of the benefits of digital technology, and leveraging museums' roles as players in larger economic and cultural ecosystems. And yet the solutions these consultants provide often fall short of the transformative results they could attain. Why? Because they are hamstrung: they don't extend into the gallery. The changes stop short of the defining moment of the museum experience, the *sanctum sanctorum*. To actually impact that core dimension of museum experience is taboo.

Of course, that is not true of all museums. Over the past 20 years or more, history and science museums have made great strides in revamping their gallery presentations in light of audience research. They have parsed "The Crowd" into demo- and psychographic profiles, experience goals and learning styles, and revised their approaches accordingly. The best among them have recognized that this is an iterative process; in these museums, ongoing prototyping and evaluation are now a way of life.

Some art museums have followed suit; several are detailed in my recent book, *Creating the Visitor-Centered Museum*, co-authored with Mimi Michaelson[1]. But the level of inside-out transformation that Nina Simon evokes in her book *The Art of Relevance*[2] is still a far shore in museum practice. Too often we prioritize our mandate to hold and protect our collections and stop short of making them relevant to today's audiences, real or potential. Too often we are zoomed way too far in on our objects, and lose sight of what people less invested might know, think, or want from us. One benefit of this book is the variety of focal lengths it affords on the museum experience, and design's potential to embed us in the lives of communities that don't necessarily think about us very often at all.

In this light, Calvi and Hover's essay (Chap. 14) is instructive. When we pull our focus back from the individual museum and its obsession with its objects, we find a larger community outside that is largely indifferent to our obsessions, and needs a story, even a superstar, to motivate their interest. In the case of the rural Dutch region known as the Noord-Brabant, they were fortunate enough to have just such a

[1] Samis, P and Michaelson, M (2017) The visitor-centered museum. Routledge, New York and London.

[2] Simon N (2016) The art of relevance. Museum 2.0, Santa Cruz, CA.

global megastar—or at least a vestigial figment thereof—on hand: Vincent van Gogh. (Not every region, museum, or cultural site is so fortunate).

From there, the conflict moves inside the museum. A struggle emerges between the museum's role as protector of authentic objects and the "facts" around them and its role as a site of experiences—preferably extraordinary ones, because if not, why bother? Where on the continuum between dry historical data and vivid voice should we land? Do the options include creative dramatizations, even poetic license? Whose side are we on: the expert-curator's or the potential visitor's, undecided as to whether to pay attention or not? How do we mediate between them?

Similarly, in a proposal that would encourage people to use their mobile devices to respond to museum shows using grist from their own daily lives, Letícia Verona and her Brazilian colleagues (Chap. 11) implicitly ask the perpetual Millennial question: Is there a place for me (and my creativity) in the narrative? Or am I to be subjected yet again to passive homage to Great (most often) White (almost always) Men?

> Naturally, this also means curators' jobs would change: from handling museum content, they would now have to look through visitor-generated content to decide what should and should not be incorporated in the exhibits. (Verona, Vivacqua & Campos, Chap. 11, p. 234)

While that may be precisely the kind of practice that Simon (2016) advocates in her book and museum, it is a far cry from most curators' image of what they signed up or were trained for. In fact, at least in the case of art specialists, their training explicitly distanced them from crowd-sourced taste or values, focusing instead on markers of distinction defined by a limited circle of *cognoscenti.* So once again, as with van Gogh, the dream of inclusiveness smashes its boat on a hard rock of museum behavior: our self-important role as gatekeepers, maintainers of the exclusive. It is no surprise, then, that after detailing two challenges to the implementation of innovative technology projects in museums, Verona, Vivacqua, and Campos (Chap. 11) acknowledge that the third one may thwart innovation before it is even tried out:

> Conceptual resistance to use technology: The public should see the artwork with no filters or digital interference; Resistance from museum personnel to learn and use new technology. (Verona, Vivacqua & Campos, Chap. 11, p. 229)

For this challenge represents Top-Down Fiat, the Veto, the Non-Starter—and it is still more present than we like to imagine. In the face of such resistance, do designers demur and focus their attention elsewhere, or do museums give them the support they need to make a difference?

And what if they don't? What is the role of designers then? To speak truth to power? Or is the client always right?

How do we deal with visitors who no longer see museums as central destinations in and of themselves (as we who work in them invariably do), but rather as interchangeable components in a larger picture-puzzle: their self-curated day, date, or vacation?

Time to zoom out again—if only to escape the bell jar. Get some air.

One caveat: while most of the solutions proposed in this book are technology-based, we should not lose sight of the fact that they are themselves embedded in larger systems, ranging from the *interpretive ecologies* (Mannion et al., 2016) described by Sabiescu and Charatzopoulou in Chap. 16 to the cultural route of Hidden Gems proposed by Vermeeren et al. in Chap. 15. Even as our society depends daily on its digital devices and the unseen networks that connect them, we still live in our bodies and often do seek refuge in museums "to oppose the overload we experience".[3]

So, while digital apps take us on mobile adventures and open up trails of wonder for some, the vast majority of our visitors still default to analog first and foremost. The more we can design for blended environments that mix the virtues of analog and digital affordances in mutually reinforcing ways to foster a context for meaningful engagement with museum objects, the better off we'll be. And the more likely that our visitors will offer their own Return On our Investment, as they reach for their phones to document and share their moments of insight and emotional connection.

Berkeley, California

Peter Samis
Associate Curator, Interpretation
San Francisco Museum of Modern Art
San Francisco
USA

References

Mannion S, Sabiescu A, Robinson W (2016) Innovate or stagnate: Disrupting the conventional audio guide. Proceedings, MW2016: Museums and the Web, 2016

Simon N (2016) The art of relevance. Museum 2.0, Santa Cruz, CA

Samis, P and Michaelson, M (2017) The visitor-centered museum. Routledge, New York and London

[3]Testimonial by museum professional in Brazil, in Verona, Vivacqua & Campos, Chap. 11, p. 235.

Contents

Editors and Contributors

About the Editors

Arnold P. O. S. Vermeeren is Assistant Professor at TU Delft, Faculty of Industrial Design Engineering and Director of the Faculty's MuseumFutures Lab. He was educated as an industrial designer and has been involved in various EU-funded projects on User Experience (UX) as well as a large variety of museum experience-related projects. His current focus is on designing museum experiences for long term engagement, using novel technologies and making connections to the world outside the museum.

Licia Calvi is a Senior Lecturer and Researcher at the Academy for Digital Entertainment at NHTV University of Applied Sciences (Breda, the Netherlands), where she teaches courses in Interactivity and in Media Theory within the Master of Media Innovation. An interaction designer by education, she has been designing interactive systems for various purposes and different domains.

Amalia Sabiescu is a communication scientist with an interdisciplinary research track at the interface between information and communication technology (ICT), culture and development studies. Her research explores the integration, use and impact of ICT in cultural and creative practice, community contexts, and intersections with issues around citizen voice, participation, and social inclusion. She is currently affiliated with the Institute for Media and Creative Industries at Loughborough University London.

Contributors

Evy Ligia Ansems Eindhoven University of Technology, Eindhoven, The Netherlands

Panagiotis Apostolellis Virginia Tech, Blacksburg, VA, USA

Sophie Boonen Muzus, Delft, The Netherlands

Doug A. Bowman Virginia Tech, Blacksburg, VA, USA

Maria Luiza M Campos PPGI, Universidade Federal do Rio de Janeiro, Rio de Janeiro, Brazil

Brendan Cassidy University of Central Lancashire, Preston, UK

Katerina Charatzopoulou Independent Researcher, Berlin, Germany

Marjee Chmiel Virginia Tech, Blacksburg, VA, USA

Teresa Consiglio Dutch Open University, Heerlen, The Netherlands

Elisa Giaccardi TU Delft - Industrial Design Engineering, Delft, The Netherlands

Alastair Gill King's College London, London, UK

Moniek Hover Academy for Leisure, NHTV—Breda University of Applied Sciences, Breda, The Netherlands

Diana C. Issidorides NEMO Science Museum, Amsterdam, The Netherlands

Ianus Keller TU Delft - Industrial Design Engineering, Delft, The Netherlands

Vassilis-Javed Khan Eindhoven University of Technology, Eindhoven, The Netherlands

Rik van der Laan TU Delft - Industrial Design Engineering, Delft, The Netherlands

Effie Lai-Chong Law Department of Informatics, University of Leicester, Leicester, UK

Maria Mortati California College of the Arts, San Francisco, CA, USA

Sara Radice Department of Design, Politecnico di Milano, Milan, Italy

Janet C. Read University of Central Lancashire, Preston, UK

Marco C. Rozendaal TU Delft - Industrial Design Engineering, Delft, The Netherlands

Hung-Chu Shih TU Delft - Industrial Design Engineering, Delft, The Netherlands

Gavin Sim University of Central Lancashire, Preston, UK

Dagny Stuedahl Department of Journalism and Media Studies, Oslo and Akershus University College of Applied Sciences, OSLO, Norway

Emma L. Tonkin School of Electrical Engineering, University of Bristol, Bristol, UK

Gregory J. L. Tourte School of Geographical Sciences, University of Bristol, Bristol, UK

Raffaella Trocchianesi Department of Design, Politecnico di Milano, Milan, Italy

Selene Uras LastMinute.com, Chiasso, Switzerland; Milan, Italy

Letícia Verona PPGI, Universidade Federal do Rio de Janeiro, Rio de Janeiro, Brazil

Adriana S Vivacqua PPGI, Universidade Federal do Rio de Janeiro, Rio de Janeiro, Brazil

Leon A. Watts University of Bath, Bath, UK

Tom Wrigglesworth University of Bath, Bath, UK

Martijn van der Heijden Fabrique, Delft, The Netherlands

Lindsey van der Lans Eindhoven University of Technology, Eindhoven, The Netherlands

Gerrit van der Veer Lelystad, The Netherlands; Dutch Open University, Heerlen, The Netherlands

JungKyoon Yoon TU Delft - Industrial Design Engineering, Delft, The Netherlands; University of Liverpool—School of Engineering, Liverpool, UK

Chapter 1
Future Museum Experience Design: Crowds, Ecosystems and Novel Technologies

Arnold P. O. S. Vermeeren, Licia Calvi, Amalia Sabiescu, Raffaella Trocchianesi, Dagny Stuedahl, Elisa Giaccardi and Sara Radice

Abstract The museum world is rapidly changing from being collection-centred to being community-centred and for the public. Apart from broadening access to collections through, for example, digitisation initiatives, new ways of involving the public more meaningfully and at various levels have emerged. Experiences inside museums have become more engaging, by extending the experience beyond the physical visit, or by involving the public in various forms of crowdsourced stewardship of collections. In this book, we explore the design implications that go along with these developments, all concerned with diversifying and making the engagement of the public in museum experiences more rewarding. We focus on the design implications associated with museums reaching out to crowds beyond their local communities, on experimenting with novel technologies and on conceiving experiences embedded in connected museum systems and large institutional ecosystems. By looking at and reflecting on trends, we attempt to sketch a picture of how future museums will change and, particularly, how they will relate to their public as a result of responding to or embracing these trends.

A. P. O. S. Vermeeren (✉) · E. Giaccardi
TU Delft - Industrial Design Engineering, Landbergstraat 15, 2628 CE Delft, The Netherlands
e-mail: a.p.o.s.vermeeren@tudelft.nl

L. Calvi
Academy for Digital Entertainment, NHTV - Breda University of Applied Sciences, Hopmansstraat 1, 4800 DX Breda, The Netherlands

A. Sabiescu
Loughborough University London, London, UK

R. Trocchianesi · S. Radice
Department of Design, Politecnico di Milano, Via Durando 38/A, 20158 Milan, Italy

D. Stuedahl
Department of Journalism and Media Studies, Oslo and Akershus University College of Applied Sciences, 4 St. Olavs plass, N-0130 OSLO, Norway

A. Vermeeren et al. (eds.), *Museum Experience Design*, Springer Series on Cultural Computing, https://doi.org/10.1007/978-3-319-58550-5_1

1.1 Trends in Museum Experience Design

In the museum world, a number of trends can be recognised that have an impact on museum experience design. For example, there is a development from museums being collection-centred to being community-centred and for the public. Additionally, the public has started to become involved in museum visits in more meaningful ways, for example, due to an increase in digitisation initiatives. This is achieved by deepening experiential engagement during the visit, by extending the museum experience beyond the physical visit or by involving the public in content generation, objects classification or other forms of crowdsourced stewardship of collections.

This book concentrates on the design of museum experiences that integrate some form of digital and networked media. However, and despite our focus on digital mediation, we acknowledge that visitor-centeredness and connected practices have been a concern for museums (or at least some museums) well before the large-scale integration of digital technologies. In a section suggestively titled 'History repeats' from their seminal work on visitor-centred practices in museums, Peter Samis and Mimi Michaelson (2017) point out that already in 1987, the Art Institute of Chicago commissioned a focus group study to gauge insights about visitor experiences, attitudes and expectations from the museum visit. The findings of that study are not less relevant today: visitors asked for more contextual information and particularly wanted to understand why an artwork is considered valuable and important for the museum. This is not very different from what museum visitors seek today. What changed, however, is the variety and complexity of forms by which museums can follow up on these expectations—not as one-way information transmission but through experiential engagements that may, for instance, accommodate creative inputs, appeal to various senses and promote collaboration and sharing of experience. Specifically, we have identified a number of trends in museum experience design: (1) dialogical engagement of the public; (2) diversifying and broadening audiences, including the nameless 'crowd'; (3) the use of novel technologies, such as the Internet of Things (IoT) and Do-It-Yourself (DIY) technology; and (4) designing for museum systems and institutional ecosystems, rather than for individual museums only.

1.1.1 From Visits to Continuous Dialogical Engagement

Museums started off as institutions focusing on collecting and preserving objects, open for the public to come and watch. The primary purpose for visitors to come to the museum was to see the original objects. A first notable shift saw the museums move from a collection focus to a visitor focus and from a mission for objects preservation and access provision to a mission of offering meaningful engagements with the collection and rewarding learning experiences for their public. The concept of 'museum experience' is the pinnacle of this historical shift, as it implies a focus on the visitor and connections between visitor and objects rather than a focus on collections. In the course of time, new types of museum experiences gradually emerged. The degree of sophistication and immersion increased exponentially when experiences started to be enhanced by the integration of interactive and digital media. In many science and technology museums, for example, visitor engagement and participation are uplifted through the use of new media (e.g. video games, interactive installations and other forms of edutainment) to encourage visitors to engage with the content on exhibit, to experiment with the techniques on show and to appropriate the visiting experience by making it meaningful and memorable. This trend is being adopted also by art museums, where it is by definition more difficult to let visitors experiment with the collections. Recent examples include the Rijksmuseum in Amsterdam, where an augmented reality app called *Paint Job*[1] (launched in 2012 by creative agency Brilliant After Breakfast) allows visitors to play with the paintings on display by 'hijacking' their content. By reappropriating the painting in this way, art gets closer to the individual and it acquires a meaning that is more personal and may, therefore, resonate longer in the visitor's memory.

Over the course of time, visitor involvement mechanisms have given more space to visitor agency and creative intention, reaching out to models in which visitors are involved as consultants or partners in co-designing museum experiences or even museum exhibitions. For example, in 2010 the Kröller-Müller Museum in the Netherlands experimented with involving a younger audience and launched *Expose: My favourite landscape,*[2] curated by children who chose the artworks to be exhibited from a sample preselected by the museum. These types of initiatives gradually have increased the involvement of visitors in museums as well as the level of social engagement among participants. One of the more recent trends goes even further than this. It focuses on a sustained engagement of people with museums and fosters connectedness between museum practice and the everyday personal experiences of those visiting the museums. For example, the project *Digital Natives* conducted by the Center for Digital Urban Living at Aarhus University, Denmark, invited young people to express their culture and everyday practices in the creation of an exhibition (Iversen and Smith 2011). Another example is Forces of Change 1960–1975,[3] an exhibition at the Oakland Museum of California in which people worked with museum staff and teaching artists to curate the objects to be exhibited through the use of both personal objects and pieces from the collection. The rich exhibition material was meant to represent the diversity of cultures and lifestyles in California from 1960 to 1975. The participative ways in which visitors interact with museums also open up new models and ways of learning about and understanding heritage and museum content. Participatory

[1]http://theinspirationroom.com/daily/2012/rijksmuseum-paint-job/.

[2]http://editie2.kmmexpose.nl/.

[3]http://museumca.org/forces-of-change.

approaches mark the transition from museum-led interpretation (under the authority of curators) to two-way conversations around heritage (e.g. McLean and Pollock 2010) and towards a conversational learning approach (Baker et al. 2002).

In terms of designing for museum experiences, the question is what are the implications of this shift towards conversational learning and continuous dialogical engagement. The experiences to be designed have changed from 'experiencing the encounter with an object' to 'experiencing interactive exhibits', and now beyond that towards designing platforms that enable two-way dialogues, multi-user content creation, collaborative activities and social learning practices. Museum experiences are thus broadened to include, for example, direct user interactions with such platforms and communication across platforms as well as more diverse ranges of activities (e.g. creative, contemplative, visual and observational) performed through digital mediation. A noteworthy development is the shift from designing short experiences within the museum towards designing long-term dialogical relationships between the museum and its audiences. Such a shift also raises issues on how to deal with curation and control, finding the right balance between the needs of the museums and the needs of public audiences.

1.1.2 From a Focus on Individuals to a Focus on Crowds

Nowadays, it is widely admitted that the desire to establish social relationships and to be actively engaged in informal learning processes are among the main expectations according to which people decide to visit a museum (e.g. see visitor categories, such as explorers, as identified by Falk 2009). However, this realisation took time to crystallise, just like it took time for museums to distinguish among and engage differently with diverse types and categories of audiences. In the early days of museum practice, 'the visitor' was an undifferentiated individual, at most with some form of distinction conferred to scholars as a special type of audience. In time, various types of (social) groups, such as families and school classes, were distinguished, with the acknowledgement that each of these comes to the museum with different needs, interests and agendas. Local communities around museums gained attention as important audiences with which museums gradually started fostering better connections for strengthening their identity and anchoring it in the local territory.

With the emergence of the Internet came initiatives for involving citizens in museum affairs. Citizen involvement was not only seen as a way to give voice to communities and enable them to have a say in the way museum exhibits were interpreted but it was also a way to link the collections to the personal experience of these communities. For example, several museum initiatives focused on engaging local communities in telling stories about objects on display or the historical period from which objects originated (see for instance the *Object Stories* project at the

Portland Art Museum[4]). The emergence of new forms of communication and collaboration over the Internet and the exponential growth of social media has made the potential outreach of museums even bigger; indeed, so big that recently some museums have started exploring the possibility of engaging the crowd—people unrelated to the museum, the geographical area or the community in which it is embedded. The potential is there for museums to no longer address only local communities and on-site visitors but to become museums 'for the global citizen', as is stated in the 2020 Strategy of the British Museum (The British Museum 2015). The focus on crowds can be seen in terms of one-way or bidirectional communication (through growing communities around museum social media sites) and culminates in crowd involvement in processes that were once exclusively carried out by institutions. Museums worldwide have already experimented with various forms of crowdsourcing: from social tagging, labelling and transcribing manuscripts through crowd involvement to co-curated experiences and exhibitions. Crowdsourcing practices are rewarding on many levels: they enrich interpretive layers for museum collections, they strengthen relationships between museums and their publics and they make audiences feel more connected, more empowered and closer to culture and the arts. Yet, existing projects show that the breadth of these phenomena is not always enough to reverberate in long-lasting or significant impacts. Indeed, some studies indicate that crowd involvement and the outcomes of their participation are oftentimes reduced to just a handful of enthusiastic or dedicated participants (Eveleigh et al. 2014). The challenge for museum experience design is to find the right balance between seeing the crowd as an undifferentiated mass and taking into account a multitude of influential factors and a number of unknowns, especially with respect to the tastes, wants, needs and interests of a diversity of audiences.

1.1.3 From Printed Labels to DIY Technology and Internet of Things

Not so long ago, objects displayed in museums were labelled with printed boards. Subsequently, displays were introduced providing general information about parts of exhibitions, audio guides to guide visitors along displayed artefacts and, gradually, also iPads as interactive labels next to exhibited objects. The Internet of Things (IoT) movement (where objects, such as those in people's daily lives, become networked) can also be expected to lead to museum experiences that become integrated in people's daily practices—at home, in offices and schools, leisure environments and elsewhere: iBeacons are already used to augment the museum experience by merging the physical and the digital: social media to share museum experiences or to contribute impressions and even ideas and content for

[4]http://objectstories.org.

exhibits design (e.g. Iversen and Smith 2011); appropriation of paintings that are printed on mugs or T-shirts is now made easier by cheaper printing technology; 3D printing is already being used for making replicas of museum artefacts as tangible memorabilia (e.g. in the British Museum and the New York Metropolitan Museum). Yet another development is the inclusion of DIY technology, such as Arduinos (e.g. Calvi and Vermeeren 2015), allowing for both museum-organised and grassroots initiatives of citizen involvement to create museum experiences. What new opportunities arise with the advent of these new technologies? How much are they empowering grassroots initiatives compared to the pre-existing ones (like blogging or video sharing)? How can we design for museum experiences that become embedded in people's everyday practices and foster more enduring connectedness between museums and their publics? These are just a few of the questions museums are confronted with by the advent of new technologies.

1.1.4 From Designing Individual Displays to Designing for Museum (eco) Systems

Originally, museums were collections of objects on display. At a certain point in time, more attention started to be paid to the way objects were displayed or to interactive possibilities around the objects. However, the design focus remained at the level of individual objects. Later on, more integral approaches were needed to better market museums and attract new audiences. Museums needed to be branded; unique identities needed to be created for them. Thus, a start was made to design experiences around the museum as a whole, instead of around individual objects only. Thereafter, the trend evolved and shifted, moving from single museums to connected museums or to museums as part of large institutional ecosystems. Looking at current EU-calls in the field of cultural heritage, there is a striking focus on museums as part of systems of connected institutes. Partnerships and networks among museums and between museums and universities, libraries, archives or community organisations have a rich potential for spearheading innovative practices and broadening the outreach and public engagement in such practices. At institutional level, they open up unique opportunities for knowledge exchange and cross-fertilisation, enabling institutions to work in convergence for identifying social needs and priorities for growth and innovation and then proposing innovative ways to meet them.

Such partnerships and networks present unique opportunities but also challenges, especially as they operate beyond the comfort zones of routine practices and processes. For instance, as part of the YOUmedia Learning Lab network,[5] the Dallas Museum of Art and the Perot Museum of Nature and Science teamed up to establish a learning lab for teens, following the principles of connected learning

[5]http://youmedia.org.

(Ito et al. 2013) and emulating the early model initiated by the YOUmedia Chicago learning lab, at the Harold Washington Public Library in Chicago (see Sebring et al. 2013). This partnership between an art and a science museum encouraged innovative explorations of convergences between art and science education. At the same time, it also meant that staff from both institutions were exploring unknown terrain and had to learn on the go how to create an experiential space for teens that enabled exploration of science and art confluences. One of the innovative approaches taken was that the Dallas Learning Lab was designed and implemented through the involvement of teens. The founders launched a survey to hear their views and collaborated with a Teen Advisory Council throughout the whole design phase, and further after the lab came into being. This example shows that partnerships between museums are deeply rewarding for multilateral thinking and innovation. Yet, designing for out-of-the-box informal learning experiences that cross disciplinary boundaries also requires out-of-the-box ideas as institutions are moving into unknown territory. In terms of designing for museum experiences, this trend implies that designers need to think further and beyond the visitor's experiences before, during and after a museum visit. Design needs to be rooted in a holistic vision that locates visitor experiences within a system of connected institutes without, however, losing sight of the museum's role within this system. The examples above show only some of the challenges this vision poses to museum experience design processes; more examples will be explored and discussed in this book.

1.2 Developing the Book Structure

A workshop was conducted at the CHI 2016 conference[6] to discuss viewpoints on the central theme of the book—how museum experience design practices are changing at present and which are the most influential factors that impact upon these changes in practice. A call for position papers (Vermeeren et al. 2016) was launched to invite potential chapter authors to submit position papers inspired by the trends discussed in Sect. 1.1. From the position papers, four themes emerged that were taken as inspiration for developing a brainstorm game to stimulate discussions among the various workshop participants. The themes were:

1. *Engaging the public*: this is about investigating the diverse modalities of engagement that museums can put forth for their visitors to make their visit (or related interaction with the physical and web presence of the museum) a memorable experience;
2. *Crowds—diverse audiences*: broadening the focus on the diverse types of museum audiences to include a more heterogeneous and somehow undifferentiated mass of people—the crowd;

[6]http://chi2016.acm.org.

3. *Opportunities through technology*: shifting the focus from the audience to the technology that museums might use to engage them;
4. *Museums as part of an ecosystem*: a further broadening of the design focus to address the ecosystems museums are part of.

1.2.1 Future Museum Experience Game: A Structured Brainstorm Game

A card game was developed as a participatory design tool to be used during the workshop for engaging participants in developing museum experience ideas. The card game was intended to inspire participants to reflect on and discuss the themes of the book as a means to better align their contributions for later inclusion in the book. Through the game, we aimed to achieve the following four goals:

1. Discuss issues related to the main topic of the workshop;
2. Highlight some crucial topics and interpret them through different filters and from diverse points of view;
3. Trigger dialogue and exchange ideas and impressions among participants;
4. Envision metaphors and scenarios around new possible ways for extending cultural experiences to a wider audience.

We used the game to mediate analysis processes through discussion and reflection. The participatory and novel dimension of designing cultural experiences can be fostered by collaborative approaches such as those used in the designed game. McGonigal (2011) notices that collaboration in games is a hard task that requires three distinct efforts: cooperation, coordination and co-creation. The first effort describes a collective action towards a common goal (i.e. developing museum experience ideas), the second means sharing resources (in this case a set of shared requirements) and synchronisation, while co-creation is a generative act, aimed at creating something that is not achievable alone (i.e. inspiring each other to come up with creative ideas for museum experience design that fulfil the complex set of requirements posed in the game).

The game consisted of three stages: (1) selecting cards and choosing one item on each card (see Fig. 1.1); (2) developing museum experience ideas based on the selected cards and card items and (3) positioning museum experience ideas in diagrams presented on large sheets. In stages 1 and 2, participants worked in teams of two, three or four people, while stage 3 was a plenary activity, confronting all participants with the ideas of the other groups and then discussing and positioning these.

The development of the actual game cards was inspired by the four themes in combination with relevant literature. Cards were divided into six categories, each of which was identified by a unique colour and an icon (see Fig. 1.1). Each card contained a number of items to choose from, as well as space for creating an extra item if desired:

Fig. 1.1 The game cards set

1. 'Types of museums' cards (purple) provided examples of different types of museums to which the experience ideas can be applied. Each museum card contained the following items: general museums; natural history and natural science museums; science and technology museums and art museums.
2. 'Cultural experience' cards (orange) included four subcategories:

    a. *paradigms or metaphors* that can be used as rhetoric narrative, containing the items: wunderkammer, game, collage, portrait, diary and time machine;
    b. *narrative* approaches, with items: hypertextual, episodic, linear (sequential), open, didascalic, ludic, ironic, poetic;
    c. *interaction modalities*, with items: multimedia, tangible, natural, bodily, performative;
    d. *resulting experience realms*, as defined by Pine and Gilmore (1999, pp. 30–38), with items: escapist, aesthetic, playful, educational.

3. 'Aims of engagement' cards (red) included three subcategories providing examples of possible museum goals that imply:

    a. *connecting what is inside the museum to something outside the museum*, with items: local territories, everyday activities, information in the wild, contemporary culture, learning aims in schools;
    b. *connecting the crowds*, with items: creating transcultural and intercultural understanding, scalability from local communities to contexts beyond that community, connecting crowds to situated museum experiences;
    c. *connecting the museums into an ecosystem*, with items: trajectories of cultural experiences through a network (coherency across various cultural

offerings), convergence of different cultural experiences within a network (e.g. art and science).

4. 'Who to engage with' cards (blue) included the three subcategories:
   a. *audiences*, with examples: crowds across the world, non-specialist audiences, younger audiences, art lovers, various target groups at the same time;
   b. *stakeholders*, with items: schools, care institutes, municipalities, heritage houses, maker spaces, design agencies;
   c. *other museums* with whom the museum can engage thanks to the experience ideas, with items: identical museum types (e.g. art museums only), related museum types (e.g. science and education museums), very different museum types (e.g. art and natural history).
5. 'Digital technologies' cards (green) provided examples of inspiring emerging technologies: mobile technologies (including AR), wearable technologies (including VR), maker movement and Do-It-Yourself technology, Internet of Things.
6. 'Ways of engagement' cards (yellow) included three subcategories based on the classification of participatory activities given by Simon (2010). These provided examples of activities aimed at:
   a. *collecting and sustaining the collection (contributory project),* with examples: crowd involvement in preservation of digital heritage, crowdsourcing;
   b. *using the collection (co-creative project)*, with items: using artworks as source of creativity, communicating through art;
   c. and *spark dialogical engagement with crowds (collaborative project)*, with items: curation by the audience, audience determines arrangement of contents.

Each group checked one item per selected card and then positioned the cards on a template to create an overview of the starting points for their idea generation (Fig. 1.2; bottom-middle). In stage 2, each group used flip-over sheets for sketching their museum experience design ideas and then summarised the idea on sticky notes for use in stage 3 (Fig. 1.2; top-right and bottom-left). In stage 3, ideas of all groups were positioned on large sheets depicting two axes along which the ideas were to be positioned (Fig. 1.2; bottom-right).

Axes in the diagrams included:

- diagram 1: term on which the applied technology would be feasible (*now—5 years*) versus length of engagement (*one time experience—continuous dialogical engagement*);
- diagram 2: place of the experience (*single place experience—trajectory of related experiences through multiple institutes*) versus size and diversity of audience (*individual person as audience—various audiences participating together, including crowds*).

Based on the position papers and the discussions during the workshop, authors were invited to rework their position papers into book chapters for a specific part of the book, using the insights gained during the workshop.

Fig. 1.2 Pictures of the workshop—top-left: short presentations of position papers; top-right: small groups developing museum experience ideas (stage 2); bottom-left: ideas developed by one of the groups (stage 2); bottom-middle: group selecting cards and checking items (stage 1); bottom-right: positioning ideas on diagrams (stage 3)

1.3 Book Structure

The 11 papers originally submitted to the workshop have been expanded and complemented by new contributions from several workshop organisers and from participants who took part in the workshop in different roles (as a keynote speaker or as attendee without a position paper).

The book is structured along the four themes, offering an inverted funnel view on trends in museum experience design, starting from the specific focus on the museum public and widening up to encompass museum ecosystems.

1.3.1 Part 1: Engaging the Public

In this part, the focus is on ways of engaging the public so as to make their visit to the museum a meaningful and memorable experience. Each of the three chapters focuses on different facets of museum experiences and diverse engagement and technology design approaches, ranging from learning through social engagement in gaming and virtual environments to inviting audiences to experiment, create and share with peers and visitors. The red thread in all the chapters is a preoccupation with designing approaches and sociotechnical environments where audiences can connect in first person, not only with the collection but also with other visitors, and put through meaningful responses in interactive environments or through creative acts. Sociality, creation and sharing are three vectors proposed throughout the chapters as a means to further dialogical engagement with museum collections. In the first chapter, Apostolellis, Bowman and Chmiel propose the development of a framework to involve large groups of visitors to engage with complex educational material in museums. C-OLiVE is the simulation game they developed to validate their framework for orchestrated learning. Boonen, van der Heijden and Giaccardi discuss the notion of amateur practice as a way to engage the audience of novice visitors with the collection of the Design Museum in London. Sim, Cassidy and Read describe how children can be involved in designing museum experiences for their peers by using augmented reality (AR).

1.3.2 Part 2: Crowds—Diverse Audiences

In part 2, the focus is broadened: from the generic notion of 'museum public' to a more heterogeneous, though somehow undifferentiated mass of people, which we have identified as 'the crowd'. Designing for the crowd does not always entail addressing unnamed, unknown audiences with unilateral messages and experiences. On the contrary, it implies diversifying and enriching the visiting experiences to appeal to and engage varied segments of visitors and users in situated, virtual or blended contexts. The chapters in here focus on diverse ways of involving crowds as audiences but also as co-creators and co-designers. What comes out as a shared concern is the importance to understand the crowd closely, even profile and segment it, so that the experiences designed for them—from digital fruition to crowdsourcing initiatives—can be meaningful and rewarding for all categories addressed.

In the first chapter of this section, Maria Mortati advocates the use of artistic experimentation and participatory practices that involve the museum, artists and the public to develop museum exhibits that cater for deeper and more meaningful visitor engagement and enable museums to reach a more inclusive visiting public. Through an exploration of a series of experimental projects, Mortati also shows how museums may find it beneficial to rethink preconceived notions of what an audience is and, on this basis, identify new frameworks and strategies for public engagement. Tonkin, Tourte and Gill propose the use of cultural media mining and social sensors to provide relevant and accessible descriptors for information objects that can support the preservation of digital cultural heritage.

Van der Lans, Ansems and Khan argue that crowdsourcing can be used by museums to craft digital experiences, all the way from concept generation and design to development and content production. They exemplify this with a study in which paid crowdsourcing was used to design and develop a museum app.

Based on the analysis of this study, they put forth a series of reflections and recommendations for museums that want to involve crowds in their experience design practices. A different stance on crowdsourcing is proposed by Wrigglesworth and Watts in the context of historical institutions. The authors propose that, beyond its immediate functional role, crowdsourcing activities have the potential to provide a meaningful experiential engagement for participants. By purposefully designing crowdsourcing experiences that are engaging and meaningful, museums also come closer to fulfilling their ethical mission. This is attained by positioning crowdsourcing not only as a way to cater for stewardship of collections but also for fostering public engagement and benefit. Their study singles out key elements that add to the meaningfulness of crowdsourcing experiences and discusses their implications for design.

Based on their long-term engagement in teaching cultural heritage and design to students and practitioners, Van der Veer, Consiglio and Uras bring a fresh perspective to museum experience design. The authors put forth a structured definition of experience, which encompasses cognitive and affective dimensions as well as attitudes and behavioural intentions towards cultural heritage. After indicating the centrality of the subjective or personal element when creating an experience, the authors discuss the importance of effectively dealing with diverse audience intentions, interests and needs during the design process.

1.3.3 Part 3: Opportunities Through Technology

In this part, the focus shifts from the audience to the technology that museums might use to mediate novel types of experiences. The array of technologies now used in museums is incredibly broad and diverse, and this part makes no attempt at a representative coverage. In the selection of the chapters, it rather aims for illustrative and diverse cases of using technology in empirical contexts, complemented by analytical and reflective contributions on the role of technology in museum experience design. Thus, three of the chapters focus, in turn, on technological mediation in diverse contexts: linking museums to external sites for enhancing experiences of intangible heritage; adoption of new technology for sociality and interactivity in museums; and novel ways of employing mobile technologies for science learning in museums. A reflective chapter complements these studies, and tackles the implications of adopting a certain design approach for the development of new museum technology and experiences.

Effie Lai-Chong Law presents a case on the development of a location-based augmented reality app for an archaeological site in the UK, which aimed to connect the archaeological objects on display in a museum to the archaeological site a person was visiting. The broader issue of technology adoption by cultural institutions is discussed by Verona, Vivacqua and Campos, with a focus on how interactive and social technology can expand the outreach and social relevance of museums in the Global South. They illustrate this with the specific case of Brazilian institutions. Rozendaal, Vermeeren and Issidorides discuss lessons learned from applying mobile technologies for on-site assessment of visitor experiences in a science museum.

To close this section, Amalia Sabiescu provides a critical reflection on the implications associated with adopting a certain paradigm for museum experience design. After examining museum usage of user-centred, participatory and lean and agile design approaches, she discusses the relations between long-term engagement with a certain design paradigm and institutional change.

1.3.4 Part 4: Museums as Part of an Ecosystem

In part 4, the focus is further extended to address the ecosystems that museums are part of and the opportunities and challenges posed by designing for museum ecosystems. These can be systems of connected cultural institutions but may also refer to the way museums are embedded in sociocultural and economic environments that need to be taken into account holistically when seeking to design comprehensive, enriching experiences for museum patrons. The chapters in this part draw on different design initiatives to illustrate diverse approaches in designing for museum ecosystems. In addition, they provide novel insights, ranging from recommendations and considerations to inform museum practice to more theoretical reflections to expand the body of knowledge on museum experience design.

Calvi and Hover discuss the complexity of dealing with museums as part of a multifaceted ecosystem in relation to the *Becoming Vincent* project and highlight the dilemmas that they had to tackle along the way to bring the project to a successful completion.

The ecosystem may also include everything that comes before or after the actual museum visit. This provides opportunities for designing new experiences around, but related to, museum interactions. This broadened perspective raises questions regarding viable ways by which a museum experience can relate to its embedding context, and how these can be effectively taken into consideration during the design process. These questions are addressed by Vermeeren, Shih, van der Laan, Calvi, Yoon and Keller through the design case of an application for the Mauritshuis museum in The Hague (the Netherlands). The chapter describes the design process and proposals for connecting museums to young adults.

Sabiescu and Charatzopoulou propose that ecological frameworks can inform and support the design of digital learning experiences in museums. Through a case study on the design of digital learning experiences in a cultural history museum, they draw attention to two sets of considerations that carry design implications: the embedding of digital learning experiences in the museum ecosystem and the role of the museum in a broader education ecosystem.

Acknowledgements We would like to thank the participants in the workshop 'Involving the crowd in future museum experience design' at CHI 2016 for their inspiring contributions, and their efforts to turn their position papers into chapters for this book. A special thank you to Anita Kreugel for proofreading parts of the book. We would like to thank as well Helen Desmond (Springer Nature) for the pleasant and fluent collaboration in the preparation of the book, and Dagny Stuedahl for initiating this process.

References

Baker AC, Jensen PJ, Kolb DA (2002) Conversational learning: an experiential approach to knowledge creation. Greenwood Publishing Group, Portsmouth

Calvi L, Vermeeren APOS (2015) DIY platform for innovative small museum experiences. Paper presented in workshop cultural heritage communities: technologies & challenges at conference communities & technologies 2015, 28 June 2015, Limerick, Ireland

Eveleigh A, Jennett C, Blandford A, Brohan P, Cox AL, Eveleigh A, Cox AL (2014) Designing for dabblers and deterring drop-outs in citizen science. In: Proceedings of the 32nd annual ACM conference on human factors in computing systems-CHI '14. ACM Press, New York, pp 2985–2994

Falk JH (2009) Identity and the museum visitor experience. Left Coast Press, Walnut Creek, 2009

Ito M, Gutiérrez K, Livingstone S, Penuel B, Rhodes J, Salen K, Watkins SC (2013). Connected learning: an agenda for research and design. BookBaby

Iversen OS, Smith RC (2011) Connecting to everyday practices: experiences from the digital natives experiment. In: Giaccardi E (ed) Heritage and social media: understanding heritage in a participatory culture. Routledge/Taylor and Francis Group, London

McGonigal J (2011) Reality is broken: why games make us better and how they can change the world. Penguin, New York

McLean K, Pollock W (2010) The convivial museum. Association of Science-Technology Centers, Washington

Pine BJ, Gilmore JH (1999) The experience economy: work is theatre & every business a stage. Harvard Business Press, Boston

Samis P, Michaelson M (2017) Creating the visitor-centered museum. Routledge, New York and London

Sebring PB, Brown ER, Julian KM, Ehrlich SB, Sporte SE, Bradley E, Meyer L (2013) Teens, digital media, and the Chicago public library. Research report. University of Chicago consortium on Chicago school research. 1313 East 60th Street, Chicago, IL 60637

Simon N (2010) The participatory museum. Museum 2.0, Santa Cruz

The British Museum (2015) Towards 2020. The British museum's strategy. https://www.britishmuseum.org/pdf/Towards_2020-The_British_Museum_Strategy.pdf Accessed 30 Sept 2015

Vermeeren AP, Calvi L, Sabiescu A, Trocchianesi R, Stuedahl D, Giaccardi E (2016) Involving the crowd in future museum experience design. In: Proceedings of the 2016 CHI conference extended abstracts on human factors in computing systems. ACM, pp 3347–3354

Author Biographies

Arnold P. O. S. Vermeeren is Assistant Professor at TU Delft, Faculty of Industrial Design Engineering and Director of the Faculty's Museum Futures Lab. He was educated as an industrial designer and has been involved in various EU-funded projects on User Experience (UX) as well as a large variety of museum experience-related projects. His current focus is on designing museum experiences for long term engagement, using novel technologies, and making connections to the world outside the museum.

Licia Calvi is a Senior Lecturer and Researcher at the Academy for Digital Entertainment at NHTV University of Applied Sciences (Breda, the Netherlands), where she teaches courses in Interactivity and in Media Theory within the Master of Media Innovation. An interaction designer by education, she has been designing interactive systems for various purposes and different domains.

Amalia Sabiescu is a communication scientist with an interdisciplinary research track at the interface between information and communication technology (ICT), culture and development studies. Her research explores the integration, use and impact of ICT in cultural and creative practice, community contexts, and intersections with issues around citizen voice, participation, and social inclusion. She is currently affiliated with the Institute for Media and Creative Industries at Loughborough University London.

Raffaella Trocchianesi is Associate Professor at the Department of Design, Politecnico di Milano. Her field is design for cultural heritage: exhibitions and museography, new technology for narrative and cultural advancement, the relation of design to humanities. She is part of the scientific board of the PhD program in design. She is Dean Of the Specializing Master in Exhibition Design, is on the steering committee of the Humanities Design Lab and a founding member of the International Forum Design as a Process. She is member of the faculty at the Master's in Design for Creative and Cultural Industries, University El Bosque, Bògotà. She was supervisor of Phd thesis including "Sociality and Meaning Making in Cultural Heritage Field." and "Designing for participation within cultural heritage."

Dagny Stuedahl, dr. polit and Professor in Media Design at Oslo and Akershus University College of Applied Sciences, Norway. Stuedahl holds a MA in ethnology, and works within socio-cultural and socio-technical theoretical framework and with co-design methods on transmedia issues in the cultural heritage sector, science centers, and museums.

Elisa Giaccardi is Chair of Interactive Media Design at Delft University of Technology, Department of Industrial Design, where she leads the Connected Everyday Lab. She is one of the recipients of the TU Delft Technology Fellowship for top female scientists, and a speaker at TEDx on the Internet of Things. She is the editor of Heritage and Social Media (Routledge 2012) and author of the chapter "How memory comes to matter: From social media to the Internet of Things" (Routledge 2016). From her pioneering work in meta-design and participatory technology to the role of the non-human in the Internet of Things, her design research reflects an ongoing concern with design as a shared process of cultivation and management of opportunity spaces.

Sara Radice holds a PhD in design. She works in the cross field of design and cultural heritage, focusing on design strategies for audience participation in digital and physical settings. She has been involved consulting and teaching activities within public and private institutions, such as Politecnico di Milano, Historical Archive of Italian Psychology, metaLAB (at) Harvard, Santa Cruz Museum of Art and History.

Part I
Engaging the Public

Heritage fruition in museums is no longer a solitary and passive experience. Museums have become socio-cultural institutions, whose social role and mission is reflected in the way they offer their collections to visitors and engage them. The visiting experience lies at the heart of true museum appreciation.

In her recent book on "The Art of Relevance"[1], Nina Simon, who is considered a visionary for her audience-centred approach to design in museums, discusses how *relevance* can become the litmus paper for museums' success stories. Relevance is the golden ratio for determining what matters to the people a museum wants to target, and what matters often implies engaging them precisely to unlock this. To do so, practices and metaphors from theatre and performance are often used to stage the visit experience, one which not only makes people connect to the collection and to each other socially, but which also refers to meanings and values. This is when the experience can become truly meaningful for museum patrons.

The three chapters under this section, all deal with the issue of relevance and public engagement, in different ways.

Apostolellis, Bowman and Chmiel propose the development of a framework to involve large groups of young visitors with complex educational material in museums. In their chapter, the focus is on learning and social engagement using serious games and virtual environments. Their notion of *orchestrated learning* explains how the audience is encouraged to interact together when inside a 3D simulation game.

Boonen, van der Heijden and Giaccardi address the novice audience of the Design Museum in London and explore ways of engaging them and of encouraging repeat visits through the notion of amateur practice. In order to lower the barrier to design items fruition, the authors propose a design intervention in the form of a Design Library. The library lends some of their objects to novice visitors who can bring them home, make them part of their everyday life, reflect on them and

---

[1]Simon N (2016) The art of relevance. Museum 2.0, Santa Cruz, CA

document this reflection via a mobile app. These reflections are collected and displayed for others (not just other visitors, but also the museum staff) to share. In this way novice visitors extend their actual visit beyond the physical walls of the museum, develop a personal knowledge on the items on display and appropriate them by unlocking their meanings and values, and finally leave a social trace of this process for others to engage with. Though in a different way than in the previous chapter, in here also the direct involvement of the visitor is encouraged and considered key for staging a rich, personal and meaningful experience. Thus, both chapters exemplify a learning-by-doing approach to audience engagement: in the chapter of Apostolellis et al., by affording interactions in a virtual environment, and in that of Boonen et al. by intervening meaningfully in visitors' daily lives.

Sim, Cassidy and Read go a step further and describe involvement through design. Their audience of children is invited to design a museum experience for their peers using augmented reality (AR). This chapter connects well to that of Boonen et al., in that it also extends the experience beyond the museum walls and encourages visitors to remain engaged with the collection in their everyday life. This can be attained by embedding the experience into their own life and appropriating it through experimentation and interpretation.

Thus, these three chapters illustrate diverse facets of public engagement in museum experiences: in terms of the *audiences* they address (from children to middle school students, from novice visitors to a more general audience of art seekers) through *different technologies* (AR, VR and mobile apps) used in various ways to elicit *diverse forms of engagement*. However, they all entail a direct involvement of the public, often through hands-on interaction with collection items. Especially the last two chapters (Boonen et al. and Sim et al.), with an emphasis either on designing experiences for others (their peers as in the chapter of Sim et al.) or in re-appropriating the collection items but embedded in a different context (often the visitor's own life context), represent strong examples of practices that help unlock the real and deep meanings of such items for the individual involved. This is where Nina Simon's notion of relevance seems to be expressed at its best.

Chapter 2
Supporting Social Engagement for Young Audiences with Serious Games and Virtual Environments in Museums

Panagiotis Apostolellis, Doug A. Bowman and Marjee Chmiel

Abstract Considering the shift of museums toward digital experiences that can satiate the interests of their young audiences, we suggest an integrated schema for socially engaging large visitor groups. As a means to present our position, we propose a framework for audience involvement with complex educational material, combining serious games and virtual environments along with a theory of contextual learning in museums. We suggest that effective learning with school groups visiting museums can occur through the facilitation of coordinated activities of young participants with appropriately designed technological mediation. We use the term *orchestrated learning* to present our rationale on how such activities can lead to enhanced learning through increased motivation and social interactions. In order to validate our framework, we built a testbed application that supports collaborative gameplay of small and large student groups. The application, named *C-OLiVE: Collaborative Orchestrated Learning in Virtual Environments*, is a 3D simulation game that allows participants to learn the process of olive oil production. The game has been used so far in three studies with 710 students in schools, summer camps, and a museum. We describe the modes of visitor involvement that were designed and tested with middle school students in the different learning settings. Finally, we present our most important findings and discuss their implications for the design of interactive digital experiences for young audiences visiting museums. These findings serve both as evidence for the applicability of our framework and as a guidepost for the direction we should move to foster richer technology-mediated social engagement of young crowds in museums.

P. Apostolellis (✉) · D. A. Bowman · M. Chmiel
Virginia Tech, Blacksburg, VA 24060, USA
e-mail: panaga@vt.edu

A. Vermeeren et al. (eds.), *Museum Experience Design*, Springer Series on Cultural Computing, https://doi.org/10.1007/978-3-319-58550-5_2

2.1 Introduction

Museums are complex social and learning environments called to satisfy the diverse interests of large crowds during a limited time visit. One of their most popular audiences in our experience is school groups visiting the museum with some learning agenda or for free exploration. In either case, students usually explore the space by themselves or participate in small group activities (e.g., scavenger hunt type of games), largely deprived of the social interactions for the whole group afforded by the nature of the space. However, there is an ever-growing voice that calls for museums to nurture the social aspect of the museum experience. Kathleen McLean and Wendy Pollock advocate the social role of the museum, as a space oriented to community building by harnessing opportunities for social engagement (McLean and Pollock 2011). Deborah Perry suggests that the visitor's primary agenda during a museum visit is "having an enjoyable social experience" and learning is merely the vehicle by which visitors achieve their goal (Perry 2012).

Nonetheless, supporting social interactions between visitors is probably not the primary agenda for most museums. What drives their efforts is engaging the public with the museum content/exhibits. Such a goal can be achieved in various ways, but as was mentioned in the introduction of this part of the book, *relevance* is probably the most crucial factor. Relevance is also indispensably connected with the visitor's *interests and beliefs*, directly affecting their *motivation and expectations*, decisive factors of learning in museums, as postulated by Falk and Dierking (2000). We agree with Nina Simon's metaphor of relevance as a key to unlock a door that leads to a memorable experience, evoking powerful emotions by finding meaning in the content discovered behind that door (Simon 2016). This can be achieved by allowing visitors to play with the museum exhibits and explore their meaning and value either by incorporating them into their own lives, as, for example, suggested by the authors in Chap. 3, or by engaging them in the process of creating novel interactive experiences through participatory design, as suggested by the authors of the fourth chapter of this part of the book. Our approach, on the other hand, involves the use of technology itself as the means for young audiences to find relevance in the experience, by appreciating the medium of delivery (i.e., digital games and social play) rather than the content. Thus, we propose that large-group interactive digital games can increase audience involvement opportunities in museums, especially for engaging students socially while being exposed to complex educational concepts and processes.

Interactivity has, indeed, been shown to be a significant component of visitor satisfaction by means of enabling multisensory dialogue, exploration/discovery, cultural connections, empowerment, uniqueness, and construction of meaning (Adams and Moussouri 2002). Moreover, digital games and high-end technology have been an indispensable part of children's culture for years, both in their leisure time and even at school (Prensky 2001). Game-based learning, a subcategory of serious games (Zyda 2005), has been studied extensively, and there is a large volume of evidence about the effectiveness of using games as a means to intrinsically motivate learners using the fun factor (Malone and Lepper 1987) and facilitate their learning by situating them in simulated experiences (Squire and Jenkins 2003; Zyda 2005; Barab et al. 2009). Interaction and its impact on learning have also been studied in the context of virtual environments (VEs), one of the primary technologies used for simulating real-world experiences. There is an abundance of evidence about the effectiveness of VEs used both for individual learning (Dede et al. 2000; Roussou et al. 2006), but also in collaborative settings such as networked classrooms (Di Blas et al. 2006; Ketelhut et al. 2007). However, in most cases, participants are deprived of social interactions due to the distributed nature of the game (e.g., occurring on individual displays over the Internet, even if participants are collocated).

Quite a few attempts have been made to merge some or all of these themes in the museum arena (see Beale 2011 for an indicative list), but they are mostly addressed to individual or family learning experiences. "Mystery at the Museum" is such an interactive game designed for the Boston Museum of Science, attempting to leverage location-aware handheld devices to engage parents and their primary-through-middle school children more deeply with the museum exhibits by encouraging collaboration between the participants (Klopfer et al. 2005). Nonetheless, research conducted by various scholars using mobile devices in museums indicated that handheld devices might motivate users to be engaged with the exhibits, but tend to inhibit opportunities for social interaction (vom Lehn and Heath 2003) and socially and physically isolate visitors (Hsi 2003). Another example project addressed to school groups of 8- to 12-year-old students is "Multimedia Magic" employed at the Samsung Digital Discovery Center of the British Museum (Doll 2012). Once more, students were divided into groups of two or three and completed various activities using tablet computers and digital cameras, undermining the opportunity for social interactions within the whole group. Attempts to engage larger audiences are usually restricted to auditoriums, mostly with specialized and proprietary technology (e.g., Dannenberg and Fisher 2001), where social interactions are limited—if not prohibited—due to space constraints. We consider that existing affordable technologies can be exploited to benefit the social engagement and collaboration of large student/visitor groups for learning purposes.

Combining our expertise in developing educational experiences with state-of-the-art technology for large audiences (Christopoulos et al. 2009), investigating the impact of virtual reality (VR) on cognition (Ragan et al. 2012), and using digital media for teaching science in renowned educational organizations (Chmiel 2009), we came to appreciate the power of games and virtual reality to engage young audiences with cultural heritage. Thus, our position supports the potential to socially engage large student audiences with complex educational material by integrating these technologies in a museum context. In the following paragraphs, we first present the conceptual framework used as the basis of our position with support from the literature. We then present the theoretical approach that guided the design of a testbed application and the experimental approach we followed to validate our hypotheses, including the most important findings from our work so far. We conclude with design implications stemming from our work and the directions we suggest researchers should take to better understand the potential impact of the proposed framework for museums.

2.2 Conceptual Framework

After exploring the major theories about learning and interactivity, and research work conducted with collaborative virtual environments (CVEs) and serious games, we extracted from these, the elements that we think can nurture the type of free-choice learning happening in museums. More specifically, collaborative games and VEs are two technologies that have been extensively studied for their educational benefits, both for individual learning as well as for collaborative settings. Similarly, the *Contextual Model of Learning (CML)* is a framework from the museum studies arena that has been suggested to predict free-choice learning in such spaces (Falk and Dierking 2000). The authors have identified various factors affecting learning in informal education spaces, categorized under three contexts: the *personal*, the *social*, and the *physical*. The main premise of our framework is that the integration of the CML with collaboration in gaming VEs can assist in enhancing the museum visitor experience and in facilitating learning in (large) student groups. We consider only factors from the personal and social contexts of the CML, as the physical context refers to factors of the actual environment that are rather fixed for the suggested collaborative setup. This is due to the fact that we propose a specific physical context where students are participating in the interactive experience by sitting in an auditorium-style arrangement. Consequently, there was not much room for varying factors such as the orientation to or architecture of the physical environment.

2.2.1 *Framework Rationale*

Our decision to combine collaborative games and VEs with the CML stems from the fact that in a social setting, these can nurture learning in two different contexts: the *personal* and the *social*. The personal context includes all the elements and the CML factors that have been shown to affect the individual experience of the game/VE user or museum visitor. These elements have been connected to enhanced *engagement* (e.g., *interactivity* and *autonomy*), which in turn has been shown to increase learning in some situations. An example from the serious games arena is Malone and Lepper's theory of *intrinsic motivation* for improving learning outcomes by making learning more fun, and thus more engaging (Malone and Lepper 1987). Moreover, students' *active participation* with imaginary worlds that are ingrained in their cultural background—by means of *beliefs*, values, and *expectations*—is believed to increase their emotional involvement and consequently learning (Dede 2009);

an example from the realm of multiuser VEs. Similarly, the CML predicts the importance of *motivation*, by meeting visitor *expectations* and satisfying their *interests* (closely related with Simon's *relevance*), for increased learning through sustained engagement during a museum visit (Falk and Dierking 2000).

The social context involves the technological elements and CML factors that are believed to contribute to the enhanced social experience of the collaborative game/VE users or museum group visitors. Elements such as *social play/interaction* and *empathy* in collaborative computer-mediated environments have been shown to increase *social presence*, especially when participants are working with or competing against friends (Gajadhar et al. 2008). Even in distributed collaborative VEs, the sense of being together (social presence) has been shown to contribute to increased enjoyment, enthusiasm, and improved knowledge and skill acquisition (Di Blas et al. 2006). At the same time, the CML predicts that increased learning derives from the opportunities for *within-group mediation and facilitation* (by more expert peers or guides), afforded by the collocation of visitors in the museum space (Falk and Dierking 2000).

Figure 2.1 depicts our conceptual framework, which identifies engagement and social presence as significant contributors to learning, and illustrates how they are affected by the personal and social context of collaborative interactions between children and technology. We suggest that this framework is helpful in arguing for our proposed position, allowing us to better present the importance of these technologies for supporting situated learning and enhanced audience involvement of young visitor groups in museums.

It is one of the basic goals of our framework to assess the effectiveness of the integration of the elements of the involved technologies and the social context factors of the CML during collocated collaboration, for increasing social presence and eventually learning. Such elements and factors have been examined in isolation about their impact on learning, and we hypothesize that their integration bears considerable potential for the orchestration of learning, in collocated groups of students (such as the ones found in museum group visits). Following our research questions, we present our testbed application and elaborate on how *orchestrated learning* can harness the situated interaction of students in the same physical space.

2.2.2 Situated Orchestrated Learning

We use the term *orchestrated learning* to denote the type of learning that occurs through the intentional facilitation of coordinated collaborative activities within a VE. Others have used the same term to describe the "coordination of learning episodes," as a means of orchestrating the interactions between learners and resources within a classroom (Crook et al. 2010). Based on our own definition, we named our framework, and consequently our testbed application, *C-OLiVE: Collaborative Orchestrated Learning in Virtual Environments*. It has been shown that encouraging collaborative activities by design through the demand of

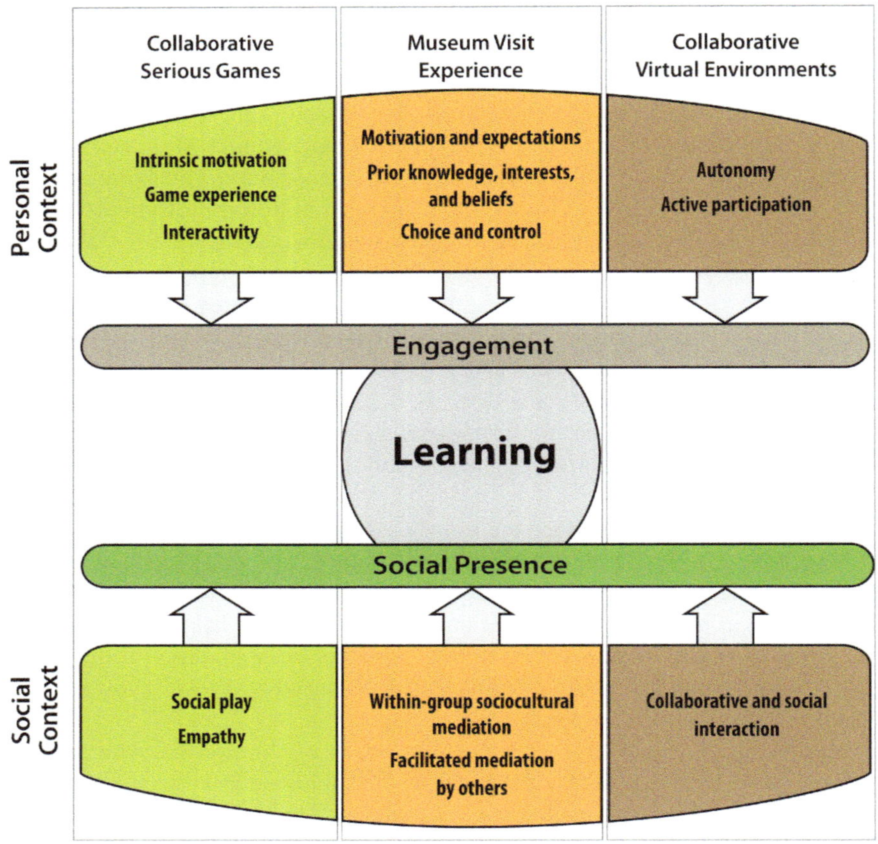

Fig. 2.1 The conceptual framework of our research position

intergroup coordination increases social (inter)actions between participants (Brown and Bell 2004), and according to our framework, we believe it will also have a positive impact on learning.

Moreover, through our literature review, we identified that the basic premise of learning occurring in VEs is the same as the one for free-choice learning spaces like museums. This has to do with the fact that the protagonist of the fictional world is engaged in realistic activities that can change the fate of the world (Barab et al. 2012), in a similar fashion that the visitor of a museum is engaged with authentic activities that reconstruct real-life experiences and concepts (Falk and Dierking 2000). Similarly, learning in C-OLiVE is achieved by engaging the students in authentic activities within a simulated environment and having them negotiate their actions in the physical space, afforded by the collocated collaborative nature of the game. Situating learners in authentic problem-solving activities is not only considered to be a major leverage of learning in physical contexts such as classrooms (Brown et al. 1989), but also one of the main benefits of learning within VEs (Dede 2009).

Furthermore, adopting this metaphor of learners as members of a musical orchestra has other connotations for our instructional approach, besides emphasizing the demand and benefits of coordinated action. Musicians are totally engaged in their performance and their actions are driven by their intrinsic passion for excellent acoustic results, similar to how games like C-OLiVE match the goal and process of the game with the learning outcomes. This engagement with free-choice tasks where extrinsic rewards are absent has been connected to increased sense of the *flow experience* (Csikszentmihalyi 1990) and also to enhanced learning due to its intrinsically motivating power (Malone and Lepper 1987). Additionally, the increased levels of fun and engagement deriving from peer collaboration within groups visiting museums (Falk and Dierking 2000), or working together in classrooms (de Freitas 2006), might in some cases reinforce learning outcomes.

Another attribute of orchestrated learning, as defined in this work, which applies aptly to CVEs and museums, is the rich sociocultural context experienced by the group members. Similar to how orchestra members participate in a shared community of practice, where common goals and understanding are necessary for its success (Lave and Wenger 1991), C-OLiVE provides a (virtual) community of workers where players have to negotiate their actions and plan a common route through distributed decision-making. Musicians can assume different levels of participation according to their skill level the same way that C-OLiVE allows players to assume more or less active roles based on their knowledge or gameplay capacity. Finally, learning is facilitated through interactions with more capable peers (musicians or players) or a tutor (conductor or curator), which has been shown to improve individual learning benefits (Vygotsky 1978). Likewise, Falk and Dierking consider the *sociocultural mediation by others*, either co-visitors or museum educators, a considerable contributor to the museum contextual learning experience (Falk and Dierking 2000).

2.2.3 Research Questions

In trying to investigate the effective merging of the elements used in our framework for achieving an enhanced museum learning experience for a group of students, we address the following research questions:

RQ1: What is the effect of the level of interactivity on learning in a gaming, collaborative VE (CVE) for more than two collocated participants?
RQ2: What is the interplay between level of interaction, game experience, social presence, and learning during within-group collaboration in physical space?
RQ3: What is the effect of culture, prior knowledge, and the style of information presentation (facilitated or not) on learning using a gaming CVE in a museum-type setting?
RQ4: How does the level of involvement of a large audience of students affect game experience, social presence, and eventually learning during collocated collaboration?

Besides this set of main questions, some other sub-questions related to factors that have been shown to affect informal learning were evaluated. More specifically, we investigated the effects of the experiment type on the outcomes; i.e., how an actual museum visit, and the expectations and motivation deriving from it, can affect enjoyment and learning, as compared to a controlled study environment. Also, we tried to gauge the students' interests and beliefs about the domain knowledge and make conclusions regarding the degree these have affected their overall experience and learning gains. Finally, motivated by our intercultural comparison, we looked at how the socioeconomic status of students, as defined by their school location and formal school assessment data, can impact learning outcomes.

2.3 Testbed Application

In order to validate our conceptual framework, we decided to develop a simulation game that supports collocated collaboration, initially for up to three players and then for a whole classroom. This is a virtual environment that teaches students about olive oil production using a game-style interface. The VE is a steam-powered olive oil factory of the mid-1900s with the actual machinery of the time, which players have to operate in order to produce olive oil. Figure 2.2 shows the virtual environment and interface for three co-players; a more detailed description of the

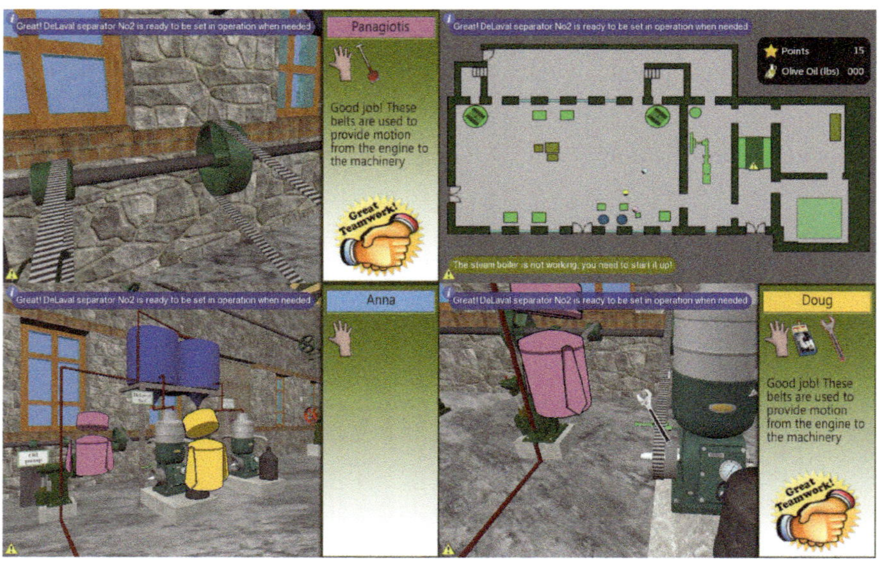

Fig. 2.2 The game interface for three players offers individual viewpoints in the virtual environment, an olive oil production factory

game and supported actions can be found in Apostolellis and Bowman (2014). We opted for a large-projected display that enables similar viewpoints for all participants and does not inhibit social interactions in any way, which is a common restriction when using immersive devices such as head-mounted displays. This application has been our testbed throughout the whole research, with modifications that enable us to respond to our research questions. Our audience is middle school students as both the dominant visitors of informal learning spaces during school field trips and avid users of gaming technology.

The topic was chosen for various reasons. First, we chose it for its suitability in enabling us to control the first two key factors of the CML's personal context (Falk and Dierking 2000): *motivation and expectations*, and *prior knowledge, interests, and beliefs*. Testing the game with different populations, having diverse cultural backgrounds, interests, and motivation to learn about the topic, allowed us to assess the effects of these factors on the game experience and learning outcomes (RQ3). Hence, the populations that we chose for our first two experiments come from the American and the Greek culture, with the latter having historically a much larger exposure to the domain knowledge, as one of the largest producers of olive oil in the world. Second, the nature of the application affords ample opportunities for collaborative activities, since the tasks that workers had to do to operate the machinery of the factory at the time involved quite a lot of manual labor. This allowed us to effectively control the level of interaction and/or collaboration, an essential component of the framework and our remaining three research questions. Last, the factory as a closed, well-defined space enables free exploration and manipulation of virtual objects increasing autonomy/control, an empowering feature both for museum meaning making (Adams and Moussouri 2002) and for learning through games and virtual environments alike (de Freitas 2006; Dede 2009).

2.3.1 Modes of Visitor Involvement with Digital Games

Since visitor involvement with digital exhibits can vary regarding the number of individuals that can interact simultaneously, we designed two major versions of the game. These versions were used to conduct three experiments with middle school students, investigating different combinations of research questions each time.

2.3.1.1 Small Group Interaction and Collaboration

The application was initially designed for one or three players to investigate how the level of interaction and collaboration could affect engagement and learning (RQ1 and RQ2). Students were exposed to the game in groups of three and assumed different levels of involvement depending on the experimental condition. In our first two experiments, we compared among three conditions: (i) students passively watching someone play the game, with some degree of facilitated involvement by the guide in the second study; (ii) one player interacting with the other two students negotiating and suggesting plans of action; and (iii) all three students playing together and performing the necessary tasks using game controllers. The first condition resembled the typical practice in museums where interactive exhibits visited by a guided group, such as (part of) a classroom, get a more passive exposure to the content of the digital experience. The second one was closer to what happens when the interactive exhibit supports only one user, in which case the other students gather around and try to participate through social interactions. The third condition was the one we suggested would afford greater engagement and social presence for all participants and eventually improved learning gains. Figure 2.2 depicts the interface with three players, after two of them perform a collaborative task (i.e., attach a belt between two pulleys).

2.3.1.2 Supporting Audience Involvement and Social Engagement

The second stage, involving a third experiment and a case study in a museum, demanded that the application support the interaction of a large group, such as a classroom (RQ4). The class was split into two groups: two *players*, who have direct agency in the game using game controllers (similar to the players in our first two experiments), and the *audience*, consisting of the rest of the class, interacting at different points with the game using tablet devices. Our initial plan involved comparing a fully passive condition for the audience, again similar to the common practice in museums, with a more involved one. However, after discussions with teachers, we opted for two interactive conditions (i.e., *low* and *high* involvement), as a means to keep the audience engaged and motivated to participate at all times. The collocated nature of the experience can also better nurture social engagement and interactions of visitors when these are somehow mediated by the technology.

The iPad interface in the low involvement condition allows audience members to attend to and register tasks happening in the game by clicking a button (see Fig. 2.3). At the end of the game, a scoreboard is presented with details about the fastest audience members, something that students are aware of from the outset for motivational purposes. Their choices, however, have no direct impact (i.e., agency) in the game.

The high involvement condition interface requires students to participate more actively in the game by providing their feedback at different prompts. Such prompts include responding to multiple-choice questions (see Fig. 2.5), pointing on the map to guide the players, or performing tasks directly in the game using the iPads. The audience's input is displayed on the main game interface (see the top-left window of Fig. 2.4).

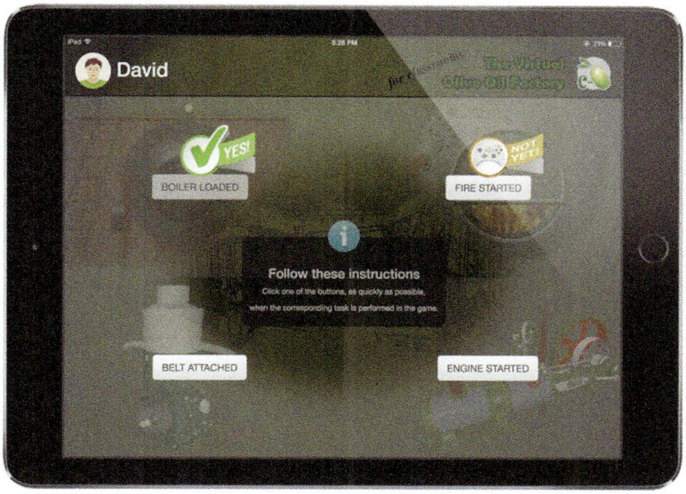

Fig. 2.3 Low involvement iPad interface

Fig. 2.4 The game interface for two players and high audience involvement, using iPads (responses appear on the top-left window), for a whole classroom experience

Fig. 2.5 High involvement iPad interface

2.4 Summary of Research Studies

We have conducted three experiments with 11- to 14-year-old students, in three different settings: summer camps, a museum, and schools. In the first two studies, we investigated the impact of collocated collaboration of small groups (three students each), varying the level of interaction/collaboration between the members. The third study was conducted with middle school classrooms, with students split into players and audience, varying the level of involvement of the audience. In all cases, we assessed the learning outcome, using a pre/posttest design (domain-specific quiz with multiple-choice questions), game experience, and social presence, using the Game Experience Questionnaire (GEQ) (Ijsselsteijn et al. 2007) and Social Presence Questionnaire (SPGQ) (de Kort and Ijsselsteijn 2007), respectively. These instruments were developed by the Game Experience Lab of the University of Eindhoven and were designed specifically for children. During our analyses, we started with exploratory statistics to identify and eliminate outliers, then ran basic correlations between our variables, and eventually used analysis of variance (ANOVA) tests to identify how the control variables affected the outcomes.

2.4.1 Study I: Small Group Game-Based Collaboration

The first study was conducted with 47 students during summer camps and after school hours in private middle school classrooms (see Fig. 2.6 for the experimental

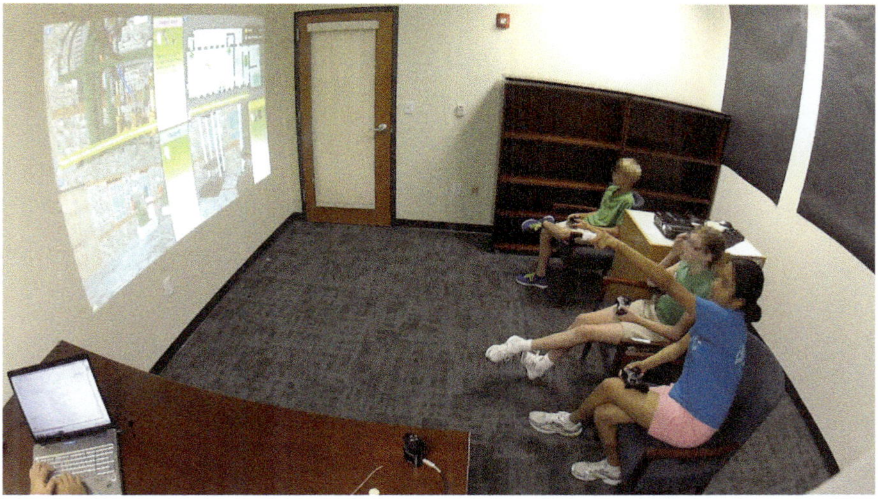

Fig. 2.6 The experimental setup of the three-player condition during our first study

setup). Analysis showed a significant association of learning gains with level of interaction, with higher levels of interaction (i.e., one or three players controlling the game) affording better score improvement in the quiz. We emphasize that this finding came only after taking into account all the variables of the experiment, using a path analysis where we predefined the directed dependencies of the variables based on prior research and our hypotheses.

Regarding game experience and social presence, which can potentially be indicators of an enjoyable social experience during museum group visits, we found that game experience (GE; measured as a construct of *immersion*, *flow*, *challenge*, *competence*, *tension*, *positive and negative affect*) was significantly higher when students had equal agency in the game (i.e., our three-player condition). Moreover, *behavioral involvement* (a measure of social presence—SP) increased with higher levels of control in both interactive conditions. On the other hand, having control in the one-player condition elicited more *negative feelings*, which is an indicator of how unequal control opportunities with digital exhibits can negatively affect the interaction (and eventually visiting) experience. A detailed report of all our findings from this study, including details about our path analysis, is included in (Apostolellis and Bowman 2014).

2.4.2 *Study II: Small Group Interactions Mediated by Culture*

The second study was conducted in Greece with 156 students—mainly in elementary grades in order to preserve our 11–14 age range—visiting a museum as

Fig. 2.7 Experimental setup of the three-player condition in a museum in Greece for our second study

part of a field trip. The setup (shown in Fig. 2.7) was very similar to our first study to enable comparison of results. We followed the exact same procedure as in the first study. We only changed the passive condition to one where the students' passive game experience was facilitated by an expert guide, providing prompts and asking questions at different points. We also gauged the students' perceived prior knowledge on the domain and expectations before the visit using the background survey, as well as their interest being satisfied and visit expectations being met using the GEQ right after the game.

Contrary to our hypothesis, the facilitated students revealed significantly greater learning gains over both interactive conditions. This was attributed to the overwhelmingly challenging nature of the digital discovery-based learning experience, which seemed beyond the cognitive capacity of this sample group. Our assumption was verified both from observations, but also from the lower performance of these students compared to the ones in the first study, despite their assumed prior knowledge due to higher culture-based exposure to the domain. We consider the main contributing factors for the contradictory findings to be the following: (a) the differences in the school grade affecting cognitive development, i.e., the cultural age being more important than the biological age (Wertsch 1985); (b) the culture-specific learning styles (Shade 1989); (c) the leading motive orientation (i.e., play or learn) (Hedegaard and Fleer 2013) influenced by the study venue; and (d) the significant cultural differences in terms of *individualism vs. collectivism* and *high vs. low uncertainty avoidance* (Hofstede et al. 2010) manifested during gameplay.

Game experience and social presence measures followed the same pattern, with increased *challenge* and *tension* in the interactive conditions negatively affecting learning, while increased collaboration opportunities elicited a higher sense of being together. Interestingly, perceived interest in the content and visit expectations being met or not did not affect learning, but was correlated with most GE and SP measures. A detailed account of this study can be found in (Apostolellis and Bowman 2015).

2.4.3 Study III: Audience Involvement with Digital Games

Our third study was conducted with 507 middle school students playing the game in classrooms, with 476 of them participating in all three study days (pretest, game, and posttest). The study was conducted inside the school's auditorium (Fig. 2.8) during normal school hours, in the context of four elective courses (six classes): Educational Technology, Business, AgriScience, and Family and Consumer Science.

There was a significant main effect of agency (in the game) on learning, with the players (i.e., students directly controlling the game) revealing significantly greater gains than the audience, in both conditions. We found no significant effect of involvement level on learning for the whole sample. However, learning gains were significantly higher for the high involvement group compared to the Low among

Fig. 2.8 Experimental setup of our third study, conducted in public middle schools

students who took the posttest 2 days after the game (N = 250), due to school schedule restrictions. This finding bears significant implications for informal learning settings, where retention of information, through a process of enculturation, is believed to be one of the added benefits of visiting museums (Falk and Dierking 2000). Furthermore, running the study in two schools with students of a highly different socioeconomic status (SES), allowed us to interpret the results in light of their varying academic performance (based on official school data). We found that students from the high SES school (N = 165) improved their knowledge of the domain, overall, significantly more than the ones from the Low SES school (N = 311). This also greatly impacts building interactive experiences for public spaces such as museums, which are visited by a diverse crowd.

Comparing GE measures for the players between the two conditions, it was interesting to find that the Low involvement condition afforded a better game experience. This might be attributed to the more vocal interventions of the audience observed in this condition (a 14% increase in talking time found through audio analysis of the recordings), substituted by the digital mediation through the iPads in the high involvement condition. This enabled Low-condition players to enjoy the game more—expressed through increased *positive affect* and *immersion*—but also made them feel more challenged as they had to attend to the audience's continuous feedback. Also, players revealed significantly higher levels of social presence, compared to the audience. A detailed description of this study can be found in (Apostolellis and Bowman 2016).

2.4.4 Case Study: Supporting Educational Activities in a Museum

The findings from the previous three studies were used to inform the design of our game to be used in a museum. The goal of this case study was threefold: increase the ecological validity of our audience interaction scheme; incorporate the game in an informal education activity for students; and test and refine the design guidelines we set as a goal at the outset. Some of the major revisions we developed based on previous experience were as follows: provide within-context information clips instead of an introductory video, include players as part of the audience by giving them iPads, enable on-the-fly switch of player/audience role, and orient the game more toward the engineering side of olive oil production. The last two points were thought to render the experience more appropriate for a science museum audience of middle-to-high school students, which was our objective for this case study.

We incorporated C-OLiVE in a minicourse at the Franklin Institute in Philadelphia, one of the most renowned science museums in the US. The minicourse consisted of two parts, the interactive game and some hands-on activities, where students can express/test their understanding of the process presented during the game. The setup of the game was identical to the one we implemented during

Fig. 2.9 Setup of student group during the case study in the museum

the third study (see Fig. 2.9), with two students controlling the game and the audience assisting with the iPads.

After the game was over, students gathered around a 9-foot long board placed on a table and participated in a collaborative activity where they had to reproduce the olive oil production process. To accomplish this, the class was split into four groups (one for every stage of the process) and used 3D-printed models of the actual machinery they saw in the videos and the game, and real-world artifacts such as olives, a belt, pulleys, pipes, etc. The task involved reading the descriptions on the board and placing the items in the provided placeholders, essentially reproducing the mechanical process that was introduced in the game. Figure 2.10 shows a fully completed board with all the items placed correctly, during a session at the museum.

Preliminary findings from this case study are mixed, both due to technical difficulties (preventing students from being fully involved in the game in some of the sessions) but also due to the different size of the groups. A common pattern we have observed is that in most groups, there were a few students that were fully immersed in the game, while the majority alternated between on- and off-topic tasks, which is detrimental to their understanding of the process. Also, students who revealed an increased comprehension during the after-game activity were not necessarily the players, like the previous studies have indicated, but rather the ones who were motivated to be engaged in the game. Gauging students' motivation to participate in most cases revealed either an interest in the topic (e.g., a girl audience member was ecstatic when offered an olive as a sample), or gameplay itself (e.g., a boy player

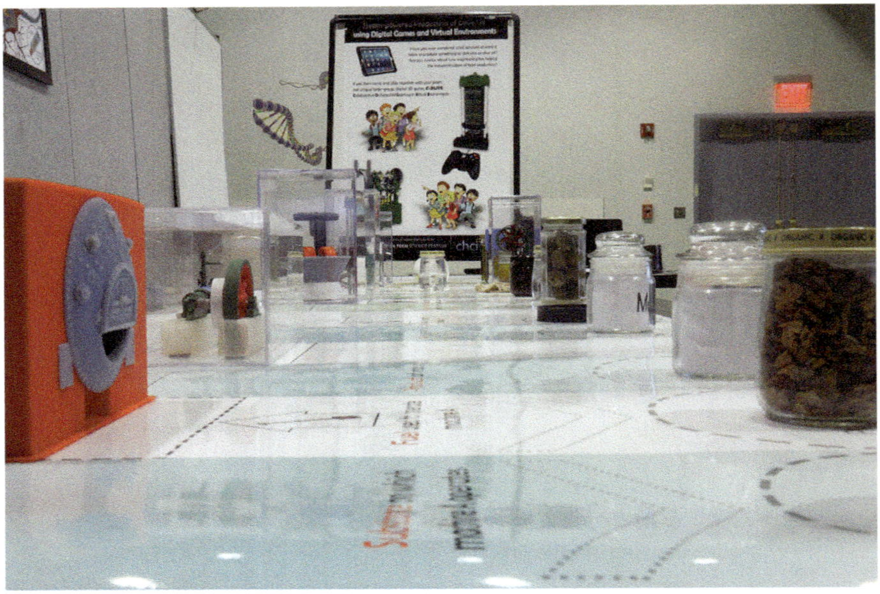

Fig. 2.10 Close-up view of a completed process board during the after-game activity

relayed that this was the second best course of the year after cooking, which he loves, because he likes games). Such anecdotal evidence clearly indicates the importance of finding relevance and matching interests for increased motivation, participation, and eventually learning. Moreover, students did not choose to participate in this program and most of them were not even aware of its theme before joining, which has an apparent impact on "free-choice" learning and expectations from the specific museum visit. Finally, size seemed to be a decisive factor regarding the level of engagement of the students, with students in smaller groups revealing sustained involvement for longer periods and decreased off-topic task incidents. A more detailed analysis of this case study will be presented in a future publication.

2.5 Implications for Designing Interactive Social Experiences for Student Groups

One of the main objectives of our research was to identify and suggest some design guidelines for effective large-group engagement with digital games in museums. Findings from our studies have given us a pretty good understanding of the ingredients of a successful group collaborative experience. As people from the museum world have suggested (Perry 2012), *collaboration* and *guidance* were found to be significant components of improved social and learning experiences during our large-group gameplay approach. Similar to Perry's recommendation, a game experience such as C-OLiVE enables visiting groups to stay together and contribute to the solution of a common problem, by encouraging discussion, negotiation, and reflection during problem-solving.

Also, guidance or facilitation was shown to be beneficial in keeping groups on-task and promoting understanding when misconceptions arose. Intrinsic motivation, although an important benefit of both (serious) games (Malone and Lepper 1987) and museum visits (Csikszentmihalyi and Hermanson 1999), was not found to be an adequate factor contributing to learning by itself during our studies. As others have argued (e.g., Kirschner et al. 2006), unguided discovery-based learning such as the type demanded during digital games can have detrimental effects on learning gains, if activities are not properly scaffolded with meaningful interventions and guidance. This was a clear finding from our second study, where students struggled to cope cognitively with the increased demands of the game and the collaboration. Moreover, the case study indicated that not all students have equal levels of motivation and interest in the topic being presented. A facilitator can identify and provide the missing link between what is relevant to those students and the theme of the collaborative experience.

A final observation affecting the effectiveness of such experiences has to do with the culture and the setting, and also the consistency of the group. We noticed there were apparent differences regarding student's teamwork attitudes between middle schoolers in a US small town setting (studies I and III), a Greek small town/rural setting (study II), and high school groups in an urban setting in the US (case study). It is difficult to make claims about the cause of the differences without further investigation, as it might be a setting effect, a culture effect, an age effect, or a combination of these. Nonetheless, our observations suggest that negative social influences are more predominant in the urban high school students, with the majority of them being more easily drawn into unrelated activities, as a means for compliance or to "fit in." This has also been found to be the case with other collaborative activities in museums, increasing the risk of off-task behavior with a companion (Packer and Ballantyne 2005), an effect that is magnified in larger groups.

2.5.1 Framework-Derived Design Guidelines

We suggest that the following design guidelines—addressing specific elements of our framework and indicating pathways to engagement and learning—can help improve the design of interactive experiences for large student groups.

- *Facilitate* the group's learning experience with frequent interventions to maintain motivation to participate, sustain engagement, and resolve misconceptions.
- Provide *equal opportunities for interaction* between participants or alternate between more and less active roles.

- Increase *agency/control* in the game, when possible, and limit passive intervals.
- Provide *within-context information* before troubleshooting instances to ensure equal levels of retention by all participants.
- Encourage *social interactions* either through the game interface (intrinsic) or by motivating participants with extrinsic rewards, if necessary.
- Take into consideration the audience, including their *cultural and societal background*, and also the setting of the informal learning experience.

This list is by no means exhaustive and constitutes just a first step toward understanding the inherent merit of digital games for the social engagement of large student groups. We acknowledge we still possess a limited view of the benefits of such experiences and suggest that further work should be carried out to better understand their potential.

2.5.2 Limitations

Although we carefully designed all experiments, there are some inherent limitations which should be taken into account when considering the aforementioned design guidelines. First and foremost, learning in informal contexts cannot be measured simply from the immediate outcomes, since a museum visit is mainly a trigger for a long-lasting learning process. The pre/posttest design used as an assessment tool in our studies bears the inherent limitations of measuring short-term learning outcomes. Ideally, learning in museums should be evaluated using sociocultural theory; i.e., understand how learning unfolds through the interplay between people acting in a social context and the "mediators" (i.e., discussions, tools, symbol systems, etc.) employed in these contexts (Schauble et al. 1997).

Furthermore, the engagement was only partially captured by the GEQ, as there was so much more happening during each game session. In all our experiments (besides the case study), we have been mostly focused on the measured "products" of the experience, mainly learning scores and self-reported game experience measures. However, as Perry (2012) suggested, "both process and product, both engagement and outcomes, are essential and intertwined components of museum visits." To address this gap in our latest experiment, we attempted to conduct audio analysis of the recordings and juxtapose the results with logged game data on a temporal scale (Miller and Quek 2012), as a means to identify behavior cues and patterns that might explain the connection between social engagement, game performance, and learning gains. However, the quality of the recordings and the setting (multiple voices overlapping in a large space) prevented us from getting usable results.

Finally, generalizations about culture should take into account the locality of the experiments. We have made rough interpretations about the differences we found between our US and Greek sample, but results cannot be generalized to the whole population of each culture. More subtle differences, such as the location regarding proximity to a metropolitan area or exposure to educational opportunities, can greatly affect results. We did try to take into account such subtleties when interpreting results in study II, but there could also exist disparities we have overlooked. Similarly, differences in socioeconomic status need great attention as this is, too, a continuum that greatly varies based on location and culture, and results can only be interpreted in the context of the specific sample presented in each research study.

2.6 Conclusion

We have argued for a need to socially involve large groups of students visiting museums in learning complex material collaboratively through digital games, as a growing part of their culture. Using our research framework, we set the basis for our position, grounding our arguments with literature on serious games, virtual environments for education, and contextual learning in museums. To investigate our ideas, we conducted three experiments and a case study with middle/high school students, and presented the most important findings as evidence. Overall, we found that learning gains are contingent on the profile of the visitors, with culture-specific learning style and cognitive development affecting the optimal means for information assimilation. Moreover, equal interaction opportunities and increased agency in the game are both contributing factors for sustained engagement during small- and large-group interactions with technology, affecting both the overall experience and the interconnectedness of the participants.

Summarizing our experiences from applying the framework and orchestrated learning approach with small and large student groups, we can share the following lessons regarding museum experience design. Starting with the challenges, we can testify that incorporating such an experience in a museum context is not an easy undertaking. Besides considerations regarding the design of the game itself, such as the age and background of the audience as mentioned before, one needs to account for logistical difficulties in setting up and administering a group experience like that. The throughput of student groups, the duration of engagement, and handling of the devices can be seen as burdens to the museum docent. Moreover, challenges may arise from the seemingly competing nature of exposing visitors to a wide range of artifacts and experiences during a typical museum visit versus exposure to the more concentrated acquisition of concepts and deep learning supported by our design; the latter believed to be more efficiently achieved through books and formal education approaches (Eisenberger 1999). The solution, we suggest, lies in combining focused initiatives in museums with specific learning goals, where museum experiences are an extension to regular school activities (Wishart and Triggs 2010). In this way, an interactive game like C-OLiVE can be seen as a learning opportunity to meaningfully integrate and disseminate knowledge across disciplines in an engaging way, also nurturing the collaborative aptitude of students, as testified by the teachers participating in our third study in public schools.

On the other hand, the rewards are mostly concerned with the learning benefit of our approach—as indicated by our findings—and the fun that students derive from such a social gaming activity. Coming back to Perry's words that a museum visit is primarily about "having an enjoyable social experience" (Perry 2012), we provided evidence that social presence not only can be rewarding by itself but can also contribute to increased learning. Nonetheless, learning outcomes—as measured during our studies—are not the sole or even the main goal of a museum visit. Having a memorable experience, one that encompasses a mixture of discovery, exploration, mental stimulation, and excitement, puts the focus on the process of learning, rather than the outcomes, and is believed to significantly contribute to a successful museum visit (Packer 2006). This idea of *learning for fun*, also one of the fundamental premises of learning games or serious games, is encapsulated in our orchestrated learning approach, in which we attempted to mentally and socially engage students in a simulated fictional scenario demanding collaborative exploration of a virtual world. Thus, we suggest that effective museum experience design should leverage the power of such theories as intrinsic motivation and flow experience (Csikszentmihalyi 1990; Csikszentmihalyi and Hermanson 1999), not just for the sake of discovering the physical space but also enabling gaming experiences in synthetic worlds that can bring large student audiences together in meaningful learning activities. Moreover, facilitation should be used to occasionally "break the flow" and—using the words of child-computer interaction expert, Panos Markopoulos (2016)—slow down the pace and allow for serendipity and social interactions to occur; a practice that was found to be beneficial during our case study in a museum.

As museums move toward a richer dialogical engagement with their audiences, both within their physical constraints but also with online and social media platforms, they should integrate new technologies to better serve and attract their young crowd's interest. Using the words of Laura Lott, President and CEO of the American Alliance of Museums, in a recent call to museum administrators, museums should "be welcoming and relevant and engaging with different and younger audiences who, frankly, experience things in different ways."[1] We hope that the work presented in this chapter contributes to a better understanding of the ways that interactive game experiences can be used toward this goal. Providing memorable experiences for young audiences and sustaining their involvement through socially rich experiences that speak in their own language has the potential to increase the relevance that these spaces have for the younger generations.

Acknowledgements We would like to thank all the Virginia Tech departments that supported our work over the years, such as the College of Engineering, the Center for Human-Computer Interaction, and the Institute for Creativity, Arts, and Technology. Also, Eric Ragan, Michael Stewart (CS); Reza Tasooji, Ellie Nikoo (School of Visual Arts); and Chreston Miller (University Libraries) for their assistance in designing the game, building the 3D models, and running the data

[1] *Laura Lott: Museums Are the Classrooms of the Future.* Article accessed online on 1/20/17 at: http://blooloop.com/feature/aam-president-laura-lott-museums-are-the-classrooms-of-the-future/.

analysis, respectively. We also want to thank Allison Loughlin from the Franklin Institute for giving us the opportunity to present the game as a case study in the museum. Last, but not least, the lead author deeply thanks his wife, Anna Delinikola, for her continuous support during all these years, also acting as a research assistant in some of the studies.

References

Adams M, Moussouri T (2002) The interactive experience: linking research & practice. In: International conference on interactive learning in museums of art and design. Victoria and Albert Museum, London

Apostolellis P, Bowman DA (2014) Evaluating the effects of orchestrated, game-based learning in virtual environments for informal education. In: Proceedings of the 11th ACM conference on advances in computer entertainment technology (ACE'14). ACM Press, Madeira, Portugal (Article 4)

Apostolellis P, Bowman DA (2015) Small group learning with games in museums: effects of interactivity as mediated by cultural differences. In: Proceedings of the SIGCHI conference on interaction design and children (IDC'15). ACM Press, Boston, pp 160–169

Apostolellis P, Bowman DA (2016) Audience involvement and agency in digital games: effects on learning, game experience, and social presence. In: Proceedings of the SIGCHI conference on interaction design and children (IDC'16). ACM Press, Manchester, UK, pp 299–310

Barab SA, Gresalfi M, Arici A (2009) Why educators should care about games. Educ Leadersh 67 (1):76–80

Barab SA, Pettyjohn P, Gresalfi M et al (2012) Game-based curriculum and transformational play: designing to meaningfully positioning person, content, and context. Comput Educ 58(1):518–533

Beale K (2011) Museums at play: games, interaction and learning. MuseumsEtc, Edinburgh

Brown B, Bell M (2004) CSCW at play: "there" as a collaborative virtual environment. In: Proceedings of the ACM conference on computer-supported collaborative work (CSCW'04). pp 350–359

Brown JS, Collins A, Duguid P (1989) Situated cognition and the culture of learning. Educ Res 18 (1):32–42

Chmiel M (2009) Game design towards scientific literacy. Int J Cogn Technol 14(2):32

Christopoulos D, Apostolellis P, Onasiadis A (2009) Educational virtual environments for digital dome display systems with audience participation. In: Proceedings of the 13th Panhellenic conference in informatics-workshop in education. Corfu, Greece, pp 265–275

Crook C, Harrison C, Farrington-Flint L, et al (2010) The impact of technology: value-added classroom practice: final report. British educational communications and technology agency (BECTA), Coventry, UK

Csikszentmihalyi M (1990) Flow: the psychology of optimal experience. Harper Perennial, London

Csikszentmihalyi M, Hermanson K (1999) Intrinsic motivation in museums: why does one want to learn? In: Hooper-Greenhill E (ed) The educational role of the museum, 2nd ed. Routledge, New York

Dannenberg RB, Fisher R (2001) An audience-interactive multimedia production on the brain. In: Proceedings of the connecticut college symposium on art and technology. Connecticut college, Connecticut, USA, pp 1–10

de Freitas S (2006) Using games and simulations for supporting learning. Learn Media Technol 31 (4):343–358

de Kort YAW, Ijsselsteijn WA (2007) Digital games as social presence technology: development of the social presence in gaming questionnaire (SPGQ). In: Proceedings of PRESENCE. pp 195–203

Dede C (2009) Immersive interfaces for engagement and learning. Science 323(5910):66–69

Dede C, Salzman M, Loftin RB, Ash K (2000) Using virtual reality technology to convey abstract scientific concepts. In: Jacobson MJ, Kozma RB (eds) Learning the sciences of the 21st century: research, design, and implementing advanced technology learning environments. Lawrence Erlbaum, Hillsdale

Di Blas N, Poggi C, Reeves TC (2006) Collaborative learning in a 3D virtual environment: design factors and evaluation results. In: Proceedings of the 7th international conference on learning sciences. pp 127–133

Doll S (2012) Digital technologies and visitng school groups. Master thesis. Department of communication sciences, University of Lugano

Eisenberger R (1999) The museum goer's motives: the social and the sublime. Visit Stud Today 2 (3):1–5

Falk JH, Dierking LD (2000) Learning from museums: visitor experiences and the making of meaning. AltaMira Press, Walnut Creek

Gajadhar BJ, De Kort YAW, Ijsselsteijn WA (2008) Shared fun is doubled fun: player enjoyment as a function of social setting. In: Markopoulos P (ed) Fun and games. LNCS, vol 5294. pp 106–117

Hedegaard M, Fleer M (2013) Play, learning, and children's development. Cambridge University Press, Cambridge

Hofstede G, Hofstede GJ, Minkov M (2010) Cultures and organizations: software of the mind, 3rd edn. McGraw-Hill, New York

Hsi S (2003) A study of user experiences mediated by nomadic web content in a museum. J Comput Assist Learn 19(3):308–319

Ijsselsteijn W, De Kort Y, Bellotti F, Jurgelionis A (2007) Characterising and measuring user experiences in digital games. In: Proceedings of the international conference on advances in computer entertainment technology (ACE). Salzburg, Austria, Austria, pp 27–30

Ketelhut DJ, Dede C, Clarke J et al (2007) Studying situated learning in a multi-user virtual environment. In: Baker E, Dickieson J, Wulfeck W, O'Neil H (eds) Assessment of problem solving using simulations. Lawrence Erlbaum Associates, Mahwah, pp 37–58

Kirschner PA, Sweller J, Clark RE (2006) Why minimal guidance during instruction does not work: an analysis of the failure of constructivist, discovery, problem-based, experiential, and inquiry-based teaching. Educ Psychol 41(2):75–86

Klopfer E, Perry J, Squire K, et al (2005) Mystery at the museum: a collaborative game for museum education. In: Proceedings of the 2005 conference on computer support for collaborative learning: the next 10 years. International Society of the Learning Sciences, pp 316–320

Lave J, Wenger E (1991) Situated learning: legitimate peripheral participation. University of Cambridge Press, Cambridge

Malone TW, Lepper MR (1987) Making learning fun: a taxonomic model of intrinsic motivations for learning. In: Snow RE, Farr MJ (eds) Aptitude learning and instruction III: Conative and affective process analysis. Erlbaum, Hillsdale, pp 223–253

Markopoulos P (2016) Towards adulthood: retrospective and reflection on IDC research. In: Keynote speech presented at the ACM interaction design and children conference. Manchester, UK

McLean K, Pollock W (2011) The convivial museum. Association of Science-Technology Centers (ASTC), Washington

Miller C, Quek F (2012) Interactive data-driven discovery of temporal behavior models from events in media streams. In: Proceedings of the 20th ACM international conference on Multimedia. pp 459–468

Packer J (2006) Learning for fun: the unique contribution of educational leisure experiences. Curator: Mus J 49(3):329–344

Packer J, Ballantyne R (2005) Solitary vs. shared: exploring the social dimension of museum learning. Curator: Mus J 48(2):177–192

Perry D (2012) What makes learning fun? Principles for the design of intrinsically motivating museum exhibits. AltaMira Press, Lanham

Prensky M (2001) Digital natives. Digit Immigr Horiz 9(5):1–6
Ragan ED, Endert A, Bowman DA, Quek F (2012) How spatial layout, interactivity, and persistent visibility affect learning with large displays. In: Proceedings of the international working conference on advanced visual interfaces-AVI '12. ACM Press, New York, pp 91–98
Roussou M, Oliver M, Slater M (2006) The virtual playground: an educational virtual reality environment for evaluating interactivity and conceptual learning. Virtual Real 10(3–4):227–240
Schauble L, Leinhardt G, Martin Laura (1997) A framework for organizing a cumulative research agenda in informal learning contexts. J Mus Educ 22(2–3):3–8
Shade BJ (1989) The influence of perceptual development on cognitive style: cross ethnic comparisons. Early Child Dev Care 51(1):137–155
Simon N (2016) The art of relevance. Museum 2.0, Santa Cruz, CA
Squire K, Jenkins H (2003) Harnessing the power of games in education. Insight 3(1):5–33
vom Lehn D, Heath C (2003) Displacing the object: mobile technologies and interpretive resources. In: Perrot,(d. 2007) X (ed) In: Proceedings of the international cultural heritage informatics meeting (ICHIM'03). Archives & Museum Informatics, École du Louvre, Paris, France
Vygotsky L (1978) Mind in society. Harvard University Press, London
Wertsch JV (1985) Culture, communication, and cognition: Vygotskian perspectives. Cambridge University Press, New York
Wishart J, Triggs P (2010) MuseumScouts: exploring how schools, museums and interactive technologies can work together to support learning. Comput Educ 54(3):669–678
Zyda M (2005) From visual simulation to virtual reality to games. Computer 38(9):25–32

Author Biographies

Panagiotis Apostolellis is a User Experience Design Analyst at the Technology-enhanced Learning and Online Strategies department at Virginia Tech. He is also an Adjunct Professor of Computer Science teaching a capstone undergraduate course on Human-Computer Interaction. He has worked professionally for many years in designing interactive experiences for museums focusing on cultural heritage and education. He holds a PhD in Computer Science and Applications from Virginia Tech, with a focus on large student group engagement during museum visits.

Doug A. Bowman is a Professor of Computer Science and Director of the Center for Human-Computer Interaction at Virginia Tech. He is the principal investigator of the 3D Interaction Group, focusing on the topics of three-dimensional user interface design and the benefits of immersion in virtual environments. He received a CAREER award from the NSF for his work on 3D Interaction, and has been named an ACM Distinguished Scientist.

Marjee Chmiel is the Director of Evaluation at Howard Hughes Medical Institute. Previously, Marjee worked at organizations such as the Smithsonian Institution, PBS, and National Geographic, leading development on award-winning educational resources. Marjee has also worked as an educational researcher, classroom teacher, and school-building leader. Her PhD is from George Mason University in Educational Research and Evaluation Methods.

Chapter 3
Design Is ~~Not~~ for Us: Engaging a New Audience for the Design Museum by Changing Their Expectations

Sophie Boonen, Martijn van der Heijden and Elisa Giaccardi

Abstract Current visitors of the Design Museum in London can be roughly divided into two types of people: experts with a background or specific interest in design and novices that are new to design. User studies in the museum revealed a lack of engagement with the novice visitors, which mostly has to do with their attitude when they enter the museum. They have relatively low expectations about their visit, assuming design is 'just not for them'. This chapter argues that in order to engage them, the museum should lower the perceived exclusiveness of design, broaden the amateur's view on what design can be, and create a lasting experience outside of the traditional museum visit. This alternative approach resulted in the proposal for a design intervention in the form of a 'Design Library'. Lending out part of the design collection to visitors enables self-documentation of user experiences through a mobile application. Collected stories are made available to (novice) visitors in the museum, broadening their definition of design. At the time of publication, the Design Library is still only a concept. Nevertheless, this project shows an interesting approach for a museum to change novices' attitude towards the subject, and thus, their expectations before they enter the exhibition.

3.1 Introduction

The Design Museum in London is a museum devoted to contemporary design in every form. In November 2016, the Design Museum moved from Shad Thames to the former Commonwealth Institute in Kensington, 34 years after its founding by Terence Conran. The move brought the non-governmental museum closer to the

S. Boonen (✉)
Muzus, Delft, The Netherlands
e-mail: sophie@muzus.nl

M. van der Heijden
Fabrique, Delft, The Netherlands

E. Giaccardi
TU Delft - Industrial Design Engineering, Landbergstraat 15, Delft, The Netherlands

A. Vermeeren et al. (eds.), *Museum Experience Design*, Springer Series on Cultural Computing, https://doi.org/10.1007/978-3-319-58550-5_3

cultural heart of London. It also gave the museum more space for exhibitions, retail and leisure. The goal is to attract a larger and wider audience, in line with the Design Museum's mission 'to inspire everyone to understand the value of design' (Chanter and Van der Heijden 2015). This ambition is not limited to its building. The museum aims to be 'the world's market square for ideas and design thinking, where audiences and professionals gather' (Chanter and Van der Heijden 2015).

As a step towards the move, the Dutch agency Fabrique designed the museum's new website in 2014. This was the start of a longer cooperation, including the design project executed by Sophie Boonen that is presented in this chapter. Boonen executed this project between September 2015 and June 2016 as her graduation project for the Master programme in Design for Interaction at the Faculty of Industrial Design Engineering (IDE), Delft University of Technology in The Netherlands.

The design process followed a design thinking approach: creative problem-solving by investigation, ideation, iteration and reflection. The focus of this project was to take user-centred design as an approach for developing ideas for engaging a larger audience with the Design Museum. The outcome of this project was the design of a service, the Design Library, which remains a concept at the time of writing this book chapter.

In this chapter, we first describe the project challenge in Sect. 3.2. During the project, studying related literature and making a comparison of museum exhibitions were all part of defining the project challenge. We give theoretical background to get an understanding of the notion of 'design expertise' and 'the role of objects in museums'. Section 3.3 highlights one of the many user studies conducted as part of this graduation project. The outcome of the user study led to reformulating and specifying the set project challenge, as described in Sect. 3.4. During the ideation phase of this graduation project, many possible solutions were created. Then iteration followed, a process of refining the concept with increasing fidelity. The solution—the Design Library—is presented in detail in Sect. 3.5, as well as how we evaluated its design. The data that resulted from the evaluation were used to determine further improvements of the concept (discussion at the end of Sect. 3.5) and draw conclusions in Sect. 3.6.

3.2 Defining the Project Challenge

At the outset of the project in 2015, the Design Museum and Fabrique had set the goal of improving the visitor experience in the then still unfinished new museum. In order to define a more specific project challenge, Boonen applied a combination of literature research and interviews with stakeholders.

An interview with Josephine Chanter, Head of Communications and External Affairs at the Design Museum, points out that visitors of the Design Museum can be roughly divided into two groups: expert and novice visitors (Chanter 2015).

1. **Expert visitors** are the (professional) design loving audience. They are familiar with different types of design. Their previous knowledge provides a frame of reference to understand and value design.

2. **Novice visitors** are a new audience that may be less familiar with the world of design. They often use a very limited definition of design—usually expensive furniture and/or fashion. They also have little experience in 'reading' it.

The museum's mission implies that the museum must attract and serve both these audiences. Also, attracting more 'design novices' becomes more important in view of the higher costs incurred by the new, larger building in Kensington.

3.2.1 Engaging Novice Visitors

Reaching this wider audience has been a challenge for the museum in the past years. Chanter remarks that the current reputation and programming of the museum is relatively specialist. People who visit the museum 'are mostly either people who are particularly interested in design or interested in the specific subject of the temporary exhibition' (Chanter 2015).

Attracting visitors to the museum is one challenge, engaging them when they do come is another. The museum's front of house staff notices a lack of engagement of novice visitors with the exhibitions. Chanter confirms this, as she refers to visitor surveys from recent years (The Audience Agency 2014). They revealed that a majority of Design Museum visitors tend not to come back after their first visit, which is an indirect result of a lack of engagement. Only 15% has visited the Design Museum before during the past year, for other museums in London that number is 31%. In order to truly engage visitors, the museum needed more than a new building.

The challenge formulated from a user-centred perspective was to create a product or service that inspires visitors who are new to design and motivates them to engage with the museum. This led to looking into the mechanisms of knowledge of and appreciation by these two types of museum visitors. Research about novice and expert visitors in a natural history museum provided more insights into the role of interaction with objects (Palmquist and Crowley 2007). As visitors become more expert in a certain field, they develop more sophisticated inquiry and begin to understand objects within their context—a larger system of interaction. Novice visitors often understand museum pieces as an individual object of study, unable to imagine them in their context or associate them with developments in society. This might result in visitors missing important bits of information and product features.

In one of their journals, Bollo and Dal Pozzolo (2005) describe how the 'ordinary' museum visitor behaves in an exhibition. They state that ordinary visitors might not know why certain objects on display are important at all. So in this case, with expertise comes intelligence, absorbing information better, knowing why designs are important and what designs are more interesting for the visitor personally.

This brings us back to the research of Palmquist and Crowley, who notice that expert visitors behave in an independent manner whereas novices expect the museum to guide their interpretations. When the museum does not provide this guidance, visitors need to focus a great part of their attention on establishing ways to interpret the experience and information. As a result, the general audience will not notice the details that tell the story about the other values of the product: its usability, how it was produced, etcetera. Let alone what sets it apart from other similar products, or what the impact was for its users or even society at large.

3.2.2 Theoretical Background

Two considerations provide insight into why the Design Museum experiences difficulties in engaging novice visitors. The first one is expertise: who decides what is good and what is bad design? Aren't we all users of design and experts of our own experience? The second consideration is the ownership of objects: what is the difference between an iPhone in the museum and the one in your pocket? The majority of the Design Museum's collection consists of industrially designed products in categories of furniture, kitchen appliances and consumer electronics. These objects were sometimes produced by the thousands and can possibly be found in many (British) households. However, there might have been remained only a few copies of a particular object over the years, carefully collected by curators of the museum. To borrow the expression from Chenhall and Vance (2013), we could say that they are '(almost) unique objects'. So why would you go to a museum to objects that are not unique?

3.2.2.1 The Definition of 'Good' Design

To the general audience, 'design' is often synonymous with expensive interior objects and fashion. People expect that the museum will teach them what is good and what is bad design. Chanter states that visitors often look for a timeline with the best cases of design (Chanter 2015). At the time of this project, the Design Museum offered neither of the two.

The question is: what is good design? Is it beautiful? Useful? Original? Innovative? There is not one definition of 'good' design; there is not even one definition of 'design'. Thus, the Design Museum wants to show a diverse view on design, covering a wide range of design disciplines. As a museum, they want to allow people to form their own opinion on design.

The Design Museum focuses on the impact of designs on the users, environment or society, for example. Sometimes it will put on a fashion exhibition, a field that fits the popular definition of design. Yet within the exhibition's subject, the museum still takes an uncommon angle. For example, the Paul Smith exhibition (Design Museum 2014) featured the designer's sources of inspiration rather than his products. In other exhibitions, some of the exhibited projects are less tangible and somewhat abstract, like the more experimental 'Designers in residence' projects

(Design Museum 2016). This makes it hard for novice visitors to understand their meaning and value. These visitors also have less specific design-specific knowledge to refer to.

3.2.2.2 'Almost' Unique Objects

It seems contradictory that design is too ordinary to merit a close look, yet too rare to be touched. Almost all designs in the Design Museum are displayed behind a glass wall (Fig. 3.1) or inside a glass box (Fig. 3.2).

To make visitors see the value of an object, the museum often uses the notion of defamiliarisation.

'After a while we just become completely familiarised and habituated to our environment, so we stop seeing things. What the museum does, it fractures that habituated looking, so that you can look fresh and see new. It should enable visitors to look differently at design', explains Helen Charman, Head of Learning at the Design Museum. Defamiliarisation was defined by Viktor Shklovsky (1917). He states: 'The technique of art is to make objects "unfamiliar" to make forms difficult, to increase the difficulty and length of perception because the process of perception is an aesthetic end in itself and must be prolonged'. This may work for art, and putting a design into a museum will make people look at them and consider their beauty. But in a museum, visitors are free to explore the exhibited objects.

Fig. 3.1 The design museum traditionally displays a collection of objects and images behind a glass wall

Fig. 3.2 Some objects are placed inside a glass box or with a 'please don't touch' sign

So they are also free to 'ignore' them, to take in only part of the information or not to take any notice of it at all.

According to Tisdale, museums only need objects 'if they do something great with them' (Tisdale 2011). He states that exhibitions should be not only educational but also unique, memorable, moving and provocative. He points out the limitations of a 'plexiglass-and-velvet-ropes approach' that favours the visual over other senses. The obvious way to experience the uniqueness of a product is to use it, to touch the object and try it out. But this is not yet possible in the museum, for obvious practical reasons.

3.2.3 Context Research

Sections 3.2.1 and 3.2.2 gave insight into how novice and expert visitors behave in exhibitions. But the visitor experience consists of much more than the actual exhibitions (Giaccardi 2012; Giaccardi and Plate 2016). It also includes exploring collections online, attending events, interaction through social media, checking reviews on websites such as Tripadvisor and purchasing objects in the Design Museum Shop. All these activities have the potential to open up the visitor experience to a more personally meaningful relationship with the objects *inside* and *outside* of the actual exhibition (Giaccardi 2012). Technology enables these personal experiences and meanings to be embedded into the objects themselves, making these experiences and meanings accessible to ordinary people. Thereby new shared spaces of interaction and values are materialised in the interaction *with* the physical object (Giaccardi and Plate 2016).

3.3 Methodology

The design challenge stated in Sect. 3.2.1 led to the main research question: how to inspire novice visitors and motivate them to engage with the Design Museum? In order to get to know the Design Museum's visitors and how they experience the museum as a whole, an explorative field study in the museum's old building took place in October 2015. At the time of this study, the Design Museum had three exhibitions going on: 'Designs of the Year 2015', 'Designers in Residence' and 'Life on Foot': an exhibition of shoe brand Camper.

To begin with, semi-structured interviews were conducted with six leading staff members of the Design Museum, from the departments of Curation, Learning and Research, Communication, Retail, Visitor Experience and Building. They were asked about their explanation of the value of design for people's everyday life, the uniqueness of the Design Museum, the role of their department for visitor engagement and their ambitions for the new museum. This was followed by 4 days of visitor research through observations in the museum and its surrounding area, visitor surveys and interviews, street interviews with potential visitors, shadowing a visitor through the museum and self-documentation of the museum visit. Research outcomes in the form of survey results, interview transcriptions, audio, video and photo recordings were gathered and coded with tags. All information was organised through an analysis on the wall. Triangulation of data resulted in conclusions and design opportunities.

This study led to several insights, some of which were not surprising to the Design Museum and some would not be relevant anymore when moving to a new building in a completely different part of London. However, one of the used research methods revealed particularly interesting outcomes and had a significant impact on the further proceeding of this project. Therefore, the method and findings of this study are highlighted here.

3.3.1 Self-documentation

On average, visitors spent about 1.5 h inside the former Design Museum, including their visit to the restaurant and museum shop (Chanter 2015). We were interested in how visitors spend these 1.5 h in the different areas of the museum. The method we focus on in this section is self-documentation, which is a powerful method for observing processes over a longer period of time; it allows the researcher to see how visitors see their museum visit. It focuses on naturally occurring interactions and routes through the museum and is therefore more suitable in this context.

This study was conducted with a group of students from Sheffield Hallam University (United Kingdom). Out of a group of 20 students, 4 of them (3 males and 1 female) were given instant cameras to document their visit in photographs (Fig. 3.3). The easier it is to self-document, the more likely it is that participants will complete the exercise. So the participants were given cards with instructions on what to take photographs of.

The research question ('How to inspire novice visitors and motivate them engage with the Design Museum?') is about *inspiration*, *engagement* and *novice visitors*. The questions that the participants were asked reflect these topics as well as the different stages of a museum visit (before, during and after the visit). The questions included are as follows:

1. *What was unexpected?*
   To find out more about the visitor's image of the experience **before** their visit
2. *What would you like to take home with you?*
   To know what's worthwhile to keep **after** their visit
3. *What inspired you most?*
   What do visitors appreciate most **during** their visit?
4. *What is your connection with design?*
   Are they novice visitors or expert visitors regarding the topic of design?

Fig. 3.3 Students were sent through the museum with instant cameras and the task to capture their visit in three photographs

Fig. 3.4 Afterwards the participants of the study were interviewed individually inside the museum cafe

The participants were asked to write down their reasons and motivations behind the choice of photographs they captured. Furthermore, they were interviewed afterwards (see Fig. 3.4), to extract the deeper values and meanings behind their answers.

3.3.2 Findings

Findings of the self-documentation study are summarised here and are contrasted with findings from observations and conversations with other visitors, as well as museum staff members. Since the main research question is around engagement,

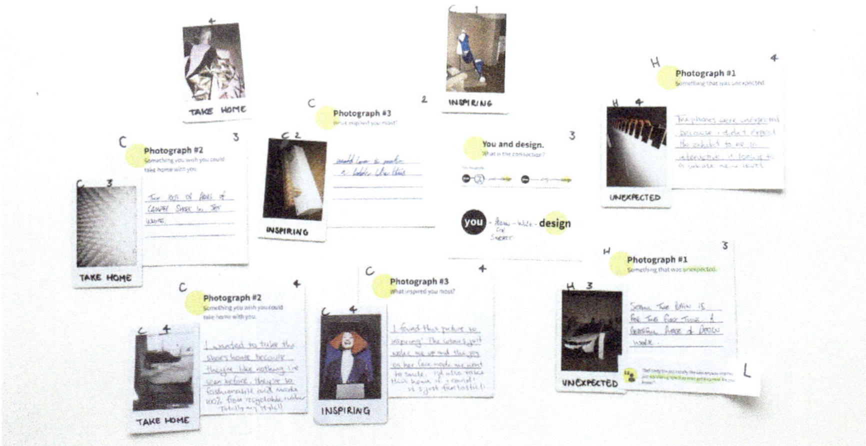

Fig. 3.5 A collection of photographs taken during the photo study with comments from participants

outcomes are structured according to broad engagement measures like time, overall enjoyment of exhibitions and depth of exploration (Fig. 3.5).

1. *Time spent*

Participants that were asked to self-document their visit with a camera spent more time in the museum's exhibition area than their fellow visitors without a camera.

2. *Enjoyment of the Design Museum compared to other museums*

Based on the observation of students in the gallery, it seemed that they enjoyed the exhibitions. This was confirmed by them in the interviews. The students mentioned the Design Museum being the most interesting museum of their study trip so far (which also included the Science Museum and the Victoria and Albert Museum).

3. *Enjoyment of exhibitions*

Observations in the museum showed that the exhibition space of 'Life on Foot' did not attract many visitors. Most visitors interviewed mentioned the highlight of their visit being 'Designs of the Year', the exhibition that was the most straightforward one of the three. It shows an overview of award-winning Designs of the Year 2015.

The 'Life on Foot' exhibition attempts to unveil the social, cultural and environmental impact of a life on foot. It has sketched concepts, prototype product and as-yet-unreleased pieces on display.

But ordinary visitors do not see this and express that they find the exhibition too commercial and just saw 'a bunch of shoes'. They missed the idea behind the exhibition, did not see the relevance of objects in the room and missed out on the main topics. It seems that people already walked in without having a clue what they could expect from this exhibition.

Participants of the self-documentation study showed a specific interest in the 'Life on Foot' exhibition. They seemed to look longer and more closely at exhibited objects and took many photographs in this exhibition space.

To illustrate this with an example (see Fig. 3.6): to the question 'What was unexpected?' participant 1 responded with a photograph of a Camper shoe prototype out of coconut, as he explains: 'I never thought you could make shoes out of coconut. That's just a whole different thing. I really like materials and manufacturing so this really appeals to me'.

4. *Depth of exploration*

Participants were immersed in less obvious parts of the exhibitions and devoted attention to understanding more abstract or conceptual designs by reading stories

Fig. 3.6 Something that was unexpected: a pair of coconut shoes, 'I never thought you could make shoes out of coconuts'

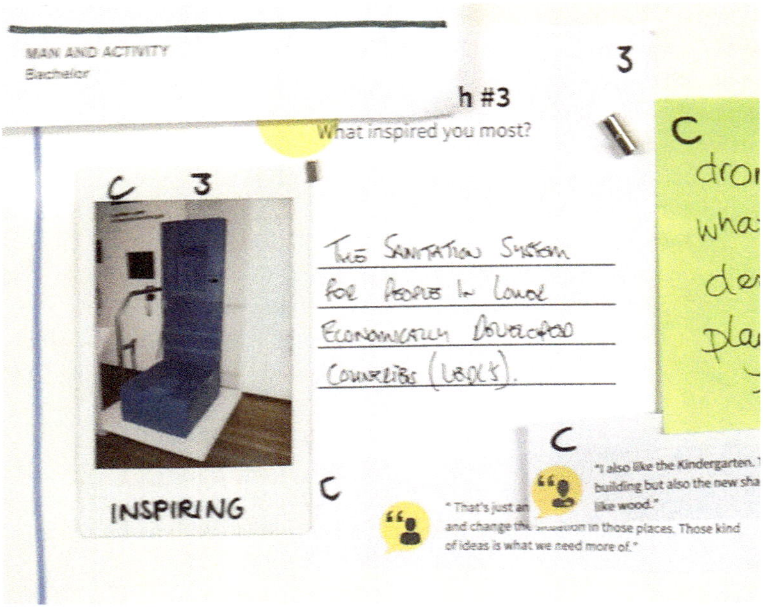

Fig. 3.7 What inspired you most: 'the sanitation system for people in lower economically developed countries (LEDCs)'

behind the objects. Participant 3 photographed a sanitation design for developing countries, one of the less straightforward designs in the exhibition of 'Designs of the Year' (Fig. 3.7).

After the self-documentation study, participants started discussing with each other what they liked in the museum and why, which made them more aware of their opinions and values in design.

Participant 2 was reminded of his past by some of the objects he saw in the exhibition. For the question 'What would you like to take home with you?', he photographed a set of assembly chairs from the Designs of the Year exhibition. He added to that: 'I like wooden things. I guess I'm just really raised with the idea that you can make a lot of things with wood. My dad always used to say; "If you want to have something, see and try if you can make it yourself first"' (Fig. 3.8).

3.3.3 Conclusion

The findings suggest that the Design Museum can have an influence on people's experience by providing clarity on what can be expected and by guiding the way they look at their exhibitions.

By telling the students to look for something 'unexpected' and 'inspiring' they already enter the exhibition with the impression that the museum will be inspiring,

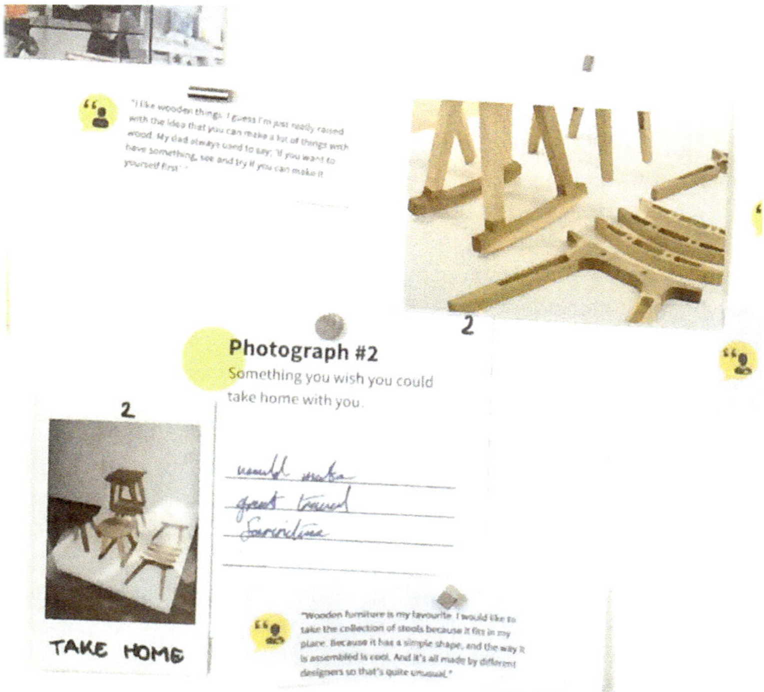

Fig. 3.8 Something you wish you could take home with you: set of wooden chairs, 'It is all made by different designers so that's quite unusual'

new and different. By handing over the camera, they were basically given the role of a design expert. You give them a symbolic permission to judge and critique the exhibitions and increase their confidence to say something about design.

So it is not only about what visitors can actually experience in the new museum, but also and perhaps more about what they expect to experience there. The more visitors enter with an open attitude, the more likely they are to engage with the museum. The research points out that novice visitors can be motivated to engage with the Design Museum by influencing their expectations.

3.4 Managing Expectations

For an important part, visitor behaviour is determined by expectations prior to a visit. Novice visitors do not get enough out of their visit and are often unsatisfied with the exhibitions because they have no idea what to expect. So in order to engage these visitors, the focus should be on the expectations before a visit instead of the experience during a visit. There lies an opportunity in designing and managing expectations. Managing expectations, however, is a broad term and can be done on different levels.

There are different types of visitor expectations. They can come from internal beliefs as well as from many different factors in the environment. Expectations come from former experiences, word-of-mouth, needs, values and opinions, the marketing mix of museums, the image of design and of museums and the Design Museum's market communication (Ojasalo 2001).

One might argue that products or services should always meet customer expectations or needs in order to achieve customer satisfaction. However, sometimes the visitors' expectations might be unrealistic, infeasible, unproductive or unjustified. In such cases, the Design Museum has to cope with visitors' expectations in a different way. It needs to shape and alter them so that the museum experience is evaluated more positively (Sheth and Mittal 1996). In other words, putting people in the right mindset for engaging with their exhibitions.

Raising expectations, however, requires striking an effective balance of high and low expectations. The danger of setting high expectations can be dissatisfaction about the visit—e.g. visitors have the expectation that 'design is a big thing, so London's only Design Museum will also be BIG'. When the actual museum is smaller than expected, visitors might be dissatisfied. On the other hand, an example of a low expectation is 'in museums you often have to read a lot and be silent, so it will be boring'. The risk of low expectations is that it might prevent people from even going to the museum at all.

The targeted audience segment of novice visitors most likely has low expectations about their visit, since they are new to the Design Museum and have little experience in the design field. When seeing the words 'design' and 'museum', all kinds of associations arise in the visitor's head. They may think of museums as heritage, history and things from the past. For most people, the idea of design is limited to fashion, furniture and consumer goods. As a result, they see design as something exclusive they cannot relate to personally. In other words, they think that: 'design is not for us'. This generates low expectations about:

1. **Accessibility:** they perceive design as exclusive and expensive.
2. **Impact of design:** think that design is just about pretty things.
3. **Personal benefit:** cannot relate design to their personal interests or own life.
4. **Lasting effect of their visit:** do not expect to get something out of their experience that lasts after their visit.
5. **Their own creativity:** they are not confident enough to share an opinion about the value of design.

3.4.1 *Desired Mindset*

What the Design Museum needs is an audience with an open mindset, but what is that mindset? Here, we wanted to connect back to the Design Museum, since they have been figuring out the answer to this question for many years. In the permanent design exhibition developed for the new Design Museum, they aim to warm up novice visitors for the rest of the museum.

The new Design Museum's permanent collection display is called 'Designer, Maker, User'. Alex Newson, curator of this exhibition, states objectives and messages about the value of design from the museum's perspective (Newson 2015). These objectives are written around four pillars of design that form the desired mindset:

1. **Design is everywhere**: Everything is designed: from the architecture of our cities and the typography that defines our street signs to the objects that we use every day. Sometimes design is even invisible.
2. **Design impacts our lives in many ways**: Design is about technological change, consumer choice, commercial manipulation and cultural expression. It has ongoing economic, political, social and environmental impact, sometimes unwanted.
3. **Design is a process**: Design combines creativity with a systematic approach to problem-solving. It starts with a brief and ends with a solution, but in between, there are many different stages. It is a collaborative process with people such as designers, engineers, manufacturers, strategists and the client.
4. **Design is happening now**. Design reflects and changes the world we live in. The future of design is full of possibilities, and the way things will be designed and made is changing—it is continually evolving.

3.4.2 Reformulating the Challenge

The reframed project challenge is to create a product or service that shapes the visitor's expectation 'design is not for us' into 'design is for us'.

With the four pillars of design in mind, we looked for a design intervention to be designed by Boonen. The objective of the ideation phase that followed was to generate ideas that don't interfere with the content of exhibitions and create something that stays, when temporary exhibitions come and go. To be disruptive and to not let ideas be restrained by the space in between the walls of the museum and to extend the experience to before and after the actual museum visit.

3.5 The Design Library Ecosystem

Based on the research and thinking presented above, Boonen designed the concept of the Design Library to address the design challenge. The concept was created in an iterative, spiral-like development design process as is common at IDE (Roozenburg and Eekels 1995). Over a period of 4 months, ideas were generated, compared, selected and tested based on the project requirements. The three most

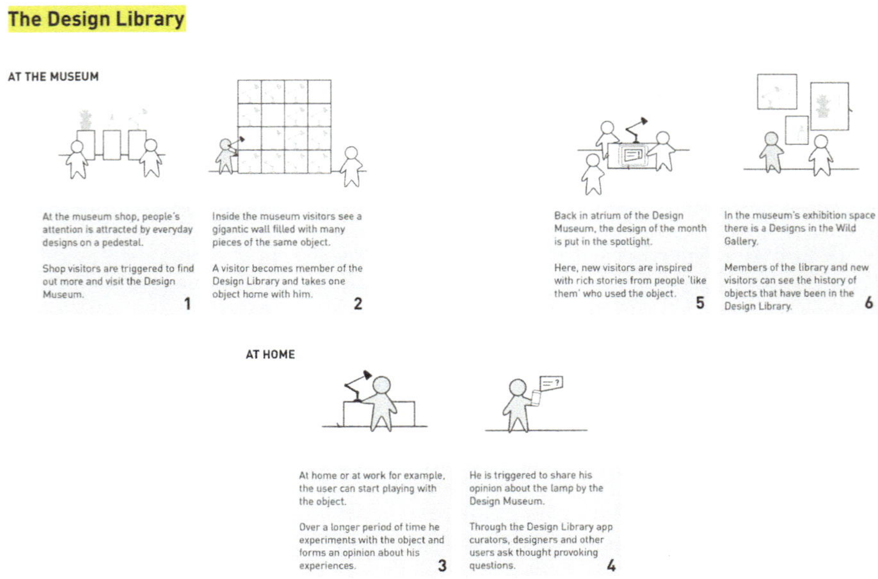

Fig. 3.9 Scenario of the Design Library in use

promising concepts were elaborated upon and presented to the Design Museum, IDE tutors and Fabrique, and finally, the chosen concept was detailed.

The schedule in Fig. 3.9 gives an overview of the Design Library concept: a service for museum visitors to borrow design objects. An app on their phone allows them to log their experiences with the object. Stories of different users around the same object are collected in a central database of design experiences. Visitors of the Design Museum encounter these stories through two free exhibits at the Design Museum, the Spotlight and the Design in the Wild Gallery, and in the museum's Shop.

3.5.1 The Design Library

The concept is designed to address needs of both expert and novice visitors and fits with objectives of the Design Museum itself:

1. It allows expert visitors that most likely are motivated to join the library to experience iconic, otherwise possibly exclusive design objects at their homes.
2. It shows novice visitors a diverse and democratic view on design, it proves that design is also for them, improving their appreciation of the museum's displays.
3. It creates a new service for the Design Museum, builds a valuable collection of data and generates visibility outside the museum building.

We envisage this works as follows. The Design Library needs active participants who are enthusiastic about taking a museum object home with them. At first, these participants will mostly be the design loving audience. By taking an object home from the museum, people can experience how it impacts their own life over a certain period time; experiencing real use, rather than only reading about facts such as material characteristics or the designers' biography. The Design Library enables exploration, learning to appreciate design by experimenting yourself.

As a result, the museum experience is extended to people's homes. It will make them feel more attached to the museum, stimulating lasting relationships between the Design Museum and its visitors.

By allowing visitors to take objects out of the museum, the museum's visibility is increased. It can reach and attract people who might not even go to museums usually: a novice audience.

By bringing design to the crowd and showing that the user is an expert, the Design Museum can show empathy with the big public. Instead of just giving background information about the designers, design process, materialisation and manufacturing of a product, the user's experiences should be included in the story of design. The user-generated content (videos, images and stories of use) enables the Design Museum to show multiple viewpoints to a certain object or topic and create a complete image. People want to see experiences of 'people like them'—people with families, business travellers or couples. Visitors are basically handed over a pair of designer glasses. Not only does it make the story more complete and rich, but it also triggers novice visitors to form and share their own opinion.

The following paragraphs describe the different elements of the Design Library ecosystem in more detail.

3.5.1.1 The Design Library at the Museum

Within the publicly accessible area of the Design Museum in Kensington, visitors are exposed to the physical embodiment of the library: a gigantic transparent wall which shows iconic design objects. The library is used to draw the visitor's attention and facilitates storage of the objects as well as distribution to the different users.

The Design Library's collection would start with everyday consumer products that are recognisable. But 'good' design is not just about form and function. For the Design Museum, good designs can also be 'controversial, promising designs that are ground-breaking in the way you interact with them' (Newson 2015). Ideally, the collection has a balance of things people would actually want to buy and, on the other hand, rather abstract objects, developing prototypes or even types of non-physical designs.

3.5.1.2 The Design Library App at Home

How long people can keep an object at their home will depend on the type of object and frequency of use. Imagine, for example, that someone borrows an Anglepoise desk lamp (Fig. 3.10) for a month. In return for borrowing the lamp from the museum, users will document their experiences by using the Design Library app.

Over the course of the loan period—in this case 1 month—the application shows comments, notifications and questions. The app enables the museum to pose specific questions to specific users at any moment in time. It triggers users to think about their experiences more thoroughly.

Every few days a curator from the Design Museum poses a new question to all users of the object. At the start, questions will be about observing surface characteristics, but after a week or so, users will be stimulated to take a closer look at the object and how they use it in their context. An example of a question asked to users in their first hours with the object is: 'How did you feel when you held the object for the first time?'. After a while, questions about the actual use and experience can be asked: 'In what angle did you position your Anglepoise lamp?'. It becomes even more interesting when the user is asked to use his own creativity and interpretation, to give the user the idea that he or she is becoming an expert: 'How would you redesign the lamp?'. Questions should allow for deeper inquiry of objects and be open, in order to have a variety of answers, which allows for new perspectives.

Fig. 3.10 An Anglepoise desk light from the design museum's collection (Source The design museum © Anglepoise)

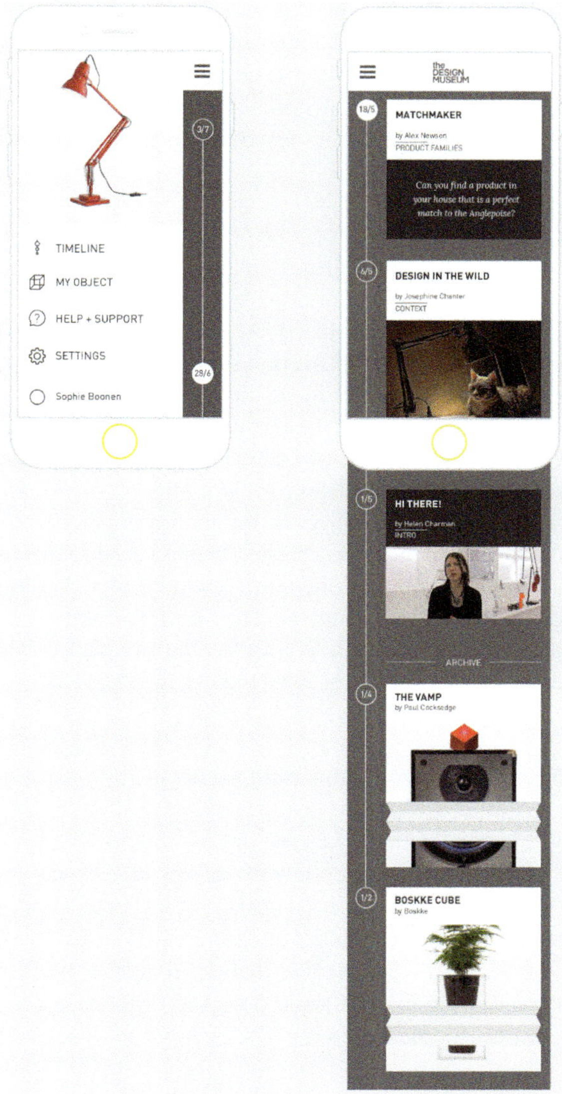

Fig. 3.11 Visual interface design of the Design Library application

The interface is designed around a timeline symbolising the loan period, see the image below (Fig. 3.11).

3.5.1.3 An Experience Database of Stories

Stories in the form of images, videos and text are gathered in an online database of experiences. Assuming there are multiple people actively using the application, a collection of experiences around an object is built up over time. This can generate valuable insights and knowledge on how different people use and value design objects, to the benefits of visitors, scientific staff (from curators to education), designers and design historians. Knowing its visitors is a valuable asset the Design Museum can have for designing a more powerful, engaging and user-friendly experience.

3.5.1.4 The Spotlight

The Spotlight is a place at the heart of the museum, in the atrium, where user-generated insights around borrowed designs are displayed. New visitors can see what 'people like them' think of a certain design object, instead of having an authoritative voice of the museum or the designer telling the story. This is the spot where novice visitors are shown that the value of design is context dependent and should be seen in relation to its users and surrounding objects.

Practically, the object of the month is placed on a pedestal and a digital information layer in the form of a display is added to the object. This display continuously shows user stories in a random order. Visitors can interact with the display by swiping through stories. They have the option to filter results based on the kind of upload (image, video or text), time and place of upload and characteristics of the user such as gender or age (Figs. 3.12 and 3.13).

3.5.1.5 Design in the Wild Gallery

While the Spotlight focuses on one specific design object, the Design in the Wild Gallery shows an overview of various objects that have been used by people so far (Fig. 3.14). The gallery consists of collected images of objects in their 'natural environment', resulting from pictures taken by users of the Design Library.

It shows novice visitors that design is for 'all of us' and everywhere around us. People recognise the same object in different environments, the natural surroundings of people's homes. The exhibition is co-created by users of the library,

Inspire me with	ANYTHING	*from*	ANYONE	*uploaded from*	ANY PLACE	*on*	ANY TIME .
	MOVIES		MALES		KENSINGTON		MORNINGS
	PICTURES		FEMALES		LONDON		EVENINGS
	STORIES		FAMILIES		UK		MONDAYS
			DESIGNERS		EUROPE		SUNDAYS
			TEENAGERS				THE FIRST DAY
							THE LAST WEEK

Fig. 3.12 Browsing through user stories by filtering on demographics and kind of upload

Fig. 3.13 Visual interface design of the Spotlight display

establishing a long-term connection with the museum. This is a permanent gallery: in this way, their image can become part of The Design Museum forever.

3.5.1.6 The Design Library Promotion in the Shop

The new museum has two museum shops: one inside the museum's building and one inside the neighbouring apartment block: the Design Museum Shop on Kensington High Street. This shop forms a bridge between the museum world and the outside world; this is the place where new (possible) visitors come across. It is an excellent way of involving people passing by, who might not have been going to the Design Museum before. A smaller depot of the Design Library here can make people aware of the existence of the service.

3.5.2 Evaluation of the Design Library

After creating the concept, Boonen organised a user test with visitors, as well as a review session with museum staff, with the goal of gathering feedback, identifying aspects of improvement and getting useful insights about developing services like this for museums.

Fig. 3.14 Artist's impression of 'Design in the Wild' gallery

3.5.2.1 User Test with Prototype

In order to have feedback from real users, a first test of the Design Library has been performed. We decided to focus the test on engaging the novice audience with the Design Museum, as this was the design challenge defined during the project. With this user test, we wanted to find out whether the concept would change the visitors' mindset: can the Design Library broaden people's view on what design is? Moreover, will it increase their ability to look at design in a critical manner?

The prototype consisted of an iPad app showing a collection of stories from the user's point of view on one single object. These stories were fictional, based on different people representing the novice audience. The digital prototype was used to demonstrate the service's potential in a way that it mimics an actual working app. The iPad and physical object were then placed on a table, giving visitors the possibility to swipe through user stories and touch the object.

The evaluation involved visitors who visited the exhibition and consisted of one question before entering the exhibition and a short questionnaire after their visit. In particular, the questionnaire was structured into various parts, regarding:

1. Definition of design: before user test,
2. Definition of design: after user test,
3. User experience,
4. Willingness to participate in service and
5. Background/level of design expertise.

During the evaluation study, people with different backgrounds were interacting with the prototype, all of them coming into the museum with an idea of design that was relevant to their own personal context (Fig. 3.15).

We found that people trusted the story better when the amount of reviews is high or when the story comes from a friend. One of the participants in the study responded: 'It's kind of like looking to reviews on Amazon but then a better or more reliable way of getting information out of people who actually used an object in their normal life. That's what you normally do, you talk to friends…'.

Participants mentioned that the stories helped them to put things in perspective. When they saw the comments, they realised how objects are actually used and what

Fig. 3.15 Find a product in your house that is a perfect match to the Anglepoise

its benefits are to the people who wrote the stories. People mentioned to be interested in the different ways objects are used. A visitor imagines: 'I think you get an appreciation for more the functional side of design. [...] Like a bike for example, it doesn't just sit there, you actually use it. So the design is used to make a physical experience better'.

There are products or services that you can only understand after you have used it for a while. One of the Anglepoise light's strengths is its constant spring mechanism, which enables freedom of movement and perfect balance. So its value is in the way you interact with it—'If I had the chance to borrow something, it would help me to understand what design really means instead of thinking that design is a style thing. For most people it is just about aesthetics'.

The Design Library is also supposed to trigger users to form and share their own opinion about design. Visitors immediately responded to the stories presented, what they thought about the object, or what objects they would like to borrow and experiment with: 'I might add some opinion about the lamp. I have one but to be honest I rather won't use it. Because I finished my studies three years ago. I used it for studying at night. But the lamp stays'.

Having a consistent design made the interface easy to interpret for users. However, using such a visual style also had an unwanted effect: users perceived the stories as too 'designed'—it did not feel like the comments came from real people. It is important to show that the displayed stories are genuine and not made up or steered too much by the Design Museum.

A sign indicated the possibility to touch and swipe through the stories on the iPad. Visitors were hesitant in interacting with it and only did this when encouraged more explicitly by the researcher.

Most visitors spent only a few minutes in front of an exhibited object or display. In this time span, visitors were not able to make sense of what they saw on the screen. First of all, there was too much text on each individual slide of the prototype. Visitors were not given an overview of comments or people having used the Anglepoise light. They need an ability to zoom out and see the overall result. Finally, there was no clear link between the display and the exhibition on show.

3.5.2.2 Review Session

In addition to this user test, a group discussion was held with eight employees from different departments of the Design Museum. Here, the main question was whether they were interested in the service and what it would mean to their own department.

The sessions started off with a presentation of the service in its entirety. Employees were then invited to give input on what should be kept and changed, for each part of the elements as laid out under 'Concept'.

The idea of the Design Library generated interest and enthusiasm among the employees. Employees even started brainstorming on the spot on their ideas for scaling up the concept or applications in other fields.

Rebecca Hossain manages the museum shop and during the creative session with staff members from the museum, she said: 'You can read all you like about an Anglepoise, but once you get it home you think: "Oh… so that's what it is!"'. In other words, the service helps 'selling' design.

From the creative session with staff members, it became clear that this concept benefits the Design Museum in learning more about their physical audience as opposed to their digital audience. It is a way to start a conversation with people, a way in: a poster.

For staff, it would be interesting to see a range of different users—in terms of demographics—using their products. David Houston, who is producer at the museum's Schools Programme, mentioned: 'What I find interesting is how an 8-year-old understands why certain things are important to adults. Why are certain things important for certain people? Who uses that, who's that making life easier for?'.

Alex Newson, one of the museum's curators, emphasised the importance of an authoritative voice of the Design Museum. To the prototype, he responded: 'Different people will respond in different ways. As an organisation, we need to make sure that we give a variety of voices back to people'.

From the museum's perspective, the main point of attention when taking this idea a step further is that the Design Library should not be too suggestive in framing the visitor's mindset. Newson responded: 'You can force visitors into only making one decision and trick them into thinking they've made that decision themselves, when actually that's the only option they had to come to. You can narrow down the options by the information that you give them'.

Employees remarked on the advantages of a service that creates many touch-points with the museum's audience, more than a traditional activity like a guided tour, a first-time visitors' kit or an introductory movie. However, when asked which person or department would be in charge of the Design Library, no conclusion could be made among the people present.

3.5.3 Discussion

The design as tested proved to elicit a positive response from people as well as to stimulate them to think more critically about their own opinions and values. However, this was not only through showing the user-generated stories but also through asking them questions in person. Explaining the service to visitors is all part of the time they need to invest in the experience. Time and attention span are scarce resources, so the service should be as simple as possible.

The proposed design opens up more questions, like how does the museum make sure objects will not just disappear? What if a visitor wants to join but is not living in London? And how will the stories be archived? This section does not give an answer to these questions; yet, it positions the concept against related work and discusses the potential of the idea as well as recommendations for further research.

Some visitors will be sceptical about the user's perspective and are more intrigued by the knowledge of the Design Museum as a research institution. For example, the Brooklyn Museum gives visitors the possibility to pose questions to their team of experts at the museum. Via an app, which is simply called ASK, visitors can message questions to curators about works of art (Browne 2014).

Allowing visitors to extend the museum experience to their homes is something that has been seen before. An inspiration for this project is the Cooper-Hewitt Design Museum in New York, which lets its visitors add a digital record of an object to their personal museum collection (Cooper-Hewitt 2014). Through the use of a pen, they make it easy and intuitive to collect and store information.

The Design Library ecosystem employs one part of its audience to create the content for the other half. As we found out, user-generated content appeals to people and stimulates them to take a new viewpoint. Some museums have been welcoming the amateur's voice inside the museum—for example, the Portland Art Museum with its Object Stories project, but mostly the visitor's contributions are limited to online (Portland Art Museum 2010).

The success of the Design Library is of course dependent on enough lenders sharing their experiences. However, we do not think that a paid crowdsourcing approach, as described by Van der Lans et al. in Chap. 7, is an option here; to get real experiences, people need to use the objects based on their own motivation, not because they're being paid.

Engaging visitors with different levels of knowledge and affinity has been and will be a challenge for most museums. The traditional approach has of course been to design exhibitions from different perspectives and levels of interpretation, and to organise guided tours and educational activities. Technology has created other ways to change the experience inside the exhibition space, like mobile wayfinding guides (e.g. the Marble Museum application—Ciavarella and Paternò 2004, or Fabrique's app for Tate—Fabrique 2016) and multimedia tours (e.g. the Van Gogh Museum tour—Museums and the Web 2015).

The Design Library adds another strategy to the pallet: change novices' attitude towards the subject, and thus their expectations before they enter the exhibition. It is somewhat similar to the sneak peek of a movie; however, the Design Library is not even connected to a specific exhibition, which significantly limits required investments.

In contrast to the museum experience described by Panagiotis Apostolellis et al. in Chap. 2, the Design Library deliberately is not meant to be a digital museum experience, and it does not involve gameplay. The Design Museum is already relatively focused on engaging their digital audience and is quite successful in this. But in terms of the people who literally drop through the door, they were not yet quite capturing that, reporting on that and acting on it. The power of the Design Library lies in how the different parts are used together. It is not about only thinking in digital or physical but about delivering a product ecosystem that serves the visitor journey across physical and digital environments, using multiple devices that are already available in our world.

The museum should give its visitors the tools to make a decision, while thinking clearly about what kind of and how many tools to give them. By choosing certain objects and asking certain questions you curate their experience. In a way, creating the Design Library is like curating an exhibition and still is work for professionals.

The Design Library demonstrates the potential for museums to go outside the physical museum building into people's homes. Looking at it through the lens of communicative ecologies (see Sabiescu et al. in Chap. 16), the Design Library forms a bridge between the communication in a locality (the museum) and people's way of life. Of course, museums are popping-up outside their primary locations regularly. Yet temporary presences in unused shops, on squares, in schools are always group activities. In this project, however, the library user enjoys a personal interaction with the museum, through the borrowed object and the app. This works perfectly for a design museum, as it collects relatively inexpensive objects, which can be easily transported and used at home. At the same time, no museum we know offers something similar, lending the concept great communication value. Would it work for other types of museums? Maybe not in lending out objects, but the idea to get something at home could work. What about museums of medicine or a zoological museum offering you a monthly exercise that will teach you more about your own or your pet's body?

Finally, it's worth reflecting on why the Design Library still is only a concept, not a reality. As the evaluation with staff proved, the new service is hard to fit neatly into existing museum structures. We think developing new services requires a holistic approach and someone in charge of it all. An example is offered by the Van Gogh Museum in Amsterdam. Fabrique developed their multimedia tour on request by the learning department, but operation staff hands out devices, the tour is promoted by the communication staff and referred to by labels hung by interpretation staff. Thus, the entire content, operation, promotion, renting out and returning was part of the design assignment. Fabrique's project manager stayed on as coordinator afterwards. This led to one million visitors using the tour (5 euros a person) in 2, 5 years (Van Gogh Museum 2017). Appointing a Head of the Design Library would be key for organisational success.

3.6 Conclusion

The uniqueness of the Design Museum is its contradicting nature: placing not so unique objects on a pedestal in the museum. This appeared to be something that was hard to understand for novice visitors who depend on the museum for guiding their interpretations.

The conducted user studies pointed out that especially these novice visitors could be influenced by the museum, changing their image on what can be expected inside. Currently, their image on design is limited, and they think that the Design Museum is just a place where you can see historical furniture behind glass. Design is not only about exclusive and expensive things, but it is about the everyday objects and environments we live with daily. Design is for all of us.

The Design Museum has the chance to lead the way and set the standard for a twenty-first-century design museum. In order to truly engage a wider range of people with the new Design Museum, they should not just offer a smooth and lovely museum visit. In the long run, it is not only about collecting the right objects and curating a blockbuster exhibition. There lies an opportunity in collecting stories, from the people themselves. Our project has repeatedly shown that people will be interested in hearing these stories. People value objects that bring back personal memories, objects that elicit an emotional response.

The Design Library is a great way of enabling active participation of visitors; there is always a reason to come back to the museum. Furthermore, the service touches upon different layers of visitor engagement. It allows visitors to discover, look at and appreciate design objects, and feel the need to collect them. Then it enables them to own museum objects for a while, in order to understand the topic of design better. Eventually it stimulates them to immerse in using the object and discuss its value with fellow users. Eventually, they can share their opinions and experiences with other people, to let them also appreciate design.

The idea was received positively by staff members, people involved in the project and most importantly the visitors. The idea of the Design Library is intriguing. It speaks to everyone; it is a service that is easy to imagine yet unexpected to be existing in a museum.

One of the most innovative aspects of this project was the user-centred approach, which led to a design intervention that crosses several museum departments. During the project, people from different departments were involved and thereby forced to think together about what they want to achieve as a museum. It encouraged the Design Museum's staff to reflect on their organisation structure and to think about the museum visit in a different way. Putting the user at the front of the experience makes it rich, and it seems to make sense for a design museum.

References

Bollo A, Dal Pozzolo L (2005) Analysis of visitor behaviour inside the museum: an empirical study. In: Proceedings of the 8th international conference on arts and cultural management, Montreal

Browne J (2014) Simply ASK. Bloomberg connects blog. https://www.brooklynmuseum.org/community/blogosphere/2014/10/06/simply-ask/ (Accessed 2015)

Chanter J (2015) (Skype interview, September 2, 2015)

Chanter J, Van der Heijden M (2015) The design museum brand proposition. Internal document of the design museum

Chenhall R, Vance D (2013) The world of (almost) unique objects. In: Parry R (ed) Museums in the digital age. Routledge, London

Ciavarella C, Paternò F (2004) The design of a handheld, location-aware guide for indoor environments. Pers Ubiquit Comput 8(2):82–91

Cooper-Hewitt (2014) The new Cooper Hewitt experience. Available at: https://www.cooperhewitt.org/new-experience/ (Accessed 2015)

Design Museum (2014) Hello, my name is Paul Smith (Design museum exhibition 2013). https://designmuseum.org/designers/paul-smith (Accessed June 2017)
Design Museum (2016) Designers in residence 2016: Open. https://designmuseum.org/exhibitions/designers-in-residence-2016-open (Accessed June 2017)
Fabrique (2016) Find your day. https://www.fabrique.com/portfolio/museums-and-heritage/tate/ (Accessed April 2017)
Giaccardi E (ed) (2012) Heritage and social media. Routledge, London
Giaccardi E, Plate L (2016) How memory comes to matter: from social media to the internet of things. In: Muntean L, Plate L, Smelik A (eds) Materializing memory in art and popular culture. Routledge, London, pp 65–88
Museums and the Web (2015) Van gogh museum multimedia tour. http://mw2015.museumsandtheweb.com/bow/van-gogh-museum-multimedia-guide-re-designing-the-visitor-experience/ (Accessed April 2017)
Newson A (2015) Design museum Kensington: permanent collection display. Interpretative plan, vol 45
Ojasalo J (2001) Managing customer expectations in professional services. Manag Serv Qual Int J 11(3):200–212
Palmquist S, Crowley K (2007) From teachers to testers: how parents talk to novice and expert children in a natural history museum. Sci Educ 91(5):783–804
Portland Art Museum (2010) Object Stories. http://objectstories.org/about/index.html. Accessed 22 Sept 2015
Roozenburg N, Eekels J (1995, 1996) Product design: fundamentals and methods. Wiley, Chichester, pp 84–93
Sheth JN, Mittal B (1996) A framework for managing customer expectations. J Market-Focus Manag 1(2):137–158
Shklovsky V (1917) Art as technique. Modern Crit Theory: Read 1988(11):16–30
The Audience Agency (2014) Design museum visitor survey 2013/14 report. Audience Finder: London Visual Arts, August 2014
Tisdale R (2011) Do history museums still need objects? Hist News 66(3):19–24
Van Gogh Museum, press release (2017) https://vangoghmuseum.nl/en/news-and-press/press-releases/one-million-interactive-guided-tours-of-the-museum-collection

Author Biographies

Sophie Boonen graduated in 2016 from the master program Design for Interaction at Delft University of Technology. During her graduation project she created a service for the Design Museum in London to stimulate people's engagement with design objects, in collaboration with strategic design agency Fabrique. She currently works as a social designer at service design agency Muzus.

Martijn van der Heijden works as a strategist at Fabrique, a strategic design agency working internationally out of the Netherlands. He has worked on many museum, cultural, travel and retail projects. Yet he remains curious to discover new strategies that fit each new client. Whether it's a museum like Tate and the Design Museum, institutes like the Koninklijke Bibliotheek and Southbank Centre or festivals like Edinburgh International Festival, Lowlands and Operadagen Rotterdam. Martijn has spoken on UX and museums at conferences like SXSW Interactive and MuseumNext. He blogs irregularly on Medium. Martijn has a MsC (cum laude) in Industrial Design from TU Delft, where he also currently advised the MuseumFuturesLab.

Elisa Giaccardi is Chair of Interactive Media Design at Delft University of Technology, Department of Industrial Design, where she leads the Connected Everyday Lab. She is one of the recipients of the TU Delft Technology Fellowship for top female scientists, and a speaker at TEDx on the Internet of Things. She is the editor of Heritage and Social Media (Routledge 2012) and author of the chapter "How memory comes to matter: From social media to the Internet of Things" (in the book Materializing Memory in Art and Popular Culture, Routledge 2016). From her pioneering work in meta-design and participatory technology to the role of the non-human in the Internet of Things, her design research reflects an ongoing concern with design as a shared process of cultivation and management of opportunity spaces.

Chapter 4
Crowdsourcing Ideas for Augmented Reality Museum Experiences with Children

Gavin Sim, Brendan Cassidy and Janet C. Read

Abstract When the target audience is children, the human–computer interaction community has firmly established the benefits of involving children throughout the design process. Participatory design methods with children have been used successfully for the design of learning. Within the context of museums, there have been shown to be benefits in children designing interactive experiences for themselves and their peers. We therefore conjecture that children can contribute towards the design of engaging learning materials for museums. With space being a premium within museums, the possibility of using augmented reality (AR) with existing exhibits is appealing. With the increased availability of off-the-shelf wearable devices, research in the field of wearable computing has grown in recent years but only a small portion of this research is dedicated to the design of wearable technologies for children. This chapter presents a study that uses specially constructed storyboards to crowdsource ideas for a VR exhibit within a museum in which children were enabled to design low-fidelity interfaces and interactions within an AR context. The storyboards that the children produced were analysed to determine whether the children understood the concept of AR. In addition, the drawings were analysed to establish the ideas generated, the feasibility of the implementation of proposed technology, the interaction methods and, finally, the educational merit. We critically reflect on the ideas proposed by the children and the methodology for generating ideas relating to museum experiences.

4.1 Introduction

Museums are integral to the development of children's minds, and they offer a unique space for exploration and learning. The United Nations Convention on the Rights of Children (CRC) claims that children should have free and full access to cultural life from birth as this fronting of cultural objects is known to encourage

G. Sim (✉) · B. Cassidy · J. C. Read
University of Central Lancashire, PR1 2HE, Preston, UK
e-mail: GRSim@uclan.ac.uk

A. Vermeeren et al. (eds.), *Museum Experience Design*, Springer Series on Cultural Computing, https://doi.org/10.1007/978-3-319-58550-5_4

active learning and promote language development for thinking and communicating (Graham 2008). Cultural objects in museums inherently foster an intrinsic motivation to learn and a desire for sustained engagement (Paris and Hapgood 2002).

Looking for effective strategies for designing engaging museum experiences for children has a long history (Caulton 1998). Many museums, depending on their size, have educational officers who are responsible for the experience of the children, insuring the content has educational value and is engaging for their visit. Museums invest considerable resources in interactive displays to attract and engage visitors who include children. With the transformation of museums from places where artefacts were displayed in static ways behind glass-fronted cabinets and where children were in the main expected to behave like adults, the museum industry has seen several shifts in its thinking from places of examination to places of exploration and from places of display to places of experience (Vom Lehn et al. 2001).

The museum experience for children has been radically rethought in recent years, and there is a clear focus nowadays on letting children interact with products in and around the museum. Thus, there is an emphasis on designing experiences around artefacts that provide greater engagement for children as they visit the museum.

Interactivity and experiences within museums have been traditionally designed with an educational focus. Early examples of interactivity relied on physical artefacts like push buttons and lift up flaps although Caulton (1998) would argue these were more hands-on than interactive as the object itself is not responding to the interaction. As information technologies became more affordable, the museum became a prime location for the integration of new technologies. Consequently, a whole new area of investigation followed, on how best to imagine and design IT-enabled interactions for children in the context of museum spaces (Cahill et al. 2011). This new area for consideration required the bringing together of two disciplines, the design of educational artefacts and the design of interactive digital artefacts.

In its early days, this space was filled with the use of a set of well-understood and easy to imagine digital props and systems including interactive surfaces, portable digital devices (like PDAs and iPads) and location-aware systems that started playing video or audio as a child came near to a product. In the excitement that accompanied this drive towards technology in the museum, much use was made of design workshops with museum staff and participatory activities with children (Smith and Iversen 2011). This chapter describes an study that acquired design ideas directly from children's use of AR technology. These design ideas provide new directions for AR interactions with children in a museum context.

4.2 Related Work

The related work in this chapter will focus on three main areas, participatory design with children, augmented reality and prototyping.

4.2.1 Approaches to Participatory Design with Children

Participatory design (PD) with children is a well-established method for engaging with children in design work (Theng et al. 2000; Alborzi et al. 2000; Frauenberger et al. 2011). Used at ideation as well as at more concrete design stages, PD with children has many guises, and the literature has established a number of ways to employ this technique to effect, see Table 4.1 for an overview (Brandt 2006; Robertson et al. 2006). In some cases (cooperative enquiry), a small group of children, heavily scaffolded and supported by adults with a range of skills, work together over several weeks to imagine and then develop a concrete solution for an intervention (Druin 1999). In other cases (design workshops), a series of workshops are held with a group of children who, less aided by adults, are facilitated towards a design idea (Dindler et al. 2010). In the third way (Fast and Furious), a larger group of children are asked for design ideas, and these are used by adult interaction designers to then infill a design solution (Read et al. 2016). Each method has its pros and cons, and each has different uses in a museum context.

The Fast and Furious practice, where designers work with children for a single session, is ideally suited towards ideation as opposed to design confirmation because children give many ideas, often disconnected, sometimes undoable and sometimes off the topic, but these many ideas are useful to guide the designers to think outside the box as they seek inspiration and child-centred detail for their work. The aim in such cases is to end up with many ideas that can then be examined by a design team for trends. A secondary aim is to generate a good representation of the children's ideas in order that some ideas can be incorporated into a design (Read et al. 2014, 2016). An approach for doing the analysis of the ideas from a Fast and Furious design session is described in Read et al. (2014), where the method is referred to as a 'crowdsourcing of ideas'.

Crowdsourcing is the practice of obtaining information relating to a project from a large number of people who may or may not be paid. The use of crowdsourcing has been applied to information technology and product development projects with some success (Leimeister et al. 2009; Poetz and Schreier 2012). In the study by Poetz and Schreier (2012), they compared designer ideas to customer generated ideas within the context of baby products. The ideas were evaluated by executives from the company in terms of key quality dimensions; these being novelty, customer benefit and feasibility. The findings revealed that the crowdsourcing process generated customer ideas that score significantly higher in terms of novelty and customer benefit, but somewhat lower in terms of feasibility. Feasibility was seen as

Table 4.1 Different PD structures and their pros and cons

PD variant	Time needed	Expert input	Children's input
Cooperative enquiry	Many weeks	Seamed into design	Seamed into design
Design workshops	3 or 4 days	Limited to facilitation	Heavily forefronted
Fast and Furious	1 day	Applied as interpretation	Sought for inspiration

a problem also in the work in Read et al. (2016), where ideas were taken from teenagers for an interactive water bottle. Within the context of this book chapter, we conjecture that the children will generate highly novel ideas, some of which might be feasible (Cassidy et al. 2015). However, the concept of customer benefit is rather outside the scope of this work, and thus, the focus will be on the alignment to educational values within prototypes of an augmented reality experience in a museum.

4.2.2 Augmented Reality

Augmented reality (AR) technologies have recently become more affordable and accessible to a wider audience than in previous years. AR has been defined as the real-time three-dimensional integration of digital information with the physical environment (Rattanarungrot et al. 2014). Three underlying technological characteristics of AR have been identified (Azuma 1997); these being combining the real and the virtual, being interactive in real time and being rendered in 3D. AR technologies are now available in a wide range of form factors from mobile phones and tablets through to wearable semi-transparent displays; there is a device capable of creating an AR experience to suit most budgets. Higher end, untethered devices such as the Microsoft Hololens are not currently designed or recommended for children 13 years of age and under, as these devices do not allow for adjustment for inter-pupillary distance (IPD). Current projection optics in devices like Hololens have binocular screens at a fixed distance from each other. This distance is based on the average user and cannot be adjusted. This measurement is not based on children's data, and thus, younger children would be more likely to experience a double image when viewing content through the device, with currently unknown health consequences. Wearable display devices aimed at children will be available and commonplace in the future as the technology improves and the cost of manufacture comes down, and the IPD issue is likely to be addressed; this is already evident in VR devices such as Oculus Rift, where the optics for each eye can be adjusted.

Designing AR systems for children, especially with a focus on education, is already a healthy research field. Studies have been performed across a range of educational levels including primary schools (Juan et al. 2008), which the work reported in this paper is situated in. In a meta-review of 26 previous peer-reviewed research projects on AR in education across the educational spectrum, AR was shown to have a number of advantages and disadvantages (Radu 2014). Learning spatial structure and function, language associations, long-term memory retention, collaboration, motivation and physical task performance could all be improved with the introduction of AR into the learning environment but the increased demands on attention when using AR can result in students missing key learning aspects. There are also usability difficulties, issues with classroom integration and issues arising from differences in learning styles, with higher achieving children seeing less of an advantage in using AR technologies and showing better learning gains through more traditional content delivery methods (Radu 2014).

Children have embraced AR associated with mobile devices such as smartphones or tablets in a playful context for some time. Successful products from Lego (Lego Fusion) and Osmo (Osmo) have shown children are receptive to these technologies. AR has also been used as a tool for children to collaborate with other children with different capabilities (Brederode et al. 2005) and also used as an assistive technology for marginalised children, particularly children with impairments related to being on the autistic spectrum (Bai 2012). In the study by Bai (2012), imaginary objects were superimposed in the real world to encourage children with autism to be involved with pretend play and encourage social interaction. Museums need to be inclusive and with schools having children with different cognitive and physical capabilities, AR offers potential to enhance the museum experience for all.

4.2.3 Technology Impacts on Choices of Participatory Design Approaches

While participatory design has been shown to work well for the design of screen-based computer systems, the complexity of modern technologies such as those used in interactive installations has been flagged up as being problematic for PD work. This problem first surfaced in museum design with the rise of UbiComp (Hornecker et al. 2006), and the solutions proposed at that time involved deep immersion with, and education around, the proposed technology. Depending on the extent to which the participatory activity is seeking many ideas, there can be a 'release' from the complexity of the technology as the children can be told to imagine anything. In a study looking at future technology (Read et al. 2016), this approach of imagining the product was used to design an interactive water bottle where the constraints were around the functionality of the bottle but where the interactivity of the technology was unspecified and left open. The children were introduced to a new concept 'Nano technology' and asked to design an interactive water bottle that could be completely digitised. In this study, all the children managed to design water bottles and many were highly novel but some were infeasible.

Many PD sessions with children result in low-fidelity prototypes that can then be evaluated either by the research team or by potential users of the system. The benefits of low-fidelity prototypes are well documented within the literature, for example, one study investigated the impact fidelity had on the user's willingness to critique the interface as part of a usability study (Wiklund et al. 1992), and the results concluded that the number of usability problems is not affected by the prototype method. This fact is useful within the context of AR as high-fidelity prototypes can be expensive and time-consuming to produce; thus, low fidelity may be sensible in the early ideation stages. But care must be taken when ideas go forward as other studies have highlighted that while low-fidelity (low visuals) prototypes can be evaluated, the lack of refined graphics may bias evaluators when comparing against other products (Kohler et al. 2012). Another study concluded that users appeared to overcompensate for deficiencies in aesthetics (Sauer and Sonderegger 2009). There are studies showing results from prototypes are equivalent to fully operational products and other studies reporting additional benefits of higher fidelity prototypes, therefore the use of mixed-fidelity prototypes which may be costly to develop (Yasar 2007). By having children create prototypes of a museum experience, it may be possible to evaluate these prototypes against many dimensions.

In Read et al. (2013), a study where children designed low-fidelity prototypes using a range of novel materials, it was shown that the materials used in prototyping heavily influenced some of the designs. In a study by Sim and Cassidy (2013) that compared low- and high-fidelity prototypes of a platform game with children, it was seen that the lower the fidelity of the prototype, the lower the game was rated in terms of appearance, interaction methods and game idea. This work, and other work, suggests that the tools and choices in relation to how children envisage their work are relevant in PD activities.

It is against this backdrop that the work reported in this chapter is situated. A Fast and Furious design activity is described in order to ideate for AR in museums. The effect of the prototyping decisions, the scope of the ideas generated and the feasibility of the ideas towards design are all discussed.

4.3 Method

4.3.1 *Participants*

The participants were 31 schoolchildren aged 7 to 9, from one UK primary school in a small village in the North of England. The children were selected as they had all previously visited the museum on a school trip, and therefore would be familiar with the artefacts. The children took part in this study during a Mess Day at the school (Horton et al. 2012). A Mess Day consists of a group of schoolchildren participating in a number of different research activities. The first author of the paper acted as the facilitator during the study; the teaching assistant and another researcher were also present to assist the children.

4.3.2 *Material*

The prototyping 'tool' used for the children was a workbook, which consisted of five pages. The first page was a brief survey capturing demographic, followed by a storyboard and three images that they needed to draw augmented reality content on. The first author of the paper visited the museum prior to this study, talked to the curators and photographed the various artefacts and layout in order to produce the storyboard. The children had access to felt tip pens and pencils with which to draw their images.

4.3.3 Procedure

The research was conducted in the children's classroom within the school and was conducted in a number of stages. Before the children came into the classroom, one of the three researchers loaded a set of PowerPoint slides onto the whiteboard and set up the MetaSpace glasses.

Stage 1: The children entered the classroom after the afternoon break and sat at their desks. The teacher introduced the research team and then one of the researchers explained the purpose of the activity, discussed the ethics surrounding their ideas and handed the children an individual workbook. Prior to the study, the research team had been advised by the teacher that the children had previously been to Ribchester Roman Museum, but when we asked the children to raise their hands if they had been there, the majority of children seemed to think they hadn't been there at all. The researcher who was facilitating the session, using PowerPoint slides, then asked the children if they knew what augmented reality was. Several children raised their hands and the researcher asked one of the children to explain what they thought this meant. The child who was selected described virtual reality in reference to the PlayStation headsets; no other children offered an alternative explanation. The facilitator then asked if anyone had seen or knew what Pokemon Go was and the entire class put their hands up. Augmented reality was then briefly explained within the context of Pokemon Go, and a video was then shown of the capabilities of MetaSpace glasses. The MetaSpace glasses were used as the discussion point as they had been effectively used to bring museum artefacts back to life (Pedersen et al. 2016), and the Hololens were still not available to developers at the time of the study.

Stage 2: The children were then asked to complete the first page of the book that simply captured some demographic data, whether they had visited the museum and if this was a positive experience, and if they had experienced augmented reality before. All the children completed this section within about 2–3 min.

Stage 3: The researcher then talked through the storyboard (see Fig. 4.1) that depicted a school visit to the museum, starting at the entrance to the museum and walking around the exhibits. The children were asked to imagine walking around with augmented reality glasses on and think about, and design, how the exhibits might come to life or be enhanced.

Stage 4: The children were then asked to turn over the booklet and a large version of the first picture was presented. The image had its transparency set to 50% so that children could easily draw on top of the image. The children were then asked

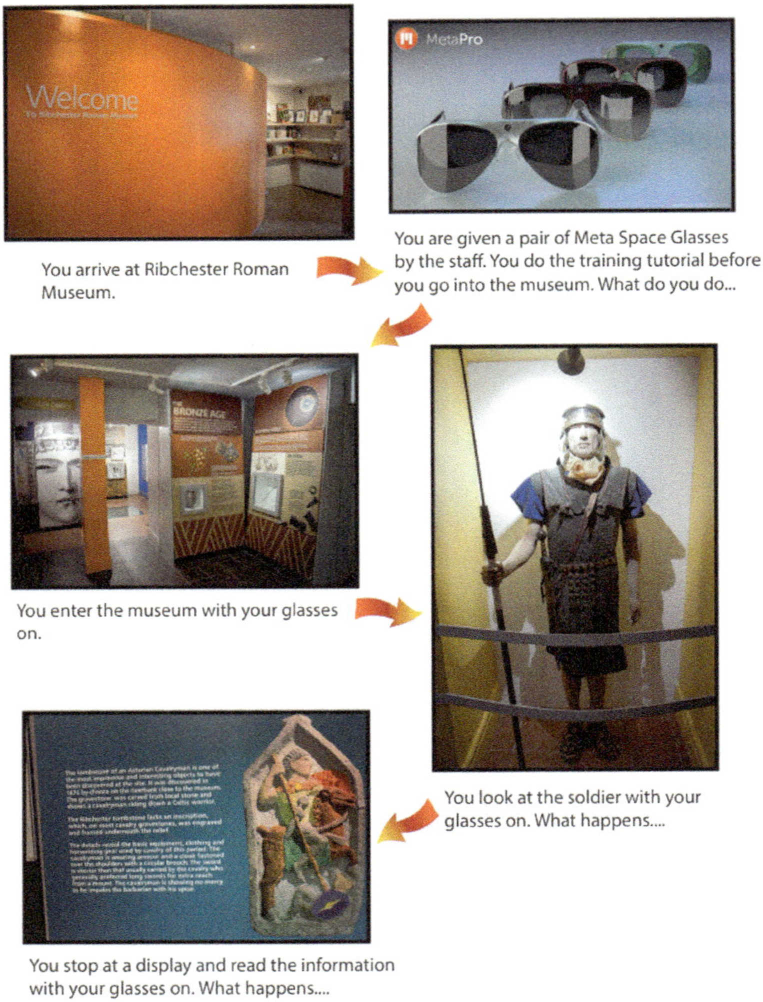

Fig. 4.1 Storyboard of the day at the museum

to draw what they might like to see as a training exercise on how to use the glasses before they enter the museum. They spent about 10 min on this exercise before they completed the next two images (scenes 4 and 5 in the storyboard).

4.3.4 Analysis

All the children who took part in the activity managed to complete at least two of the three drawings relating to augmented reality within the museum. As would be expected, children provided drawings that varied in quality and level of detail. Some of the drawings were difficult to interpret while other children provided a written description of the interaction and described the scene.

The analysis of children's drawings is an established method in the area of child–computer interaction (Xu et al. 2009) and in other subject disciplines such as environmental studies (Barraza 1999) and health (Backett-Milburn and McKie 1999). Drawings are used to enable children to communicate and express their ideas without being prohibited by language skills. The pictures that the children produced were analysed to determine whether the children understood the concept of AR. In addition, the drawings were analysed to establish the ideas generated, the feasibility of the implementation of proposed technology, the interaction methods imagined and, finally, the educational merit of the design idea. The analysis was performed in two stages, in the first stage each of the three pictures relating to the scenes in the storyboard (training, soldier and sign) were analysed, using content analysis, to establish what was drawn, and the frequency of elements. A single image from a page from a child's drawings could potentially have a number of different elements (see Fig. 4.2), and therefore, each unique 'idea' element was coded separately (as done in Read et al. 2014). Once all the images had been analysed, two researchers merged the data into themes.

The second stage of the analysis was to re-examine the images to determine whether they were feasible within the context of AR technology. The capabilities of AR technology were identified from the literature and the functionality of HoloLens as:

Fig. 4.2 Example of children's drawing of training activity

- Spatial mapping enables a detailed representation of real-world surfaces in the environment to be identified. For example, it can establish the walls, ceiling and floors.
- Marker-based tracking: The tracking of objects in the real world using fiducial markers. These are usually distinct asymmetrical monochrome patterns and have the least resource overhead when tracking.
- Object recognition tracking: The tracking of a tangible real-world object, such as a toy. Unlike marker and image tracking (where the digital markers/images to be tracked can just be provided to the system), object tracking will require some kind of training in order to recognise the object to be tracked. For example, the Vuforia AR SDK (www.vuforia.com) makes use of a 'Scanner App' to train AR software to recognise real-world 3D objects.
- Surface/markerless tracking: The tracking of flat surfaces in order to place augmented content on it. This functionality can be accomplished with a depth camera and can serve as a way to achieve markerless tracking without the need for full spatial mapping.
- Image tracking: The tracking of objects in the real world using an image as a marker. This helps make the tracking marker more integrated into the environment. For example, objects to be tracked could contain an image of a company logo, cartoon character or any relevant image for the content being tracked. Both image markers and fiducial markers need to be asymmetrical to track well.
- Interaction Techniques
  - Hand: uses hand gestures to interact with the AR content,
  - Head: uses the accelerometer within the glasses to interact,
  - Gaze: uses eye tracking to interact with objects and
  - Voice: the user would give verbal commands.

The same two researchers then examined each image to determine whether it was feasible within AR and how it might be implemented. There were a number of images that would require more than one technology, for example, see Fig. 4.2.

The image shown in Fig. 4.2 is the entrance to the museum. The white space below the images is where children were encouraged to describe their drawing and interaction methods. In this example, the child had drawn a range of objects including a tank, bird, a tie fighter and described the tank firing sweets. Figure 4.2 could be implemented simply by using maker-based tracking; however if the sweets fired from the tank needed to remain on the floor or hit objects, then this would require spatial mapping of the environment. For instances like this shown in Fig. 4.2, with multiple options, the images were coded against all feasible techniques. When children incorporated interaction with objects into their drawings, these were coded against the feasible interaction techniques, for example, eye gaze and hand gesture.

4.4 Results

Of the 31 children, only 9 (29%) reported having previously visited the museum. Four children (13%) indicated that they had experienced augmented reality before having played Pokemon Go. Therefore, the majority of the children had limited knowledge of the specific museum (although the teacher reported otherwise that these children had visited the museum in a previous term) and augmented reality.

The first of the three scenes that the children were asked to complete was the training session. This session represents the moment when the children enter the museum and first puts the glasses on. All of the children managed to create a drawing for this. These drawings were analysed, and the themes that the children had drawn are shown in Table 4.2.

In total, 16 different themes emerged from the children's drawings with the most popular being animals, with 14 (45%) of the drawings containing an animal of some sort; these ranged from rabbits to dinosaurs. Weapons also featured heavily within the designs along with people, rockets and various random shapes. The majority of the designs were not unique to an individual child; out of the 16 themes, only 3 were unique, those being a door, bike and flower. In total, 23 out of 31 drawings for this scene contained visuals that were animated, for example, rockets and animals flying around the room, and one contained a soldier who would attack the gift shop lady. Although the remaining images were static, they did enable some interaction, for example, one contained a bowl of fruit that you could pick up and eat, and another required you to move a cupcake around the room.

For the second scene, the soldier, again all 31 children managed to complete a drawing, with 17 themes emerging, see Table 4.3.

The soldier had more unique categories than for the training image, with seven items only appearing in one drawing. The most popular item again was animals, followed by weapons and persons. For this image, eight (8) of the children opted to customise the soldier, for example, one placed a snorkel on his face, others put a beard on him and one child drew arrows sticking out of him. In this instance, there were 22 drawings that contained some form of animation, ranging from the soldier attacking you, the volcano erupting to spiders running over the soldier's arms. Again, the static images enabled levels of interaction. For example, a sword could be picked up and this interaction would enable you to then fight the Roman soldier.

Table 4.2 The children's drawings for the training session

Drawing	Freq.	Drawing	Freq.	Drawing	Freq.
Animals	14	Food	5	Door	1
Weapon	8	Soldier	4	Bike	1
Rocket	7	Speech	3	Flower	1
Person	7	Pencil	3	Flying book	1
Shapes	7	Water	2		
Weather	5	Building	2		

Table 4.3 The children's drawings for the soldier

Drawing	Freq.	Drawing	Freq.	Drawing	Freq.
Animal	9	Shape	5	Soldier	1
Weapon	8	Ghost	5	Flower	1
Change soldier	8	Spaceship	2	Weather	1
Person	8	Robot	2	Background	1
Speech	7	Car	1	Food	1
Castle	6	Volcano	1		

Table 4.4 The children's drawings for the sign

Drawing	Freq.	Drawing	Freq.	Drawing	Freq.
Animals	7	Shapes	3	Phone	1
Person	4	Weather	2	Castle	1
Ghost	4	Speech	2	Angels	1
Flowers	3	Pacman	1		

The final image was the sign, and seven of the children did not complete the drawings; it might have been that they spent too long on the first two images and simply ran out of time. Of the 24 drawings that were completed, the themes are displayed in Table 4.4.

For the sign, 11 themes emerged and again animals were by far the most popular, followed once again by people and in this instance ghosts. There were four unique design ideas, with one child drawing a Pacman game and another incorporating modern technology into the artefact with a phone. The sign also incorporated a lot of animated objects, with 18 examples being shown in the drawings; this included the horse the person was on animating into a bird flying around. Once again, static content enabled a level of interactivity, for example, you could dress up the statue as shown in Fig. 4.4.

Following the first analysis, the drawings were then analysed to determine whether they were feasible, and all the children's designs appeared to be feasible within the context of AR. Table 4.5 shows the technology that would be required within AR to implement the children's design.

The children did not have any designs that required surface markers or imaging tracking technologies. For the training exercise, many of the designs would potentially be implemented with marker-based tracking. This interaction could be achieved through the use of fiducial markers attached to the wall, when the child wearing the technology looked at the spot the digital content would then be displayed. For example, one of the drawings depicted a cave woman dancing and a pencil writing 'come and enjoy the museum' next to her. Other more complex interactions would require spatial mapping as shown in Fig. 4.3. In this example, the environment would need to be mapped so that the two soldiers fighting (bottom right-hand side of the image) could be placed within the environment, the stones could be placed on the floor and the collision detection based on throwing the stones could be implemented.

Table 4.5 The technology that would be required to implement the children's designs

	Training	Soldier	Sign
Spatial mapping	8	19	4
Marker-based tracking	24	10	19
Object recognition	0	8	1
Surface markers	0	0	0
Image tracking	0	0	0
Input hand	7	7	3
Input head	5	1	1
Input gaze	3	2	1
Input voice	0	1	0

Fig. 4.3 Two soldiers fighting and ghosts added to a picture of a soldier

For the soldier, many of the designs would have required spatial mapping as items were being attached to the soldier in such a way that the child could interact with him, for example, children placed beards on him and other children added war wounds to him. There were still a number of instances in which marker-based tracking could be used, with the marker placed either to the side or behind the soldier. For example, in Fig. 4.3, when the child looked in the direction of the soldier, the marker would be recognised and the ghosts would appear.

For the final scene, the sign, the vast majority of the images would simply require marker-based tracking. However, there were a number of images that demonstrated some form of interaction, for example, Fig. 4.4 requires the person to dress the person in the tombstone, and there is also the option to place make-up on the person.

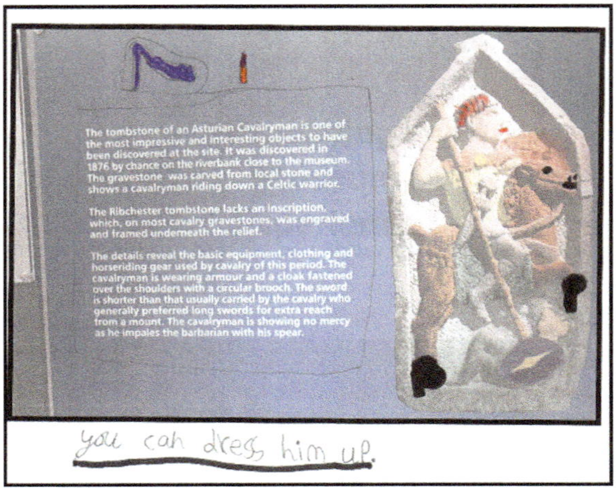

Fig. 4.4 Interactive content added to the sign

4.5 Discussion

The children used a low-fidelity approach to creating prototype ideas relating to the museum. The majority of the children (87%) reported that they had not experienced AR before but were able to contribute design ideas conveyed in their drawings. In this study, the research aimed to understand whether children could contribute design ideas to enable AR to be incorporated into a museum, and it was evident that they could with some limitations. This result is in line with the work by Cassidy et al. (2015) who used participatory design activities with children within the context of AR and play. In the study by Cassidy et al., 10 themes were identified from the drawings, with item information, item augmentation and instructions being the dominant themes, and there was very little in the way of interactive items. In the museum study reported in this chapter, the majority of the drawings required no interaction, which aligns with the study of Cassidy et al. (2015). It may well be that without experience of the technology or a full understanding of the capabilities of AR, they struggle to imagine the interactive capabilities of the technology. It is also possible that the 'tool' used, being a 2D drawing of an interactive space, limited the possibility to describe the interaction. In Read et al. (2013), this effect was mitigated against by having children make images of their prototype ideas over a period of time but this technique would be problematic for children of this age making drawings.

It was evident when examining the drawings that the ideas offered very little in educational value. Although it was anticipated that the children would be able to add content to the images, it was conjectured that this might relate to the Romans but this was not the case for the majority of images. The only items that really related to the Romans that were added were swords, shields and castles but the majority of items drawn were unrelated. It may well have been the children did not know enough about the subject domain, and therefore struggled to imagine Roman artefacts that could enhance the images. In other studies using participatory design, children have struggled to incorporate educational content often just designing things they perceive to be fun (Sim et al. 2014) and even when sensitising techniques have been used they have struggled to produce ideas with direct educational value (Sim et al. 2016). Further work is still required to find ways of ensuring the content is relevant and offers educational value. It may be that design workshops or cooperative design methods may be more suitable as these design techniques would enable the children to refine their designs over a longer period of time. In this study, the children were exposed to the technology, the concept and expect to complete three drawings within an hour; this time limit may simply have been too short a duration. Despite this limitation, the children did contribute many imaginative ideas.

The drawings that the children created were highly diverse and imaginative. There were seven themes that spanned all three scenes; these were as follows: animals, weather, weapons, persons, shapes, speech and flowers, and interaction is present in all the design. The types of ideas that are generated when the themes are examined at a higher level related to four categories:

- Augmented visuals that animate and can be interacted with.
- Augmented static visuals that can be interacted with.
- Visuals or objects that can communicate to the child.
- Visual description of interaction methods.

The drawings within these categories mainly focused on items that would amuse the children and were perceived to be fun. For developers of systems, these insights might offer valuable data in which the educational material could be further embedded or scaffolded around. The use of other stakeholders within the museum may be required to shape the designs further, for example, the educational officers may add educational value to these designs. Alternatively, it may be necessary to have input from educational officers to what additional content should be associated with the artefact and use this as the starting block for the design.

There is also the ethical debate as to whether the design ideas are appropriate for children within the context of a school visit. For example, the interaction depicted in the drawings often focused on fighting the soldiers. For example, one of the drawings required you to throw stones at the soldiers, others required you to fight the soldier with a sword and it showed the soldier getting wounded if you hit him. This type of activity although perceived to be fun by the children may not necessarily be appropriate within the context of a school visit as it could be perceived to be promoting violence.

The feasibility of taking the drawings and turning them into a high-fidelity prototype was also investigated, and all the designs were feasible within current technology. The use of fiducial markers is perfectly acceptable for static environments, but poses challenges when the environment to augment is dynamic and also involves user manipulation of objects. In situations that require this kind of interaction, spatial mapping would be a more appropriate approach. This result has not proven to be the case in other studies that used crowdsourcing to generate ideas (Poetz and Schreier 2012). The two main technologies that would be required to take the drawings forward are spatial mapping and marker-based tracking. Within a museum, care would need to be taken on the location of the marker to ensure it is in the field of view and not obscured by the artefact, as it is highly unlikely that markers could be physically attached to the artefacts due to a risk of damaging them. Spatial mapping would be significantly more expensive to implement than marker-based tracking, and therefore, it may be sensible to prototype marker-based tracking and evaluate this interaction within the context of museums before moving to using other AR technologies. Care needs to be taken when evaluating the technology as the results may be skewed due to the novelty of the AR. If the same type of experience is depicted within each artefact, then the overall experience may be diluted; thus, care needs to be taken to ensure it is not a passive experience. Despite these concerns, marker-based tracking has successfully been used within museums for interacting with phones and tablets (Chen et al. 2014); thus, it is conjectured they would also work with headsets.

From the results, it is difficult to establish how effective the method was for generating museum experiences. Using this approach would enable a designer or developer to understand content that may appeal to children; however, many of the ideas generated had little relevance to both the location and the scene in question. Despite this result, if the aim was to crowdsource ideas as part of the first iteration of a development process, then it could be argued the method was a success. All the children generated ideas with certain themes occurring across all three scenes. This data would enable ideas to be taken forward to the next iteration or feed into the development of a high-fidelity prototype. It is clear that there were some limitations of the approach such as the duration, the lack of understanding of the AR capabilities around interaction and lack of educational value in the designs. These issues may be addressed by increasing the duration, having the children visit the museum prior to the study and letting them experience the technology before they engage in the PD session.

4.6 Conclusion

This study set out to determine whether, through the use of low-fidelity prototyping techniques that incorporated a storyboard, children could understand the concept of AR and design museum experiences and produce design ideas. It was evident from the pictures which the children drew that AR was understood: the children drawings often depicted animated content with a few of them also incorporating interactivity, which is essential within AR. However, the relevance of the drawings to the museum context is somewhat questionable and may be an artefact of the study design. There were a few items of relevance most notably sword, shields and castles but the majority were rather generic to items you might imagine children to enjoy, e.g., rockets, flowers and dinosaurs. The items that were drawn, when analysed to determine whether they were feasible with AR technology, proved to be plausible through the use of either spatial mapping or marker-based tracking. Overall, the results are encouraging in that children could contribute feasible ideas that developers could take forward into higher fidelity prototypes or museums could use these ideas to enhance the fun within the museum artefacts.

Further works are required to determine how the method can be enhanced to ensure that the drawings are more aligned with the museum artefacts. This may be through a process of ensuring the children have more experience of the subject domain, in this instance the Romans. The novel technology did not appear to impact on their creativity or imagination but the lack of interactivity meant many of the designs were not fully utilising the full capabilities of AR and ways in which this could be better incorporated into the ideation stage is still required. Further work could also investigate whether the ideas generated are age specific; this study used children aged 7 to 9 with the majority being 7 and 8. Perhaps the same themes would emerge from older children. This experiment would be important to produce as museums need to appeal to children of a diverse age range, and it may be uneconomical to design AR experiences that are adaptive based on the age. Further work would need to be performed to obtain feedback from the museum on the design ideas and the impact they may have on the wider visitor experience.

Acknowledgements We would like to thank the children from class 3 at Heskin and Pemberton Primary School for participating in this study and contributing their ideas.

References

Alborzi H, Druin A, Montemayor J, Platner M, Porteous J, Sherman L, Hammer J (2000) Designing StoryRooms: interactive storytelling spaces for children. In: Paper presented at the proceedings of the 3rd conference on designing interactive systems: processes, practices, methods, and techniques

Azuma RT (1997) A survey of augmented reality. Presence: Teleoperators Virtual Environ 6(4):355–385

Backett-Milburn K, McKie L (1999) A critical appraisal of the draw and write technique. Health Educ Res 14(3):387–398

Bai Z (2012) Augmenting imagination for children with autism. In: Paper presented at the proceedings of the 11th international conference on interaction design and children

Barraza L (1999) Children's drawings about the environment. Environ Educ Res 5(1):49–66

Brandt E (2006) Designing exploratory design games: a framework for participation in participatory Design? In: Paper presented at the proceedings of the ninth conference on participatory design: expanding boundaries in design, vol 1

Brederode B, Markopoulos P, Gielen M, Vermeeren A, De Ridder H (2005) pOwerball: the design of a novel mixed-reality game for children with mixed abilities. In: Paper presented at the proceedings of the 2005 conference on Interaction design and children

Cahill C, Kuhn A, Schmoll S, Lo W-T, McNally B, Quintana C (2011) Mobile learning in museums: how mobile supports for learning influence student behavior. In: Paper presented at the proceedings of the 10th international conference on interaction design and children

Cassidy B, Sim G, Horton M, Fitton D (2015) Participatory design of wearable augmented reality display elements for children at play. In: Paper presented at the 2015 7th computer science and electronic engineering conference (CEEC)

Caulton T (1998) Hands-on exhibitions: managing interactive museums and science centres. Psychology Press, London

Chen C-Y, Chang BR, Huang P-S (2014) Multimedia augmented reality information system for museum guidance. Pers Ubiquitous Comput 18(2):315–322

Dindler C, Iversen OS, Smith R, Veersawmy R (2010) Participatory design at the museum: inquiring into children's everyday engagement in cultural heritage. In: Paper presented at the OZCHI, Brisbane

Druin A (1999) Cooperative inquiry: develping new technologies for children with children. In: Paper presented at the SIGCHI conference on human factors in computer systems: the CHI is the limit, Pittsburgh

Frauenberger C, Good J, Keay-Bright W (2011) Designing technology for children with special needs: bridging perspectives through participatory design. CoDesign 7(1):1–28

Graham J (2008) Close encounters with culture: museums and galleries as part of the early years foundation stage. Renaissance North West, Manchester

Hornecker E, Halloran J, Fitzpatrick G, Weal M, Millard D, Michaelides D, Cruickshank D, De Roure D (2006) UbiComp in opportunity spaces: challenges for participatory design.In: Paper presented at the proceedings of the ninth conference on participatory design: expanding boundaries in design, vol 1

Horton M, Read JC, Mazzone E, Sim G, Fitton D (2012) School friendly participatory research activities with children.In: Paper presented at the CHI 12 Extend Abstracts, Austin Texas

Juan C, Beatrice F, Cano J (2008) An augmented reality system for learning the interior of the human body. In: Paper presented at the 8th IEEE international conference on advanced learning technologies, Santander, Spain

Kohler B, Haladjian J, Simeonova B, Ismailovic D (2012) Feedback in low vs high fidelity visuals for game prototypes. In: Paper presented at the games and software engineering, Zurich

Leimeister JM, Huber M, Bretschneider U, Krcmar H (2009) Leveraging crowdsourcing: activation-supporting components for IT-based ideas competition. J Manag Inf Syst 26(1): 197–224

Paris SG, Hapgood SE (2002) Children learning with objects in informal learning environments. In: Perspectives on object-centered learning in museums, pp 37–54

Pedersen I, Gale N, Mirza-Babaei P (2016) TombSeer: Illuminating the dead. In: Paper presented at the proceedings of the 7th augmented human international conference 2016, Geneva, Switzerland

Poetz MK, Schreier M (2012) The value of crowdsourcing: can users really compete with professionals in generating new product ideas? J Prod Innov Manag 29(2):245–256

Radu I (2014) Augmented reality in education: a meta-review and cross-media analysis. Pers Ubiquitous Comput 18(6):1533–1543

Rattanarungrot S, White M, Patoli Z, Pascu T (2014) The application of augmented reality for reanimating cultural heritage.In: Paper presented at the international conference on virtual, augmented and mixed reality

Read JC, Fitton D, Horton M (2013) Theatre, playdoh and comic strips: designing organic user interfaces with young adolescent and teenage participants. Interact Comput 25(2):183–198

Read JC, Fitton D, Horton M (2014) Giving ideas an equal chance: inclusion and representation in participatory design with children.In: Paper presented at the proceedings of the 2014 conference on Interaction design and children

Read JC, Fitton D, Sim G, Horton M (2016) How ideas make it through to designs: process and practice. In: Paper presented at the proceedings of the 9th Nordic conference on human-computer interaction

Robertson T, Mansfield T, Loke L (2006) Designing an immersive environment for public use. In: Paper presented at the Proceedings of the ninth conference on participatory design: expanding boundaries in design, vol 1

Sauer J, Sonderegger A (2009) The influence of prototype fidelity and aesthetics of design in usability tests: effects on user behaviour, subjective evaluation and emotion. Appl Ergon 40 670–677

Sim G, Cassidy B (2013) Investigating the fidelity effect when evaluating game prototypes with children. In: Paper presented at the proceedings of the 27th international BCS human computer interaction conference, London, UK

Sim G, Horton M, Read JC (2016) Sensitizing: helping children design serious games for a surrogate population. Serious games, interaction, and simulation. Springer International Publishing, pp 58–65

Sim G, Read JC, Gregory P, Xu D (2014) From England to Uganda: children designing and evaluating serious games. Hum-Comput Interact 30(3–4):263–293

Smith RC, Iversen OS (2011) When the museum goes native. Interactions 18(5):15–19

Theng YL, Nasir NM, Thimbleby H, Buchanan G, Jones M, Bainbridge D, Cassidy N (2000) Children as design partners and testers for a children's digital library.In: Paper presented at the international conference on theory and practice of digital libraries

Vom Lehn D, Heath C, Hindmarsh J (2001) Exhibiting interaction: conduct and collaboration in museums and galleries. Symb Interact 24(2):189–216

Wiklund M, Thurrot C, Dumas J (1992) Does the fidelity of software prototypes affect the perception of usability. In: Paper presented at the proceedings of the human factors and ergonomics society annual meeting, Atlanta, USA

Xu Y Read JC, Sim G, McManus B, Qualter P (2009) Children and smart technologies: can children's experiences be interpreted and coded. In: Paper presented at the HCI 2009 people and computers, Cambridge

Yasar A-U-H (2007) Enhancing experience prototyping by the help of mixed-fidelity prototypes. In: Paper presented at the Mobility, Singapore

Author Biographies

Gavin Sim is a Reader in Human Computer Interaction at the University of Central Lancashire. He is a member of the Child Computer Interaction Group with research interests in the areas of user experience, usability and participatory design within a wide variety of contexts. He is chair of the BCS Interaction group and regularly publishes and reviews for international conferences and journals.

Brendan Cassidy is a Senior Lecturer in Human Computer Interaction at the University of Central Lancashire. His research interests include the design of novel interaction devices and design for augmented and virtual reality technologies. Brendan has worked in interaction design for 12 years and is currently Principle Investigator on the We Are Able: Displays and Play project. An EPSRC funded project (EP/L027658/1) examining how wearable augmented display technologies can help children with different capabilities collaborate and play better together.

Janet C Read is a professor of Child Computer Interaction at the University of Central Lancashire. She is the Director of the Child Computer Interaction (ChiCI) research group at UCLan. Internationally known for her work on designing and evaluating technologies for and with children. She is editor of the International Journal of Child Computer Interaction and has over 100 peer reviewed publications within the area of CCI and HCI.

Part II
Crowds—Diverse Audiences

The chapters in this section engage analytically, critically and reflectively with the opportunities opened up and challenges posed by conceiving of museum audiences as crowds and configuring new ways to engage them through design. The chapters all have a common feature in their concern to involve crowds not as passive audiences but as active users, co-designers and co-creators. Different approaches to crowd engagement and crowdsourcing are introduced and examined, from crowd involvement through participatory design to engagement in the design of interactive experiences and large-scale data mining for mapping the evolution of audience discourses, interests and tastes.

Maria Mortati's chapter illustrates new modes of participatory engagement in art museums, in response to three distinct challenges and possible responses through design: first, moving from exclusively elite voices in heritage interpretation towards more inclusive approaches that integrate audience perspectives and community voices; second, facilitating enhanced art appreciation and understanding for the uninitiated, by offering pre-visit digitally-mediated experiences; and third, moving from passive to participatory engagement in museum spaces, afforded, for instance through the provision of shared creative spaces for artists and museum visitors.

The chapter by *Tonkin, Tourte and Gill* treats the challenges posed by social and technical change on our abilities to access and use digital cultural heritage in sustainable ways. They propose crowd mining as a viable solution for digital cultural heritage preservation and access, to ensure taxonomies and descriptors for information objects are aligned to the interests of relevant audiences. The authors exemplify how the evolution and changes in audience discourses around cultural heritage can be mapped and understood through long-term statistical studies of social media platforms such as Twitter and Tumblr. The chapter concludes that to maintain relevance in knowledge and information management for digital heritage, it is important to think and work beyond silo models. This implies involving direct users, but also involving other institutions, to avoid narrow or biased views of users and user activities.

The next two chapters examine the relationships between crowdsourcing and experience design from two distinct perspectives: first, focusing on the power of crowdsourcing to design rewarding experiences for museums; and second, designing crowdsourcing engagement as a meaningful experience in itself, with direct benefits derived by the voluntary participants.

Van der Lans, Ansems, and Khan make a case for crowdsourcing as a means to design museum experiences and generate content for interactive applications. They introduce and analyse the process of creating *BrainChain*—an app for which the design, content generation and content curation were crowdsourced through a combination of paid crowdsourcing and voluntary visitor involvement. The chapter also addresses an important issue in crowdsourcing: incentives to participate. The authors propose that paid crowdsourcing is a solution, but voluntary crowdsourcing can be encouraged by integrating playful and game-like interaction patterns, which can trigger visitors to contribute to content creation, communication and evaluation. Whilst oftentimes crowdsourcing initiatives are evaluated in functional terms, oriented towards outcomes, the last chapter by *Wrigglesworth and Watts* place an accent on the potential of participatory initiatives to be beneficial as well for the users taking part. This implies that it is important to consider from the onset the quality of the user experience, and design crowdsourcing platforms and initiatives that support meaningful interactions with museum collections and content. The authors propose a series of design lenses or perspectives, which can be adopted to enhance the experiential qualities of crowdsourcing engagements.

In the last chapter, *Van der Veer, Consiglio and Uras* propose that the design of museum experiences can be inspired by giving greater attention to the relations between audiences and cultural artefacts. The authors define the concept of 'experience' by singling out four essential components that characterise these relations: cognitive understanding, emotional engagement, behavioural intentions and attitudes. This approach opens up new ways of thinking about and designing for diverse types of audiences, defined by distinctive modes of relating with cultural artefacts.

Together, the chapters offer a variety of perspectives and approaches for enhancing museum experience design for and with audiences as crowds. In so doing, they also contribute to re-assessing ideas of what a crowd is, and of how to conceive and approach crowds to afford rewarding experiential engagements. Crowds may be nameless, however distinct categories of stakeholders or audience profiles may be identified within them, such as proposed in Maria Mortati's chapter, where crowds are profiled as the arts uninitiated, or the excluded.

Chapter 5
Experiencing the Art Museum: Methods for Public Engagement

Maria Mortati

Abstract Methods for interactive, socially engaged art museum experiences are explored. They examine the utility of developing larger, institutional philosophies to specific techniques via case studies at the U.C.L.A. Hammer Museum, the Oakland Museum of California, and the Walker Art Center. Employed by a spectrum of practitioners such as artists, designers, and museum professionals, these approaches created new avenues for interaction. Specifically, artists entering into visitor services to drive institutional evolution, techniques for engaging atypical visitors, and approaches for engaging with "the crowd" with ephemeral art movements.

5.1 Introduction

It is well documented that museum attendance has been declining in the United States since the early 1980s. The roots of attrition are complex. They stem from changing demographics to the public's lack of early experiences with museums and art. These feed into a perception that museums are not relevant to them. (Wyrick 2014) According to arts engagement studies, in recent years we have been "…in the midst of a seismic shift in cultural production, moving from a 'sit-back-and-be-told culture' to a 'making-and-doing-culture.' Active or participatory arts practices are emerging from the fringes of the Western cultural tradition to capture the collective imagination (WolfBrown 2011)."

Art museums have explored these two phenomena directly by bringing arts practitioners with experience in participatory design or socially engaged art into the visitor experience. Some of these efforts are directly concerned with how to engage more people given that they are not art lovers and *connoisseurs*. Others are less concerned with questions around arts literacy; they are more interested in participation or perception of institutional sense-making. They address questions such as,

M. Mortati (✉)
California College of the Arts, 4354 23rd Street, San Francisco, CA 94114, USA
e-mail: maria@mortati.com

A. Vermeeren et al. (eds.), *Museum Experience Design*, Springer Series on Cultural Computing, https://doi.org/10.1007/978-3-319-58550-5_5

"What can a museum be (now)?" or "What might happen if we bring different practitioners on board to engage with the life and operations of the museum?"

Institutions have different models of how and why to bring in artists and how to work with them. We will explore these models via three case studies. These are projects I have developed as an individual contributor, and in collaboration with staff, other artists, and participants. The first project, at the UCLA Hammer Museum, brought in artists to address the space of Visitor Services. The second, at the Oakland Museum of California, brought artists into engage with their non-visiting public. Lastly, the Walker Art Center, created a public space outside of the museum for artists and the public to manifest open-ended, socially engaged projects.

Public engagement is by nature, experimental. Whether as an art practice or the desired outcome, it is specific to the community and institution in which it occurs. While is no one approach, there are methodologies that make this work possible.

5.2 Case Study: U.C.L.A. Hammer Museum Artist Residencies in Visitor Services

The U.C.L.A. Hammer Museum (Hammer) is a contemporary art museum in Los Angeles. In 2009, they were awarded an arts innovation grant with the objective to "…create a new kind of interactive museum: an artist-driven visitor engagement and education program that encourages daily contact among visitors, artists, and museum staff (James Irvine Foundation 2009)…"

For the first year of the residency, they invited Machine Project, a Los Angeles based not-for-profit arts organization whose mission is "to produce cultural programming that inspires audiences to become creatively active by imagining, participating and relating in new ways to the arts and sciences—utilizing a range of techniques, such as informality, humour, and surprise…" (Machine Project n.d.). During the course of their residency, Machine Project produced 26 projects in conjunction with 300 artists.

The museum identified "visitor services" as a focus for their residency, and defined the general visiting public as their audience. No distinctions were made with regards to demographics or artistic literacy. They wanted artists to come up with creative solutions or catalysts for things that were traditionally considered infrastructure, not art. These included mundane issues, such as how to find the bathroom, or where to buy tickets. Other examples were how to get people into unused spaces, or simply ways to put unused spaces into play. Oftentimes, these engaging experiences seemed ridiculous on the surface. Yet they were also a critique of how the museum used its spaces and welcomed its visitors.

When Machine Project Director Mark Allen invited me to participate in the residency, it struck me choosing wayfinding as an area of exploration would be challenging to do in an interactive and engaging manner. This is especially true as a "museum sense-making" type of project, i.e., how do we understand the institutions, not simply the contents. Wayfinding is traditionally the domain of architects and designers. A clear map and wall signs are the standard. It is a problem often solved in an efficient and seamless manner, blending into infrastructure, and regardless of audience literacy.

The Hammer Museum site is complex. It is situated on the same site as the Occidental Petroleum Corporation Headquarters. They share entrances, parking facilities, atrium, and café. Depending on what entrance you use, it can be confusing to identify where the museum entrance is, and to understand where one is in the space.

The organized and logical thinking that is essential to create a good map was not necessarily a constraint for the artists looking at this problem. The fact that wayfinding was a problem for the museum was not our primary concern. What mattered to us was to find a way that would engagingly get visitors around the site, and help them participate (however opaquely) in the conversation the artists were having with the museum *and* the public through the residency.

I explored ways to navigate visitors around the site. These approaches ranged from variations on the familiar "breadcrumb trail" (a progression of signs that point the way) to more iconoclastic concepts bordering on the absurd. Mark and I had identified the atrium entrance as the main area for orientation. It is a large space with many entries and exits. It provided an ideal opportunity to orient the visitor in the building.

After dozens of iterations, we came up with the idea of using a mechatronic hand mounted on top of a model of the building to point the visitor in the direction they wanted to go (Mortati 2014b). We started out quite small, playing with the notion of creating an architect's model of the museum inside a vitrine. It would house a large rotating hand inside so visitors could look down into it and have an overview of where to go. However, in order for our project to make itself understood as a way experience, (and not as an object in a vitrine), it became clear that the interactive experience needed to dominate the visual field enough to make an impact for visitors.

Working with local fabricator Matt Jones and programming by artist Ben Dean, the interactive evolved into a structure seven feet wide by eight and a half feet high. It became a 3D animatronic sculpture mounted atop a large "model" of the museum. The sculpture pointed people toward different parts of the Museum or to themselves; depending on the button they pushed (Figs. 5.1 and 5.2).

We borrowed from the vernacular of science museum interactives in using Happ buttons that lit up when a location was pressed. Driven by an Arduino, the motor would whir and the hand would slowly point in the chosen direction: tickets, galleries, theater, café, you.

The anecdotal evidence showed that it (or "the big hand") was surprisingly effective at getting people around. It was an object made for the visitor, and called attention to their concerns, not the concerns of the museum or the (other) artwork in its location, its orientation, and its language.

For the museum, however, there was a lot of internal controversy during the residency with this particular project. It created discussion and tension about signage, the role of the artist, the ability of the museum to allow confusion around authority, artwork, and the building envelope itself. Much of this discussion happened among the staff, between the artists and the staff, and anecdotally, among the

Fig. 5.1 Interacting with the giant hand. Source: Machine Project

Fig. 5.2 Button interface. Source: Machine Project

public. While there was the talk of keeping it up for a year or perhaps even accessioning it, as a solution to the tension, the museum and Machine chose to leave it up for only a month.

Was it artwork? Perhaps, but it was not a traditionally accessioned object. Was it design? Perhaps, but it took over the space, creating another problem while theoretically solving the first one. The museum was ultimately concerned that in calling so much attention to their wayfinding problem we would limit the functionality of our approach as a navigational tool and overemphasize the difficulty of their layout.

With the public as its primary concern, this initiative provided the opportunity for the multiple constituents to participate in the question of the artist as a problem solver, the functions of design, and the needs of operationalizing experimentation.

"Machine's wayfinding proposals… made the Hammer's infrastructural concerns part of the art that it displayed. The value of this, from a public engagement perspective, is that the museum becomes a more dynamic and approachable entity—and one that includes the public in discussions about the nature and function of the museum. The invitation to think critically about the museum itself is a gambit that implicitly extends to the art: it sends visitors a clear message that the museum is a space in which art serves as the basis for a conversation about values in which they are welcomed to participate (Allen and Agsten 2012)."

By borrowing the interaction language more familiar in science museums of button-pushing and whirring motors created a familiarity for the visitor. Having the freedom (however fleeting) to make the experience adequately dominate the field of view created a piece that was effective in function and in critique. The artist as a problem solver is a tricky assignment. The artist as a catalyst to explore and discuss is more in line with how they work.

In the end, the project resulted in the following outcomes:

- Engaged dozens of artists and staff with the questions of museum as a self-aware entity into which the public is invited
- Evolved the institution's socially engaged curatorial practice
- Documentation and sharing through conferences, video, and the widely disseminated "Machine Project Hammer Museum Public Engagement Artist in Residence Report (Ibid)."

5.3 Case Study: Appropriating the Collection at the Oakland Museum of California

In 2014, the Oakland Museum of California (OMCA) began an institution-wide initiative to address the discrepancy that their immediate neighbors fell well outside of their typical visiting public (James Irvine Foundation Arts Innovation Grant 2009). The OMCA has long been a progressive institution. In 2011, they did extensive work on exhibitions and programming and reframed themselves as a "visitor centric institution." (Henry and Mclean 2011) With this new initiative, they intended to build up attendance and engagement with these non-visiting neighbors. Much of this nearby, potential audience consisted of the visitors who do not tend to frequent museums, and in terms of art, come armed with little prior knowledge.

The city of Oakland is extraordinarily diverse in terms of ethnic makeup: White (34.5%), Black or African American (28%), Asian (16.8%), and Latino (25.4%)

(United States Census Bureau 2010) Most of the non-white communities lived in high concentrations adjacent to the museum.

"Becoming familiar with your neighbors is the first step. Research that focused on learning about them should be undertaken with the same enthusiasm that has already gone into learning about your [museum] and the artifacts it houses. What you need to know has nothing to do with [art] history or your particular [museum's] narrative. It has to do with everything surrounding it (Vagnone et al. 2016)."

Through this initiative, the museum invited me to do a project of my own choosing and agreed to pair me with a single local family. Given that I had little experience with their neighbors, and that my more traditional museum work tended toward larger constituencies, I felt that working on a more intimate scale would prove more fruitful in building relationships, both for the museum and for me. Thus, this project fell under the second type I mentioned at the outset of this chapter: engaging audiences beyond the usual art lovers and connoisseurs.

The museum connected me to a Latino family with three children: two young boys and a middle school aged girl who spoke a mixture of English and Spanish. Mother and daughter had been to the museum via school trip, while the rest of the family had never visited.

The OMCA is a comprehensive institution and I chose to work with their art collection (vs. their history or science collections). At the time, the art galleries seemed as if they stood the most to gain from a socially engaged project. And art seemed a subject that has more universal subject rather than the specificity of history or science. The project culminated into a series of interpretive pedestals throughout the art galleries with a video installation at the start. These were supported by a series of public events, led by the family, hosted by the museum, and facilitated by myself.

When looking for explanations for why certain communities do not visit museums, a common response is that these communities do not see themselves reflected there (James Irvine Foundation Arts Innovation Grant 2009). Playing on the idea of reflections, I titled my project *Tell Me Where the Mirrors Go*.

My original proposal was structured around connecting the internal lives of the family at home with the art collection in the museum. I wanted to suggest that these works in the museum are not the domain of the few. Instead, they are the ideas of the many, and for many. The concept was that over a period of visits, the family would identify works of art they resonated with and that they wanted to have represented in their home. The museum was going to de-install their chosen artworks, and we would install full-scale recreations in the family's home. The in-gallery artworks would be replaced with large-scale photographs of the family at home with "their" artworks.

However, at the beginning of the project, this family did not have a permanent home. They had a series of temporary living arrangements and were living in a motel. This changed the focus away from visually representing ownership of ideas and more toward letting the project evolve in an improvisational way. The museum was supportive of this shift.

I wanted to find out if the question of not seeing themselves reflected was true for this family. We began working together through a series of in-person meetings at the site and in their motel. I listened to what they had to say about their experiences or impressions of the museum, their impressions with art, and their desires for a role the museum could play in their lives.

It took a few visits to the museum (Fig. 5.3) and at their temporary home before we achieved a level of comfort with one another. In all cases, the family was incredibly generous with their time and attention. They were honest and candid, despite the fact that they were often being recorded.

They talked about what they thought of the collection, the museum itself, and its value. The father said that he thought the museum was a bit "boring", but he also said that he hoped his kids would want to visit; he wanted them to have the opportunity for informal education encounters. This softens the art museum myth: that the collections themselves are somehow continuously inaccessible to certain publics (Weil 2002).

"A lot of people don't like to come to museums. I don't know why… Maybe they don't… sometimes we have a lot of problems before [we] think about go(ing) to museums. When you think about rent, first, I'm sure you could walk around in my area, and you could interview people who never go to the museum."—Margaro, father (2015).

My objective for the project was still to insert their presence into the art viewing moment (for all visitors). To again, let them choose where they saw themselves reflected, and to make that visible to the museum staff and the public.

Instead of photos of them inside at home with works of art (again, not possible), I integrated their first-person perspectives adjacent to individual works of art that had resonated with them.

Fig. 5.3 Author (left) and family (right) at the museum. Source: Alex Rapine

The project resulted in three primary in-gallery components that spanned media, interpretive layer, and events, with everything bilingual, prioritizing Spanish. The in-gallery experience began with a mini-documentary near the entrance of the gallery. Following were eight pedestals (Fig. 5.4) directly adjacent to works of art that each family member resonated with. On each pedestal were images of the individual family member, and their commentary engraved in two languages. It was created to have the feel of a semi-permanent object. I chose this route versus a comment card or flat graphic format to underline the importance of their place in this "museum of California." No one could ignore or overlook these objects. The series of public events were bilingual tours of these chosen artworks, with the mother of the family performing the role of translator.

A popular refrain I heard from artists, designers, and curators were 'why will they care about art?' inferring that because they were struggling economically and/or ethnically, the idea for them to engage with the museum was ridiculous. On the contrary, during both in-gallery and post-project interviews, the mother said that she welcomed the opportunity to see another "plane" above the fray of daily life.

In follow-up interviews and meetings after the project, the family reported that they visited more often and that they felt a sense of ownership of the museum. For the museum, the details of the project, including the video, were shared with staff. A number of them expressed the impact it had on how they prioritize their work going forward. The specificity of a single family was successful towards fostering a sense of connectedness between staff and their community.

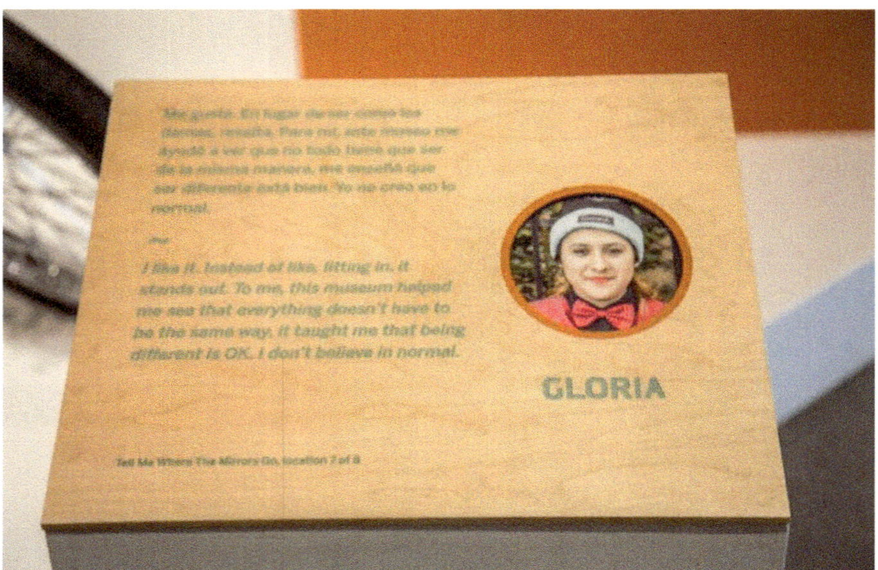

Fig. 5.4 Pedestal with daughter's commentary. Source: Odell Hussey

During the course of the grant, projects by other regional artists explored the vein of demographics and the museum. For example, one was a large, community-driven exhibition developed by local artist Chris Treggiari and OMCA Curator of Social Practice Evelyn Orantes called "Oakland I Want You to Know…" It was a participatory installation about the impacts of gentrification on West Oakland, driven by economic forces in the greater San Francisco Bay Area (Abbey-Lambertz 2016).

Director of the OMCA Lab, Kelly McKinley provided high-level findings on the impact of the grant initiatives:

"We know that over the duration of the project we attracted over 80,000 new visitors to the Museum. We also increased the diversity of our audience with now over 50% of visitors being people of color. We have surveyed staff each year to see how their perception of the museum's and their own commitment/understanding of community engagement has shifted (McKinley 2017)."

In my work with museums, I engage with large groups or constituencies to find commonalities, or to distil ideas into a format that will resonate or make sense to them. Working in such an intimate way underscored how much more impact one-on-one interaction can have on those involved in the project, as well as those who view it.

In the end, the project resulted in the following outcomes:

- Provided the museum with a better understanding of their public
- Gave the museum tools for engaging their neighborhood through first-person engagement
- Created a sense of ownership of the museum for this formerly non-visiting group
- Enabled artists and staff to produce work that actively engaged with the subject of demographics and institutional relationships
- Documentation and sharing through conferences, talks, and video.

5.4 Case Study: Public Engagement at the Walker Art Center's Open Field

In 2009, the Walker Art Center, a contemporary art museum, noticed that the field adjacent to their building was being used in an ad hoc fashion, and began to formulate a question:

"What form of public park could emerge from the context of a contemporary arts center?" (Peters and Schultz 2012)

The general public was making it their own: dropping by and having picnics, playing games, and hanging out, but they were not necessarily coming into the museum. In 2009, the Education and Community Programs department began to develop a 4-acre green space on the campus as "a shared space for creative gatherings, unexpected interactions, and idea exchange (Ibid)." It was transformed into an area for programing with an outdoor café, a tool shed to hold games and art-making supplies, and of course, a large, grassy field (Fig. 5.5). They named it Open Field, and established it using the framework of the commons (Fig. 5.5).

In brief, "commons" is a general term for shared resources used in political economic theory (Hess 2006). Commons are defined by these shared resources and are managed by guidelines and theories that help groups to share them. In the context of Open Field, the Walker extrapolated the concept to explore creating a sense of shared ownership between the public and the museum, in an area, the public was already using.

Embracing an inclusive sensibility and aesthetic, Open Field went on to initiate and support dozens of art, design, research residencies, projects of the public's own creation, and large-scale popular events. It was an experiment in participation and public space, which over the course of 3 years engaged approximately 92,000 people (Mortati 2014a). In this sense, the larger project was both a "museum sense-making" project as well as an effort to expand the audience beyond the norm.

From a purely logistical perspective, this scale of participation requires extensive support. The Open Field team created accessible guidelines for participation which were posted on their website. They made it clear how to propose projects, what kind

Fig. 5.5 Walker Art Center's Open Field amenities included a tool shed (filled with art activities and games), cafe, worktables and the field itself. Source: Author

of support to expect, and how to use a public calendar, all of which came together as an "etiquette" guide for the field.

I was invited by the Walker to create two Open Field projects. The first was an interactive video project and the second focused on an experimental art movement from the mid-twentieth century.

5.4.1 People Imitating Cats: Interactive Video Project

It is impossible to write about Open Field without mentioning the unexpected success of their 2012 spontaneous project, the Internet Cat Video Festival. In brief, CatVidFest (as it became known) was the first-ever, crowd-sourced video festival that celebrated the phenomenon of people watching cat videos. The Walker Open Field team developed an online jury of artists, enthusiasts, and friends to review an estimated 4,000 submissions that were winnowed down into a final reel. Screened outdoors one evening on the field, the Walker did not know whether to expect a few hundred or a thousand people. In the end, 10,000 people showed up.

"We assumed when we were assembling the clips that people would be eager to see new videos, but in actuality, the greater joy was sharing the experience of watching very familiar videos with each other (Walker Art Center 2014)."

My first project was for the 2013 CatVidFest. I developed and deployed a public interactive titled *People Imitating Cats* (Fig. 5.6). It was a mobile recording cart, shaped like a cat's head, and it roamed the Minnesota State Fair, the site of that years' festival. It was a relatively simple interactive that recorded videos of the attendees imitating cats. The recordings were played back to an audience of 11,000 during the event, amplifying the absurdity, and joy of people gathering en masse to watch cat videos.

Fig. 5.6 People imitating cats interactive. Source: Author

5.4.2 FluxField Projects—Engaging the Ephemeral

In 2014, Open Field invited a number of artists and practitioners to explore the art movement Fluxus. This was in parallel to the Center's exhibition *Art Expanded, 1958–1978,* a large show of art and media from their collection of the "expanded arts scene," (Walker Art Center 2014) a large part of which included Fluxus. Their invitation to me was to do research in the archives and create public engagement projects on the field in relation to the movement.

Fluxus took shape in the mid-twentieth century, and is a loosely defined, international collection of artists, designers, poets, and performers. Their work spearheaded a moment in time where artists began to upend traditional art forms though informal and distributed collaborations.

"I think of Fluxus first and foremost as the loose network of artists in the late 1950s into'60s who first carried the name—who understood art as inseparable from everyday life, and vice versa, and performed lots of public experiments accordingly. And who also constantly disagreed with each other about what "Fluxus" was about. I think of names like John Cage, George Maciunas, Alison Knowles, George Brecht, Nam June Paik. So in that sense, I think Fluxus is people."—Rachel Jendrzejewski (Holloway 2014)

With few prerequisites for prior-knowledge and a performative and playful sensibility, Fluxus is fertile territory for interpretation and engagement. Its lingua franca was instructions in the form of written or visualized "scores." Fluxus artists wrote, shared, and performed these simple written instructions (Fig. 5.7). One artist

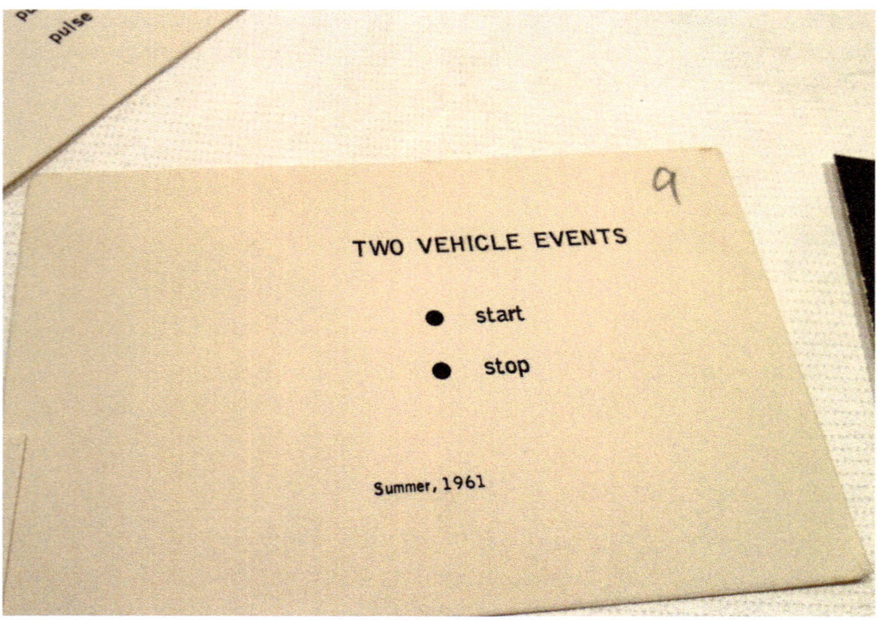

Fig. 5.7 Fluxus score, walker archives. Source: Author

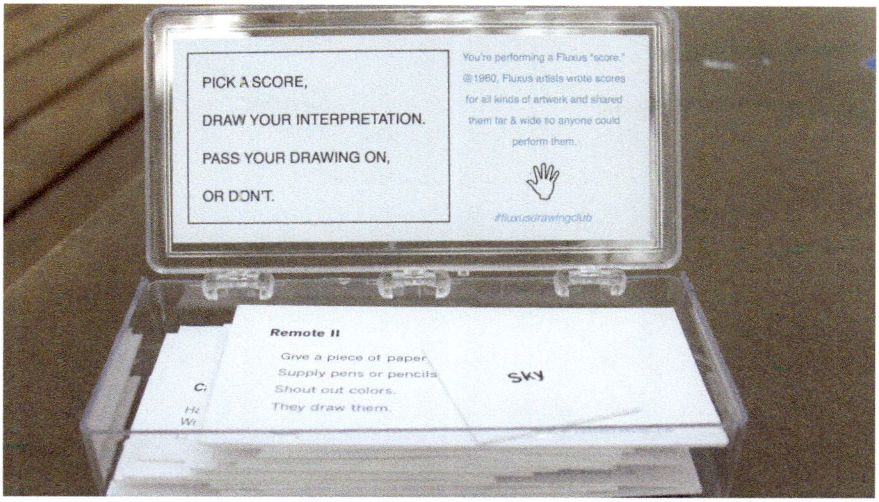

Fig. 5.8 Fluxus scores for drawing club. Source: Author

could craft a score; pass it on to another to "perform" in their manner, their place, maybe even at the same time.

My residency culminated in a participatory event called Fluxus Drawing Club, and an installation of Fluxus scores called FluxField Interpretive Trail on the adjacent field for the public to wander through.

Fluxus Drawing Club was a collaboration between myself and Minneapolis artist Margaret Pezalla-Granlund. Drawing Club, a collaborative and participatory drawing event, was already a weekly Open Field program, which we used as our platform. Together we designed scores, creating a series of Flux Kits with light (do you mean fun? Or what could another word be) instructions printed inside (Fig. 5.8). The public sat out at the picnic tables and "drew" scores (Fig. 5.9). For background at the event, I asked Margaret and her family to record their reading of an essay by Fluxus founding father, Dick Higgins: "A Child's History of Fluxus" (1979). Visitors spent the evening engaged with the scores, drawing, sharing, and posting them on a purpose-built mobile display board.

Because they already had an established program, I could easily propose a project without the pressure of attracting participants. The museum was also able to quickly connect me with local collaborators, allowing me to spend most of my time on developing ideas and producing the work, making it possible to easily produce a second and complimentary project.

For FluxField Interpretive Trail, the second project of the event, I generated a series of interpretive panels that made connections between the (rambunctious) spirit of Fluxus with the playful, experimental spirit of Open Field (Fig. 5.10). The Fluxus philosophy that (their) art was "neither an exhibition of objects or a performance, but somewhere in between." (George Brecht, Wikipedia). These scores included commentaries on Fluxus ("The most ambiguous club in the art world"),

Fig. 5.9 Fluxus drawing club event. Source: Author

quotes from founding Fluxus artists, and observations of the actual field ("Need Sod"). Hashtags became an organizing principle of the trail which I used as labels to suggest whether a score was foundational, descriptive, or invitational. The field served my project well by allowing people to participate in an experiential yet low-stakes manner.

In art education or interactive contexts, we often talk about learning goals and visitor outcomes because of an intervention. What do learning goals look like in a relatively free-choice public space such as the contemporary art center when we explore these questions in tandem with practitioners and the public? How do we, as a field, work iteratively to uncover those questions?

"The learning goals in contemporary art museums seem to be particularly difficult to define. Are we hoping that visitors walk away with a greater knowledge of the art world, studio practices, issues in contemporary society or all of these things (Di Salvo 2012)?"

Fig. 5.10 Scores on the field. Source: Author

The Open Field construct gave both the public and practitioners of many disciplines, a framework in which they could produce social projects of their own creation. For artists and practitioners, it fostered new, more social art forms, by giving them space, access to intellectual resources and operational support.

Another important result of the Open Field project is what it did for the staff and artists who worked in and on it. The impact of the project is still being felt as their work continues to evolve in more social ways. Having the space and support to do these types of projects builds internal capacities and skills in practitioners inside and outside the museum, all toward future engagement.

The projects were not intended to be permanent. Open Field was "…an experiment in participation. It was less about audience attendance and more about shifting audience perception of the Center. We wanted to expand the idea of what a museum could be by intentionally inviting and mixing up different kinds of people and experiences (Schultz 2017)."

In the end, the project resulted in the following outcomes:

- Expanded and better understood their public
- Moved a number of the audience from "public" to "participant"
- Engaged dozens of museum practitioners, artists and lay people in a new form of interaction
- Helped develop a new curatorial practice across the art museum and art education field

- Expanded and enriched the rigor of the Walker's Education and Community Programs Department
- Created new persistent relationships with other groups and individuals in Minneapolis and nationally
- Disseminated the work in print, video, and through conferences to foster other projects and artists in this space

In the context of the 4 years of Open Field, my projects were simply two of several hundred projects. What's interesting is how they demonstrate the flexibility (and durability) of this construct. By providing the public and artists an open space to participate and foment, it fostered a new wave in art and social practices with the intellectual rigor of contemporary art, and the inclusivity of the public sphere.

5.5 Conclusion

The projects described in this chapter share a common desire to reach outside the traditional boundaries of the museum in an attempt to build a closer bond with their institution and their public (however directly or indirectly). The varied approaches to this goal can be a useful reminder that there is no universal solution.

In many of these projects, the museums become a little more pliant by not taking themselves too seriously. Social positioning and tonality are useful tools to employ when your public might be unfamiliar or uncomfortable with what seems to be a formal, authoritarian place.

"The presence of curious giggling children at the Hammer can certainly help to relax a museum's stereotypical stuffy atmosphere (Bastien 2010)."

While it might seem ridiculous to build a large, mechatronic hand for wayfinding at the Hammer, it ultimately created understanding about how artists best work: less as problem solvers and more as catalysts for exploration.

It is also important to understand the community that each museum serves. The OMCA created space to explore myths and realities of their neighboring public through a multiyear grant initiative. The project I cited, an intimate and open-ended engagement with a local family, not only changed the way the family viewed the museum, but it also had a profound effect on the way the museum staff viewed their roles and responsibilities.

With the Open Field project, the Walker used an outdoor space to reach beyond the museum walls and bring the museum to the public. CatVidFest used the cultural sense-making apparatus of the Walker to share a social phenomenon. FluxField was an example both of making space for new practices, and of highlighting an aspect of art history that does not take itself too seriously. By breaking down multiple barriers between the public, who might be intimidated by or indifferent to art, and the museum, which might be unsure how to reach new audiences, unexpected connections could occur. Playfulness and humility can be powerful tools for engagement.

While for the sake of your project you may need to differentiate, in the end, there is no clear-cut distinction among visitors, staff, and artists. "Visitor Centric" describes museums where the visitor is the primary concern. This is a very important step, however, it puts all the focus on the visitor. Artists and systems that bring in other players into the museum (and sometimes they are the visitors) take the museum beyond a simple transactional or binary relationship. These projects engaged public, staff, and artists, frequently blurring the lines among all of those groups.

References

Abbey-Lambertz K (2016) Oakland artists take on gentrification as tech boom threatens their city Huffington post. http://www.huffingtonpost.com/entry/oakland-gentrification-art-installation_us_579bac86e4b0693164c1374e Accessed 3 Mar 2017

Allen M, Agsten A (2012) Public engagement artist in residence, machine project hammer report. https://hammer.ucla.edu/blog/2012/04/machine-project-201011-a-report/. Accessed 1 Mar 2017

Bastien J (2010, July 18) Machine project sounds out the boundaries of the museum experience at the hammer with bells, Guitars And Houseplants. Retrieved March 1, 2017, from http://dailybruin.com/2010/07/18/machine_project_sounds_out_the_boundaries_of_the_museum_experience_at_the_hammer_with_bells_guitars_/

Di Salvo BJ, Di Salvo C (2012) Walker kitchen lab [Web blog post]. https://walkerkitchenlab.wordpress.com/

Henry B, Mclean K (2011) How visitors changed our museum: transforming the gallery of california art. James Irvine Foundation. http://museumca.org/files/HowVisitorsChangedOurMuseumBook.pdf

Hess C (2006) Research on the commons, common-pool resources, and common property. http://dlc.dlib.indiana.edu/dlc/contentguidelines. Accessed 1 Mar 2017

Higgins D (1979) A child's history of fluxus. Lightworks 11–12:26–27

Holloway L (2014) Artists respond to fluxus. http://blogs.walkerart.org/ecp/category/general/page/2/. Accessed 3 Mar 2017

Machine Project-Hammer Museum (2012) https://hammer.ucla.edu/artist-residencies/2009/machine-project/. Accessed 1 Feb 2017

Machine Project, About Us. (n.d.) http://machineproject.com/archival/about/. Accessed 19 June 2017

McKinley K (2017) Oakland museum of California N.C.A.F. Grant assessment. E-mail

Mortati M (2014a) A fluxfield research residency. http://blogs.walkerart.org/ecp/2014/10/02/a-fluxfield-research-residency/. Accessed 11 Mar 2017

Mortati M (2014b) Design intentionality and the art museum. Intentionally designed spaces, March 2014, 34–39. http://name-aam.org/resources/exhibitionist/back-issues-and-online-archive. Accessed 1 Feb 2017 (Print and online)

Peters S, Schultz S (2012) Open field: conversations on the commons. Walker Art Centre, Minneapolis. https://shop.walkerart.org/products/open-field-conversations-on-the-commons-online-version

Schultz S (2017) Open field. E-mail

United States Census Bureau (2010) Bay Area Census, City of Oakland Alameda County. http://www.bayareacensus.ca.gov/cities/Oakland.htm.. Accessed 19 June 2017

Vagnone FD, Ryan DE, Cothren OB (2016) Anarchist's guide to historic house museums. Routledge, Taylor and Francis Group, London

Walker Art Center, Art Expanded, 1958–1978 (2105) https://walkerart.org/calendar/2014/art-expanded-19581978.Accessed 19 June 2017
Walker Art Center, (2014) Internet Cat Video Festival. http://web.archive.org/web/20140101000000*/http://www.walkerart.org/internet-cat-video-festival. Accessed 19 June 2017
Weil SE (2002) A cabinet of curiosities: inquiries into museums and their prospects. Smithsonian Institution Press, Washington
WolfBrown (2011) Getting in on the act. Response from James Irvine Foundation. https://www.irvine.org/arts/what-were-learning/getting-in-on-the-act
Wyrick G (2014) All together now: teens and museums. J Mus Educ 39(3):231–35. http://museumeducation.info/wp-content/uploads/2014/08/JME.v39.03-2.pdf. Accessed 3 Mar 2017

Author Biography

Maria Mortati is a designer, artist, and educator working in the museum field. Her area of expertise is in public interaction design and social practice. Her work encompasses exhibition development and design, performed in close collaboration with museum staff, boards, and local communities. Her work explores mechanisms for engagement through exhibit platforms, installations, public events, and writing. Maria has worked for and with a variety of institutions such as: the Baltimore and Dallas Museums of Art, the Exploratorium, the Sainsbury Wellcome Centre, U.C.L.A. Hammer Museum, and the Walker Art Center. She is a frequent panelist on the subject of innovative and experimental museum practice. Maria teaches in the Graduate Interaction Design Program at the California College of the Arts, has a B.F.A. in Studio Art from the University of Colorado, and an M.F.A. in Design from Stanford University.

Chapter 6
Crowd Mining Applied to Preservation of Digital Cultural Heritage

Emma L. Tonkin, Gregory J. L. Tourte and Alastair Gill

Abstract Accessible systems, in digital heritage as elsewhere, should 'speak the user's language'. However, over long time periods, this may change significantly, and the system must still keep track of it. Conceptualising and tracking change in a population may be achieved using a functional and computable model based on representative datasets. Such a model must encompass relevant characteristics in that population and support predefined functionality, such as the ability to track current trends in language use. Individual published viewpoints on any given platform may be observed in aggregate by means of a large-scale text mining approach. We have made use of social media platforms such as Twitter and Tumblr to collect statistical information about anonymous users' perspectives on cultural heritage items and institutions. Through longitudinal studies, it is possible to identify indicators pointing to an evolution of discourse surrounding cultural heritage items, and provide an estimate of trends relating to represented items and creators. We describe a functional approach to building useful models of shift in contemporary language use, using data collection across social networks. This approach is informed by existing theoretical approaches to modelling of semantic change. As a case study, we present a means by which such ongoing user modelling processes drawing on contemporary resources can support 'just-in-time' pre-emptive review of material to be presented to the public. We also show that this approach can feed into enhancement of the data retrieval processes.

E. L. Tonkin (✉)
School of Electrical Engineering, University of Bristol, MVB, Woodland Road, Bristol BSB 1UB, UK
e-mail: e.tonkin@bath.edu

G. J. L. Tourte
School of Geographical Sciences, University of Bristol, Bristol, UK

A. Gill
King's College London, London, UK

A. Vermeeren et al. (eds.), *Museum Experience Design*, Springer Series on Cultural Computing, https://doi.org/10.1007/978-3-319-58550-5_6

6.1 Introduction

It is a familiar observation that digital cultural heritage brings with it new challenges. One such challenge is the effect of long-term technical and societal change on our ability to access and make use of digital objects held within heritage databases. Materials that surround and support access to these resources, such as indexing metadata, also suffer from various forms of degradation.

Just as such materials, especially those intended for machine to machine (m2m) usage, may refer to or depend on unavailable or obsolete technologies, information intended for human consumption may suffer from processes of obsolescence. For example, resources or accompanying material may use terminology that is no longer current, or which has acquired unintended or problematic connotations, or which is in any other sense inaccessible to the reader. Hence, these materials are also a subject for digital preservation (Brunsmann 2011). Similar issues and principles apply in contemporary information access contexts. The processes of information sharing between expert practitioners and non-expert members of the public are similarly dependent on the ability to bridge between communities. Consider for example the discussion in the work of Abu-Shumays and Leinhardt (2002) of the role of the *docent*, or volunteer guide, as intermediary between public and professional.

A great deal of existing work in knowledge and information management has focused on related problems, such as the development of knowledge structures designed to support user-focused changes made to information systems such as collection catalogues and search engines. Consider, for example, the use of adaptive indexing to allow indexing terms to converge towards user-supplied vocabulary (Furnas 1985), provision of facilities enabling user-supplied terms to be used, reused and combined flexibly with formal knowledge structures such as ontologies (Weller 2007) user-centred evaluation of library indexes (Carlo Bertot et al. 2006), and formal representations of user journeys through information spaces, enabling past user experience to be called on in future systems engineering (Canter et al. 1985). Many institutions make use of ontologies or taxonomies designed to allow for the use of variant terminologies in describing technical aspects of cultural heritage objects; an example is the Getty Vocabularies published by the Getty Research Institute. Such structures are available for reuse by other institutions, leaving open the key problem of how these should evolve with different times and concepts. Several further examples of such works are concisely discussed in this chapter.

Digital preservation is a significant focus for cultural heritage organisations. Museums, libraries and archives increasingly work with digital objects, as documented by the significant and growing literature on the challenges of digital preservation (Hedstrom 1997). Long-term digital preservation refers to 'processes, strategies and tools used to store and access digital data for long periods of time', according to Factor et al. (2009, p. 6:1). The time period in question is sufficiently long that technologies, formats, hardware, software and technical communities are likely to change.

There is Kuny (1998) a risk of a 'digital dark age', in which data from the digital age is lost irrevocably. Digital preservation attempts to mitigate such risks, a process which often involves some sort of maintenance: format shifting of digital objects, for example, can resolve problems of format, hardware and software obsolescence.

In this chapter, we explore the issues which contribute to a 'digital dark age', and propose an approach—identifying promising related work in human–computer interaction and information retrieval—to enhance usability of digital data in the future. Whilst we acknowledge that this alone cannot mean that a digital dark age—or similar lack of usability or access—is averted, it can begin to help researchers consider some of the issues in this area.

Our research interest is not solely in preservation of access to data across a large temporal gulf. Similar issues of accessibility and usability arise in contemporary contexts; Burrows et al. (2015) describe the benefits of 'actively develop[ing] a shared language' between specialist system designers/implementers and end users. We have a keen interest in this area and hope to explore the adaptation of the methods in this chapter to support such developments. Cultural heritage catalogues, as large semi-structured datasets, offer an opportunity to evaluate the effects of cultural and contextual change over time.

In the following, we review long-standing research which has contributed to our understanding of usability and accessibility concerns presented by online/digital catalogue information. We then discuss in more detail how these and other related issues of digital preservation affect the cultural heritage sector. In particular, we focus on search and retrieval process relating to catalogues, as this is a core function of first- and second-generation cultural heritage organisation informatics as well as a key architectural component underlying implementation of additional functionality: education, study and enjoyment.

This leads us to our proposal, which we believe will provide a new insight in detecting the early signs of possible digital dark ages in this sector. Specifically, we believe that since language is the 'currency' both in indexing catalogues and in search and retrieval behaviour, it makes sense to accommodate potential changes or differences in usage which may provide a barrier to use for a proportion of those accessing it. By automatically considering linguistic differences, we can identify cases in which performance of mitigating maintenance actions may reduce impact of change, adding further information to support the active curation processes implemented by cultural heritage professionals. In particular, we suggest that data drawn from social sensors and cultural media mining could usefully support such processes of revision.

Whilst the main body of this chapter deals with digital infrastructure, we remark that objects and their surrounding data are accessed in a variety of physical and online contexts. Many of the issues described in this chapter are relevant across online and physical contexts.

6.2 The Usable Catalogue

In the context of digital cultural heritage, interest in understanding the strengths and weaknesses of the online (electronic) catalogue grew with the evolution of the Web. Notably, the online library catalogue significantly pre-dates broader digital cultural heritage efforts. Consequentially the following literature review considers evidence drawn from studies of the library catalogue as well as more recent studies focusing directly on cultural heritage. We begin with a discussion of the electronic catalogue, before moving onto physical and hybrid interactions with the system.

Two influential papers by Christine Borgman, published a decade apart, document the development of online catalogue usability between 1986 (Borgman 1986) and 1996 (Borgman 1996). Key issues identified included misunderstanding of system features, lack of use of advanced search techniques and difficulty in identifying appropriate subject headings ('headline labels' for relevant categories). Two key types of user knowledge were identified (Borgman 1986): knowledge of search syntax, semantics, structure and system, and knowledge of the conceptual aspects of search methodologies. In the later paper (Borgman 1996), Borgman adds

- conceptual knowledge—in which a person 'seeking knowledge or meaning [...] must formulate a query in terms of the content of information entities' [or proxies],
- understanding of query implementation—the semantics of the catalogue system, and
- technical skills allowing the user to navigate the computer interface and query syntax (syntactic knowledge).

Significantly, Borgman also noted the effects of various factors relating to the catalogue user, such as personality, age and experience, on user search behaviour.

In the 1990s, key questions about cultural heritage were asked about both physical and online visitors: wants, needs and strategies for information access (Cunliffe et al. 2001). In general, a greater focus was placed on developing well-informed *user models* (see Sect. 6.2.1),—patterns of use, visitor aims, information needs and search strategies.

'Next-generation' features (Hildreth 1987) gained interest and currency, eventually entering the mainstream of catalogue design. Examples include faceted navigation, attempts at correcting user error via methods such as spellchecking and automated format validation, enriched search metadata, ranking of search results and greatly simplified interface design, lessons learned from the simple, sparse search interfaces offered by search engines such as Google (Breeding 2007). Further innovations (Wilson 2007) are often focused on active, ongoing user participation. Increased interest in the Semantic Web (Dokoohaki and Matskin 2008) has facilitated further enrichment of catalogue records by providing technical scaffolds on which to build and datasets against which to work, prompting redesigns by major catalogue holders such as the Library of Congress (Lafrance 2016).

6.2.1 User Modelling

At the core of these developments is the placement of the user at the centre of design, development and deployment. One may work directly with users to establish user preferences and needs a process of user-centred design. However, it is not always possible at design time to fully anticipate uses that may arise during the operating life of a given software product, and for that reason, systems may be designed to *adapt* to changing circumstances (Van Velsen et al. 2008). Such systems, to quote Van Velsen et al. (2008, p. 261), 'alter aspects of their structure, functionality or interface on the basis of a user model generated from implicit and/or explicit user input, in order to accommodate the differing needs of individuals or groups of users and the changing needs of users over time'.

A user model is a structure that describes some aspect(s) of the user and their behaviour. For example, one may capture simple statistics about visitors: age, background, level of education, number of visits. A more complex model might aggregate information about visitor behaviour and context, working from several sources—that is to say that, as well as storing direct evidence such as electronic search histories (explicitly coded interactions with the system), further information may be gleaned from observing a visitor's actions. How does the visitor approach the collection? How does he/she act? What additional contextual information is available about him/her? (Ruotsalo et al. 2009)

User models typically consist of generalisations built from aggregated data. There are, consequently, ethical issues associated with their use. Trust and privacy are sometimes cited as a concern (Van Velsen et al. 2008). In particular, such data is sometimes collected without user awareness of this activity (Kobsa and Schreck 2003), a practice which conflicts with contemporary data protection legislation such as European data protection regulations. Various strategies have been proposed to mitigate this, such as anonymisation of contributors (Kobsa and Schreck 2003). However, since subsequent research demonstrates that it is possible to de-anonymise ('re-identify') participants in many cases given adequate information (Ohm 2009), the developer working in this field must build consideration of the ethical and legal implications into each stage of her work.

As we see, the technical evolution of cultural heritage systems is bound closely with the developing story of research themes such as personalisation (Ardissono et al. 2012), ubiquitous computing (Kuflik et al. 2012) and augmented reality (Wojciechowski et al. 2004).

In the following pages, we consider the evolution of metadata creation and use, as it moved from 'one person's view' (a manually created resource) to an automated indexing approach trained (taught) using an aggregate of individual human judgements, and thence towards interface design that explicitly acknowledges variation in user interests, preferences and goals. In Sect. 6.3, we discuss the extension of systems into the physical domain, as experienced by visitors standing within the physical borders of the museum. We consider the role of the museum as expressed by the International Council of Museums, and demonstrate the centrality of the visitor to each goal provided in this definition. In Sect. 6.4, we briefly introduce our research into the use of social sensors to capture contemporary texts relating to a museum and to related artefacts and activities, providing an aggregate model usable to support ongoing maintenance activities on textual material.

6.2.2 *Populating a Catalogue*

6.2.2.1 Manually Contributed Metadata

Traditionally, catalogue information is manually generated by expert cataloguers chosen from subject experts in the field. It typically contains elements drawn from a controlled vocabulary (a taxonomy or list of subject headings) as well as free-text elements that may contain any choice of string input by the user.

As this process involves expert input, cataloguing is an expensive process. In some of its more expansive forms, cataloguing work is broadly viewed as prohibitively expensive. From time to time, efforts have been made to reduce cost by involving non-expert contributors: in the Great Depression, for example, non-experts were hired via the Welfare To Work platform to contribute to extensive cataloguing of historical records (Baltimore City Archives 2014). In more recent years, the annotation platforms offered on the Social Web provided further support for non-expert annotations (Trant 2009), although opinions differ on the utility of the outcome, which are sometimes viewed as privileging serendipity over structured search (Chan 2007; Van Laere et al. 2014).

6.2.2.2 Automated Metadata

A further development is that of automated metadata generation (automated indexing). Theis approach evolved since the 1970s (Stevens 1970), latterly encompassing areas such as image and multimedia resource indexing. A wide variety of methods are used to extract specific types of information, from extraction of textual features and video captions to extraction of image features. Because the features extracted are seldom directly comparable to the types of metadata created in a traditional catalogue record, there is often a semi-supervised training process necessary to 'translate' findings to compatible catalogue terms.

Although, prima facie, automated metadata extraction systems may be viewed as free from the variable human biases that characterise manually contributed metadata, it is important to recognise that many such systems are trained against exemplars of human performance in a given task, and hence are designed to approximate human performance as closely as possible. Consequentially, such systems replicate the biases common to the training set (Islam et al. 2016). As the audience changes, and as the material ingested by the museum itself continues to evolve, assumptions made during system calibration about dataset features and distribution are likely to require revision, a task that is likely to be either expensive or technically challenging (Pan and Yang 2010).

6.2.3 The Search and Retrieval Process

In a basic search process, the user simply formulates a search query by providing a few words. By interrogating the index of objects, making use of catalogue data, the service is able to identify and return matches. This process draws heavily on the user's ability to generate appropriate search key terms, ordinarily with little prompting from the interface. S/he is likely to be supported by second-generation site features such as search query processing via a thesaurus built into the interface and automated error identification/correction: such thesauri are not automatically updated and require ongoing work to maintain.

6.3 Interactive Cultural Heritage: Collaborative Performance and (Re)Construction

The increasing focus of the 2000s on supporting user activity beyond catalogue search and discovery heralded further research projects and practical developments focusing on a holistic understanding of the role of a cultural heritage platform. Broader platform functionality is intended to support individual participant needs, whether they are acting as a student, self-directed learner, an individual planning a physical visit to the museum, subject expert or teacher (Fantoni 2006). Supporting the data and workflow requirements for a given role involves extensive information about the participant, the material held within collections, the physical context and contexts of creation (provenance) and curation of the object. A broad understanding of these goals implies access to a great deal of extrinsic information in broad terms, an understanding of the object's place in the world. In pursuit of such goals, data about navigation of a museum, particularly shared navigation, may be collected and used to enrich an existing user model.

6.3.1 Personalisation

Personalised access to museums, libraries and archives was explored during the 2000s by many high-profile cultural heritage institutions (Borgman 2003). The Rijksmuseum, for example, created a service called Cultural Heritage Information Presentation (CHIP) (Wang et al. 2007). This stored 'likes' and 'dislikes' expressed by the user, a 'non-obtrusive collection of user data' designed to underpin generation of personalised tours.

Under the name 'personal digital collections systems', functionality allowing users to select items from a museum's catalogue for a personalised collection was implemented by many museums, including the Museum of Fine Arts in Boston, the National Museum of Australia and Tate Online (Marty 2011). These systems were popular with a subset of users (Fantoni 2006), although often collections were abandoned shortly after creation (Fantoni and Bowen 2007), causing suggestions that the outcome of such systems is 'a landscape of "lost" personal museums' (Marty 2011).

It is not clear whether the ephemeral nature of an individual's interaction with a cultural heritage system—creating and abandoning, or discarding, a list—genuinely implies that the interaction is incomplete or superficial, as the literature often suggests. It is partially as a consequence of the short-lived nature of many visitor interactions, however, that many institutions have chosen to work with external services, often commercial in nature. These allow the institution to indirectly provide functionality such as social bookmarking or personal digital collection, rather than providing the service themselves.

Introduction of a dependency on social websites heightens the risk of a 'digital dark age' (Jeffrey 2012). Whilst it is not clear that either a self-hosted service model or an external service is sustainable, it is clear that the attrition rate for social websites is high (Tonkin 2015). Where external services are used, it is likely that information (such as course notes, expert or public comment and further annotation) is not captured by the institution itself. Consequentially, such interactions may be both ephemeral and unobserved by the museum itself, unless action is taken to observe and document patterns of usage. As an aside, even this manner of observation is increasingly challenging, as web technologies continue to develop, impacting on the technical accessibility of web services for purposes such as archiving of information (Kelly et al. 2013).

6.3.2 Co-visiting and Shared Spaces

In the catalogue-focused examples shown in the previous section, systems are designed with the individual user in mind: one visitor's journey (physical or virtual) represents a completed interaction. In practice, a broader understanding of visitor activity is useful. ARCHIE (Van Loon et al. 2006), for example, explored 'co-visiting'—interactive learning within the physical borders of the museum. Contextual models of learning—in which sociocultural, physical and personal context influence and contribute to interactions with objects and subsequent learning—were explored (Falk and Dierking 2000; Van Loon et al. 2006). Projects such as Sotto Voce explored co-visiting and the creation of shared audio media, exploring shared listening in interaction (Aoki et al. 2002), whilst Dini et al. (2007) explored location-aware mobile gaming for cooperative learning.

6.3.3 The Mission of the Museum

These activities reflect what Lin and Gregor (2006), citing the International Council of Museums (ICOM), describe in a vision statement as the mission of the museum:

> A museum is a non-profit, permanent institution in the service of society and its development, open to the public, which acquires, conserves, researches, communicates and exhibits the tangible and intangible heritage of humanity and its environment for the purposes of education, study and enjoyment.

This definition contains an omission, likely intentional: in stating that a museum is 'open to the public', the target audience is defined as broadly as possible. The intended purposes of the interaction are clearer: communication for education, study and enjoyment. Perhaps this simply reflects the span of ICOM's membership—given over 20,000 museums, it is to be expected that a variety of answers might be given to the question, 'who is this museum primarily intended to serve?'

Yet the importance of specifying the intended audience is made clear by content preservation standards, such as the OAIS reference model (Lavoie et al. 2002), which identifies what it refers to as a 'designated community'—a construct possibly including several different groups—as a prerequisite for digital preservation activities. This follows when one considers any test of the success or failure of the museum in achieving its stated goals: *communicating*—with whom? Supporting study *by which students?* A wholly open mandate is problematic to evaluate. Goals must be made concrete and achievable.

In any case, this definition offers a series of items that a museum must support: the requirements of education, study and enjoyment. The evidence suggests that provision of a service capable of providing all three of these is an ongoing process that is deeply dependent on a strong and contemporary understanding of the visitor. In particular, we suggest that ongoing service provision in the museum context, in particular, requires careful monitoring and proactive response to changes in user behaviour, profile and context.

It is not yet clear in what time span issues associated with the types of change process monitored by 'long term' digital preservation become significant to each of these activities. Metrics for establishing the quality of engagement with the visitor, on the other hand, are well established, in general. For the virtual visitor, a body of literature exists on website design and associated metrics for evaluating enjoyment (Lin and Gregor 2006; Lin et al. 2008). A broader literature on factors associated with enjoyment in human-computer interaction, such as flow (Ghani and Deshpande 1994), suggests a link between enjoyment and level of challenge (a factor associated with individual level of certain forms of pre-existing knowledge). Education and study may be viewed as relating to pre-existing formal knowledge, to lived experience, to exposure to contexts, peers and experts with shared areas of interests and to learning opportunities (Ito et al. 2013).

We suggest that the effect of ageing on each key aspect of the museum's mission is a useful area of study, in that the frequency of intervention and hence the sustainability of any institution's services is greatly influenced by this factor. In the remainder of this chapter, however, we will not consider these services further. Rather, we will, by reference to relevant theory, consider the effect of ageing on one relatively straightforward element of the system: the museum catalogue and its accompanying index.

6.4 The Ageing of Cultural Collections

We are familiar with the marks of time. On stone, we expect to see erosion where water once flowed or generations of visitors have walked; on skin, liver spots and crows' feet. Some of these marks are informationally rich physical clues to the experiences lived by other visitors in past years, such as a well-worn passage in a book, or the scuffed floor where furniture once stood. A great deal of recent research on digital preservation has focused on forms of erosion that affect digital objects themselves, such as lack of compatibility with modern software (Factor et al. 2009). The structural conveniences that accompany these objects—the texts and interlinks that provide context and render the material searchable and accessible—are generally engineered for a shorter timescale. What are the effects of age on the tertiary indexes and metadata structures that accompany those objects and make them actionable resources, such as catalogues of digital heritage material?

There are relatively few studies of the effects of age on catalogues over a significant period of time. There are various reasons for this, notably the fact that online catalogues are of themselves a fairly recent phenomenon. The opportunity to observe issues that occur over the long term, as in long-term data preservation scenarios, has therefore been limited. Confounding factors may also be identified. As we see above, catalogue interfaces have typically undergone significant amounts of re-engineering as new technologies and standards are developed and gain in popularity. Where funding exists, cultural heritage organisations will often look to state-of-the-art research, implementation guidelines and even upcoming trends in interface design to overhaul aspects of their online and public presence, meaning that the presentation of information is likely to change rapidly and often, even if the information itself is edited relatively infrequently. This adds a confounding aspect to any longitudinal study. Waterfield's review (Waterfield 2000) of the development of art cataloguing demonstrates the significance that pragmatic, idealistic and nationalistic concerns took in this nascent field, discussing the complex interplay between the factors mentioned above.

We must, therefore, look for evidence from indirect sources, such as theoretical and experimental research, which may inform our hypotheses about digital preservation issues on the humble museum catalogue and the information it contains.

6.4.1 The Problem of Ageing Indexes and Potential Mitigation

6.4.1.1 Studies in Recognition and Term Generation

A contemporary text is written with an audience in mind, according to the author's perception of the strategies that will most effectively transmit his or her point. The same is true of catalogue entries, particularly elements that serve an interpretive or contextual purpose, such as descriptive text.

A subtle effect of passing time is an ongoing change in the style of written and spoken speech. Terminology, in particular, undergoes ongoing processes of change, with terms falling out of favour and being replaced by alternatives. A similar effect occurs between speech communities, which may prefer different terminology to others. Despite this change in preference, low-frequency lexical items are typically still recognised long after falling out of regular use. However, low-frequency words are not well recalled (Lohnas and Kahana 2013).

Thus, as an unmodified index continues to age, the search process is compromised by increased user difficulty in generating the necessary search terminology—a subtle but measurable process. The search process becomes slower and more error-laden, and the accessibility of the collection consequentially reduces despite the fact that the index itself has not changed at all.

In practice, catalogue and index are not immutable: they are frequently updated for particular purposes, ranging from addition of new items to correction of existing entries for various purposes. A high-profile recent review of Rijksmuseum metadata, for example, saw the alteration of over a hundred items containing racially charged terminology (Siegal 2015). User complaints have been identified as a factor in the decision to review the metadata.

6.4.1.2 Mitigation

Taking these things together, we use them as our motivation and basis for addressing digital preservation within cultural heritage institutions.

Words come and go from fashion. In some cases, historical or outmoded terms may cause offence. In others, they may cause a breakdown in understanding or ability to retrieve certain information. A strongly data-driven and frequently updated set of user profiles facilitates detection of both conditions. Yet the museum as an operating context introduces particular complexities. The ‘user’ of a museum is not clearly defined. Consider, for example, reuse of museum resources, which may be considered by many individuals or groups for a wide variety of purposes, from the sheer joy of collection[1] to academic research.

6.4.1.3 Scalable, Sustainable Information Sourcing

To gather information, an institution may reach out to the public, perhaps directly working with museum visitors or, as proposed by Wrigglesworth and Watts in Chap. 8, volunteers. Crowdsourcing, as van der Lans et al. explain in Chap. 7, is an

[1]Analysis of the social collection website Pinterest (Mull and Lee 2014) shows that users of the site self-report as finding the process both enjoyable and inspiring.

alternative approach that, though it may come at a cost, offers the possibility of receiving input from participants across the world. The downside of both approaches is simply the paucity of available agents; in a large collection of items, most will receive little attention. It is therefore commonplace to consider the coexistence of participant-driven approaches with observations generated elsewhere: that is to say, we assert that a machine-driven 'shallow reading' (Etzioni et al. 2006) of a broad variety of sources can usefully support cultural heritage in various tasks related to catalogue maintenance.

As an institution, it is preferable to schedule preventative maintenance in good time than to discover issues that have significantly inconvenienced large numbers of users. Thus, it is proposed that ongoing and non-invasive methods of data collection are used to identify cases in which catalogue (or, more frequently, thesaural) maintenance may become necessary, such that the proposed changes may be reviewed and implemented as part of the routine of data preservation.

6.4.1.4 Recording Change, Purpose and Provenance

In addition, metadata versioning can be put in place to help reflect changes in our understanding of the object (Zavalina et al. 2015). The addition of extra information within the metadata, or accompanying the metadata, allows us to record explanations for the changes made being able to add extra information within the metadata record to provide explanation surrounding the changes made. The metadata surrounding an object, be it digital or physical, is itself a living record, with a chain of provenance that tells its life story.

The provision of service infrastructures to support maintenance tasks in preservation is a fairly common pattern: various digital preservation frameworks have been proposed to this end, including OAIS. These often focus primarily on concrete tasks such as ensuring the ongoing technical accessibility of the materials held and on ensuring that adequate metadata records are stored. For this purpose, necessary technical infrastructure, such as registries of document formats, format validators, etc., are provided. Whilst these standards do not exclude ongoing user modelling, tracking of audience engagement and so forth, they also do not explicitly mandate such activities. Yet it is only through interaction and observation of those engaging with materials that a cultural heritage organisation can establish whether they are achieving their goals.

At times, explanatory information is explicitly provided by archivists; however, the contexts in which such decisions are taken is often not explicitly encoded. We suggest that efforts should be made to capture this information and, perhaps more importantly, to ensure that the information captured is informationally rich. This implies, from the metadata design perspective, providing rich provenance and annotation capabilities.

6.4.1.5 Aggregate User Data Collection Through Social Sensors

Where created user data is viewed as of interest, an appropriate social sensor may be used to evaluate specific dimensions of social annotations or interactions, such as information shared, emotional responses and geographical localisation (Resch et al. 2015). A social sensor is a source of information—which could be anything from a mobile or pervasive computing device to information sequences gleaned from Web services such as Web tools—Flickr, Twitter, search engine queries and activities and so forth (Rosi et al. 2011)—which tells us something interesting. Social sensors are used for an increasingly significant set of purposes. For example, using a sensor of this kind it is possible to rapidly detect earthquakes (Sakaki et al. 2010) through automated review of Twitter posts, and to provide sufficient information about everyday life in cities to support decision-making for city councils and utilities (Domingo et al. 2013) and characterise social interactions within a group (Bell et al. 2011) using information from mobile devices.

6.4.1.6 The Use of Social Sensors for the Museum Observatory

We propose the use of a set of social (Manovich 2011) and corresponding sensors operating on cultural and political data (e.g. Zeng and Greenfield 2015) that, in combination, represent a Museum Observatory. Such an observatory allows the museum, in an automated manner, to look out at the constellations of human activity and discourse that surround it and to identify and react to ongoing processes of change. For example, such an observatory might process data relating to news reports referencing the cultural institution, in order to get a sense of the context in which it operates and the discussions surrounding it at a formal level. In addition, social media may provide indications of the concerns of the general public (or sections of the general public). Inclusion of more structured data such as the catalogue search terms (or those in relation to the website), will also allow a more focused perspective on users of the cultural institution's resources.

The incorporation of a wide range of relevant resources which form the immediate ecosystem of the museum, enable a broad and varied view of its context. This observatory could then be integrated into the museum catalogue, for example, by generating relevant terms for automated (or semi-automated) annotation of objects, or for identifying and generating new relationships within the catalogue (e.g. between objects or between different indexing terms, or between objects and indexing terms). Although itself an actor in the ecosystem, the museum is one among many. We argue that to remain accessible to the visitor, the museum must retain an active connection with the general public and along with its wider context. Such an observatory may act as a virtual mirror on an institutional level (Gloor et al. 2010). It would, as the poet Robert Burns once put it, 'the giftie gie us/To see oursels as ithers see us!'

Such infrastructure, although cheap by comparison with the human-led processes which it can inform, is far from free: we remark, however, that such observatories do not need to exist in large numbers. In the case of larger institutions, they will most likely have the expertise and resources to create, and curate, such and observatory. However, smaller institutions may need to form consortia or create links with the larger institutions; as with significant manual infrastructural efforts such as the development of openly accessible thesauri or taxonomies, the work is better shared than individually replicated.

6.5 Social Sensors in Corpus Review: A Preliminary Exploration

We developed an initial prototype for the purpose of investigating the feasibility of this approach. A large number of museums, both in the United Kingdom and internationally, have published metadata of varying levels of comprehensiveness describing their collections. In some cases, providers also offer contextual material such as information about the artist, prior provenance and history of artefacts. In our initial study, we selected a network of UK-based museums as the subject for our work, for several reasons. First, extensive contemporary material about the institution's holdings had been made available online under an appropriate licence.[2] Second, we were aware that further relevant material, such as historical guides from the earliest days of this institution, has now been digitised by the Getty Research Institute. Additionally, we had already developed a corpus of statistical information characterising online discussion about several institutions, including Tate (Kontopoulos et al. 2016).

In an initial study, quantitative methods have been explored to support direct comparison with modern corpora drawn from the same topic area and corresponding repair processes. Material drawn from social sensors is considered as a source for data relating to impact and effect, as well as an entry point into relevant online discourse. From this pilot study, we provide a few manually derived examples.

6.5.1 What People Say: Methods for Sensing Change Through Observation of Contemporary Data Sources

Contemporary social media platforms frequently provide an application programming interface (API) that makes material provided by users of these platforms, such as text or multimedia content, available to software. Programmers can straightforwardly work with these interfaces by making use of libraries available in many

[2]https://github.com/tategallery/collection, available under the Creative Commons Public Domain CC0 licence.

contemporary programming languages such as R and Python; in our case, we primarily made use of Python in our research.

In our initial work, we began by focusing on two such platforms: the microblogging and social networking websites Tumblr and Twitter. Each of these platforms can be searched for content relating to certain keywords, although Twitter restricts search matches to contemporary material (normally within the last few hours or days), whilst Tumblr allows searching of material from the entire history of the site, with the exception of material posted by since-deleted accounts. We began by exploring a confined space: published material directly relating to a particular museum. This was used as a starting point from which to identify cliques, in the social network sense (which is to say, clusters of people—or, sometimes, agencies such as news agencies or, indeed, museum social media accounts—between whom there exist many links, such as cross references, mentions or 'likes').

Through this means, we built up a corpus of material relating to the institution in its many facets—a building; a destination; a sequence of events, of exhibitions, of performances; individuals associated to it directly (for example, the subject of specific exhibitions). Caught, also, in this web, we see people, places and things that are more tangentially connected, such as people producing comparable or relevant work, collaborating institutions, relevant news, and so forth. So, too, do we find references to activities directed by educational institutions—reading material for a course, for example. In itself, such material can be accessed serendipitously—by happy chance, perhaps, something interesting for a reader may be found. It is valuable in part, even through direct inspection, for its exuberant presentation of the multiplicity of faces presented by the institution; indeed, many institutions already seek to characterise electronic participation and interaction.

Less directly, this material also provides us with a reference point: speaking informally, it tells us a little more about the way people write, what they say—and what they do not. There are, of course, limits to the use of this resource, and obvious objections; any corpus is limited in scope, and the contributors to the corpus may or may not have contemporary relevance to a given institution. A shallow reading is only the beginning of the process. To work with a corpus such as the one described above, we need good, relevant questions, complementary datasets and supplementary information.

Whilst we do not propose to go into technical detail in this chapter, we note that methods to achieve various relevant tasks have been reported elsewhere. Consider, for example, the problem of identifying new uses of existing terminology within a corpus (Dorow and Widdows 2003). Solutions to this problem allow us to identify existing words that now hold different meanings or connotations, especially problematic connotations. Methods from recent research (Hamilton et al. 2016) show promise in robustly identifying term sentiment in a new corpus of text. Such methods allow us to identify words that hold positive or negative connotations, allowing systems to track change in the way that terms are perceived and the connotations that they have. Using graph-theoretical methods, it is also possible to identify orthographic changes (that is, changes in the way that words are written) over long periods of time.

By comparing large amounts of text taken from similar subject areas written over very distinct periods of time, we find that using sample corpora we are able to demonstrate differences, the extent of the differences, and, in general, to identify pathways that can be used to bring material up to date.

6.5.2 Examples of Use

Consider as a first case the comparison of historical materials with contemporary material: we take several examples of artwork titles from an open catalogue, and evaluate them against our corpus. A proportion of terms simply do not appear in randomly sample modern corpora, or if so, appear very seldom; others have gained or lost connotations over the years.

One example of an uncommon term is ‘Newsmongers’, the title of an artwork by Sir David Wilkie.[3] The term is defined by the Oxford English Dictionary as referencing a gossip. From the artwork and its accompanying taxonomic information (which includes ‘reading, writing, printed matter’ and ‘newspaper’), it is not clear that the reader would interpret this term accordingly. An example of the latter—a term used in a manner which is now considered archaic—is in the title of a piece by Gilbert Stuart Newton, ‘Yorick and the Grisette’. The Oxford English Dictionary reminds us that a grisette is a common edible woodland mushroom, and, historically, referred to a young working-class Frenchwoman.[4] Neither definition is common on social media; in fact, a grisette is also a type of beer, and this is overwhelmingly the most commonplace use of the term today. There exist two parts to this problem: detection of the fact that the connotations of the token ‘grisette’ have changed over time, achievable given sufficient information through the use of frequency and co-occurrence information, and selection, by evaluation of the context of use of the term, of appropriate equivalent terms.

Identification of candidate terms is not always straightforward and sometimes, as here, there are no straightforward and commonplace equivalent terms available to us. In other cases, as with the Caravaggio artwork, ‘The Decollation of St John’, there is a more widely accepted alternative term (i.e. ‘beheading’) readily usable in its place. Such simple cases are straightforwardly automated, and can be achieved in the context of ‘just-in-time’ service provision.

The identification of problematic terminology is useful in that it allows for the helpful provision of (for example) an adaptive thesaurus, accompanying glossary or an explanatory note. The automated nature of this approach enables it to reach into the ‘long tail’ of a museum’s collections, where serendipitous encounters with confused visitors are somewhat less likely to spark spontaneous review of accompanying data.

---

[3]http://www.tate.org.uk/art/artworks/wilkie-newsmongers-n00331.

[4]https://en.oxforddictionaries.com/definition/grisette.

Beyond description of individual holdings, we have not yet spoken about encounters with a museum—with temporary exhibitions, for example, which attract visitors and comment during their lifetime. Our published findings (Maronidis et al. 2016) show that exhibitions, tours and events are prominent in social media datasets. If we aim to compare perspectives on cultural heritage items, we must also consider the contexts in which they encounter, and perhaps also (as a matter of future work), how they react to the work within this context.

6.6 Discussion

This study has given us confidence that text analytic methods based on the distributional hypothesis, twinned with topic-comparable corpora from distinct temporal or social contexts, can be used both to describe the gulf that lies between the two corpora, and to identify strategies that enable the construction of knowledge structures that facilitate the bridging of the gap. We expect to report more extensively on this work in an upcoming publication.

Maintaining relevant and accessible descriptors for information objects (i.e. a usable catalogue) is a time-consuming task. That said, data-driven approaches are themselves time-consuming. Data collection is a lengthy task, although it can be automated to a large extent; maintenance of software is time-consuming and potentially expensive. For a single institution, data-driven approaches may not be an economical solution.

It is therefore recommended that efforts continue to be cast as collaborative between multiple cultural heritage institutions and groups likely to make use of the data. Siloised models of operation are commonplace, but, as in this instance, there is much to be gained from collaboration between institutions.

It is also worth noting that sampling methodology has a significant impact on the relevance and accuracy of the results. An observer receives a partial and biased view of user activities and responses, so there is a risk that an institution may overfit their solution, hence further reducing the accessibility of the result.

6.7 Conclusion

Digital preservation of cultural heritage often focuses on digital objects or digital proxies of physical objects, however, museums require significant surrounding infrastructure to fulfil their mission which includes both the core function of search and discovery of information, as well as supporting visitors in education, learning and enjoyment.

In this chapter, we have begun to explore the impact of language change in accessing catalogue information. Given that the catalogue function is a key element of cultural heritage sites, the cumulative result of this process may cause a significant decline in accessibility of information. One proposal to potentially mitigate this might be the use of social sensors and cultural media mining. In this paper, we have proposed that the collection of this kind of information from open data sources could be used to provide a landscape from which to understand and interpret catalogue information. By automatically and periodically collecting this information, in a manner that takes into consideration ethical concerns, it becomes possible for the catalogue/index to model—and therefore take account of—changes in common understanding or usage of language, with a view to cultural context, including specific search terms. This therefore may go some way towards supporting proactive maintenance of museum infrastructure as it is currently supported for digital object formats. We hope that by doing so, this may begin to address the problems of catalogue accessibility with relation to averting a digital dark age. Such an approach may also contribute to supporting the increasingly extensive objectives of cultural organisations in supporting education, study and enjoyment.

We hope to explore the use of similar linguistically inspired approaches across heterogeneous groups for practical purposes. One such approach is the support of system development by identifying problematic or specialised jargon. A second is to provide support for detailed analysis of specialised cataloguing approaches and practices, which is of use in the normalisation of catalogue metadata, and in the sociological study of practices in a specialised field.

References

Abu-Shumays M, Leinhardt G (2002) Two docents in three museums: central and peripheral participation. Learning conversations in museums, pp 45–80

Aoki PM, Grinter RE, Hurst A, Szymanski MH, Thornton JD, Woodruff A (2002) Sotto voce: exploring the interplay of conversation and mobile audio spaces. In: Proceedings of the SIGCHI conference on human factors in computing systems, pp 431–438

Ardissono L, Kuflik T, Petrelli D (2012) Personalization in cultural heritage: the road travelled and the one ahead. User Model User-Adapt Interact 22(1):73–99. https://doi.org/10.1007/s11257-011-9104-x

Baltimore City Archives (2014) Transcribing and inventorying the records of Baltimore City, 1905–1940. http://baltimorecityhistory.net/research-at-the-baltimore-city-archives/transcribing-and-inventorying-the-records-of-baltimore-city-1905-1940/

Bell S, McDiarmid A, Irvine J (2011) Nodobo: mobile phone as a software sensor for social network research. In: 2011 IEEE 73rd vehicular technology conference (VTC Spring), pp 1–5. https://doi.org/10.1109/VETECS.2011.5956319

Borgman CL (1986) Why are online catalogs hard to use? Lessons learned from information-retrieval studies. J Am Soc Inf Sci 37(6):387–400

Borgman CL (1996) Why are online catalogs still hard to use? JASIS 47(7):493–503

Borgman CL (2003) Personal digital libraries: creating individual spaces for innovation. In: Nsf post-digital library futures workshop

Breeding M (2007) Next-gen library catalogs. Library technology reports, pp 10–13

Brunsmann J (2011) Product lifecycle metadata harmonization with the future in OAIS archives. In: International conference on Dublin core and metadata applications, pp 126–136

Burrows A, Gooberman-Hill R, Coyle D (2015, 12) Shared language and the design of home healthcare technology. In: Proceedings of the ACM conference on human factors in computing systems

Canter D, Rivers R, Storrs G (1985) Characterizing user navigation through complex data structures. Behav Inf Technol 4(2):93–102

Carlo Bertot J, Snead JT, Jaeger PT, McClure CR (2006) Functionality, usability, and accessibility: Iterative user-centered evaluation strategies for digital libraries. Perform Meas Metr 7(1):17–28

Chan S (2007) Tagging and searching: serendipity and museum collection databases

Cunliffe D, Kritou E, Tudhope D (2001) Usability evaluation for museum web sites. Mus Manag Curatorship 19(3):229–252

Dini R, Paternò F, Santoro C (2007) An environment to support multi-user interaction and cooperation for improving museum visits through games. In: Proceedings of the 9th international conference on human computer interaction with mobile devices and services, pp 515–521

Dokoohaki N, Matskin M (2008) Personalizing human interaction through hybrid ontological profiling: cultural heritage case study. In: Ronchetti M (ed) 1st workshop on semantic web applications and human aspects, (SWAHA08), pp 133–140 (In conjunction with Asian Semantic Web Conference)

Domingo A, Bellalta B, Palacin M, Oliver M, Almirall E (2013) winter) Public open sensor data: revolutionizing smart cities. IEEE Technol Soc Mag 32(4):50–56. https://doi.org/10.1109/MTS.2013.2286421

Dorow B, Widdows D (2003) Discovering corpus-specific word senses. In: Proceedings of the tenth conference on European chapter of the association for computational linguistics, vol 2, pp 79–82

Etzioni O, Banko M, Cafarella MJ (2006) Machine reading. In: Aaai, vol 6, pp 1517–1519

Factor M, Henis E, Naor D, Rabinovici-Cohen S, Reshef P, Ronen S, Guercio M (2009) Authenticity and provenance in long term digital preservation: modeling and implementation in preservation aware storage. In: First workshop on theory and practice of provenance, pp 6:1–6:10 Berkeley, CA, USA: USENIX Association

Falk JH, Dierking LD (2000) Learning from museums: visitor experiences and the making of meaning. Altamira Press, Lanham

Fantoni SF (2006) Web-based solutions: save it for later. http://www.artsprofessional.co.uk/magazine/article/web-based-solutions-save-it-later

Fantoni SF, Bowen JP (2007) Bookmarking in museums: extending the museum experience beyond the visit. In: Trant J, Bearman D (eds) Museums and the web 2007

Furnas GW (1985) Experience with an adaptive indexing scheme, vol 16(4). ACM, New York

Ghani JA, Deshpande SP (1994) Task characteristics and the experience of optimal flow in human-computer interaction. J Psychol 128(4):381–391

Gloor PA, Oster D, Raz O, Pentland A, Schoder D (2010) The virtual mirror: reflecting on the social and psychological self to increase organizational creativity. Int Stud Manag Organ 40 (2):74–94

Hamilton WL, Clark K, Leskovec J, Jurafsky D (2016) Inducing domain-specific sentiment lexicons from unlabeled corpora arXiv:1606.02820

Hedstrom M (1997) Digital preservation: a time bomb for digital libraries. Comput Humanit 31 (3):189–202

Hildreth C (1987, Spring) Beyond Boolean; designing the next generation of online catalogues. Libr Trends 647–667

Islam AC, Bryson JJ, Narayanan A (2016) Semantics derived automatically from language corpora necessarily contain human biases. CoRR. arXiv:1608.07187

Ito M, Gutierrez K, Livingstone S, Penuel B, Rhodes J, Salen K, Watkins SC (2013) Connected learning: an agenda for research and design. Digital Media and Learning Research Hub

Jeffrey S (2012) A new digital dark age? Collaborative web tools, social media and long-term preservation. World Archaeol 44(4):553–570

Kelly M, Brunelle JF, Weigle MC, Nelson ML (2013) On the change in archivability of websites over time. In: Aalberg T, Papatheodorou C, Dobreva M, Tsakonas G, Farrugia CJ (eds) Research and advanced technology for digital libraries: international conference on theory and practice of digital libraries, TPDL 2013, Valletta, Malta, 22–26 September 2013. Proceedings, pp 35–47. Springer, Berlin. https://doi.org/10.1007/978-3-642-40501-3_5

Kobsa A, Schreck J (2003) Privacy through pseudonymity in user-adaptive systems. ACM Trans Internet Technol (TOIT) 3(2):149–183

Kontopoulos E, Riga M, Mitzias P, Andreadis S, Stavropoulos T, Konstantinidis K, Tonkin EL (2016) Pericles deliverable 4.4: modelling contextualised semantics. PERICLES project

Kuflik T, Kay J, Kummerfeld B (2012) Challenges and solutions of ubiquitous user modeling. In: Krüger A, Kuflik T (eds) Ubiquitous display environments, pp 7–30. Springer, Berlin. https://doi.org/10.1007/978-3-642-27663-7_2

Kuny T (1998) The digital dark ages? Challenges in the preservation of electronic information. Int Preserv News 17:8–13

Lafrance A (2016) Archaeology's information revolution - the Atlantic. https://www.theatlantic.com/technology/archive/2016/03/digital-material-worlds/471858/. Accessed 02 Mar 2017

Lavoie B, Alexander M, Rieger O, Bradley K, Sergeant D, Day M, Woodyard D (2002) Preservation metadata and the OAIS information model. A metadata framework to support the preservation of digital objects. Technical report. OCLC Online Computer Library Center, Inc., Dublin, OH. http://www.oclc.org/content/dam/research/activities/pmwg/pm_framework.pdf

Lin ACH, Gregor SD (2006) Designing websites for learning and enjoyment: a study of museum experiences. Int Rev Res Open Distrib Learn 7(3)

Lin ACH, Gregor SD, Ewing M (2008) Developing a scale to measure the enjoyment of web experiences. J Interact Mark 22(4):40–57

Lohnas LJ, Kahana MJ (2013) Parametric effects of word frequency in memory for mixed frequency lists. J Exp Psychol Learn Mem Cogn 39(6):1943–1946

Manovich L (2011) Trending: the promises and the challenges of big social data. Debates Digit Humanit 2:460–475

Maronidis A, Chatzilari E, Kontopoulos E, Nikopoulos S, Riga M, Mitzias P, other (2016) Pericles deliverable 4.3: content semantics and use context analysis techniques. Technical report. http://urn.kb.se/resolve?urn=urn:nbn:se:hb:diva-11750

Marty PF (2011) My lost museum: user expectations and motivations for creating personal digital collections on museum websites. Libr Inf Sci Res 33(3):211–219

Mull IR, Lee S-E (2014) "Pin" pointing the motivational dimensions behind pinterest. Comput Hum Behav 33:192–200. https://doi.org/10.1016/j.chb.2014.01.011

Ohm P (2009) Broken promises of privacy: responding to the surprising failure of anonymization. UCLA Law Rev 57:1701–1777. https://ssrn.com/abstract=1450006

Pan SJ, Yang Q (2010) A survey on transfer learning. IEEE Trans Knowl Data Eng 22(10):1345–1359. https://doi.org/10.1109/TKDE.2009.191

Resch B, Summa A, Sagl G, Zeile P, Exner J-P (2015) Urban emotions — geo-semantic emotion extraction from technical sensors, human sensors and crowdsourced data. Progress in location-based services 2014. Springer, Berlin, pp 199–212

Rosi A, Mamei M, Zambonelli F, Dobson S, Stevenson G, Ye J (2011) Social sensors and pervasive services: approaches and perspectives. In: 2011 IEEE international conference on pervasive computing and communications workshops (percom workshops), pp 525–530. https://doi.org/10.1109/PERCOMW.2011.5766946

Ruotsalo T, Mäkelä E, Kauppinen T, Hyvönen E, Haav K, Rantala V, Matskin M (2009) Smartmuseum – personalized context-aware access to digital cultural heritage

Sakaki T, Okazaki M, Matsuo Y (2010) Earthquake shakes twitter users: real-time event detection by social sensors. In: Proceedings of the 19th international conference on world wide web. ACM, New York, pp 851–860. https://doi.org/10.1145/1772690.1772777

Siegal N (2015) Rijksmuseum removing racially charged terms from artworks, titles and descriptions. New York Times. http://nyti.ms/1SQeoEX
Stevens ME (1970) Automatic indexing: a state-of-the-art report
Tonkin EL (2015) Supporting unsupervised context identification using social and physical sensors (Unpublished doctoral dissertation). The University of Bristol
Trant J (2009) Studying social tagging and folksonomy: a review and framework. J Digit Inf 10(1)
Van Laere O, Bordino I, Mejova Y, Lalmas M (2014) Deesse: entity-driven exploratory and serendipitous search system. In: Proceedings of the 23rd ACM international conference on information and knowledge management. ACM, New York, pp 2072–2074. https://doi.org/10.1145/2661829.2661853
Van Loon H, Gabriëls K, Teunkens D, Robert K, Luyten K, Coninx K, Manshoven E (2006) Designing for interaction: socially-aware museum handheld guides. NODEM 06-Digital Interpretation in Cultural Heritage, Art and Science
Van Velsen L, Van Der Geest T, Klaassen R, Steehouder M (2008) User-centered evaluation of adaptive and adaptable systems: a literature review. Knowl Eng Rev 23(3):261–281. https://doi.org/10.1017/S0269888908001379
Wang Y, Aroyo LM, Stash N, Rutledge L (2007) Interactive user modeling for personalized access to museum collections: the Rijksmuseum case study. User modeling 2007. Springer, Berlin, pp 385–389
Waterfield G (2000) The origins of the early picture gallery catalogue in Europe, and its manifestation in victorian Britain. Art in museums, pp 42–73
Weller K (2007) Folksonomies and ontologies: two new players in indexing and knowledge representation. Appl Web 2:108–115
Wilson K (2007) Opac 2.0: next generation online library catalogues ride the web 2.0 wave! Online Curr 21(10):406
Wojciechowski R, Walczak K, White M, Cellary W (2004) Building virtual and augmented reality museum exhibitions. In: Proceedings of the ninth international conference on 3d web technology. ACM, New York, pp 135–144. https://doi.org/10.1145/985040.985060
Zavalina OL, Shakeri S, Kizhakkethil P (2015) Metadata change in traditional library collections and digital repositories: exploratory comparative analysis. In: Proceedings of the 78th ASIS&T annual meeting: information science with impact: research in and for the community. American Society for Information Science, Silver Springs, pp 146:1–146:5
Zeng R, Greenfield PM (2015) Cultural evolution over the last 40 years in China: using the Google Ngram viewer to study implications of social and political change for cultural values. Int J Psychol 50(1):47–55

Author Biographies

Emma Tonkin holds a PhD in computer science from the University of Bristol, where she works as a Senior Research Associate in Electrical and Electronic Engineering. Her current employment involves data mining and management on an interdisciplinary EPSRC-funded sensor-based healthcare project, SPHERE. She has many years of research experience in digital cultural heritage at UKOLN and at the Department of Digital Humanities, King's College London.

Gregory Tourte is a Senior Research Associate at the University of Bristol in the School of Geographical Sciences, where he started as a system administrator for the research group's supercomputer and used this opportunity to research data management due to the large quantity of data being generated. He continues his work with deep time climate modelling within the Bristol Research Initiative for the Dynamic Global Environment (BRIDGE).

Alastair Gill is a researcher and developer in the Department of Digital Humanities, King's College London. His research focuses on the interaction of technology with the social processes of communication and collaboration. In particular, his work focuses on language to study influence and knowledge construction online, as well as the expression and perception of characteristics such as personality, emotion and trust, and he has published widely in these areas. He holds a Ph.D in Informatics from the University of Edinburgh.

Chapter 7
Paid Crowdsourcing as Concept and Content Generator to Enhance Museum Experiences

Lindsey van der Lans, Evy Ligia Ansems and Vassilis-Javed Khan

Abstract Current design and development practices for technologies in museums are costly and difficult to scale. We present a case study that shows that paid crowdsourcing is a viable approach for the design of a Museum app from concept to the development of a working prototype, and the creation of scalable content for over 80 museums worldwide. The concept that was developed is a quiz-type mobile app, the content of which was collected by existing crowdsourcing platforms. Our work extends prior studies of crowdsourcing in cultural institutions by reporting on the process, platforms, and data we utilized so that other institutions could replicate them. Paid crowdsourcing of content for a mobile museum application creates opportunities for new museum experiences that fit into the modern technological society. This emerging crowdsourcing approach addresses the evolving museum trend of being community-centered. The case study shows interesting opportunities for content modification regarding decent and up-to-date information which can make the application self-sustaining.

7.1 Introduction

Museums, nowadays, face several challenges. Among these, two important ones are related to the need to attract and sustain visitors, and viable ways to integrate modern technology. It should not come as a surprise that there might be a link between the two aforementioned challenges. Visitors are more likely to be more technology savvy and often might expect an interactive experience within museums. To face these challenges, museums are shifting from being collection-centered to being community-centered. The decision to take a community-centered approach further opens up more specific questions that museums may face: How to keep the visitors engaged during their visit in the museum? How to let remote crowds contribute to an interactive experience?

L. van der Lans · E. L. Ansems · V.-J. Khan (✉)
Eindhoven University of Technology, 5612 AZ Eindhoven, The Netherlands
e-mail: v.j.khan@tue.nl

A. Vermeeren et al. (eds.), *Museum Experience Design*, Springer Series on Cultural Computing, https://doi.org/10.1007/978-3-319-58550-5_7

To tackle these questions, one approach is by using social media. Through social media, such as Facebook and Twitter, museums try to directly communicate with the visitors, try to engage them more by promoting their services and products, and thus, attempt to build loyalty and encourage repeat visits (Padilla-Meléndez and del Águila-Obra 2013). However, the application of social media for museums is often limited in scope to marketing and promotional activities. Additionally, many museums do not fully exploit the potential of social media to engage and give voice to visitors, so that audience interactions are often passive or superficial.

Another approach for enhancing the visitor experience is the use of modern technologies within the museum's premises. Museum visitors are often confused by the purpose of technology in museum premises and it takes time for them to understand what to do (Csikszentmihaly and Hermanson 1995). A popular approach used within the premises of a museum is combining education and entertainment, called edutainment, to enhance one's learning experiences. For example, gamifying elements supported by technology can increase visitor engagement (Hamari and Koivisto 2015). Examples of other technologies to enhance visitor engagement include mobile-device-based walking tours or touch screens for requesting more information. A drawback of using these technologies, for the visitors seems to be that they find it difficult to divide their attention between the device and the environment (Ghiani et al. 2007). Moreover, one study reports that another drawback of this approach is that even if the target group consists of young people, designers may need to spend a lot of effort in explaining the task beforehand (Stuedahl and Smørdal 2015). Using technologies that are not intuitive inside a museum may affect the visit experience. Prior work shows that letting visitors contribute makes technology around museums more user-friendly and more approachable (Fidas et al. 2012). One approach that we like to suggest in this chapter revolves around the engagement of the crowd in codesigning or contributing additional content for designing technology.

A different way of creating positive experiences would be to let the local community contribute with private stories and experiences to historical sites and objects. More specifically, local communities can contribute by social activities or categorizing objects. In this way, the community is a producer and consumer of the created content (Stuedahl 2011). That involvement could lead to creating a sustainable relationship with the local heritage (Giaccardi and Palen 2008). One benefit for local community involvement is to provide a venue for community members to express their perceptions, interpretations, and expectations of their local heritage. A novel approach to connect to the local community is presented in Chap. 3 of this volume authored by Boonen, van der Heijden and Giaccardi, in which the visitors take museum objects home for a few weeks and then write stories about them, which then go back to the museum. Such approaches, although very useful and truly engaging with the museum's collection, are obviously limited to local aspects of communities and are hard to scale beyond a museum's locality.

Crowdsourcing is a rather novel socio-digital phenomenon that makes use of an ad hoc community that has the ability to scale beyond the local community. There are already a limited number of cultural institutions that have utilized crowdsourcing for a variety of purposes (Carletti et al. 2013; Oomen and Aroyo 2011). More specifically, prior literature reports six uses of crowdsourcing by cultural institutions: correction and transcription, contextualization, complementing collection, classification, co-curation, and funding (Oomen and Aroyo 2011). However, to our knowledge, no research efforts have been published in which paid crowdsourcing is tried as an alternative approach to developing technology and content (that does not directly contribute to the artifacts) of museums. Although in prior initiatives new assets have been created through crowdsourcing (Carletti et al. 2013), there is no study to the best of our knowledge that utilizes paid crowdsourcing to develop technology and content that is adjacent to the main collection (i.e., not enhancing the actual museum collection) and supports the visitors' experience in the museum itself. Furthermore, museums in the past have developed their own systems to support crowdsourcing initiatives (Carletti et al. 2013). Yet, only few museums have the resources and know-how to actually develop their own crowdsourcing systems. But nowadays, there is a plethora of crowdsourcing platforms that can be used or combined and repurposed for the needs of museums.

We wish to contribute to the literature by presenting a study that evidently shows that paid crowdsourcing—in combination with input from social networks—is a viable alternative for helping museums to: (1) ideate technological concepts; (2) decide which ideas are best; (3) design the visuals; and (4) develop the content for digital artifacts and experiences. In this paper, we present our experiences with paid crowdsourcing in developing a mobile application from scratch and generating its content having the crowd on the steering wheel. In this way, we present an alternative to the aforementioned approaches by reaching out to a crowd beyond local communities for the design of novel learning experiences in the museum that are technically and financially feasible and sustainable.

7.2 Method

Although there are different definitions of what crowdsourcing is, for our work we adopt a broad, encompassing definition:

"*Crowdsourcing is an umbrella term for a variety of approaches that harness the potential of large crowds of people by issuing open calls for contribution to particular tasks*" (Geiger et al. 2012).

It is evident that this definition includes paid crowdsourcing but does not exclude other platforms such as social networking systems.

The backdrop of the research we report in this chapter was a two week project, part of a postgraduate module taught at our university, on utilizing (as many as possible) crowdsourcing platforms for design research with one of the end results being developing an app. At the start of the project, the team chose three topics: a Recipes app, a Photography app, and a Museum app. The topic chosen by the crowd was a Museum app. Subsequently, we asked the crowd by using a crowdsourcing platform what kind of functionalities the application should have.

Moreover, we crowdsourced the application's visual design. The next step was to create content for the application, by asking the crowd to come up with questions. To test the usability of the application, we used another crowdsourcing platform. Finally, the programming of the application was crowdsourced as well. In Fig. 7.1 the six stages are shown in an overview. We want to highlight that no stakeholders from museums were consulted due to time limitations. In the following section, we present in detail our process and results.

7.3 Process and Results

7.3.1 Need Finding with Crowds

In the first step (out of six), our team of three researchers held a brainstorm session in which three topics were chosen:

1. A Museum app for the purpose of encouraging users to visit museums by unlocking riddles;
2. A Recipes app for the purpose of creating new recipes with the crowd while playing a game;
3. A Photos app for the purpose of getting photos by people one crossed paths with.

In the next phase, we asked the crowd to: (1) rank the ideas from one to three, and (2) explain their reasons for their first choice. The results are shown in Fig. 7.2. We distributed the survey link in several platforms: Facebook, Twitter, Google+, LinkedIn, WhatsApp, and Skype. Eventually, 77 responses were collected in 20 hours and 29 participants ranked the Recipes app at the first place (Fig. 7.2).

Due to the favorable comments, we decided to work on the Museum app for which 26 participants ranked this in the first place. This is because participants were elaborating the most on the reason why they would like to have this application. First, a simple word count showed that participants used on average 24 words (SD = 29) to describe why they choose the Museum app. In contrast, this was only 13 words on average for the Recipes app (SD = 14). In Table 7.1 one can find some sample statements.

The quotes show that the Museum app seemed to be more appealing and participants felt more passionate about it, compared to the Recipes app. This is why we continued with the Museum app concept. This finding shows that it may be rewarding to have a mix of quantitative and qualitative measures to evaluate the

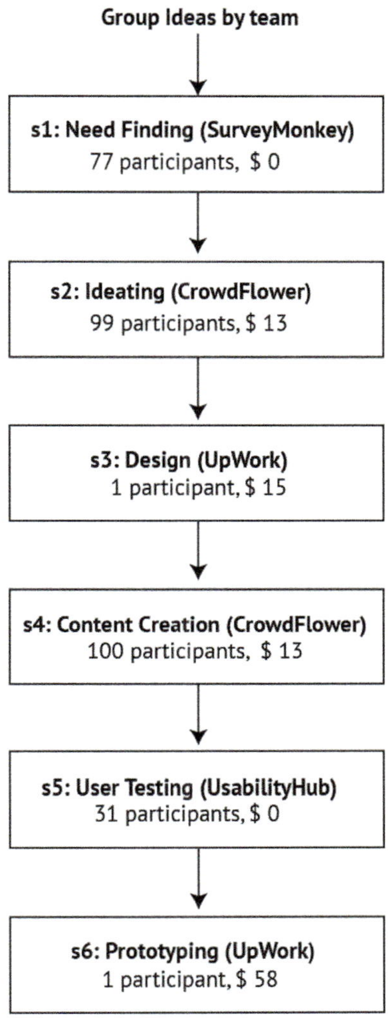

Fig. 7.1 Stages of the design process including the amount of crowd workers engaged, the utilized platform and the total costs for each step. For example, in Step 2 (S2) we utilized CrowdFlower by asking 99 crowd workers to help us come up with ideas about application features with a total cost of $13

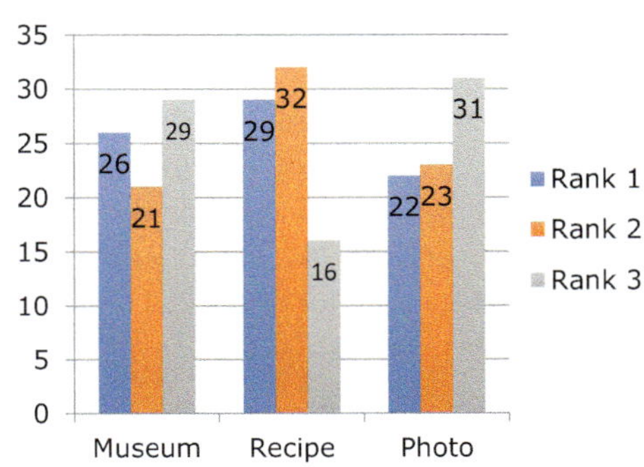

Fig. 7.2 Utilizing paid crowdsourcing to rank ideas that were themselves crowd-driven. The crowd (N = 29) ranked the Recipes app idea as most interesting but when looking at the arguments it was clear that the Museum app idea was the most favorable

crowd's responses during a design process. In our case, if we had not asked the open question we would have decided to continue with the Recipes app.

7.3.2 Ideating with Crowds

To specify the goal of the Museum app, we decided to detail a design statement: *Design an application which educates people about art/museums by making use of crowd wisdom: collectively working on cultural heritage in a fun and engaging way.* This design statement was based on how people can be intrinsically motivated, such as by sharing experiences and making learning situations fun (Csikszentmihaly and Hermanson 1995).

We first identified 14 different functionalities, six different rewards and four different names for the app. We then asked the crowd to show their preference for functionalities and rewards. Workers could select multiple options. Moreover, they were asked to vote for the name they liked best. For the data collection, we launched a survey on CrowdFlower.[1] This is a platform where surveys can be set up and distributed to all workers registered in this platform. We paid contributors $0, 10 for every completed survey. In one hour, we received 99 responses from 36 different nationalities. Workers were told that they were contributing to the design of a Museum app, which would contain game elements.

After counting the data for the potential functionalities (in total 557 votes) seven main functionalities were selected based upon the highest rating (more than 40 votes—see Table 7.2). The same approach was taken for the rewards. In total 206 votes were received, and out of the six options, three main rewards were selected (more than 40 votes). Forty contributors chose the name "BrainChain" for the app, instead of Mucation (22 votes), BrainTrain (16 votes) or BrainGain (21 votes).

94 workers mentioned that they would play this game and 89 workers said they would be motivated going to museums by this game. Tables 7.2 and 7.3 show the different kinds of rewards and functionalities that contributors voted for.

7.3.3 Designing with Crowds

The next step after identifying the application functionalities was to come up with a design for the app. Our initial idea was to crowdsource some different designs and then let the crowd decide which design they liked the most. However, since there was only one UpWork[2] contributor (lady from Odessa, Ukraine) that offered to work for free, out of 15 offers that ranged approximately from $0 to 60, we decided

[1]www.crowdflower.com.

[2]www.upwork.com.

Table 7.1 Sample results of the qualitative input from the crowd, with the reason why they preferred the app (either Museum or Recipe)

Museum app	Recipe app
"I would like to go to a museum more often. Somehow I always fail to do this"	*"I like to cook"*
"Look at that, it's great for people to learn about art and history on a playful way! Think actually about simple museums and other touristy stuff in your own Neighborhood that we seem to forget because we live here and don't care anymore"	*"Love cooking"*

Table 7.2 The rewards workers could choose from. We actually used the first three ones for the concept

Rewards	Votes
Free tickets to go to a proposed place to solve the next assignment	56
Coupons (can be spent anywhere)	47
Discounts on museums in general	46
Congratulation badges related to specific levels	24
Fixed amount of Points for solving an individual and crowd assignments	21
Medals related to specific levels	15

to work with her due to our limited budget (for our project we had a budget of $100). She wanted to improve her design skills and this gave her the opportunity to do so, as she was coached by the designer in our team. We developed a paper prototype and this was sent to her and after an iterative process with our team's designer, the first design was received within three days (see Fig. 7.3). The interesting element, in terms of design process, is that the role of the designer, in our team, shifted from being active on designing to monitoring the crowd contributor. The final design is shown in Fig. 7.4. Our results show that even with limited -or perhaps no- budget but rather for learning purposes, crowdsourcing platforms could assist museums in generating designs (Table 7.3).

7.3.4 Creating Content with Crowds

Our application needed questions as content. Instead of coming up with these ourselves, we decided to crowdsource the questions by again using CrowdFlower. The task description for contributors was to become quizmasters, and we asked the following questions: *What is your favorite museum?* and as a follow-up: *What quiz question can you ask about the museum collection?* We also asked what their favorite art piece is in that museum and as a follow-up: *What question could you ask about this art piece?* Out of 100 responses, we could actually create 115 open

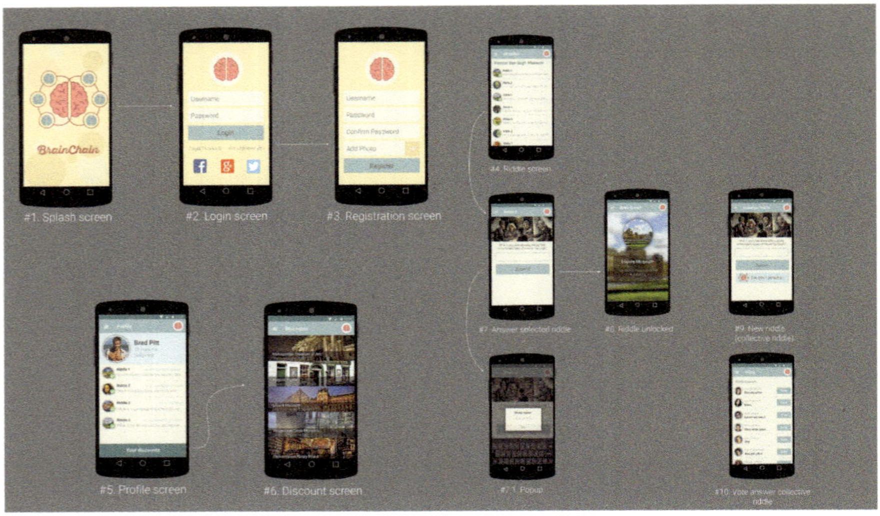

Fig. 7.3 First Graphic Design crowdsourced through UpWork (graphic design done by a worker from UpWork)

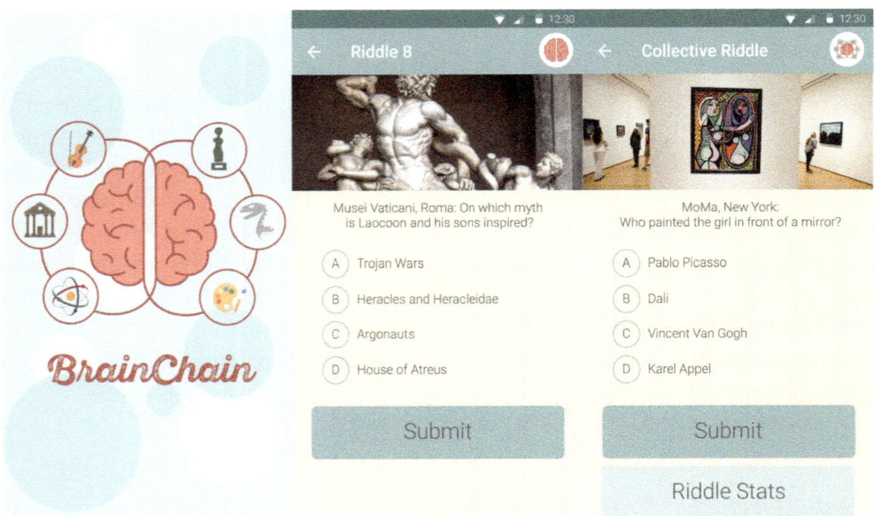

Fig. 7.4 Final BrainChain design. Screenshot of the landing page and the collective and individual questions

questions. From this input we used only 25 questions for the first prototype, to make it work in the short amount of time we had for our project (see Appendix 1 for the 25 selected questions). Our results show that there is a plethora of diverse

Table 7.3 The functionalities contributors could choose from. We actually used the first seven rows for the concept

Functionalities	Votes
Different Museum themes (architecture/sculptures/paintings etc.)	62
Receiving "points" by giving an individual correct answer	62
Difficulty levels	53
Extra reward for entering a certain level	46
Chatbox to chat with other users	42
History of solved assignments	43
An overview of reviews of museums	40
Receiving "points" by giving a collective correct answer	36
Limited attempts to solve the assignment (e.g., three attempts)	35
Connecting to social media	34
Limited time to solve the assignment (a countdown)	33
Having a look in another museum somewhere in the world, through someone else's "eyes"	28
Share your location with other users	24
An overview of which museums your friends visited	19

Table 7.4 Results of content creation through CrowdFlower. The task description and metrics

Content derived from: CrowdFlower
Task: Imagine being a quizmaster and create questions about your favorite museum
Metrics
Time to complete the task: 4 h
Responses: 100, 95 useful
Worker Nationalities: 35
Paid: 10 cents per participant
Number of museums: 80
Questions: 115

content that can be created in a short time and with a small budget with paid crowdsourcing for creating museum related quiz questions (Table 7.4).

7.3.5 Testing with Crowds

Having the design and the content, the next step was to test this with the crowd. UsabilityHub[3] is another crowdsourcing platform that offers several kinds of design tests. At this platform, we earned "karma points" by contributing to others' projects.

[3]www.usabilityhub.com.

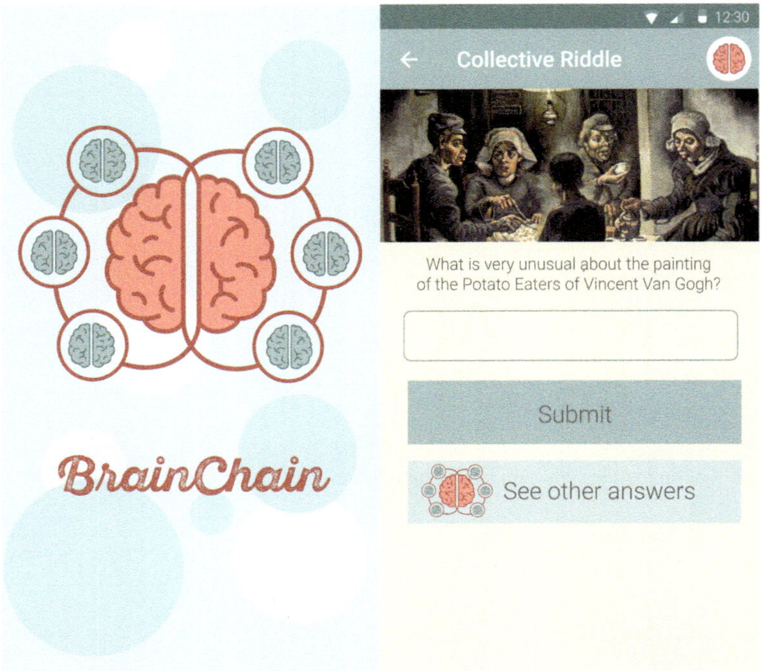

Fig. 7.5 Screens which were checked for usability, focusing on the functionality, and the intention of the application (graphic design done by a worker from UpWork)

Being a worker or a contributor in this sense means filling in questionnaires or participating in preference or flow tests. With the karma points, we could "pay" our own contributors and therefore, were able to stick to our tight budget.

The first test we conducted was a short questionnaire about the design of our app. In total ten participants were asked. The purpose of this test was to find out what people would expect after tapping on a user interface element. The following questions were asked about Fig. 7.5:

Imagine you are going to the museum, where you see advertisements with this picture of a mobile app.

1. *What do you think the application is about?*
2. *What would you expect to happen when you click on submit?*
3. *What would you expect to happen when you click on see others?*
4. *What would you expect to happen if you click on the brain image in the upper right corner?*
5. *Do you have any design recommendations?*

Most workers thought the application was a brain game (5 out of 10) or a museum quiz (3 out of 10). Other responses were that it was to boost imagination or to share expert knowledge. We also asked what they would expect after clicking on the submit button. The results showed that they expected to see the right answer after submitting it and they also wanted feedback. This is something we did not think about at that stage. Beforehand, our idea was that they would go to the home screen instead of seeing the right answer. The brain icon was interpreted as a way of going to the home screen or to settings. The workers were also asked to give suggestions about the design. The only feedback we received was that the readability of the text in the buttons should be improved.

The second test was a *flow-test* and was also conducted at UsabilityHub. Ten workers were asked to complete the following tasks: *you are going to (1) play an individual game, (2) choose game 4, (3) submit the answer, (4) go back to the main screen, (5) check discount, and (6) go back to the main screen*. The first task was not completed, and this was probably due to the confusing task description. We could have asked them to click on an individual game. For task (3) submitting the answer, they might have thought that they would have had to write an answer, which was not necessary for continuing the test. The lesson we learned from this, is that instructions need to be piloted before asking the crowd workers to participate in the test, as there can be unexpected unclarities in the formulations of the instructions.

The last test was conducted on UsabilityHub. This was a *preference test* with 11 workers. The purpose was to test which logo would better convey the purpose of the app. We provided a short description of the application and then contributors had to choose between two alternative logos (see Figs. 7.4 and 7.5). Ten out of the eleven people chose the current design (Fig. 7.4). The overall time of receiving answers from participants from UsabilityHub was very short: between 10 and 15 min per test.

7.3.6 Prototyping

As aforementioned, the aim of the project was to explore what and how existing crowdsourcing platforms could be used for the development of a Museum app. After designing an interactive prototype in Axure, we uploaded that again in UpWork together with a detailed task description. After one hour, there was a response from a Ukrainian developer who was willing to program a working prototype. Due to our limited time schedule, the programmer had only one day left for programming the application and therefore, he only coded part of the app. Our experience shows that it was easy to find a programmer for a reasonable amount of money. The programmer was paid $58 for about 24 hours of work.

7.4 Discussion

In this study, we aimed to demonstrate that paid crowdsourcing—in combination with input from popular social media networks—is a viable alternative for helping museums to: (1) ideate technological concepts; (2) decide which ideas are best; (3) design the visuals; and (4) develop the content. In our study, we asked crowd workers to contribute to the creation of a Museum app in relation to these four activities. The design process of the BrainChain app unfolded in a short time span of two weeks, carried out by a team of three people plus the different workers in crowd sourcing platforms and with a limited budget of $100. This shows that the four activities can be carried out efficiently by making use of existing crowdsourcing platforms. This is an important finding, as until now museums have engaged with crowds by developing their own platforms (Oomen and Aroyo 2011). Our study shows that it is not necessary to design and develop a completely new platform since existing platforms were used. We expect that the resources and know-how to design novel crowdsource-based systems to engage with crowds can be limited for museums. Thus, our study suggests that to overcome this lack of resources and know-how, museums can use existing crowdsourcing platforms.

Moreover, our study revealed three main learning points about how to make use of existing crowdsourcing platforms to develop an (crowdsource-based) application for visitor engagement. These learning points relate to

(1) awareness of existing crowdsourcing platforms including their benefits and shortcomings,
(2) knowledge of how to use them effectively, and
(3) experience in combining them.

Our case study showed that the right type of existing crowdsourcing platforms need to be found to get started. The existing crowdsourcing platforms differ in their focus (crowd creation, crowd voting, crowd wisdom or crowd funding), their expenses, quality control, and immediacy (Geiger et al. 2012; Scholz 2015). In our case, mainly crowd creation platforms were used for the design and content creation of the mobile application. Although crowd creation platforms related to design contests (e.g. DesignCrowd[4]) often ask for starting fees beyond our budget, low-cost, bid-oriented and yet, immediate crowdsourcing platforms exist as well. These platforms allow crowdsourced workers to improve their skills. For example, in our study, multiple potential workers responded to the design proposal for the Museum app which was posted on the crowdsourcing platform of UpWork.[5] Subsequently, one of the UpWork workers offered to work for free in order to learn and expand her online portfolio. Since her graphic design deliverables of the mobile application exceeded our expectations, we did financially reward her to show our appreciation of the smooth collaboration and the high quality of deliverables.

[4]www.designcrowd.com.

[5]www.upwork.com.

Positive feedback, online reviews or recommendations could also be a reward option due to the value of reputation. We want to highlight that we do not advocate unreasonable, low payment for designers working in crowdsourcing platforms. We merely report our findings which were based in the limited budget and time we had in our hands due the course's constraints. We did observe the need of learning and getting better by practising and at least the designer we found turned to crowdsourcing platforms to fullfil that need. Future work should look more carfefully into how to support that need without financial compromise.

Aside from finding the right platforms, the crowd needs guidance (Dow et al. 2012). The development of the Museum app demonstrated that paid crowdsourcing can be a viable approach for ideating technical concepts, decision making, graphic design, and content creation. Nevertheless, to receive such fruitful design outcomes it matters how the crowd is involved by the initiator. It needs to be clear for the crowd what is expected from them and it needs to be appealing to generate productive outcomes. Therefore, our advice is to let the crowd know that they are part of the application development. In this case study, the crowd knew what the application was about, why their participation was important, and how their input was going to be used. Contributors were triggered as well by playful storytelling. Moreover, a responsive, proactive attitude of the initiator was required throughout the graphic design, because immediate and online feedback on visuals was essential for establishing common ground. When we as commissioners were not able to give feedback on the multiple design outcomes of the UpWork worker, the crowd was asked to make a design decision through crowd voting. Therefore, our advice is to use other platforms when needed to avoid providing vague feedback which could impede the creative process. Throughout the study, we asked the crowd to make a decision which was in turn provided to the UpWork worker. This type of workflows that utilize crowd workers in a chain of events within the design process is also known as crowd algorithms (Bigham et al. 2015). Both approaches of coaching the UpWork worker properly and involving other crowdsourcing platforms for decision-making went hand in hand and thereby, fostered an immediate and fruitful design process.

Aside from the investigation of what and how existing crowdsourcing platforms should be used, our view on the functionalities of the application matured over time, because we became more familiar with crowdsourcing ourselves. The Museum app developed, BrainChain, provides the opportunity for content creation and is regarded as being adaptable to renewed exhibitions due to the content evaluation of the crowd. However, research is still needed to find out how the content can be managed accurately by the crowd without the help of cultural heritage experts. A way to do this is, for example, to let the other users evaluate potential quiz questions, which already happens in the Question Factory of Trivia Crack. This allows for checking the questions on accuracy (Crawley 2015). Therefore, it is possible to let the crowd actively create and evaluate digital museum content as an attempt to enrich the user experience in museums by providing flexibility in modification. Since museum collections can change rapidly, frequent and perhaps automated content management by the crowd is required for maintaining accurate quiz questions.

By providing the opportunity to add questions to the Museum app, the visitor experience is captured. An added question about an artifact can show where the user has been and how an artifact is perceived. Chapter 12 by Rozendaal, Vermeeren, and Issidorides will elaborate more about capturing the user experience. By conceiving museum audiences not only as museum quizzers but as the creators and validators of museum content, they actively take part in and are part of museum design and content creation processes, as demonstrated by the case of the BrainChain app. Based on this experience, we envision the BrainChain app to be self-sustaining and cost-effective, an example of how paid crowdsourcing can be fruitfully employed in other museum experience design projects.

This process also enabled us to further develop our views on the importance of strengthening interconnections between audiences and museums and to enhance visitors' engagement. In this case study, we wanted to create a mobile app by the crowd for the crowd in order to enhance visitors' experience. As written by Csikszentmihaly and Hermanson (1995): "*... one of the major underdeveloped functions of museums is to provide opportunities for individually meaningful experiences that also connect with the experiences of others.*" In our study, this idea of being connected to the experience of others is reflected in the functionality that all people are contributing to the collective quiz questions of BrainChain. By taking part in (e.g., being a gamer) and being part of (e.g., contributing to the content creation) the BrainChain app is envisioned to go beyond the usual visit by conceiving museum experiences as interconnected through the contributions of crowds not tied to the proximity of a single museum. Such an approach could even go beyond local communities and single museums, e.g., it could be applied for constellations of different cultural institutions connected through the interpretive acts and creative activities of diverse crowds. Thereby, such an approach could potentially contribute to people's international museum experiences and would go from museum experience design focused on a single museum to an approach that fosters connectedness across multiple museum audiences and even multiple museums (Shih et al. 2016).

Museums may face challenges about how to keep the visitors engaged and how to let the visitors contribute to content creation. Paid crowdsourcing is an alternative to marketing oriented social media and limitedly scalable (local community) attempts for developing technology that is adjacent to the main collections and enhances visitor's experience. We believe that digital crowdsourcing media are likely to foster greater public engagement. However, in our study, we could not investigate in depth the potential for increased public engagement, and therefore, we suggest that this is an aspect to be validated by future research.

Furthermore, we acknowledge that it is yet unknown whether museums themselves are able to undertake such a design process. The desirability and capacity to engage in similar design processes still needs to be evaluated within the remit of specific museums. However, we hope with this chapter to contribute to the proliferation of such usage. An important lesson learned from our study is that while experimenting with existing platforms we (as a design team) experienced that our role shifted from being designers toward being facilitators of design, which required changing our mindset (Radice 2014). Although we were in control as facilitators, to a certain extent direct control was given to the crowd to make design choices about BrainChain, especially when we did not have the answer. Facilitating a design and development process rather than having the expertise to actually perform it might better suit museum employees. Prior research has shown that when involving "unwitting participants" contributes to inspiring technologies that cultural heritage experts could not think themselves (Díaz et al. 2016). In essence, crowdsourcing affords the entry of a limitless pool of "unwitting participants" in the domain of museum experience design.

7.5 Conclusion

Paid crowdsourcing is relatively unexplored as being an effective and efficient approach for participatory museum experiences. The case study of BrainChain, which we reported in this chapter, shows how paid crowdsourcing can be a method for museums, not only for ideation, design, and software development but also for content creation. Our experience shows that during this process our role shifted from designers to facilitators of the design process. All throughout, crowd workers needed both clarifications and feedback, which implies as well that the overall process can be time-consuming. Future facilitators of such crowdsourced design processes should take into account that it does take time to review the crowd input, however, acknowledging as well that the crowdsourcing process has the potential of becoming self-sustaining. Furthermore, providing emerging digital technologies for crowdsourced Museum app content is likely to create opportunities for visitor engagement in more rewarding participatory museum experiences and provide new avenues and models for community building around museums. Using paid crowdsourcing means reaching out to people way beyond the museum walls and potentially to people from all over the world.

While crowdsourcing platforms differ in their costs, quality control, and immediacy, decent content creation is mainly dependent on how the crowd is involved. Future research is needed to cover the subjects of incorporating accurate adaptability in crowdsourced content creation and the peer review mechanism, the (software) development of the application itself and the evaluation of the application in the context of use. Finally, although existing crowdsourcing platforms could be used in their current form to support design and technical activities in museums, future research can also look into the development of specialized crowdsourcing platforms that exclusively focus on museums and cultural heritage institutions.

Acknowledgements We thank Tudor Vacaretu for his contribution during the project, moreover, we would like to thank Olga Kovalska, the designer from Upwork for her contribution related to the UI design of the BrainChain app. Lastly, we thank the USI program and specifically Ivor Grisel for his support of our research work.

Appendix 1 Quiz questions provided by Crowdflower workers (in bold the right answers)

#	Museum	Question	Answers
1	Philippine Museum, Manila	Who made the Spoliarium?	**Juan Luna**
			Luna Juan
			Picasso
			Dali
2	Indian National Museum, NewDelhi	How many art pieces does this museum have?	**200,000**
			250,000
			100,000
			500,000
3	Paschendale 1917, Zonnebeke, Belgium	What is the museum about?	**Fight of Paschendale**
			Victory of Paschendale
			Loosing of Paschendale
			Constitution of Paschendale
4	National Historic Museum, Sofia Bulgaria	Who made the Samara flag?	**Nuns**
			Soldiers
			Wife
			Themselves
5	National Historic Museum, Sofia Bulgaria	How many Items you can find in the museum?	**650,000**
			100,000
			1000,000
			500,000
6	Salarjung Museum, Hyderabad	What is a talking clock?	**English bracket clock**
			French Clock
			Russian Clock
			German Clock
7	El Prado, Madrid	In which century Madera made Las Meninas?	**17th**
			16th
			15th

(continued)

(continued)

			18th
8	Musei Vaticani, Roma	On which myth is Laocoon and his sons inspired?	**Trojan Wars**
			Heracles and Heracleidae
			Argonauts
			House of Atreus
9	Louvre, Paris	Who painted the Mona Lisa?	**Leonardo da Vinci**
			Rembrandt
			Dali
10	Louvre, Paris	How many works are exhibited?	**35,000**
			20,000
			15,000
			45,000
11	Cappella Sansevero, Napoli	Who sculptured the Veiled Christ?	**Giuseppe Sanmartino**
			St. Antonio
			Davor Salhi
			Michelangelo
12	MoMa, New York	Who painted the girl in front of a mirror?	**Pablo Picasso**
			Dali
			Van Gogh
			Karel Appel
14	The museum of vintage ladies dresses, Kiev	When is the first lace parasol created?	**1772**
			1872
			1672
			1972
15	Victoria, Kolkata	Who is the architect of the museum?	**William Emmerson**
			Jean Paul Gaultier
			Henry Berkeley
			Anthony Lake
16	Athens Museum, Athens	Are all the statues in the museum complete?	**No**
			Yes
17	Museum for physics, Brussels	Where is this the Iguanodon found?	**Bernissart**
			Anvers
			Brussels
			Liege
18	Imperial Museum, Janeiro	Which year the museum starts their historic collection?	**1943**
			1843

(continued)

(continued)

			1899
			1950
19	Kiev Museum of Russian art, Kiev	When is Boris and Gleb painted?	**14th century**
			13th century
			15th century
			16th century
20	Museum of Macedonia, Skopje	Which artifacts are from Kokino?	**Cans and Jars**
			Plates and cutlery
			Pots and pans
			Jewelry
21	Ancient Museum, Thessaloniki Greece	What flag symbol had the ancient Macedonians in Greece?	**Vergina Sun**
			Vergina Moon
			Dorgina Sun
			Dorgina Moon
22	Hagia Sophia Museum, Istanbul	What do the mosaics reflect?	**Christian Iconographics**
			Islamic Iconographics
			Jew Iconographics
			Hindu Iconographics
23	Reina Sofia, Madrid	What type of art is in Reina Sofia?	**Modern** and **Contemporary art** Renaissance
			Midevil
			Bauhaus
24	Victoria Museum, Vijayawada	Who is the founder of the NIZAM Dynasty?	**MIR QAMARUDDIN Khan**
			Mir Ahmed Ali Khan
			Mir Hidayat muhi udin
			Mir Said Muhammad
25	Rijksmuseum, Amsterdam	Who Painted the “Nightwatch”?	**Rembrandt**
			Van Gogh
			Karel Appel
			Mondriaan

References

Bigham JP, Bernstein MS, Adar E (2015) Human-computer interaction and collective intelligence. Handbook of collective intelligence, vol 57

Carletti L, McAuley D, Price D, Giannachi G, Benford S (2013) Digital humanities and crowdsourcing: an exploration. In: Proctor N, Cherry R (eds) Museums and the Web 2013. Silver Spring, MD. http://mw2013.museumsandtheweb.com/paper/digital-humanities-and-crowdsourcing-an-exploration-4/

Crawley D (2015) How trivia crack dev Etermax created a global sensation from Buenos Aires. http://www.pocketgamer.biz/feature/61358/trivia-crack-global-sensation-buenos-aires/. Accessed 4 Jan 2016

Csikszentmihaly M, Hermanson K (1995) Intrinsic motivation in museums: what makes visitors want to learn? Museum News 35–61

Díaz P, Aedo I, Bellucci A (2016) Integrating user stories to inspire the co-design of digital futures for cultural heritage. In: Proceedings of the XVII international conference on human computer interaction. ACM, p 31

Dow S, Kulkarni A, Klemmer S, Hartmann B (2012) Shepherding the crowd yields better work. In: Proceedings of the ACM 2012 conference on computer supported cooperative work. ACM, pp 1013–1022

Fidas C Sintoris C, Yiannoutsou N, Avouris N (2012) A survey on tools for end user authoring of mobile applications for cultural heritage. In: Proceedings of the IISA, workshop on mobile, hypermedia applications for culture

Geiger D, Rosemann M, Fielt E, Schader M (2012) Crowdsourcing information systems—definition, typology and design. In: Thirty third International conference on information systems, Orlando 2012

Ghiani G, Paternò F, Santoro C, Spano D (2007) Interactive games in multi-device environments to enhance the learning experience of museum visitors. In: Technology Enhanced Learning, ERCIM, vol 71

Giaccardi E, Palen L (2008) The social production of heritage through cross-media interaction: making place for place-making. Int J Herit Stud 14(3):281–297

Hamari J, Koivisto J (2015) Why do people use gamification services? Int J Inf Manag 35:419–431

Oomen J, Aroyo L (2011) Crowdsourcing in the cultural heritage domain: opportunities and challenges. In: Proceedings of the 5th international conference on communities and technologies. ACM, pp 138–149

Padilla-Meléndez A, del Águila-Obra AR (2013) Web and social media usage by museums: online value creation. Int J Inf Manag 33(5):892–898

Radice S (2014) Designing for participation within cultural heritage. Participatory practices and audience engagement in heritage experience processes (Doctoral dissertation, Politecno di Milano). https://www.politesi.polimi.it/handle/10589/89798?locale=it

Scholz N (2015) The relevance of crowdfunding: the impact on the innovation process of small entrepreneurial firms. Springer Gabler, Wiesbaden

Shih HC, Yoon JK, Vermeeren APOS (2016) Positive emotions for inciting behavior—playing with paintings to enhance museum experiences. In: Proceedings of design and emotions 2016, 27–30 September 2016, Amsterdam, NL

Stuedahl D (2011) Social media and community involvements in museums. A case study of a local history wiki community. Nordisk Museologi 1:3–14

Stuedahl D, Smørdal O (2015) Matters of becoming, experimental zones for making museums public with social media. CoDesign 11(3–4):193–207

Author Biographies

Lindsey van der Lans (M.Sc.) has a background in Applied Cognitive Psychology from Leiden University. At the moment she is completing her PDEng degree (Professional Doctorate in Engineering) in User System Interaction at the Eindhoven University of Technology. Her interest is to improve people's life by creating valuable experiences which are supported by the use of technology. Special interest goes to persuasive design.

Evy Ansems (M.Sc.) is a designer with an educational background in Industrial Design and Human Technology Interaction. Evy designs for rich user experiences; from translation of the user needs into wireframes, mock-ups, and prototypes. In an iterative design process, Evy applies knowledge from the social sciences to the challenges and opportunities of new, interactive technologies.

Vassilis Javed Khan currently is assistant professor at the Industrial Design Department at Eindhoven University of Technology in the Netherlands. His research interests include crowdsourcing, mobile interaction design and UX of virtual environments. He earned his Ph.D. in HCI at Eindhoven University of Technology and Masters in Computer Engineering at the University of Patras, in Greece.

Chapter 8
The Value of User-Centric Crowdsourcing for Cultural Heritage: Fostering Emotional Engagement with Integrity

Tom Wrigglesworth and Leon A. Watts

Abstract Historical museums and institutions are turning to crowdsourcing initiatives to help collect, organise and preserve information. The systems being deployed are designed with usability and data validity as their primary concern. However, participatory projects also provide an opportunity for institutions to fulfil their ethical remit to engage the public with their digital collections. In this chapter, we (a) place the role of crowdsourcing initiatives in terms of the ethical concerns of cultural heritage institutions and (b) take a preliminary step in theorising experience design concepts to integrate these concerns with crowdsourcing initiatives. We propose that the design of such systems should take into account the experiential qualities of the volunteer's work. The aim of taking such an approach would be to place more emphasis on these initiatives as participatory processes that are beneficial not only to the institution but also to the individuals taking part. We report a study carried out in collaboration with the American Air Museum, part of the Imperial War Museums in the UK. An image classification system is deployed in gallery to explore participants' reflections on their user experience and to identify components of engagement that can be targeted for design work. Our findings suggest that a volunteer's emotional connection to the crowdsourcing content is correlated to their appreciation and enjoyment of the task. We go on to propose a set of design perspectives derived from further analysis of the participants' qualitative experiences of the task.

8.1 Introduction

Crowdsourcing initiatives are growing in popularity amongst museums and historical institutions as a means to collect new data and enhance their existing collections (Ridge 2014). As such, the need for reliable and valid data places constraints upon the design of crowdsourcing systems and an emphasis on

T. Wrigglesworth (✉) · L. A. Watts
University of Bath, Bath, UK
e-mail: T.A.D.Wrigglesworth@bath.ac.uk

A. Vermeeren et al. (eds.), *Museum Experience Design*, Springer Series on Cultural Computing, https://doi.org/10.1007/978-3-319-58550-5_8

error-free operation and other strictly functional aspects of usability. However, user experience as a whole encompasses much more than this. In this chapter, we argue that user experience has a fundamental impact on the nature of interactive engagement with cultural heritage, and consequently on the capacity of crowdsourcing to promote meaningful participation by existing and new audiences of volunteers.

Many initiatives past and present have provided meaningful work for communities of enthusiasts (Ridge 2014; Straub 2016). The motivations for taking part can be varied and are dependent on personal context and identity (Raddick et al. 2010; Rotman et al. 2012). However, it is only really a small number of deeply interested enthusiasts/hobbyists that make up the large percentage of contributions (Eveleigh et al. 2014; Suh et al. 2009).

We argue that if we are to take museums' principle of institutional integrity into account, systems should be built that engender respectful and transparent relationships with their volunteers. From this ethical standpoint (see the UK Museum Association's Code of Ethics[1]), a museum has an active role in society to (a) provide meaningful work for public participation, (b) cultivate new audiences beyond those with existing deep interests, and (c) be respectful of their volunteer's well-being. Placing emphasis on the amplification of positive aspects of user engagement when designing these systems may be a method of moving towards fulfilment of the three principles simultaneously.

We report a study carried out in collaboration with the American Air Museum, part of the Imperial War Museums in the UK. An image classification system was deployed in gallery to explore participants' reflections on their user experience and to identify components of engagement that can be targeted for design work. We place particular emphasis on the emotional component of engagement due to its noted importance in prior museum visitor research (Falk and Dierking 2013). Our work addresses the lack of research relating to the role of emotional engagement in crowdsourcing tasks.

8.2 Crowdsourcing for Museum Collections

Digitisation of museum collections and advances in web technologies have allowed museums to open up their collections to the public. Many museum websites now have a searchable online collection such as the Rijksmuseum[2] in the Netherlands, the Imperial War Museum[3] in the UK or the Holocaust Memorial Museum[4] in the

[1]See Sect. 8.3 of the Museum Association Code of Ethics: https://www.museumsassociation.org/download?id=1173810.

[2]https://www.rijksmuseum.nl/en/.

[3]http://www.iwm.org.uk/collections.

[4]https://collections.ushmm.org/.

USA. These collections are sometimes curated into online exhibitions, but for the most part they exist as searchable databases for academic researchers and interested individuals. In this way, they are primarily useful to people who know what they are looking for and not casual visitors.

Crowdsourcing initiatives provide an alternative means in which people can encounter a museum's collections whilst also taking part in meaningful work on behalf of the museum. The popularisation of these systems can perhaps be seen in the success of the early Zooniverse[5] citizen science movement. Volunteers take part in transcribing and classifying media in order to aid scientific research. Some of the most successful of these projects have been Galaxy Zoo (classification of galaxies), Snapshot Serengeti (classification of wildlife) and Old Weather (transcription of ship logbooks).

Crowdsourcing initiatives can be classified in a number of ways (Oomen and Aroyo 2011). Wiki-type project participation, in which volunteers complement an existing collection in some way, usually requires a level of prerequisite knowledge. The American Air Museum website, for example, is collecting data about the military personnel, civilians and aircraft connected to the US Air Force Britain during World War II. In order to contribute to this project, the volunteer must either (a) know or possess information about a person or aircraft (perhaps be a family member) or (b) have research skills, enthusiasm and knowledge relating to the subject matter. These criteria raise the barrier to entry for general public engagement. Classification and transcription-type tasks, on the other hand, require little or no prerequisite knowledge. Participants simply need to analyse an image within the structure of the system, usually answering a classifying question or transcribing text within the image.

It is important to consider why museums are attracted to launching crowdsourcing initiatives. The (UK) Museum Association Code of Ethics[6] outlines ethical principles for museums as public institutions. The code was developed as a collaborative process between museum stakeholders, members of the public, funders and interest groups across the sector. The code adopts three principles:

1. **Public Engagement and Public Benefit**—Actively engage and work with existing audiences and reach out to new and diverse audiences; Promote meaningful participation with museums; Use collections for public benefit—for learning, inspiration and enjoyment.
2. **Stewardship of Collections**—Acquire, care for, exhibit and loan collections with transparency and competency in order to generate knowledge and engage the public with collections.
3. **Individual and Institutional Integrity**—Act in the public interest in all areas of work; Build respectful and transparent relationships with staff and volunteers to ensure public trust in museum's activities.

---

[5]https://www.zooniverse.org/.

[6]https://www.museumsassociation.org/ethics/code-of-ethics (see additional guidance version).

Museums are attracted to crowdsourcing initiatives as a solution to high work load projects that are just not possible with limited resources available to them. When taking this perspective, a museum's motivation to build a crowdsourcing project is to fulfil the stewardship aim and to enhance an existing collection through data collection. However, as Owens (2014) notes, crowdsourcing provides a convenient solution not only to fulfil stewardship-oriented aims of the museum but also satisfy the aim to engage the public with their collections. In doing so, the museum should not take advantage of the volunteers as cheap labour.

If we are to adhere to the principles set forth by the Museum Association, the work in which they participate should be meaningful, enjoyable and inspire learning. The initiative should actively seek to engage new audiences rather than rely on a small selection of enthusiast hobbyists. Designing initiatives that fulfil these criteria, in turn, may be said to fulfil the institutional integrity principle; ensuring a respectful relationship between the institution and the crowdsourcing volunteers. This is an active effort on the museum's part to design engaging experiences that are inclusive, meaningful and satisfying.

8.2.1 User Engagement in Crowdsourcing

A user's values, motivations, goals and interactions with a system contribute to their user experience. User experiences are multifaceted since they describe matters of relevance and value to users. As such, one of the key facets of user experience is the extent to which a person finds their interactions with a system engaging. User engagement in Human–Computer Interaction is a term used to refer to the emotional, cognitive, behavioural and temporal relation between a user and a system (O'Brien 2010; O'Brien and Toms 2008). In simpler terms, it is a quality of a user's experience that gives emphasis to positive aspects of interactions (Attfield et al. 2011). How we term positive engagement is dependent on the user and the system designer's goals. If there is a mismatch of perspectives, users or designers may not see the values and meanings that matter to one another.

From the museum's perspective, we can use the principles set out by the Museum Association's Ethics Code as mentioned in the previous section. Desirable outcomes towards *public engagement and public benefit* may be learning, inspiration, enjoyment and meaningful participation. The user's goals may or may not be congruent with these ideal ethical aims of the museum. We can look to existing literature to better understand volunteers' motivations and positive aspects of their engagement with crowdsourcing systems.

O'Brien and Toms developed a framework for engagement through a study based around user encounters with web search, online shopping, gaming and webcasting applications (O'Brien and Toms 2008). The framework consists of four phases: a point of engagement, a period of sustained engagement, disengagement and re-engagement. Within the period of sustained engagement, they identified a number of attributes of engagement that contributed towards a user's positive engagement with a system: focused attention, perceived usability, endurability, novelty, aesthetics and felt involvement.

8.2.1.1 Designing for Reliability

In crowdsourcing system design, challenges relating to data and system usability and functionality take precedence over user experience related attributes. In some ways, the need for reliable and valid data may overbear upon an experience-centric approach to design. Classification systems are simple and structured systems because they need people to give reliable and valid information as a primary function. There is perhaps a dichotomy between designing for usability and designing for user experience. Using video game design as an example Cook (2008) has noted, if the game Super Mario Bros was designed to be usable the result would simply be a button labelled ‘Rescue Princess’. The user would click the button and achieve their goal. This is a purely usable system that streamlines user activity towards its main goal but not one that would result in a positive experience for the user/player. In a similar way, crowdsourcing systems designed for usability around data validity may not support positive attributes of engagement that give rise to positive user experience.

8.2.1.2 Designing for Engagement

Designing for engagement may have to be underspecified and open to customisation to support dynamic personalisation (Deterding 2015). However, valid and reliable data is at the core of crowdsourcing system and so should not be compromised for the sake of user experience. Without the collection of useful data, the crowdsourcing work being undertaken loses its meaning. Due to the importance of usability to classification tasks, crowdsourcing system designers employ a number of mechanisms to promote engagement without the need to compromise data validity.

The Old Weather ship logs transcription project uses gamification and social features to encourage user engagement with the project. The system awards points and ranks to top contributors allowing volunteers to become ‘captain’ of a ship if they made the most transcriptions from the relevant log book (Eveleigh et al. 2013). This competitive mechanism was found to be motivating and rewarding to some users, ignored by others and even contributed to the decision to cease participation by some.

Another mechanism used by the Old Weather project is the use of narrative feedback. As the coordinates of the ship are transcribed from the logbook, a ship’s course is plotted across the map. This led to some volunteers becoming more emotionally attached to a certain ship and gave way to a sense of identification and exploration of the past (Blaser 2014).

The addition of social features has also been used to promote social engagement around a project's content. The American Air Museum website incorporates a user activity feed on their front page to engender a feeling that the site is an active social space. The Zooniverse Galaxy Zoo project encouraged the use of forums to promote work and conversation around the project's content and inspire volunteer-led scientific discovery (Straub 2016).

Motivations for participation amongst volunteers can vary and so cannot be distilled to a single underlying motivational factor. Intrinsic and extrinsic factors, such as altruism, personal interest, learning, competitiveness and sociality can all be motivations to take part in an initiative (Raddick et al. 2010; Rotman et al. 2012). It is typical for a crowdsourcing project to have a skewed pattern of participation; most of the work is done by a small percentage of the system's user-base. For example, 94% of volunteers only contribute to 15% of the input in the Old Weather project (Eveleigh et al. 2014). In this way, the 'crowd' can be thought of as a group of dedicated enthusiasts supported by a large number of 'dabblers'. Referring back to the code of ethics, we might consider a museum's role to actively reach out to and engage with new audiences. With regards to crowdsourcing initiatives, this could extend to 'flattening' this skewed pattern of participation by actively designing to engage those beyond the core enthusiast group and thus making the resources spent on building such systems of greater value to a larger percentage of the public.

The present study sought to understand the energising and attenuating factors that lead to engagement in the context of historical classification systems. We have proposed that designing for user engagement can be a mechanism for meeting the public engagement, stewardship and integrity aims of a museum.

8.2.2 Emotional Engagement in Museums

As discussed in the previous section, designers of crowdsourcing systems can target particular components of user engagement to energise through design mechanisms (For example, the forums on the Zooniverse project aim to energise social engagement around the content). In the present study, we draw focus to the emotional component. This is based upon prior research in visitor emotion in the physical museum and findings from our previous exploratory study. The emotional aspect of engagement can broadly be thought of as the affective experiences of user's interactions with a system (O'Brien and Toms 2008). Falk and Dierking note that emotion has long been thought of an important part of the physical museum experience but to a large extent has been poorly understood (2013, p. 191).

Dierking connects emotions, motivation and interest in informal learning environment of science and technology museums (2005). She argues that emotion is a vital part of learning and the formation of memory. She goes on to provide three reasons for effective free-choice learning; (a) visitors experience ideas on their own terms with an autonomy to attend exhibits depending on prior knowledge and interest, (b) the institution provides a safe, comfortable environment in which they are free to encounter and pursue ideas and (c) visitors can see and experience how the encountered ideas apply in the context of the real world. To Dierking, emotions experienced as part of this personal context are fundamental constituents of learning.

There is some evidence to suggest that a visitor's emotional state is an important factor in exhibition design. Studies show that after visiting an emotionally arousing exhibition a visitor's level of reflection and long-term learning is higher when compared to visitors of a less arousing exhibition within the same museum (Falk and Gillespie 2009).

In a previous study (Wrigglesworth and Watts 2016), we explored museum visitors' sensemaking process as they encountered a set of historical images. Each image was accompanied by a set of verbal prompts to elicit meaning-making by the visitor. The responses were analysed through a grounded theory methodology (Strauss and Corbin 1994) to identify components of engagement with historical information. The qualitative responses were analysed to expose the salient components of engagement. Several of these emergent components can be said to be pertinent to emotional experience:

Empathising—The participant talks about how they think the people in the photograph are feeling.

Responding emotionally—The participant makes reference to their own feelings about the photograph content.

Seeking personal connection—The participant seeks to know more personal information about the subject.

The personal context seems to be important in this sensemaking process. Although a photograph can be understood as a factual representation of circumstances, when actively engaged by an individual it becomes a mirror in which their own experiences, prior knowledge and feelings are reflected. This is exemplified by two individual's different reactions to the same photograph during a pilot study; the photograph depicts US bombers on a bombing run.[7] One lady was moved to tears and was noted saying 'You sometimes forget about the people involved'. A man took a contrasting view and cheered the bombers on, 'Well, they got what was coming to them'. In both cases, the participants were emotionally involved with the content of the photograph, but their emotional reaction was a result of their own personal context. The man's reaction was perhaps more understandable when later in the museum cafe he was heard reflecting on the photograph and explaining to family members that his relatives were heavily bombed in Coventry during the war. Such emotional connections to content may serve as a mechanism for engaging visitors with historical content.

People visit a war museum knowing that they will likely encounter media that evoke negative emotions; images of violence, death and suffering. The lady that cried may have experienced unpleasant emotions as she was moved to tears. These

[7]Photograph FRE 8474 available at http://www.americanairmuseum.com/media/10185.

negative emotions, however, do not necessarily mean that her experience as a whole was negative. People have been found to enjoy and appreciate experiencing negative emotions when playing video games (Bopp et al. 2016). Entertainment audiences voluntarily expose themselves to unpleasant feelings (Bartsch 2012; Oliver and Raney 2011). People seek entertainment to satisfy their psychological needs and move towards well-being. Sad and moving films can satisfy a viewer's eudaimonic motivations; an individual's search for deeper insight, meaning and self-actualisation (Bartsch 2012; Bartsch et al. 2014; Tamborini et al. 2010).

The present study aims to explore the findings of this prior research in relation to museum crowdsourcing activities. We explore the relationship between the felt emotional involvement to those depicted in historical content (as suggested by our previous study), reflective and meaningful entertainment and enjoyment (as suggested by museum motivations and the prior work in entertainment experience studies). As covered in previous sections, by targeting components of user experience (in this case emotional) in this way, we aim to explore how crowdsourcing can provide an opportunity for a museum to fulfil its aims of public engagement, stewardship and integrity simultaneously.

8.3 Study

8.3.1 Study Rationale

We have argued that public engagement and integrity should be reconciled with the data-driven aims of a museums mission when designing crowdsourcing systems. In the study reported herein, we partly focus on one particular aspect of user experience: emotional engagement with the crowdsourcing task content. Our previous studies (Wrigglesworth and Watts 2016) have suggested that museum visitors respond emotionally to historical content and prior research in entertainment psychology and media communication has shown that users have a psychological need for emotional gratification.

The first part of the study focused on five operationalised components of engagement: positive and negative affect, connectedness, reflection and enjoyment. The relationship between these components has been explored to test the hypothesis that feelings of connectedness with people depicted in the photographs relate to enjoyment and reflection of the crowdsourcing task. Further to this, we used a post-task interview to provide qualitative data and provoke participant's reflection about their experience of the task. From this, we hoped to acquire a complementary and rich data set to explore emergent components of engagement that may be targeted for design work.

8.3.2 *Quantitative Measures*

Five measures were developed from the relevant literature. All survey measures consisted of a 7-point Likert scale. A reliability analysis was conducted for each scale (see Table 8.1). All measures had a high-reliability rating (Cronbach $\alpha > 0.8$).

8.3.2.1 Panas

The Positive Affect Negative Affect Schedule (PANAS) is a widely used set of two 10-item mood scales to measure both positive and negative dimensions of affect (Watson et al. 1988). In the present study, we used the scale to assess the positive and negative dimensions of a participant's mood during the task as a whole. It treats positive and negative affect as orthogonal to each other rather than opposing poles on the same scale (Ekkekakis 2013).

8.3.2.2 Connectedness

A scale was developed to assess the extent to which participants felt empathetic and connected to the people in the photographs. The scale was adapted from Bartsch's *emotional engagement with characters* scale (2012). The wording of the scale items was changed to be relevant to photographs rather than apply to television and films as they do in the original. For example, the general statement '… because I identify with the characters' outlook on life' was adapted to '… I was able to put myself "in the Shoes" of those depicted in the photographs'.

… I had a connection to the people shown in the photographs
… I understood how the people in the photographs were feeling
… I was able to put myself 'in the shoes' of those depicted in the photographs
… I was able to relate to those depicted in the photographs
… I cared about what happened to those shown in the photographs.

Table 8.1 Reliability analysis results for each scale

Variable	Cronbach's α	N of items
Connectedness	0.915	5
Reflection	0.893	5
Enjoyment	0.873	4
PANAS positive	0.917	10
PANAS negative	0.944	10

8.3.2.3 Reflection

A scale was used to measure the extent to which a participant was provoked to think about meaningful subjects. This was adapted from a contemplativeness scale developed in prior research (Bartsch 2012; Bartsch et al. 2014). This measure is pertinent because, as well as being a measure of contemplative entertainment, museums aim to provide the public with opportunities for inspiration and learning.

… I was inspired to think about meaningful issues
… I was inspired to gain new insights
… I thought about meaningful events in the world
… I thought about myself in relation to others
… I found the task thought-provoking.

8.3.2.4 Enjoyment

Enjoyment was measured using a scale developed and validated for measuring enjoyment of computer games (Ryan et al. 2006). As with reflection, it was used in this instance as a measure that is desirable from the museum's point of view to satisfy public engagement motives. The scale was reduced to five measures for brevity in the survey.

… I enjoyed doing this activity very much
… This activity was fun to do
… I would describe this activity as very interesting
… While I was doing this activity, I was thinking about how much I enjoyed it.

8.3.3 *System Design*

The study was conducted using a custom-built web-based image classification. The design of the system was largely influenced by two existing designs: the Zooniverse citizen science classification platform and the American Air Museum's in-gallery image classification interactive tables.

A user was presented with a photograph and a simple multiple-choice question regarding the content of that photograph. For example, 'Is there a person in this photograph?' A simple question logic tree determines which question will be asked next. There were two main logic branches: questions regarding people and questions regarding aircraft. When the user reached the end of a logic tree, the system moves onto the next photograph. This approach is used in most classification systems including the Zooniverse Labs system[8] and can be said to be paradigmatic of such systems.

The questions were adapted from the AAM's own in-gallery crowdsourcing system. This was so they were emblematic of a museum's desired classification-tag output in relation to the content. The photographs were from the AAM's Roger Freeman Collection; a collection of $\sim$15,000 photographs of the US air force and civilians in Britain during World War II. A total of 12 were used in the present study to keep the study session time to a reasonable length. Six were chosen that depicted people and six to depict aircraft. This was to keep the set balanced in regards to the question logic tree focus (People and Aircraft). The order in which the photographs appeared was randomised to combat order biasing effects.

8.3.4 Study Context

The study took place in the American Air Museum's Georgia Frontiere gallery, a room separate from the main museum hall. The gallery contains two crowdsourcing interactive tables that were designed by the museum (and on which the study's task questions were based) and the roll of honour for the 8th Airforce. It is regarded as a quieter and more reflective space than the main museum hall.

The museum does not have a strong narrative trail and is open plan. The gallery is positioned at the back of the hall, so visitors are therefore likely to have passed by and looked at exhibits on the way. Therefore, there may be framing effects introduced by this configuration, as people think about the exhibits they encounter before reaching the study location.

8.3.5 Participants

Participants were recruited from visitors to the American Air Museum. They were approached by the researcher and asked if they would like to take part in a short experiment for the museum. A total of 31 participants took part in the study (74% Male, 26% female). The age demographic was largely skewed to people aged 45–55 and 55–65 age categories (39% and 32%, respectively). This is in line with the demographics for the American Air Museum website visitors as reported by their Google Analytics. The sample can therefore be said to be representative of the American Air Museum's current audience.

[8]https://www.zooniverse.org/lab.

8.3.6 Approach

A mixed methods approach was used for the present study. Quantitative measures were used to explore correlations between, positive negative affect (PANAS) and the emotional connectedness, enjoyment and reflective nature of the crowdsourcing task. Data was gathered by a survey when the user completed the task. The survey consisted of three pages. The first was a PANAS survey headed by the question 'How did you feel during the task' and given a Likert scale ranging from 1 to 7 for each affective word (1 being 'not at all' and 7 being 'very much'). The second page was the engagement component survey measuring connectedness, reflection and enjoyment. Participants were asked the extent to which they thought the statements were true on a Likert scale of 1–7 (1 being 'not at all' true and 7 being 'very true'). The third and final page asked participants for their demographic data (gender and age category). The order of the Likert scale terms was randomised for the first two pages for each participant, in order to reduce ordering bias effects.

The quantitative survey was followed by a short semi-open interview. This was conducted to gather rich data about the participant's engagement with the system to complement and elucidate any findings from the quantitative data. Participants were asked about their experience using the system in regards to the task as a process and to elaborate upon their thoughts and feelings about the specific content they encountered. The length of the interview ranged from 5 to 10 min depending on how much the participant had to say.

The audio recordings of the post-task interviews were transcribed and then coded line-by-line. An open-coding process was used to allow for codes to emerge from the data (Saldaña 2009). These open codes were then developed into concepts as the coding progressed. The categories were in constant flux as the analysis proceeded; concepts were created and merged as they were constantly being compared to each other.

8.3.7 Study Procedure

The study procedure took the following form: Participants were asked to read the study briefing on the introduction screen. This briefing explained that their help was needed to classify the museum's large collection of photographs. They were told that they would have to complete 12 photographs and the task would be followed by a survey and short interview.

The participants were then left to complete the task. Upon finishing, they were thanked and then asked to proceed with the survey. On completion of the survey, they were asked to take part in the interview.

8.4 Results

8.4.1 Survey Results

A Pearson's product-moment correlation coefficient was computed to explore the correlational relationships between the five variables. The results can be seen in Table 8.2.

There is a strong positive correlation between enjoyment and positive PANAS ($r = 0.745$, $p < 0.001$), and moderate positive correlations between connectedness and positive PANAS ($r = 0.544$, $p < 0.01$), and to a lesser extent, reflection and positive PANAS ($r = 0.440$, $p < 0.05$). Negative PANAS has no significant correlation with any of the variables.

Connectedness, reflection and enjoyment all hold moderate correlations to each other; enjoyment and connectedness ($r = 0.671$, $p < 0.001$), enjoyment and reflection ($r = 0.647$, $p < 0.001$) and connectedness and reflection ($r = 0.681$, $p < 0.001$). This may suggest that connectedness, reflection and enjoyment are all constituent parts that make up a positive experience with a crowdsourcing task.

Table 8.2 Pearson's correlation results for the five factors

Correlations						
		PANAS positive	PANAS negative	Enjoyment	Connectedness	Reflection
PANAS positive	Pearson Correlation	1	0.098	0.745[b]	0.544[b]	0.440[a]
	Sig. (2-tailed)		0.601	0.000002	0.002	0.013
	N	31	31	31	31	31
PANAS negative	Pearson Correlation	0.098	1	−0.204	0.033	0.083
	Sig. (2-tailed)	0.601		0.271	0.859	0.659
	N	31	31	31	31	31
Enjoyment	Pearson Correlation	0.745[b]	−0.204	1	0.671[b]	0.647[b]
	Sig. (2-tailed)	0.000002	0.271		0.000085	0.000036
	N	31	31	31	31	31
Connectedness	Pearson Correlation	0.544[b]	0.033	0.671[b]	1	0.681[b]
	Sig. (2-tailed)	0.002	0.859	0.000085		0.000025
	N	31	31	31	31	31
Reflection	Pearson Correlation	0.440[a]	0.083	0.647[b]	0.681[b]	1
	Sig. (2-tailed)	0.013	0.659	0.000036	0.000025	
	N	31	31	31	31	31

[a]Correlation is significant at the 0.01 level (2-tailed)
[b]Correlation is significant at the 0.05 level (2-tailed)

Figure 8.1 shows a flattened three-dimensional graph that visualises the correlations between connectedness, reflection and enjoyment. The vertical line on the graph represents the reflection mean (17.58) and the horizontal line represents the connectedness mean (18.0).

8.4.2 Post-task Interviews

The coding process for the transcribed interviews resulted in a pool of 28 concepts. The concepts from this pool were further analysed and abstracted into six categories with an interpretive sensitivity for engagement (See Table 8.3 for results). Sensitivity to engagement refers to interest or disinterest in respect of the activity. These categories often contain what can be considered opposed concepts, for example, the category of motivations contains both motivating (altruism) and demotivating (unclear goals) concepts.

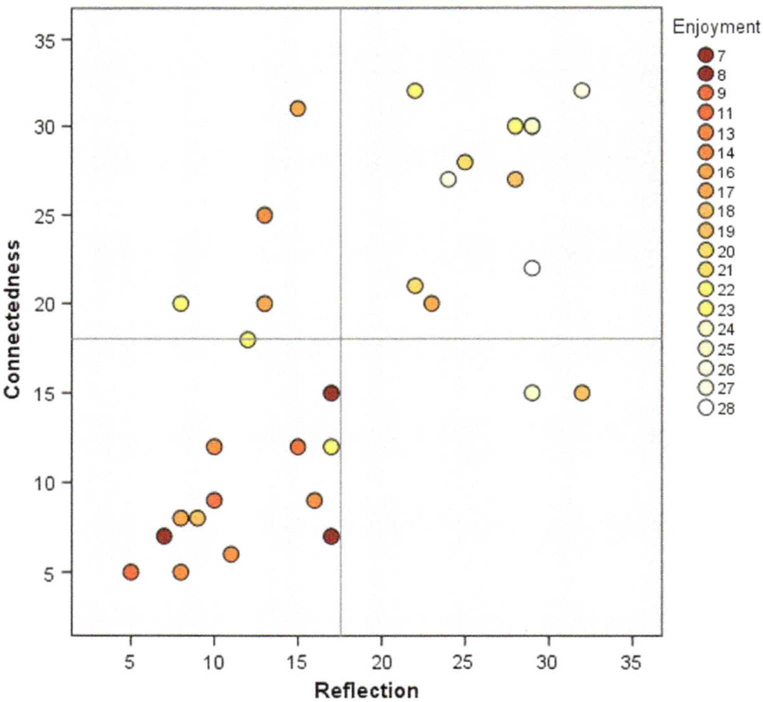

Fig. 8.1 Three-dimensional graph showing the correlation between connectedness, reflection and enjoyment

Table 8.3 Categories and the concepts they were developed from

Categories	Concepts
Altruistic motivations	Altruism, institution identity, building something of value, feeling work was meaningful, unclear goals, question ambiguity
Novelty	Seeing something new, over-familiarity, repetitiveness, losing attention, appreciating social history
Resonance with prior interest	Familial connections, identifying, not identifying, photography interest, social history interest, location interest, aircraft interest, vocation interest
Opportunities for depth	Concentrating on the task, shallow engagement, learning
Emotional involvement	Showing emotional reactions, empathising, visual impact, stories, appreciating social history, not emotional
Task temporality	Losing attention, task process changing over time, concentrating, repetitiveness

8.4.2.1 Altruistic Motivations

Participants often cited altruistic motivational reasons for enjoying or appreciating the task. Taken as a whole, this category can be thought of as the motivation to take part in meaningful work for the common good. Helping a museum was seen as a good thing to do in itself, *'I felt like I was I thought I was helping you guys out by doing it'*. To some, identification with the particular museum fuelled this altruistic motivation, '*If I got to it because I was looking at the Duxford website that might sway you, because you might think you want to support them*'. Some participants liked to feel part of something bigger than themselves, *'I think it's kind of neat to play a part and to assist'*.

The task was meaningful because the work was focused on important world events, '*World War II is a huge point in our history and I think it's becoming obsolete and, not being forgot, that's not the correct word, but we need to continue on a legacy because it's such a massive, important thing, so, that's why I would do it*'. In contrast to this, some people seemed to find that *unclear goals* had the opposite effect, '*I didn't know how I was contributing really, I suppose*'. This was either from them not understanding the project aims as a whole, or that they struggled to understand how the answers they gave related to the classification tags.

8.4.2.2 Novelty

Participants were particularly engaged by the content of the photographs that seemed to be novel to them in some way. '*You see things you don't normally see. You see them doing their everyday things... you know*'. Much of this novelty factor was relating to the social history aspect of the photographs; seeing people act out their lives and duties rather than looking at the aircraft or the technical side of war, '*I guess I'm not into all the planes side of things, I'm more into looking at the social side of things, how they relaxed and all that kind of thing'*. This can perhaps be a consequence of finding certain types of images overly familiar, '*I've seen a lot of similar photos before, so I wasn't very surprised by any of it'*. Images of grounded aircraft or bombers flying in formation seemed to have a lower novelty factor than the *behind-the-scenes* photographs such as those showing men and women relaxing together. However, the influence of this component may be dependent on the participant's prior interests. Many were pushed on in the task by the curiosity of which photograph they would see next.

8.4.2.3 Resonance with Prior Experience or Interest

Engagement was reported to be energised by photographic content that was in accordance to the participant's identity and personal interests. This could be directly related to what the photograph was depicting, '*I like the technical ones because I'm a bit of a nerd on the technical ones with the planes and stuff'*. Sometimes a participant's familial connection was a bridge to amplify engagement with the photograph content and the task as a whole, '*Both my grand-fathers fought in world war two on the American side, one of my grandpas landed at Omaha beach on D-Day, so it all kind of ties in, so I found it all very interesting*'.

In contrast to this, engagement may be attenuated by a participant not identifying with the task, '*I guess it's more for people that are more interested in the war museum*', or identification with only a certain aspect *'[I liked] Looking at the crew, the uniforms, the equipment; the actual airborne bombing didn't do much for me'*. The most common expressions of personal interest in the photograph content included interest in social history, the aircraft depicted and vocational connections.

8.4.2.4 Emotional Involvement

When participants reflected upon the photographs that they found most interesting, they often talked about their engagement from an emotional perspective. Some people described how seeing certain photographs affected them, '*Some of the ones of planes that were dropping bombs I thought was shocking kind of to see the action and the flak you know*'. This was often due to the visual impact of the photograph depicting dramatic scenes such as bombers in action, '*The planes bombing and that are just impressive, you know it's a horrible thing they're doing, but they just look impressive*'.

The social–historical scenes provoked more contemplative emotional involvement as participants would think about and empathise with the people they saw, '*Just looking at things like the clothes and the food they ate; I guess just thinking about how they felt when they were in the situation*', and '*I liked to see some of them where there were people going to have their food, they looked exhausted, so that you know that's what I mean you can see, you can sort of get into it*'. This deeper reading into each photo perhaps led some participants to think about the stories behind those in the photographs, *'I mean yeah, they are all interesting, each one tells a really specific story, it's really interesting'* and (when asked what they found interesting), *'Well, a planes a plane. Shouldn't say that too loud should I? I think it's individual's stories and how things were different'*.

In contrast to this, some people found that their emotional involvement was attenuated by their focus on the classifying task, *'So mostly I was trying to answer the questions—I'd turned off the emotion button [laughs]'*.

8.4.2.5 Opportunities for Deeper Engagement

Some participants found that there were no opportunities for deeper engagement with the subject matter or that the task was not meaningful to them, *'I felt like I was just doing a service for you guys'*. Their concentration was, for the most part, focused on the task activity; analysing the photographs to reliably answer the questions, *'I was just answering the questions as opposed to looking at the photograph with any meaning'*. Some expressed an interest to learn more about the subject matter such as where the photograph was taken or who the people in the photograph were, *'You didn't know if that was at Duxford or if it was in the other US airbases or it was in North Korea or South Korea so the interesting bit would be a direct connection to Duxford'*.

8.4.2.6 Task Temporality

The temporal aspect of engagement emerged in a number of ways. Some noted that they felt that their attention to the task waned as the time went on, *'A bit too long, but I would have gone to 10 rather than 12, I was starting to lose attention at the end'*. This may have been due to the repetitiveness of the simple questions and structure of the system, *'You could almost predict the questions, you almost went into autopilot slightly'*. Some people may have been happy to go along with the repetitive nature of the task because of altruistic motivations, *'A little bit mechanical, but obviously you told me there was a purpose to it so I was quite happy to go along with that'*.

In contrast, some reported that as they proceeded with the task it became easier once the initial ambiguity had been overcome, *'As I went along, the more you got into it, the more you actually studied it'*.

8.5 Discussion

The present study has explored the role of engagement in crowdsourcing using an historical image classification system. We found that the *emotional connectedness* to the people depicted in the images was positively correlated to two desirable elements of volunteer experience (from the museum perspective): *reflection* about the subject matter and *enjoyment* of the task. All three of these factors were significantly correlated with positive affect. Negative affect had no correlation to any of the factors. This may suggest that connectedness, reflection and enjoyment are all components that result from or contribute to a positive experience with a crowdsourcing task.

However, the data does not suggest causality. From this data alone, we cannot yet say that designing for this type of emotional engagement leads to higher reflection and enjoyment, only that if one is present we are likely to find the others. Given the prior research in emotional engagement in physical museums (Dierking 2005; Falk 2009; Falk and Dierking 2013; Simon 2010) and the emergent component of 'emotional involvement' and 'resonance with prior interest' (perhaps better termed as *personal context*), it is reasonable to suggest that it is a salient part of visitor's experience that carries over into crowdsourcing applications.

To further explore the volunteer's perspective of their engagement with the task, we collected qualitative data by conducting semi-structured interviews. The interpretation of this data yielded six categories of user engagement: altruistic motivations, novelty, resonance with prior interest, emotional involvement, opportunities for deeper engagement and task temporality. These components may not be considered exhaustive but they are the most noteworthy and prominent in the present study. We can operationalise these findings by developing the categories into design lenses: ways of viewing design work from a given perspective (Deterding 2015).

8.5.1 Emotional Involvement

The *emotional involvement* construct comprises of feelings of connectedness, emotional impact and narrative involvement in regards to the crowdsourcing task and its content. This might manifest in design work in a number of ways. As mentioned previously, the Old Weather project encourages volunteers to become attached to the ships they encounter as they transcribe log books. This is done through visual feedback of the ship's journey as the coordinates are transcribed. The narrative unfolds as they work and the volunteers feel involved in the story (Blaser 2014).

8.5.2 Resonance with Prior Interests

As we have suggested before, emotional involvement is influenced by a volunteer's personal context and the content's *resonance with prior interests*. Interests in regards to the material encountered in the present study varied from social history, technical and aircraft, vocational interests or familial connections. Designing for a variety of interests can be quite challenging. Some Zooniverse projects enable multiple work flows to be followed. This is akin to setting up different sets of classification questions that focus on different aspects of classification. For example, The American Air Museum's in-gallery system uses four branches of classification enquiry: people, aircraft, places and documents. Giving users a choice for the branch to follow may help them direct their work towards their own personal interests. Another possible solution would be to give the volunteer a choice of images to tag next rather than just present them with a random one.

8.5.3 *Altruism*

Museums are social institutions, so people regard their crowdsourcing work as being part of that social enterprise. They see value in it and are therefore motivated by the *altruistic* aspect. A number of design features can be employed to amplify this component of engagement. Community features and social translucent mechanisms can help engender the feeling that the volunteer is working meaningfully as part of something bigger than themselves. This could be implemented through community activity feeds, project progress bars, records of contributions, messages of thanks from the museum, clear project goals, and updates about the how the museum is using the output from the project.

8.5.4 *Novelty*

Novelty is a component of engagement that relates to seeing something new, a sense of discovery or feeling behind-the-scenes in some way. Previous research has shown that when a volunteer is informed that they are the first to encounter a particular image, their contribution increases (Jackson et al. 2016). Informing the volunteer with a notification is a simple design mechanism to this end.

8.5.5 *Opportunities for Deeper Engagement*

A problem with crowdsourcing and especially classification systems is that the museums do not know much about the *specific* content being shown. That is why crowdsourcing is being used in the first place. This makes it difficult to provide *opportunities for deeper engagement* such as learning. Beyond providing links to general learning resources about the subject matter, social design features can be employed. Integration of forums with the system allows volunteers to further develop their interests through conversation around the crowdsourcing content. Zooniverse's Galaxy Zoo project is an exemplar of the benefits taking this approach can have. Volunteers led their own research activity resulting in a new category of 'Green Pea galaxies' being discovered (Straub 2016).

8.5.6 *Task Temporality*

Over time, attributes of engagement with a task may attenuate. This can be due to the loss of attention and tiredness, the repetitive nature of the task, or perhaps a degrading of positive components of engagement such as loss of novelty. We may be able to frame this in terms of balancing volunteer skill level and the challenge level of the task, a building block of flow theory (Csikszentmihalyi 1996). As volunteers master one level of analysis such as answering simple questions (Is there an aircraft in this photograph?) we might offer them a more challenging variation on the task that requires a higher level of skill (What type of aircraft is this? Here are some reference photographs to help you).

These perspectives aim to align design of crowdsourcing systems to user motivations and desired outcomes. The context and content of a specific system may 'naturally' accommodate certain components more than others, e.g. the personal aspect of transcribing an artist's notebook may more easily afford *emotional involvement*. Design work that amplifies the positive aspects of these components (and removes the attenuating aspects) should lead to volunteer satisfaction and well-being. The ultimate aim of this approach is that a museum is able to fulfil its remit to cultivate engaging experience for volunteers, which in turn means that the museum is respectful of the volunteer's needs and going some way towards fulfilling the institutional integrity principle.

8.6 Limitations and Future Work

The study was limited by a number or factors. First, due to the exploratory nature of the study, the data only shows correlational relationships and not causal relationships between the factors. There was a relatively low number of participants (n = 31), therefore certain statistical methods such as factor analysis could not be applied reliably. The visualisation of the data in the graph, the lack of correlation to negative PANAS, and the consistency of connectedness and reflective components appearing in the qualitative data, all suggest the correlations to be plausible. However, now that this exploratory study has exposed these correlations, larger scale studies should be conducted to confirm these findings and to further explore the underlying causes.

Another limitation was that the study took place in a physical museum context and not online as the target system would in practice. This may have coloured what people might have experienced and so lays a constraint on what we might be able to say in terms of designing engagement for crowdsourcing. The survey results may also have been influenced by this. Museum visitors may be more receptive to or reflective about experiences at the museum as opposed to at home. However, the use of museum visitors as participants is perhaps justified because by visiting the museum, they have demonstrated an interest in the subject matter of the system and so their motivations and interests may be more representative of a typical crowdsourcing crowd.

The study was conducted using historical photography and so the exposed components of engagement may be more relevant to humanities projects in which people and the past are present in the crowdsourcing content. We have tried to generalise these findings in the discussion and design lens perspective. Also, in reporting this study, we have outlined an approach to conducting research into investigating user engagement which can be applied in multiple contexts.

8.7 Conclusion

We have taken the position that museum crowdsourcing projects should be designed to fulfil the ethical principles of public engagement and benefit, stewardship of collections and institutional integrity. We have argued that the cultivation of positive user engagement can lead to volunteer satisfaction and well-being. A particular focus to our perspective is the emotional component of engagement due to prior research in physical museum settings, prior exploratory work and the lack of related research in the context of crowdsourcing systems.

The present study explored the relationship between five potential factors that contribute to positive user experience with a historical classification system: connectedness, reflection, enjoyment and positive and negative affect. Further to this, we explored the felt engagement from the volunteer's perspective through the conduct of interviews and qualitative analysis.

Our quantitative study has shown emotional connectedness and relatedness to be components of enjoyable and positive user experiences. Six categories emerged from the data that reflected a user's engagement with the classification system: emotional involvement, altruistic motivation, novelty, resonance with prior interest, opportunities for deeper engagement and task temporality.

We reason that using these components of user engagement as design lenses when designing crowdsourcing systems can lead to more positive volunteer experience and thus fulfil the public benefit and institutional integrity principles of a museum's ethical remit.

References

Attfield S, Kazai G, Lalmas M (2011) Towards a science of user engagement (position paper). WSDM workshop on user

Bartsch A (2012) Emotional gratification in entertainment experience. why viewers of movies and television series find it rewarding to experience emotions. Media Psychol 15(3):267–302

Bartsch A, Kalch A, Beth Oliver M (2014) Moved to think. J Media Psychol 26(3):125–140

Blaser L (2014) Old weather: approaching collections from a different angle. In: Crowdsourcing our cultural heritage. Ashgate Publishing, Ltd

Bopp JA, Mekler ED, Opwis K (2016) Negative emotion, positive experience? In: Proceedings of the 2016 CHI Conference on Human Factors in Computing Systems-CHI'16. ACM Press, New York, pp 2996–3006

Cook D (2008) Lost garden: the princess rescuing application: slides. http://www.lostgarden.com/2008/10/princess-rescuing-application-slides.html. Accessed 9 Feb 2017

Csikszentmihalyi M (1996) Flow and the psychology of discovery and invention. Harper Collins, New York

Deterding S (2015) The lens of intrinsic skill atoms: a method for gameful design. Hum-Comput Interact 30(3–4):294–335

Dierking LD (2005) Museums, affect, and cognition: the view from another window. In: Cobern WW, Tobin K, Brown-Acquay H, Espinet M, Irzik G, Jegede O, Alsop S (eds) Beyond Cartesian dualism: encountering affect in the teaching and learning of science. Springer Netherlands, Dordrecht, pp 111–122

Ekkekakis P (2013) The measurement of affect, mood, and emotion: a guide for health-behavioral research

Eveleigh A, Jennett C, Blandford A, Brohan P, Cox AL, Eveleigh A, Cox AL (2014) Designing for dabblers and deterring drop-outs in citizen science. In: Proceedings of the 32nd annual ACM conference on Human factors in computing systems-CHI'14. ACM Press, New York, pp 2985–2994

Eveleigh A, Jennett C, Lynn S, Cox AL (2013) I want to be a captain! i want to be a captain!: gamification in the old weather citizen science project. In Proceedings of the first international conference on gameful design, research, and applications, pp 79–82

Falk JH (2009) Identity and the museum visitor experience. Sci Educ 94:302

Falk JH, Dierking LD (2013) Museum experience revisited. Left Coast Press, Walnut Creek

Falk JH, Gillespie KL (2009) Investigating the role of emotion in science center visitor learning. Visit Stud 12(2):112–132

Jackson CB, Crowston K, Mugar G, Østerlund C (2016) Guess what! You're the first to see this event. In: Proceedings of the 19th international conference on supporting group work-groUP'16. ACM Press, New York, pp 171–179

O'Brien HL (2010) The influence of hedonic and utilitarian motivations on user engagement: the case of online shopping experiences. Interact Comput 22(5):344–352

O'Brien HL, Toms EG (2008) What is user engagement? A conceptual framework for defining user engagement with technology. J Am Soc Inform Sci Technol 59(6):938–955

Oliver MB, Raney AA (2011) Entertainment as pleasurable and meaningful: identifying hedonic and eudaimonic motivations for entertainment consumption. J Commun 61(5):984–1004

Oomen J, Aroyo L (2011) Crowdsourcing in the cultural heritage domain. In: Proceedings of the 5th International Conference on Communities and Technologies-C&T'11. ACM Press, New York, p 138

Owens T (2014) Making crowdsourcing compatible with the missions and values of cultural heritage organisations. In: Crowdsourcing our cultural heritage. Ashgate Publishing, Ltd, pp 269–280

Raddick MJ, Bracey G, Gay PL, Lintott CJ, Murray P, Schawinski K, Vandenberg J (2010) Galaxy zoo: exploring the motivations of citizen science volunteers. Astron Educ Rev 9(1):269–280

Ridge M (2014) Crowdsourcing our cultural heritage: introduction. In: Crowdsourcing our cultural heritage. Ashgate Publishing, Ltd, p. 306

Rotman D, Preece J, Hammock J, Procita K, Hansen D, Parr C, Jacobs D (2012) Dynamic changes in motivation in collaborative citizen-science projects. In: Proceedings of the ACM 2012 conference on computer supported cooperative work-CSCW'12. ACM Press, New York, p 217

Ryan RM, Rigby CS, Przybylski A (2006) The motivational pull of video games: a self-determination theory approach. Motiv Emotion 30(4):344–360

Saldaña J (2009) The coding manual for qualitative researchers. The coding manual for qualitative researchers. Sage Publications Ltd

Simon N (2010) The participatory museum. Museum 2.0, Santa Cruz. http://www.participatorymuseum.org/read/

Straub M (2016) Giving citizen scientists a chance: a study of volunteer-led scientific discovery. Citiz Sci: Theory Pract 1(1):5

Strauss A, Corbin J (1994) Grounded theory methodology: an overview. In: Handbook of qualitative research, Sage Publications, Thousand Oaks

Suh B, Convertino G, Chi EH, Pirolli P (2009) The singularity is not near. In: Proceedings of the 5th international symposium on wikis and open collaboration-WikiSym'09. ACM Press, New York, p. 1

Tamborini R, Bowman ND, Eden A, Grizzard M, Organ A (2010) Defining Media enjoyment as the satisfaction of intrinsic needs. J Commun 60(4):758–777

Watson D, Clark LA, Tellegen A (1988) Development and validation of brief measures of positive and negative affect: the PANAS scales. J Pers Soc Psychol 54(6):1063–1070

Wrigglesworth T, Watts L (2016) Emotional connections with the past: exploring engagement with historical images from an online museum collection. Submitted for publication

Author Biographies

Tom Wrigglesworth is a Research Engineer from the University of Bath who is conducting research in collaboration with the Imperial War Museums. His work is centered on the community activities surrounding the American Air Museum's crowd-sourced online archive. He is interested in studying the sensemaking of historical information and in the development of tools that support meaningful engagement with online museum collections.

Leon A. Watts researches the effects of digital mediation on human communication, towards the facilitation of positive and equitable contributions to joint activity. His work has particular concern for contexts in which feelings are material to the creation of valued outcomes. He takes an interdisciplinary approach to communication contexts, combining psychological, and computational expertise in his analytical and design work.

Chapter 9
One Museum, Multiple Doors—Design for Experience of Living Cultural Heritage for Different Stakeholders

Gerrit van der Veer, Teresa Consiglio and Selene Uras

Abstract We define cultural heritage, drawing on UNESCO, as tangible and intangible artifacts (e.g., tools, dresses, symbols, languages, decorations, buildings, stories, songs, rituals, etc.) that are developed in a culture. Based on teaching academic courses on design for cultural heritage and on work we did in relation to various collections of cultural heritage, we developed a taxonomy that distinguishes different types of stakeholders for cultural heritage collections. Different stakeholders vary in their needs and in the intended or expected experiences. For a culture to survive generations of participants, individual cultural heritage artifacts need to be maintained as well as be available for examination and (responsible) use. We propose that for being understood by new generations, the documentation for each artifact should include: (a) a description of the current state as well as of its original state; (b) an account of the original context of its creation and of its creator(s) in the context, a history of use, maintenance, changes, evolving role in the culture; and (c) a diary of use and maintenance by the current (temporal) owner(s). Cultural heritage artifacts often move into departments of public museums that should cope with a growing variety of intentions and needs between culture scholars, amateur culture participants and the general public. However, presentation of cultural heritage museum exhibit that provides optimal information for a scholar may be boring for the general public. Solutions are discussed in terms of museum business models, ICT support, and logistics, and involvement of cultural heritage related communities.

G. van der Veer (✉)
Voorhof 33, Lelystad, Netherlands
e-mail: gerrit@acm.org

G. van der Veer · T. Consiglio
Dutch Open University, Heerlen, The Netherlands

S. Uras
LastMinute.com, Vicolo de' Calvi, 2 Chiasso, Switzerland
e-mail: selene.uras@gmail.com

S. Uras
Milan, Italy

A. Vermeeren et al. (eds.), *Museum Experience Design*, Springer Series on Cultural Computing, https://doi.org/10.1007/978-3-319-58550-5_9

9.1 Introduction

During the last 6 years, we have been teaching university courses on "Design of ICT support for Cultural Heritage" in a variety of different cultural contexts (Uras, Consiglio, van der Veer 2015b):

- bachelor design projects of about 200 student-hours in a faculty of architecture in Italy;
- a 20 student-hour course for consultants of cultural institutes as part of a project on the Internet of Things in the Netherlands,
- biannual courses (80 student-hour each) for master students in a computer science faculty, department of usability engineering, working in 3-person design teams, mostly in collaboration with some students from a university of fine arts in China;
- a 20 student-hour course for (Spanish) students working in three-person teams: a mixture of computer science MSc students and museum curators.

In these courses, our students provided example cultural heritage artifacts and collections, from their own participation in diverse cultural environments. The examples featured a diversity of objects, including: musical instruments; historic costumes; Chinese historic furniture; Chinese paper cutting; rural dance games; historic memorial ceremonies; archeological pottery remains; etc. After we had some initial experience with this course type, we realized that our students often needed some initial support in identifying what are the individual artifacts for which to provide experience and information, and for what type(s) of audience this should this be made available. Based on this understanding, from then on in each course we proposed that students should start with:

- Identifying the main types of cultural heritage artifacts in an environment or a collection. This implies asking questions such as: Is this the unique choreography, and/or the traditional costumes, and/or the inherited music? As sometimes the same dance is performed on new, contemporary, music, or danced in contemporary outfit.
- Identifying "secondary" objects that belong to one or more of the primary objects (historic pictures or recordings of the dance; documents of events).
- Identifying the different types of stakeholders involved in various aspects of the living culture: maintaining and providing the primary artifacts, teaching the use of the artifacts, teaching active participation in the culture, documenting the cultural history or the current culture and events, regular participants in events, novices, and interested public that might turn into novices.

Besides this, we and our students are involved in maintaining collections of cultural heritage objects, e.g., A society for historic costumes in Sardinia; A Spanish museum of historic as well as contemporary folk music instruments and a related music school in Spain; A collection of seventeenth to nineteenth century art musical instruments in the Netherlands; A museum for the history of early movies; A collection of early movie projectors; A collection of early stereoscopic pictures and magic lantern slides as well as the early projectors for these; and a collection of (mainly Dutch) twenty and twenty-first century radio plays. We discovered that in all these domains the curators of both private and public collections struggle with the challenge of accommodating the interests of the various types of visitors that comprise the public of their collection and related performances, and we are developing a design approach to handle this diversity of visitors in a way that supports the viability of this type of collections. We consider our growing insight may be of benefit for other types of (museum) collections as well.

Thus, in this chapter we will share and discuss our insights on designing Information and Communication Technology (ICT) support for cultural heritage collections, both when these are still maintained in their original cultural context and when the artifacts have been moved to a general museum with broader content and, consequently, with public that varies more in knowledge, interest, and intentions regarding their experience of the artifacts.

First, in the forthcoming section, we define what we mean by cultural heritage. Based on that, we describe (in Sect. 3) an ontology to structure a collection of cultural heritage artifacts such that people who want to participate in the original culture will be supported in their various needs. We will discuss how to provide access to relevant knowledge on cultural heritage; how collections of cultural heritage in the course of the time move from the original community storage to general museums; how museums are currently often enforced to reconsider their business model and to provide service first of all to the general public; and discuss why this requires a special attention and measures to continue support to the original culture of cultural heritage collections.

In Sect. 4, we will show how to support the different stakeholders of cultural heritage artifacts and collections. Different stakeholders do need different types of experience, which can be accommodated by providing a choice of resources and dedicated venue. Finally, we will show how a separate route through the museum can be provided without splitting the general collection management.

9.2 Cultural Heritage: An Ontology and Stakeholder Experiences

Uras, Consiglio, and van der Veer (2015a) state*: "Cultures develop in societies, by people co-developing and sharing artifacts … of many types: languages, rules, gestures, physical objects, documents, stories,* etc. *The artifacts are the product of the culture and, at the same time, the main way to keep the culture. As the people living in the culture will die, the artifacts are needed to keep the culture alive. They are inherited by new generations of members of the culture. Since the artifacts get used, and transferred, they change, get worn out, acquire additional meaning and lose some "previous" meaning, and finally may get lost, or lose their original function and* *meaning. After that, these artifacts are no longer cultural heritage but just heritage, and at the same time the culture may be in immediate danger of dying".*

UNESCO (2017) states: "*The term cultural heritage encompasses several main categories of heritage:*

- *Tangible cultural heritage*
  - *movable cultural heritage (paintings, sculptures, coins, manuscripts)*
  - *immovable cultural heritage (monuments, archeological sites, and so on)*
  - *underwater cultural heritage (shipwrecks, underwater ruins, and cities)*
- *Intangible cultural heritage: oral traditions, performing arts, rituals*".

Our concept of Cultural Heritage is based on both sources: The concept indicates all types of artifacts listed by UNESCO, as far as they are related to a living culture - as tools to be used by people who aim at continuing participation in a culture, as documents to understand the history of the culture for learning and teaching, or as fragile artifacts that will inform and inspire copiers and makers of new tools.

9.2.1 An Ontology

To support systematic analysis and design for the domain of cultural heritage, we distil key concepts from our definition that help structure the artifacts in the cultural domain and relate this to the different people that participate in the culture and keep the culture alive. We note that cultural heritage refers to tangible and intangible artifacts that are kept by (mostly temporal) owners (a person, institute, museum, or community). A dictionary-like definition of culture, in this respect, refers to the set of shared attitudes, values, goals, and practices that characterizes a community, and the integrated pattern of human knowledge, belief, and behavior of the Participants in the culture (Merriam Webster 2017).

In each culture, people may participate in one or more of several roles. Focusing mainly on the active participants in the culture, we identify three roles: scholars, amateurs, and the general public.

Scholars actively support maintenance and knowledge of the culture, the artifacts, and their use in the living culture: collectors, restorers, and curators, makers of facsimiles, expert performers, researchers of artifacts or of the history of the culture. Based on the examples that students introduced in our courses and the collections we worked with we discovered that there may be many different types of scholars that are related to a single type of cultural heritage objects and collections, so expanded our definition of scholar to include all who are considered experts by the cultural community. Our concept of scholar will, consequently, include all who are considered that are in fact studying, preserve, renovate, copy, or even update tangible as well as intangible cultural heritage. So far, we studied a broad variety of cultural domains and communities, e.g.:

Radio play communities: Individual plays and series of plays have authors, actors, sound technicians, radio station managers, restorers of historic sound tracks.

Musical instrument cultures: Individual instruments have makers (designers, and builders), facsimile makers, experts in analysis (e.g., dendrology) measurement and description, restorers (including experts in woodwork, metal, textiles, paint), climate experts, players, and teachers of all this.

Historic early films: Experts on the history of movie styles, players, studios, authors, technical experts on safe storage, maintenance and restauration of nitrate, and acetate film, and experts on color preservation and color restoration, and digitization technicians.

Rural dancing games: First of all, there are the local "official experts ", mostly older people who learned the games from their ancestors and are currently educating the younger (and sometimes are documenting the current details of the choreography and the valid rules). Based on our expanded definition above, all people who are participating in the game are a type of scholars, as are the people who provide the props (chairs, ribbons) and prepare the layout of the playground.

Amateur is our label for a member of the audience that is willing and able to take the role of member of the culture, knowing, appreciating, and understanding the culture and actively participating in, and supporting, exhibition and performances. In various domains that featured in our courses, the distinction between scholar and amateur is vague: the audience in some cases will be allowed to participate on certain occasions (join the chorus or the dancers, contribute knowledge they inherited from their parents). In most domains, amateurs are not supposed to adjust or change artifacts or rules. Participants in a culture mostly gradually develop into their role, based on living (or even literally being born) in a society where the cultural practices are still actively being performed and attended.

Especially in public collections like in museums, there is a 3rd role indicating interested people who are not members or participants in the culture: The general public. This audience might be excited about inspecting objects and events that appear strange as well as intriguing or beautiful to them.

There are other approaches to museum and cultural heritage audience segmentation, from which we mention the one developed by Falk and Dierking (2013), who report an analysis of museum visitors' intended experiences where they identify six different types: *Professionals*; *Hobbyists*; *explorers*; *facilitators*; *experience seekers*; and *rechargers*. The types *Professionals* and *Hobbyists* are equivalent to our roles of scholars and amateurs, respectively. The other types mentioned (*explorers, facilitators, experience seekers*, and *rechargers)* are, from our point of view, different sub-types of what we label general public. Our analysis focusses on cultural heritage and its main stakeholders at a higher level of granularity, and, consequently, we do not discuss these differences here. In Sect. 9.1 of this volume, we find two chapters that show a focus on a different type of museum visitors that in our analysis is a part of the general public: Apostolellis, Bowman, and Chime (Chap. 2, this volume) focus on "young audiences", school groups and students; and Sim et al. (Chap. 4, this volume) on "children". Both publications consider a subgroup of what we label, "the general public" (no scholars or amateurs in relation to the domain of the museum). On the other hand, Boonen, van der Heijden, and Giaccardi (Chap.3, this volume) make a distinction between "expert visitors" (we would label them scholars) and novice visitors (part of the general public) in the context of a museum of design.

9.2.2 Cultural Heritage and Stakeholder Experiences

We are particularly interested in how museums should deal with the variety of intentions and needs of the stakeholders of cultural heritage collections. In this section, we focus on how the various stakeholders of cultural heritage experience the way the museum provides them the service they need: Will they be able to find the knowledge they are looking for? Are they able to perceive and understand the artifacts as displayed, rendered, or represented? In current human-centered design approaches the concept of experience is often used to indicate in a holistic way the quality of use of a service. UXPA (2017) describes the concept in their Usability Body of Knowledge Glossary:"*User Experience (UE): Every aspect of the user's interaction with a product, service, or company that make up the user's perceptions of the whole.*"

The concept of experience needs to be defined in relation to stakeholder types. We refer to Vyas and van der Veer (2006a), where the concept of experience is defined in four distinctive but related components, which we apply to the stakeholders' needs and goals related to the cultural heritage artifacts:

(a) understanding the meaning of the artifacts,
(b) emotional aspects related to the perception and use of the artifacts, including esthetical valuation,
(c) triggered intentions and actions in relation to the artifacts, and
(d) attitude towards the artifacts (for instance being attracted to them or wanting to avoid a relationship with them).

For different types of stakeholder roles these aspects may have rather different content, for instance: a music player may (a) understand in some professional way the score of the song to be played, (b) consider the score to be too much prescribing the performance to allow individual creative expression, as well as too complicated to be well performed without more practice, (c) is triggered to execute the score in a way that fit the instrument and the context of the event, and (d) would prefer this score not to be part of the current performance. For a regular member of the audience each of these aspects will have a rather different content, though (a) there is certainly an aspect of understanding the relation between the score on the musician's desk and the sound, (b) the playing will evoke some emotional reactions, (c) the listener will build an appreciation that in the end will trigger applause, and (d) the listener may decide not to return to the music hall if the same music will be played.

Scholars in the types of cultures that we analyzed mostly consider their role to be a mixture of a profession or a mission. Their intention is to keep the culture alive and to keep it integer, by both supporting development and maintaining authenticity. They live the culture, they continue to learn as well as to teach, to study and guard the artifacts as well as to provide responsible access to the amateurs to experience the true heritage. And they are aware that their continued devotion is required to keep the culture alive. The different types of scholars that are distinguishable in some cultures each may aim at, or need, different experiences: manipulating original historic artifacts like 100-year-old costumes or 300-year-old flutes is needed for maintenance, for measurement and for some type of analysis, though makers of copies in most cases are completely happy and well documented through the availability of pictures, descriptions, and measurements.

An amateur contributes to the culture in several ways, from being a sense-making audience at events, to (financially or politically) contributing to a healthy context.

Scholars and amateurs are both needed to keep a culture alive, as stated by the Khan Academy (2017): "'Culture' refers to *the integrated pattern of human knowledge, belief, and behavior that depends upon the capacity for learning and transmitting knowledge to succeeding generations*". Like scholars, amateurs will only continue to experience the living culture first hand if they remain open to learning as well as open to let their peers learn, and if they continue to attend and participate.

These two categories of stakeholders in a culture may regularly shift between their roles of scholar and amateur: being authors of a novel and readers of other prose, one day a performer and the next day a member of the audience, making a flute and then listening to someone else playing it.

The general public, on the other hand, will aim at a completely different type of experiences: To them, the cultural heritage object collection is an opportunity to meet novel objects in an unknown context. If at first sight the context is attractive enough to them and, if the encounter keeps them interested, they will start their exploration, be entertained and develop a rather new experience that may include (following the conceptual analysis of Vyas and van der Veer 2006a and 2006b):

- Developing an understanding of functions and meaning of the artifacts and their cultural context;
- Acquiring an impression of the emotional values of the culture and its artifacts;
- Acquiring a tendency to act regarding the exposition (buying documentation, discussing with peers, leaving) and possibly to interact with it when appropriate and available; and
- Feeling attracted (or the contrary) to the culture as understood so far, which might even result in an intention to learn more or join.

9.3 Private Collections and Museums

Cultural heritage artifacts (e.g., the physical objects, the scripts, the rules, the stories, the rites, or the values) are the actual items that allow transfer of a culture between its participants and between generations. These artifacts need to be kept and made available to the participants in a culture. The artifacts originally are being developed in their culture, are being used for generations (hence "heritage") and owned by successive individual amateurs and scholars or by a community of these. At a certain moment, they are explicitly considered heritage, get the special treatment as such (their historic value is acknowledged, repair is now considered restoration, use is restricted or safeguarded to restrict wear) and they are carefully stored in safe climate conditions. Their use and their state are recorded (especially for intangible artifacts), and copies of tangible objects are being made and used when possible.

Gradually these utensils develop into collection items, regarded as the authentic items of the culture that the scholars will need to study and the amateurs might be allowed to inspect and in special cases even handle in controlled conditions.

Most collections of cultural heritage artifacts originate in the original culture, and are kept there to facilitate learning and teaching as well as to provide a feeling of authenticity and to support the collective memory of the cultural stakeholders.

9.3.1 How to Provide Access to and Document a Collection

During our teaching practice, we and our students developed an approach to identify cultural heritage objects, to categorize and describe relevant knowledge, and to preserve the knowledge of the cultural heritage objects for current and future stakeholders. Based on this approach, we designed a structure where, for each artifact, at least three types of knowledge need to be available, if possible incorporated in a website or at least a hypertext structure based on a content management system:

- A history of each object. Figure 9.1 shows samples of a student project on developing a not-public tablet tool for a cultural heritage community on historic costumes, which shows that even the general history may well contain private details referring to individual ancestors of current members of a culture. Inside the original culture this may not cause problems, though it could be inappropriate to provide these details to the general public.
- A description of the object (see Fig. 9.2) seems relevant also for the general public, though the appreciated amount of details (and the size of pictures or video clips to be downloaded) may be different for different roles. For example, a 10-page restoration report on an eighteenth century violin (including chemical analysis of the varnish or a dendrography of the soundboard wood) analysis may be exciting and extremely informative for a scholar who wants to consider this

(a)

(b)

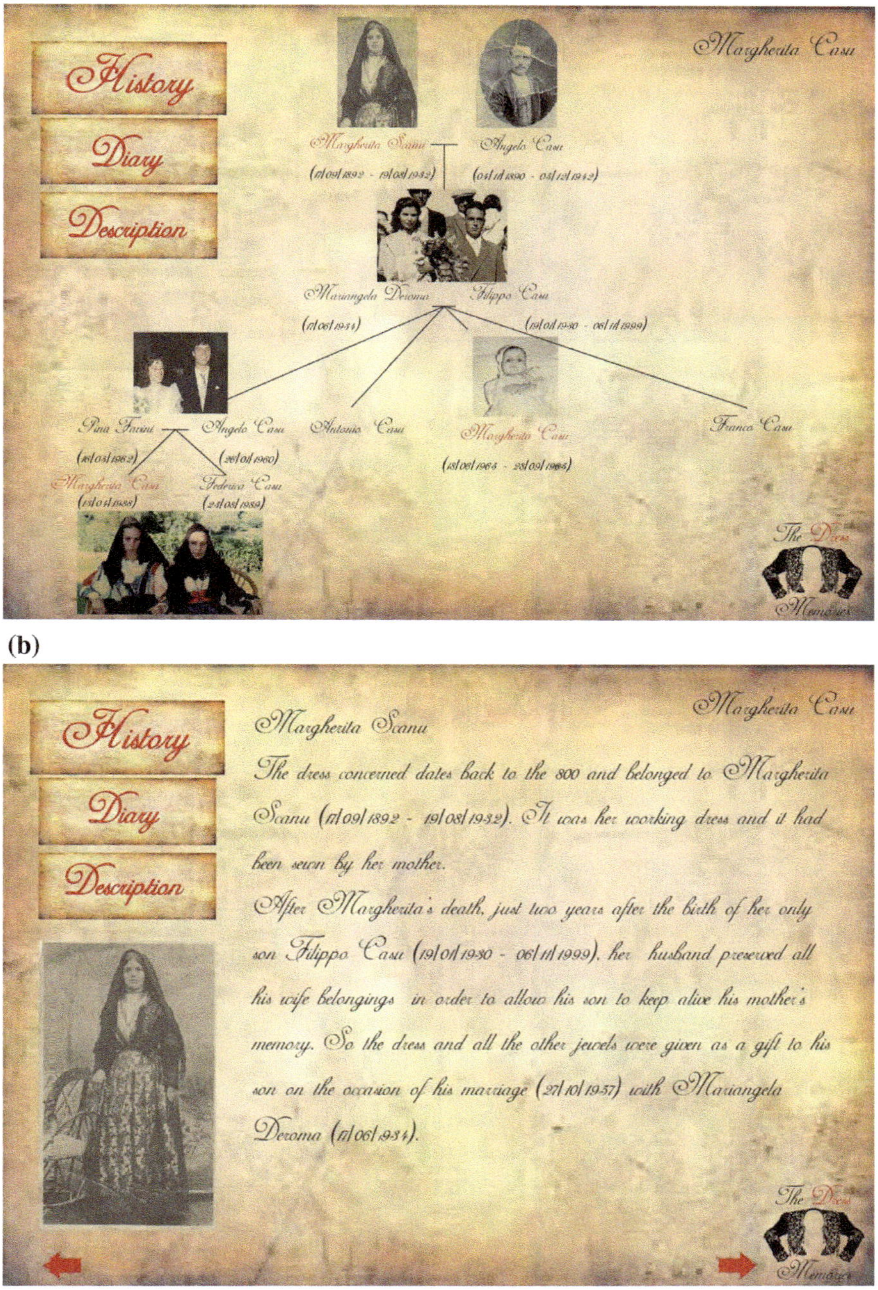

Fig. 9.1 General representation of the history of one artifact, a historic costume (**a**) and specifics of a single period (**b**)

Fig. 9.2 Description of one element of composed artifact. The details on the jacket may be interesting for a scholar who needs to provide a copy for the annual festival, though not necessarily for amateurs dressed in this facsimile at the festival

type of analysis for an artifact he is supposed to describe, and totally boring for a member of the general public who might just want to know how high the restoration price was and how long the process took. For an amateur, pictures showing before–after differences might be a relevant and instructive type of description.

- A diary of the activities related to the object as far as the current temporal owner is keeping it (see Fig. 9.3). Diaries need to include all relevant knowledge needed to understand the actual state of the artifact at a given time as well as the background of all changes. Consequently, there will be data that contain private information on the current owner or keeper, or on others who manipulated the artifact (including amounts of money paid for services, people involved in cases of abuse). Often, diaries are at least partially considered to be for the eyes of the current keeper only, and a change to a new responsible stakeholder requires careful decisions on what to keep and whom to allow access to this on what date (Our courses contain a separate lecture entitled "What if the owner dies").

For the collections that we ourselves are involved with, we often need more different categories of specific information, like restoration, multimedia, and a separate account of the original culture. For example, Fig. 9.4 shows an entry page of one artifact in a collection of 17—19th Western musical instruments. Authorized

Fig. 9.3 Entry in a diary of a single artifact

visitors (who did acquire a login and access) may go to various categories of information:

- a detailed description including measures, material, pictures, a scan—relevant for scholars with a technical role (restorers, copyists);
- a video recording with a URL of the specialist player, details of the strings and the bow used, a facsimile of the original score and transcription of the score as performed;
- the history of previous owners and the music they performed with the violin—relevant for historians of the culture;
- an account ("diary") of what happened with the violin while in the custody of the current owner, including facsimiles of programs of performances where the violin was played, invoices for assurance during these events—part of the diary may well be considered private to the current owner and will not be made available through a login;
- a detailed restoration report including pictures and an indication of techniques applied;
- description, referenced by period publications, on the location and culture of origin, relevant facts known about the author (where he was an apprentice, who was his successor, who ordered or bought his instruments)—relevant for players who are looking for a match between a piece of music and the best instrument to play it.

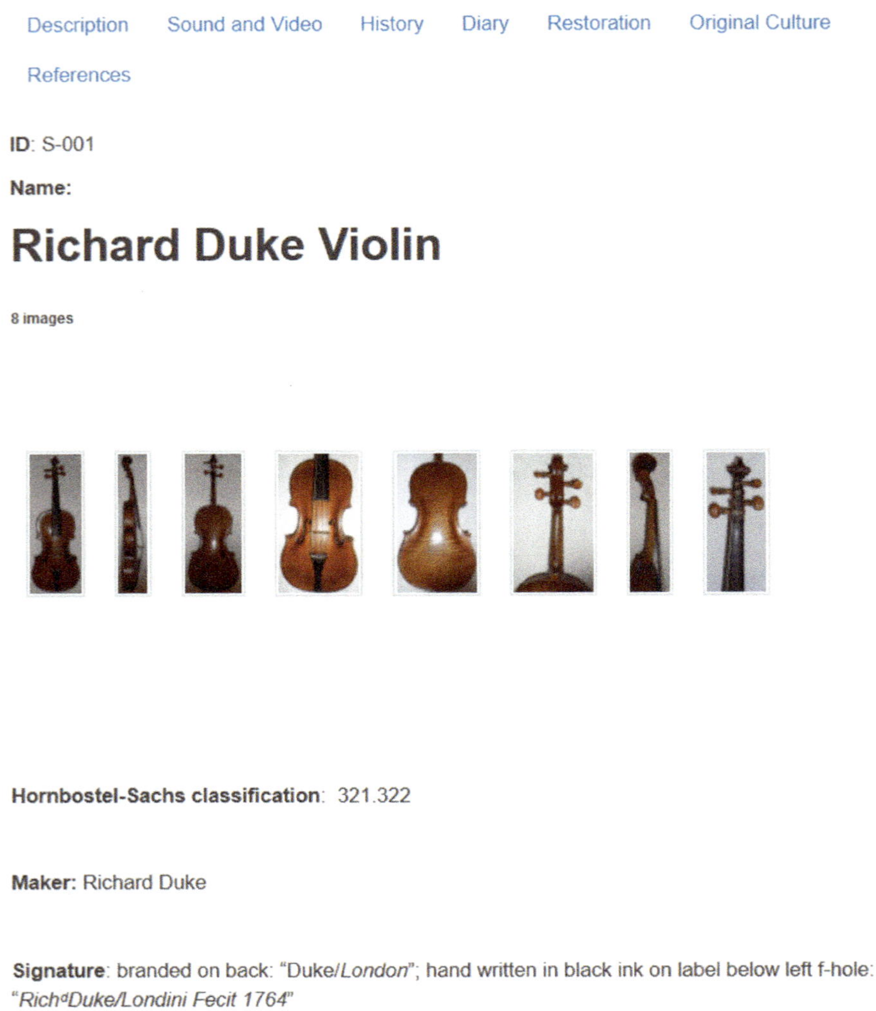

Fig. 9.4 Entry web page for a single artifact in a collection of historic musical instruments for access a login is required)

9.3.2 *Collections Often Move to Museums*

Cultural heritage collections require special logistics (space, climate and lightning control, timely maintenance, protection against damage and unmonitored manipulation), devoted curators, and documentation, as well as a stable financial base to guarantee continuity of all this. Over time, collections grow. A private collection of folk musical instruments that we visited in Spain contains currently 5000 physical objects. The artifacts are kept in a large storage facility, each tagged with simple paper label with a unique number that corresponds to a numbered paper card in a set of boxes. Regularly, different selections from the collection are exhibited in museums. The documentation needs to be manageable, and ICT support (including a content management system) becomes compulsory.

One requirement is an ontology of these artifacts that allows finding the related documentation in the system, based on a classification that is accepted and usable for scholars in the culture and experts in the domain, e.g., for any type of musical instrument collection the current classification based on Hornbostel and Sachs (1914).

The other requirement is a safe and valid way to authenticate and identify physical cultural heritage artifacts and to relate these to the entries in the database. To this end the current state of the art includes the use of RFID tags to locate specific artifacts in large storage contexts and to identify an individual artifact (for any stakeholder who is not a real expert in this matter), and QR codes to allow easy connection with a relevant internet location that contains information unique to the artifact. Expectedly, soon, a safer way of tagging (that promises a better defense against forgeries as a side effect) will be the use of PUF NFC readable tags (Yu and Devadas 2017) that may be connected to the physical object in a tag inlay or embedded in a paper label.

For large collections, the development and maintenance of this type of ICT support often turns out to require too much from the individual volunteer stakeholders and even from the original cultural community if this is a private group. Hence, the collection is in danger of being corrupted, being sold in pieces, or otherwise disappearing. In that case, political or legal bodies (a municipality, a foundation) may take over or may be constructed, and the collection develops into a public museum or is incorporated in an existing one. This seems to be the fate of many important and famous collections. In fact, most museums with collections of cultural heritage found their origin precisely in the mechanism sketched above.

9.3.3 Museums in Trouble

So far so good: Till a few decades ago, in the domains and museum practices we are aware of, there were many thriving examples where societies of friends of a culture supported museum activities (including performances by scholars of the domain attended by amateurs), where private collections were donated or sold for a token price, and where the curator collaborated in a responsible way with scholars who needed to manipulate the artifacts in order to support the living culture (e.g., for making valid replicas). The collections on display were intended for the original stakeholders, and so was the information available. If a member of the general public would enter the space, which was a relatively rare occasion, the visit would often be short since no expectations or needs had explicitly be triggered, though visitors did not experience this as something negative.

However, political and societal situations change, and museums in many cases had to decide for a change in business goals and business models. In the last couple of decades, we perceive a common view that museums should serve the general public in all its variety (including children or enterprises), should aim for a profit, should advertise the cultural state and vision of the political body that controls them and of the corporate sponsors that are replacing the financial support of cultural communities. Museums, in this situation, should conform to new visions of what is a good balance and dosage of information, entertainment, aesthetics, and variety.

In the domains of historic costumes and of historic musical instruments we have seen striking changes: rather complete costume collections, even if they may keep their fashion gallery, lose visibility due to changing exhibitions in relation to temporary interests triggered by events in other domains. For instance, London's Victoria and Albert Museum celebrated 100 years of Hollywood filmmaking, and staged a film costume exhibition, which was exciting for the general public that discovered a relation to other simultaneous cultural events. At the same time, world famous large and important collections of historical musical instruments in the same London museum and in the "Gemeente Museum" at The Hague completely disappeared: Parts were silently taken over by specialist museums, larger parts are supposed to be in store without a curator being in control and with information unreachable for scholars. These cases include large parts of the collections that originated from donated private collections that once belonged to their original living cultures.

9.3.4 New Venues Bring Traffic Issues

These museums do not have a choice: The management needs to conform to the new political and cultural visions of their authorities. Their new business models require them to provide opportunities for patrons to organize a reception in museum premises that should be exciting and fit for the occasion. They are supposed to provide an appropriate mix of learning and entertainment for families with children, and to provide accommodation for visitors to have a drink and a chat in an amusing environment (Victoria and Albert Museum 2016); all of this for a consumer price that allows a healthy financial profit.

In current museums, different types of visitors will meet quite different types of traffic: In the fashion gallery visitors will not encounter many other visitors, whilst the thematic exhibition on movie costumes may be crowded. The more an (often temporal) exhibit attracts the general public, the more space and routing is an issue, and at the same time, the more the exhibit could be in danger regarding climate conditions and damage.

Historic textiles and historic artifacts with certain types of coloring and dyed decoration may be deteriorating if light is too strong for a long period, but visitors should be able to see what is displayed. With heavy traffic, these conditions are contradicting each other.

9.4 Dealing with Different Stakeholders

In the previous sections, we have seen that in the current situation authorities that are responsible for the business goals and business process are no longer mainly the community of members of a culture. This poses problems with respect to the needs of the main stakeholders of the culture, that are different from the needs of the general public. To find solutions for this, we need to get more insights into these differences and the differences in services a museum might provide. Thus, we analyze how different stakeholders are aiming at different experiences. Subsequently, we propose an approach to provide differentiation in access, information, and services.

Museums and comparable institutes that keep cultural heritage collections need to maintain a long-term survival strategy. This includes a sound financial support model (which may well be based on a mixture of corporate sponsorship, entrance fees and commercial activities, and support from the cultural community as far as it still exists).

Preserving artifacts certainly has always been part of the mission statement of most museums. Keeping cultures alive by keeping cultural heritage available for the participants of the culture, however, may for many modern museums have become a secondary task, often inherited from a different business goal in the past, or from a business model of a previous collection that was adopted.

Consequently, cultural heritage collections disappear without a trace or are explicitly repelled. If this is about to happen, the original culture needs to act, to negotiate with the sponsors, and to find a way to make the authorities accept maintenance and support to allow the members of culture access to whatever they need. For example, when the Gemeentemuseum in The Hague, Netherlands, changed its mission, focused explicitly on art, and stopped exhibiting the large (internationally famous) musical instrument collection, the role of curator for the collection was made redundant. Through pressure from scholars who specialized in historic music performers, the main part of the collection is available for members of the culture. The current website of the museum (Gemeentemuseum 2017) states: "*The music collection was one of the highlights at the opening of the Haags Gemeentemuseum in 1935, but is no longer displayed today. Nowadays, the museum's exhibitions focus on fine art, decorative art and fashion. The music collection is however of a high standard and uniquely valuable in terms of the history of music. It is kept under controlled climate conditions, and musicians, students and other researchers may view the instruments in the reading room on request.*" The related library has been moved to the National Library of the Netherlands, parts of the instruments were moved to the Rijksmuseum in Amsterdam, and volunteers collaborate with the museum to keep the collection in stock available for scholars to analyze, describe, and measure the artifacts.

9.4.1 Different Stakeholders Need Different Types of Experiences

Famous museums like the Rijksmuseum Amsterdam offer possibilities for business events. Incentive Europe (2017) publishes: "*A cocktail reception or gala dinner in the Rijksmuseum is a unique experience in a very special environment, one your guests won't forget!*" The Rijksmuseum is considered to be among the major tourist attractions in Amsterdam, where visitors are allowed to film or take photographs of the museum as long as they do not use lights, flash or tripod (Traveldudes 2017). The general public in a museum including families with children, school groups, corporate sponsors and their guests, all expect something amusing and entertaining. This includes the opportunity to get some easy explanation to understand exciting unknown things as well as things that are supposed to be new or interesting; to interact with artifacts, the context, and with people like themselves; to get a scent of emotions that might be appropriate regarding the exhibit and the context, and to have a generally enjoyable time during their stay. In addition, they may well feel the need to build some memory of this occasion: a souvenir, a picture, some easy documentation or even a pointer to what more could be found in this building might be highly appreciated and, if needed, paid for.

Regarding collections of cultural heritage (a museum may well have a variety of these in their premises), the members of the culture will have very different expectations and needs. Scholars (e.g., the musicians specializing in historic practices that study the collection in the Gemeentemuseum, The Hague) will need all of the below:

- Hands-on experiences: measurements, actual use, maintenance, and restoration —all of which should be carefully monitored by a responsible curator, documented, and restricted to the bare minimum. The good news is that there will be a restricted number of scholars who need this, that they may collaborate and cooperate (providing each other with measurements taken, attend a joint session of actual use, and document this on multimedia). E.g., when an instrument has been measured, it is common among scholars to provide drawings, pictures, and measurements to each other or even to publish these (e.g., FoMRHI 2017);
- Access to documentation regarding each artifact as sketched before (e.g., related to Figs. 9.1, 9.2, 9.3 and 9.4)—history, complete description, restoration reports; etc. as well as access within reason regarding the diary information. On the other hand, scholars should understand, and can be requested, to provide any available new insights, findings, recordings, and references;
- Access to the full collection, including whatever is stored in the depot.

Amateurs will expect the true experience of the living culture. This includes at least the opportunity to inspect the original artifacts as well as documentation as far as there are no privacy issues regarding the current owner. They will understand restricting issues regarding climate control, damage prevention, and lighting regulations. This also includes the opportunity of participating, as a knowledgeable audience, in actual use by scholars—performances where dresses are used in a relevant context (e.g., a staged ceremony) or musical instruments are being played in a concert.

9.4.2 Split the Venue, Keep the Richness of Multiple Resources

In various cases that we analyzed, we noticed a need for diverse spaces with functions that match the needs and intended experiences of the various visitors and stakeholders. For example, in several collections of musical instruments that we or our students investigated, the collection was on display for all, including the general public, and some simple descriptions were available that did not require any expertise to understand.

In one case, only the general public was served: an exhibition in the History Museum in Puertollano in 2005 commemorated the musical culture from the time of Don Quijote (a novel written in 1605 by Miguel de Cervantes) by showing historic pictures of period Spanish instruments and rather simple "reconstructions" of the instruments depicted: certainly, interesting for the general public but disappointing for amateurs and scholars. These latter were likely to know quite well that many actual music scores of that time and context existed as well as original instruments, and were well aware of performances and recordings by groups like those led by Jordi Savall based on original manuscripts and performed on original instruments or faithful copies. This exhibition only had a single door: for the general public.

On the other hand, we find the Horniman Museum in London that, next to an easy entrance for the general public that allows access to a selection of the collected items, provides scholars with facilities like clearly described procedures to access the many artifacts in the depots, and even policies and procedures to request a loan —a second, if not physical, door to the collections. For amateurs, there is a 3rd entrance through the internet, where all artifacts in the collections are visible, though only with very small pictures, often randomly categorized (e.g., there are 32 "traverse flutes" and 12 "flutes" that are in fact traverse flutes), featuring descriptions that often lack relevant details and with indications of whether some of them are on display often incorrect.

The curators of some musical instrument collections, based on requests, decided to allow (only known specialist) players to use instruments to play in controlled conditions, separated from the rooms with display cabinets. Professional builders of facsimiles asked for, and were allowed to, take measurements and make pictures of details, again under supervision and in a safe environment. In one case, the measurement and analysis resulted in the expert developing life-size construction drawings to allow amateur builders to study these in their own environment.

Some cultural heritage collections in the domain of music are part of institutes for professional music education, like the Museum of Musical Instruments at the Royal College of Music in London. The museum shows in fact nearly all its cultural heritage artifacts, in a display that clearly aims at the students and staff, an audience that is mostly of the category "amateur". The general public will not find in this display and content too much to be excited about, but for scholars, the curator is most of the time available to provide additional access and information. The same situation is the case for the Musical Instrument Museum in St Cecelia Hall, part of the University of Edinburgh. Amateurs and scholars will find a rich collection with a lot of exemplary documentation, and a helpful curator to provide access whenever needed and at all possible, where the general public will probably never know about it and would not be challenged to enter, browse, and study. This type of specialized museums seems able to survive financially because of their relationship with an educational institute in a related domain, and, consequently, shape their "door" to fit the intended specialized audience.

In the same domain of musical cultural heritage, the musical instrument museum in Markneukirchen, Germany, seems to mainly aim at amateurs, providing over 3000 historical instruments and related artifacts. However, in one of the buildings (in fact with a separate door), there are bizarre exhibits like the largest tuba in the world, the largest accordion in the world and the largest violin (14 feet)—completely irrelevant for amateurs but a favorite background for tourist selfies.

In the case of the historic costume, we learned there are national and international organizations that state annual meetings where original costumes will be shown to experts, and even worn in a safe environment. For the general public, there seems to be only the experience of seeing dancers dressed in copies of original costumes at festivals.

Based on our cases we have identified needs that seem to exist in almost all cases, for a way to safely exhibit to all participants of a culture as well as to the general public, as well special environments for close examination, for manipulation, and under strict conditions even for use:

- A museum shop seems to be relevant for almost any type of visitor. Providing easy to understand and appreciate souvenirs will mainly serve the general public and corporate sponsor guests. Though, once in the shop they can be seduced to browse and may well discover there is more in the collection, and even consider the status of amateur to a culture that seems to be exciting enough (information provided electronically through, for instance, CDs, and well-designed books may be a first step to embracing a culture).
- Food, drink, reception, and meeting facilities, for the general public, for families with children, and for special events organized by corporate sponsors. Museum management might have good reasons to be less nervous if the drinking crowd is not too close to the most well-known painting in the collection.
- For members of a culture, there is a need for entrance to a library of archival material and documentation. Some types of access (related to the state and

possible sensitive content of the documents) may need to be monitored or restricted to certified scholars.
- As far as space can be made available, scholars and amateurs will be able to walk their dedicated galleries, mostly without the need of a guide (whether audio or human). On the other hand, a member of the general public who happens to enter such a specialist room might feel the need and will appreciate a guidance that highlights "specialties" which may be either artifact that look "extreme" or that are related to a well-known story (such as the hat worn by Napoleon at Waterloo, the largest violin in the world).

For offering these types of access, professionals and experts are needed. e.g., for the shop, for the library, as guides or for monitoring the audio guides, for monitoring manipulation by scholars. Maybe not all of them need to be (full time) employed by the museum organization: in the case of cultural heritage collections, the original community may well be able and willing to provide recognized scholars that volunteer or are in other ways working on behalf of the interested community. These volunteers often will be happy to work, both for the benefit of their living culture and for developing appreciation for their culture by the general public.

9.4.3 Different Doors (and Routes) with United Management

One of our student groups came to the course based on their expertise as consultants on the internet of thing. They introduced us to the metaphor of multiple roads through the world of things and of knowledge related to the things, and they suggested that (at least conceptually) a museum could have separate doors:

- The general public may be served best by providing them with a nice and smooth route along exhibits and installations that are easy to appreciate and that are safe for crowds. Obviously, food and drinks, as well as the shop should be strategically located in this tract.
- A separate and appropriately indicated VIP door could lead to special event facilities, designed for the purpose and, at the same time, making specific use of the museum context (some special exhibits, the newest sponsored acquisition).
- Amateurs will often enter especially for "their" section. Make sure they will be able to find it immediately (also on the museum website, for example trying to locate the historic costume collection for the Victoria and Albert Museum). For this group, availability of objects is more important than being provided with a carefully crafted aesthetic experience
- Scholars will sometimes need access to artifacts in store, as well as to the archive and library. Guided by them, this will also be the case for amateurs.

For the display of cultural heritage objects, the main question is what is safe to be responsibly made available, and in which environmental conditions (humidity, temperature, lighting). Members of the culture will understand the restrictions in this respect.

For amateurs, some examples of cultural heritage objects will often be appreciated, though in their route this could well be copies that show how the objects originally looked: They will be happy to experience what people in the old days had available. Often copies are fine, and for some types of experience they may even be handled: Some museums successfully provide look-alikes of historic costumes for making pictures, or copies of musical instrument mechanics to allow touching and manipulation.

In the same way, new technologies can be applied: even the concept of mummification (whether this is in fact still cultural heritage or just a far cry from a past culture) can now be studied through a video clip (New Scientist 2016) that gradually shows the unpacking of a mummy till the bare bones and beyond, just the metal amulets. And, in the same domains, New Scientist (2016) shows how kids may get a feel of mummification practices or even be practiced by children on a Barbie doll (Kidsactivitiesblog 2016).

Providing access to these technologies in the route that is dedicated for amateurs will certainly support the intended experiences. Moreover, techniques like augmented reality with the use of the omnipresent smartphone will allow visitors to find vivid references to (use of) the exhibits in the past. Museum websites could contain additional information specifically intended for members of cultures related to the cultural heritage collections, as illustrated before. This information could, obviously, be password protected if only qualified scholars should have access.

By designing separate routes and indicating them carefully for the diversity of visitors, both the crowds and the specialists may be served better and with much less frustration. Successful engagement of these groups may also hopefully provide arguments for the various stakeholders (from authorities to cultural communities to sponsors to the general public) to provide more support, financially as well as by explicit opinion, to maintain museums and collections to serve everyone.

9.5 Conclusions

Communities of people united by their living culture, even if they are no longer able to preserve their cultural heritage privately, depend on the availability of access to the artifacts of their culture. Currently, cultural heritage artifact collections often move to museums where these collections become part of a much larger and much more heterogeneous content. Based on our teaching and our collaboration with curators of cultural heritage, and guided by the vision on cultural heritage by UNESCO, we developed an approach aiming at keeping these artifacts available for the participants of the original culture. Consequently, we focus on the participants of the culture, their different roles in the culture and their needs and intended experience of the artifacts.

Obviously, a museum aims at serving many different stakeholders, including sponsors and the general public, with interest, knowledge, and intended experiences that may differ largely from the needs of the stakeholders of the specific culture. Communities of people united by their living culture, and consequently motivated to keep their cultural heritage, need a very different type of services from the museum. We showed how some museums accommodate this goal through specialized websites, others by providing access to knowledge and artifacts that are kept invisible for the general public, whereas other museums currently do not manage to provide adequate service to support the survival of cultures that are dependent on access to their heritage.

In this chapter, we illustrated the types of access, representations, and knowledge that are relevant to keep a culture alive when the artifacts are preserved in a museum. The metaphor of separate doors and dedicated routes through the collection to welcome diverse stakeholders of a culture (amateurs who live and learn the culture, and scholars who actively research and teach the culture) illustrates our current understanding of how museums can actively support the survival of cultures, and, at the same time, support the general public that will have rather different knowledge, interest, and intended experiences for cultural heritage artifacts.

Acknowledgements We thank our students, and the scholars and amateurs involved in the cultural heritage collections that allowed us insight into their content, operations, and logistics.

References

Falk JH, Dierking LD (2013) The museum experience revisited. Left Coast Press, Walnut Creek, CA

FoMRHI (2017) The fellowship of makers and researchers of historic instruments. Accessed from http://www.fomrhi.org/

Gemeentemuseum (2017) Gemeentemuseum Den Haag, collections, applied art, musical instruments. Accessed from: https://www.gemeentemuseum.nl/en/collections/musical-instruments

Incentive Europe (2017) Presenting: the new and improved Rijksmuseum. Accessed from http://www.incentive.nl/en/incentivenews/english-presenting-the-new-and-improved-rijksmuseum/

Khan Academy (2017) Peoples and cultures. In: Arts and humanities > Art of AfricaAfrican > Art, an introduction. Accessed from https://www.khanacademy.org/humanities/art-africa/african-art-intro/a/peoples-and-cultures

Kidsactivitiesblog (2016) Mummification: let's Mummify Barbie! Accessed from kidsactivities-blog.com/9140/mummification-lets-mummify-barbie

Merriam Webster (2017) An encyclopaedia Britannica company: definition of culture. Accessed from Merriamwebster website: https://www.merriam-webster.com/dictionary/culture

New Scientist (2016) Mummy X-rays let you peel its body to reveal insides. Accessed from www.newscientist.com/article/dn25619-mummy-x-rays-let-you-peel-its-body-to-reveal-insides

Traveldudes (2017) Rijksmuseum in Amsterdam: a major tourist attraction. Accessed from http://www.traveldudes.org/travel-tips/rijksmuseum-amsterdam-major-tourist-attraction/59122

Uras S, Consiglio T, van der Veer GC (2015a) Keeping cultural heritage alive – opportunities with ICT. In: HCITOCH 2015, human-computer interaction, tourism and cultural heritage

Uras S, Consiglio T, van der Veer GC (2015b) Teaching design for living memory. In: HCITOCH 2015, human-computer interaction, tourism and cultural heritage

UNESCO (2017) Definition of cultural heritage. Accessed from http://www.unesco.org/new/en/culture/themes/illicit-trafficking-of-cultural-property/unesco-database-of-national-cultural-heritage-laws/frequently-asked-questions/definition-of-the-cultural-heritage/

UXPA (2017) http://www.usabilitybok.org/glossary Victoria, Albert museum. (2016). Eating and drinking page, Accessed from www.vam.ac.uk/visiting/visitor-information/#eating-drinking

Von Hornbostel EM, Sachs C (1914) Systematik der Musikinstrumente. Zeitschrift fuer Ethnologie, 553–590

Vyas D, van der Veer G (2006a) Rich evaluations of entertainment experience: bridging the interpretational gap. In: Proceeding of ECCE-13. ACM Digital Library, pp 137–144

Vyas D, van der Veer G (2006b) Experience as meaning: some underlying concepts and implications for design. In: Proceedings of ECCE-13. ACM Digital Library, pp 81–91

Yu M-D, Devadas S (2017) Pervasive, dynamic authentication of physical items. Commun ACM 60(4):32–39

Author Biographies

Gerrit van der Veer is a university researcher since 1961 in Cognitive Psychology, Ergonomics, and Computer Science, on HCI, cultural differences, and ICT for cultural heritage. He taught in Belgium, Germany, Spain, Italy, Romania, The Netherlands and China. He is currently supervising PhD Students in Italy and the Netherlands and teaching courses at the Maritime University of Dalian (China).

Teresa Consiglio is PhD researcher in Computer Science at the Open University of the Netherlands. She holds a Ph.D. in e-Learning Development & Delivery. Her research interests include: instructional design, design and technologies for cooperative and collaborative learning also in different cultural contexts, design processes, blended learning, adult learning, and cultural heritage. She has published in the area of human-computer interaction.

Selene Uras is UX researcher in the Italian headquarters of an international media group, collaborating with other research groups on Service Design, and patient-centric collaborative tele-rehabilitation. She received a Master Degree in Psychology in 2002, and a PhD in Computer Science in 2008. Her research interests center on improving the understanding of users' desires and needs to ameliorate their experience.

Part III
Opportunities Through Technology

Most of the chapters presented in this book use technology as a means to reach out to new audiences, to provide them with a meaningful and memorable experience inside or around the museum, and to connect across institutions and communities. Those grouped in this section however, focus more specifically on the ways technology can engage and connect audiences and on how this affects the experience itself and can offer new design opportunities.

Technology has a long history of use in museums (take, for example, museum audio guides) but the way it is used and understood today has changed by putting more emphasis on the visitor's experience and even on the *total* or immersive experience, that is one where either more senses are triggered (like in a virtual reality experience) or one where the visitor, by being an active participant, uses technology as a means to live a more relevant experience for them (see Part 1). Therefore, it is primarily the experience (and not the technology) that seems to be again the core element and common thread connecting the five chapters in this section, an experience where technology is a means to evoke that experience.

We see this for instance in *Law*'s chapter. This chapter presents a location-based app for a small archaeological site in the UK, which can be augmented with audio and visual information from a nearby museum. This use of the technology is quite innovative, as few examples are documented where co-located sites are connected virtually through an on-site experience of one of the involved places. This allows visitors to build connections with the content that would otherwise not be possible and to broaden their experience and fruition of it.

Verona, Vivacqua and Campos deal with technology, or rather the lack of it, in museums of the Global South. Based on an empirical study conducted in Brazil, the authors discuss the challenges faced by local museums when seeking to adopt and employ new technologies. Interestingly, they name conceptual resistance to technology use as one of three fundamental challenges museums face. The chapter envisages as well opportunities opened up by the use of social and interactive media as a way to connect across museum stakeholders and to enrich visitor experiences.

Mobile technology is the central theme in the chapter of *Rozendaal, Vermeeren and Issidorides*, though used not to enhance but rather to capture the visitor experience by asking visitors to self-report their experiences in an on-the-spot, automated way. Drawing on a study carried out in a science museum, the chapter shares insights and recommendations to integrate this experience assessment technology in the overall visit experience, to process the resulting data to better understand it and, finally, to relate the captured experience to the museum itself and its exhibition.

Finally, *Sabiescu* critically reflects on three design approaches to the use of technology in museums, namely user-centred design, participatory design and Lean and Agile methodologies, all positioned within an overarching visitor-centredness frame. These design approaches or paradigms represent systematic ways by which museums deliver value to their patrons through the experiences designed and delivered. The chapter further argues that long-term work within a certain design paradigm can have an impact on how museums develop enduring relationships with their patrons and communities, and may echo in changes within their organisational structures and practices.

What connects all these chapters is the assumption that technology is only a means and not an end in itself. What technology to use is debatable and depends on the context and the people addressed. This choice "is not neutral, but it is *value laden*", as Sabiescu rightly states. Overall, the visitors and their experience remain at the centre of the design process.

Chapter 10
Augmenting the Experience of a Museum Visit with a Geo-Located AR App for an Associated Archaeological Site

Effie Lai-Chong Law

Abstract The experience and learning effect of visiting a museum associated with an archaeological site located nearby can be augmented by a location-based app designed to explore the site. In this chapter, we describe the design of such an app for a relatively small archaeological site called Thetford Priory in England. The design and development of the app was a multidisciplinary and inter-sectoral effort. A survey was conducted with 164 children aged 10–11 years old from five different schools to evaluate the usability and user experience of the app and the learning effect of deploying it. Results of the survey indicated that the enjoyability, ease-of-use, and understandability of the app were generally high, and that the users tended to download the app and recommend it to others. Overall, the main implication we can infer from the research study is that new mobile and interaction technology, when carefully designed, can be a powerful tool in enhancing and disseminating the value of cultural heritage and in utilising the complementarity of museums and their associated sites nearby.

10.1 Introduction

In Europe, popular archaeological sites such as Pompei in Italy, Delphi in Greece, and Stonehenge in the UK are widely visited and well-researched. In contrast, much less attention and research effort has been drawn to a number of relatively smaller but important archaeological sites, which could have elicited higher appreciation as cultural heritage and attracted a higher number of visitors if they were better known. More important, they would have better been exploited for educational purposes (Wishart and Triggs 2010). The potential benefit of improving the popularity of these sites is that they can not only stimulate local economies but also encourage community-building and identity-building in both rural and urban areas. To realise such a potential, one obvious recommendation is to enhance the accessibility and

E. L.-C. Law (✉)
Department of Informatics, University of Leicester, Leicester LE1 7RH, UK
e-mail: lcl9@le.ac.uk

A. Vermeeren et al. (eds.), *Museum Experience Design*, Springer Series on Cultural Computing, https://doi.org/10.1007/978-3-319-58550-5_10

appeal of these sites. Nonetheless, the challenge is that typically for small archaeological sites, the data and artefacts are not available or presented in forms that are meaningful to general audience.

In recent decades, we have witnessed major developments in the techniques of archaeological survey, the use of geographic information systems (GIS), 3D scanning and modelling, and theoretical work on place and space have all expanded our understanding of how people, sites, artefacts and landscapes fit together. Astonishingly, the potential of exploiting the emerging technical and theoretical knowledge to augment visitors' experience in an ancient landscape and environment of an archaeological site with their experience in a (typically co-located) museum dedicated to the site has been under-explored. This can be attributed to the fact that visitors are usually engaged with archaeological material on a site (with no artefacts) or in a museum (with no site). Developing mobile digital apps with the use of augmented reality (AR) to narrate histories vividly is regarded as a promising approach to enhance the meaningfulness, accessibility and enjoyability of visiting such sites, especially for a non-specialist public audience. Furthermore, like all other mobile educational tools, such apps should be grounded in strong pedagogical frameworks to foster learning. In our project *Representing Reformation* (RR) funded by the Arts and Humanities Research Council (AHRC) in the UK, we developed such a mobile app to explore a relatively small archaeological site known as Thetford Priory in England. In the following, we first briefly describe the motivation and historical background underpinning the project and the app. Then we depict the design of the app in detail, followed by a report on the evaluation results of a survey that aimed to evaluate the usability, user experience and learning effect of the app.

10.2 Motivation and Historical Background

Representing Reformation (RR)[1] is an interdisciplinary science and heritage project exploring the multifaceted lives of the Howard Dukes of Norfolk—the most prominent noble family during the era of Reformation. The three-year project studied the Howard Tombs, two of which were originally planned to stand in Thetford Priory, Norfolk, England, but were moved to 60 km away in Framlingham after the priory's dissolution by Henry VIII. The surviving remains of Thetford Priory include the lower walls of the church and cloister, along with the shell of the priors' lodging and, reached by a pathway from the main site, an almost complete 14th century gatehouse. The ruin is of high educational value for the intriguing history of reformation dated 400 years ago. Specifically, the project RR aimed to deliver to the public an AR-based iOS app that contextualises the research findings

[1]http://representingreformation.net/.

Fig. 10.1 Framlingham Parish Church (left) where the tombs were re-erected after they had been moved away from Thetford Priory (right) (photos source: Wikipedia; Creative Commons: CC BY-SA 3.0)

in situ of the priory. The app can be used as an educational resource by schools to engage students and by the local museum 'Ancient House of Thetford Life'[2] to attract more visitors (Fig. 10.1).

10.3 Design of the Mobile App

The design and development of the app were driven by the meticulous collaborative efforts of a multidisciplinary team consisting of historians, archaeologists, museum experts, curators, game designers, human-computer interaction experts, pedagogical experts and space research experts, who provided their expertise in 3D scanning and modelling. Technically, the app was implemented by a professional game company, *Enigma Interactive,*[3] which worked closely with the academic partners, who provided the content and resources.

Users may access help for further information. The access is displayed as an overlay on the map of the priory (Fig. 10.2). The six Interest Points (red dots with '?' and the green dot with '?') are displayed in their appropriate locations on the map. Selecting 'Where to next …' suggests the next Interest Point to visit. The next Interest Point will flash prompting users to either walk to the Interest Point or select it directly on the map. 'Where to next …' will lead users around the Priory on a predefined route. If the user has already visited the next predefined Interest Point, this will be skipped and the user will be prompted to visit the next point. Once a user has accessed or visited an Interest Point on the map, the point will be displayed as visited. Users may still access or revisit the point if required.

[2]http://www.museums.norfolk.gov.uk/Visit_us/Ancient_House/index.htm.

[3]https://www.enigma-interactive.co.uk/work/university-of-leicester-thetford-priory-tablet-app.

Six different QR codes are generated to represent the six Interest Points on the map. On selecting to scan a QR code, the application will change to camera/ scanning mode allowing users to scan QR codes. The scanning interface will also let users exit scanning mode. On successfully scanning a QR code, the appropriate Interest Point will highlight on the map, prompting users to select the Interest Point.

10.3.1 Basic Concepts

The mobile app enables geo-located AR of the artefacts found at the dissolved Thetford Priory site to tell stories about their relevance to the Howards and the findings of this project. There is a narrative to the physical exploration of the site clustered by themes on the funerals and tomb monuments of the Howard family with Second and Third Duke being most prominent characters. Six Interest Points (A–F) are:

A. Dukes of Norfolk were powerful and important
B. Second Duke had a spectacular funeral at Thetford Priory
C. Second Duke's tomb at Thetford Priory
D. Tombs were covered in meaningful things
E. Second Duke's body was moved to Lambeth
F. Clues to the Third Duke's tomb were found at the Priory

Using GPS location, the app can test whether the user is onsite or offsite. If onsite, the user can explore and access Interest Points by walking to them or by selecting the Points directly on the interactive map. If offsite, GPS navigation is disabled and users can access the Interest Points by selecting them directly on the map or scanning a QR code. The main app navigation is represented as an illustrated map of the Thetford Priory site (Fig. 10.2 with the five numbered dots and related notes).

The six Interest Points (IPs, A–F) feature formatted text areas, imagery and video (Table 10.1). Each content area is designed to display the supplied content in the most appropriate format. After visiting all six IPs, the 'Conclusion Screen' will be presented to prompt users to find the location of the Third Duke's tomb (NB: a historical puzzle is yet to be resolved). This screen is also used to provide key points the user has been given whilst using the app. If the user is onsite, the current location of the device will be displayed on the map. Users will be taken into the camera mode with the 3D render of the tomb being displayed over the device's camera display. Users may rotate the image around the horizontal axis to position the tomb. If offsite, the user will have to identify the location of the tomb by selecting a point on the map; selecting will add a location marker onto the map, users may change this location by selecting another point. On selecting a location, the '*I think the tomb was here…*' button will be displayed. Clicking it will lead to the conclusion videos.

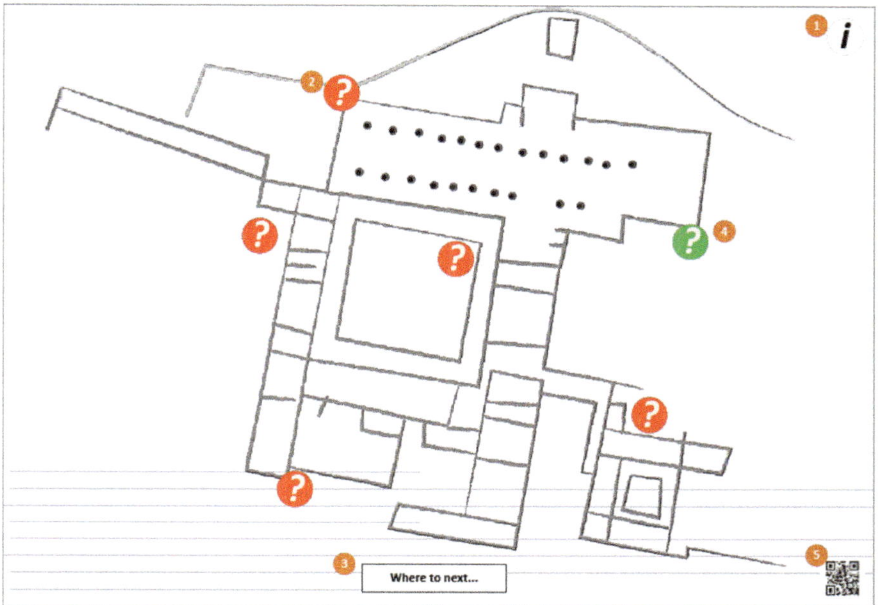

Fig. 10.2 The main navigation map as an illustrated map of Thetford Priory

10.3.2 Pedagogical Design

The field of mobile learning (or 'mlearning') has grown over the last decade in several related fields, including HCI and technology-enhanced learning (TEL) (Vavoula and Sharples 2009), from small-scale case studies to larger international initiatives, commercial projects and institutional programmes. The emergence of location-based technologies, countrywide Internet access and increasingly powerful multimedia capture and display has brought new opportunities to enhance learning in settings outside the classroom (Brown 2010). Specifically, the following areas of research and practice where mobile technologies feature have been identified (Sharples and Kukuluska-Hulme 2010): handhelds in the classroom, mixed reality learning, personal informal learning, distance and online education, learning across contexts and between informal and formal settings. An interesting implication is the use of mobile technology for field and school trips with a particular emphasis on the pedagogical gains that can be made through the use of location-based technologies to bridge formal and semi-formal (outside the classroom) settings.

Our app employs an inquiry-based design (Healey 2005) that attempts to mimic the research process of the project. It can facilitate the realisation of our aim to encourage user-led investigation of the site while communicating some of the project's findings and the type of work researchers in academia conduct. Specifically, we identify which media are required for different Interest Points (A–F),

Table 10.1 Six Interest Points (IPs) with Generic Learning Outcomes and associated attributes

IP	Media required	Learning styles served	Generic Learning Outcomes (GLO)	Relevance & personal meaning
A	Photo of terracotta roundel and Hampton Court roundel; Voiceover for 'Dukes are important'	**Dynamic learner**: there is a logical induction here; seeing one element as the clue to something bigger **Analytical learner**: using source material to compare to something else you know	**KU** (know that the roundel was part of the priory, and that it is similar to that in Hampton Court, and how that might indicate style and wealth) **ABP** (reflect on how and why a family 400 years ago behaved the way they did – decided to self-fashion themselves in a particular way)	How we use material things to project our own style and image today
B	Video of actors discussing 2nd Duke's funeral Picture of funeral from that time	**Imaginative learner**: constructing a picture of what happened, and empathising with what it would have been like to be at the funeral **Common sense learners**: how funerals worked, what happened, and who did what	**KU** (understand what a Tudor funeral was like) **AV** (empathise what it was like to be at a Ducal funeral; and respect how Tudor people mourned their dead)	The rules of our own (and other) public festivals and events Today's ceremonies around life and death
C	3D reconstruction of 2nd Duke's tomb 2D image of 2nd Duke's tomb 3D scans of fragments from 2nd Duke's tomb	**Imaginative learner**: seeking meaning from the empty vault, and imagining the presence of the tomb **Analytical learner**: knowing what experts think the heraldry on the tomb means, and the significance of where the fragments were found	**KU** (know that the tomb was here and looked a particular way) **EIC** (be surprised by the presence, scale and placement of the tomb) **S** (be able to perceive the augmented space of the priory)	Our spatial awareness and literacy
D	2D snapshot of 3rd Duke's scanned tomb Pop-up videos describing sections of 3rd Duke's tomb	**Analytical learner**: asking what these symbols mean; learning by thinking through the ideas around symbols and signs on the tombs; learning from expert views on the symbols and signs	**KU** (make some sense of the symbols on the tomb) **S** (know how to read some symbols and heraldry) **AV** (be sensitive to what Tudor people did with their tombs to commemorate and communicate things)	How we read and communicate through non-textual signs and symbols Why and how we mark a death – through (for instance) memorialisation, eulogy or obituary

(continued)

Table 10.1 (continued)

IP	Media required	Learning styles served	Generic Learning Outcomes (GLO)	Relevance & personal meaning
E	Photo of where 2nd Duke's body is in Lambeth and of Lambeth parish church Plaque with relevant information in Lambeth	**Dynamic learner**: seeking solution to the mystery of the missing body; processing the information offered and seeking to test theories of where the body might be **Imaginative learner**: asking why a body would be moved	**EIC** (think innovatively about what may have happened to the 2nd Duke's body) **AV** (acknowledge why the body was moved)	The role of sacred places in the respect for the dead How evidence can be lost over the passage of time The change in the built landscape around us (the lost priory, the Lambeth café …)
F	Animation Rotatable 3D construction of 3rd Duke's tomb Image of a dig at the priory	**Dynamic learner**: seeking and reflecting upon the possibilities presented by the fragments; responding to the idea of different hypotheses; engaging with the idea that the extant tombs can become something else **Common sense leaner**: seeking a solution to the problem of the fragments; seeing the tombs and the fragments as a problem-solving activity; engaging with the practical application of laser technology to history	**KU** (know and follow the project's 'working hypothesis' around the tombs, and how the team came to it) **EIC** (be inspired by the project's approach; and able to identify the innovative thoughts around Heritage Science) **AV** (empathise with how the Howards had as a family to respond to the Dissolution)	The impact of politics and religion on our lives, our families our self-identity How research works, how different academic disciplines are different How technology affects how we see the past.

which learning styles to be served, and what learning outcomes to be expected, and what relevance and personal meaning to be implied (see Law et al. 2013 for details). For our project RR, we embrace the Generic Learning Outcomes (GLO) framework. The GLOs are underpinned by a broad definition of learning which identifies benefits that people gain from interacting with museums, libraries and archives[4]:

[4]http://www.inspiringlearningforall.gov.uk/toolstemplates/genericlearning/.

- Knowledge and Understanding (KU)
- Skills (S)
- Attitudes and Values (AV)
- Enjoyment, Inspiration & Creativity (EIC)
- Activity, Behaviour & Progression (ABP)

10.3.3 Challenges and Beta Version Prototype

As described above, the design of the app was first focused on the creation of the bespoke map (Fig. 10.2) and then on the integration of the GPS location finding functionality, which was used to inform onsite users where they were (the blue dot in Fig. 10.3) and to trigger off the next Interest Point (the six points A–F explained above) by making it blink. When visitors were close to an Interest Point, pictures, expert videos and interactive 3D renders of some of the important objects found by archaeologists would become accessible (Fig. 10.4).

The alpha version of the app was thoroughly tested in the field by the project's partners. The main challenge was the precision of the GPS location finding in the archaeological site, which is relatively small to allow accurate estimation.

Fig. 10.3 The mobile app used onsite in the Priory; the blue dot indicates the position of the user (the beta version)

Fig. 10.4 The mobile app showed the pictures, videos and other educational resources

10.4 Evaluation

Evaluation is an integral part of the developmental lifecycle of any interactive system, given the importance of interplay between user experience evaluation and system redesign (Law and Abrahao 2014). As the app developed for the project RR was aimed to be a mobile learning tool, a specific evaluation framework should be employed, which is described subsequently.

10.4.1 Evaluation Framework for Mobile Learning App

The evaluation strategy is informed by the six challenges of evaluating mobile learning (Sharples and Kukuluska-Hulme 2010; Vavoula and Sharples 2009; Vavoula et al. 2009) and the three-level framework proposed to addresses these challenges (Vavoula et al. 2009). The challenges include: capturing and analysing learning in context and across contexts (school, local visitors, museum and priory site), measuring the processes and outcomes of mobile learning activities (learner-led inquiry), privacy issues (visitors using their own technology), the usability of the technology which is not personal (project supplied iPads), assessing in/formality of the learning setting (visitors and school field trips), and considering how well this fits into the wider organisational and socio-cultural context (the local museum, community and schools).

The three-level framework aiming to address these challenges is relevant to our mobile app (Vavoula and Sharples 2009). The micro-level assesses usability issues; a meso-level examines the learning experience including the breakthroughs and breakdowns that occur in the process. Finally, the macro-level considers how well the technology is integrated into the existing socio-cultural context, in this case the local museum, which facilitates visitors and educational field trips. This final level especially helps assess the impact of the application on the local community. A variety of mainly qualitative methods need to be used at different stages, including focus groups, semi-structured interviews and ethnographic observation of the application in use, Google Analytics, user feedback reviews and questionnaires. Within the lifetime and resources of the project, we were only able to evaluate the micro-level—usability and user experience issues of the app, and the preliminary meso-level in terms of learning.

10.4.2 Methods

10.4.2.1 Instrument

As mentioned, the museum Ancient House of Thetford Life is linked to the archaeological site Thetford Priory. The museum is often visited by school children to learn about the British history of the Reformation era. It also attracts tourists, scholars, amateur historians and archaeologists and the like. Typically, after visiting the museum, visitors walk to Thetford Priory. The evaluation of the app was incorporated into this typical journey. To facilitate data collection, we opted for a paper-based questionnaire. However, for a handful of cases, upon the consent of the visitors, the 'shadowing' technique (Hagen et al. 2005) was employed; results of these cases are not reported in this chapter. To avoid overwhelming the visitors with a long questionnaire and to minimise the time they needed to spend in filling it out, especially for school trips, the questionnaire was made to be short and highly accessible (Fig. 10.5).

10.4.2.2 Participants

Altogether 164 school children aged 10–11 years old (Grade 6 when they study the related British history at school) were involved in the evaluation of the app. They came from five different schools in the vicinity of Thetford and took part in the study as part of their excursion of visiting the museum and the archaeological site. The five schools are designated as S1, S2, S3, S4 and S5. Overall, the participants were gender balanced: 50% female and 50% were male. 46% of the participants chose the option 'most days' with respect to the question on Computer Usage, 26% indicated that they used computer every day whereas 10% showed that they hardly ever used computer (Table 10.2).

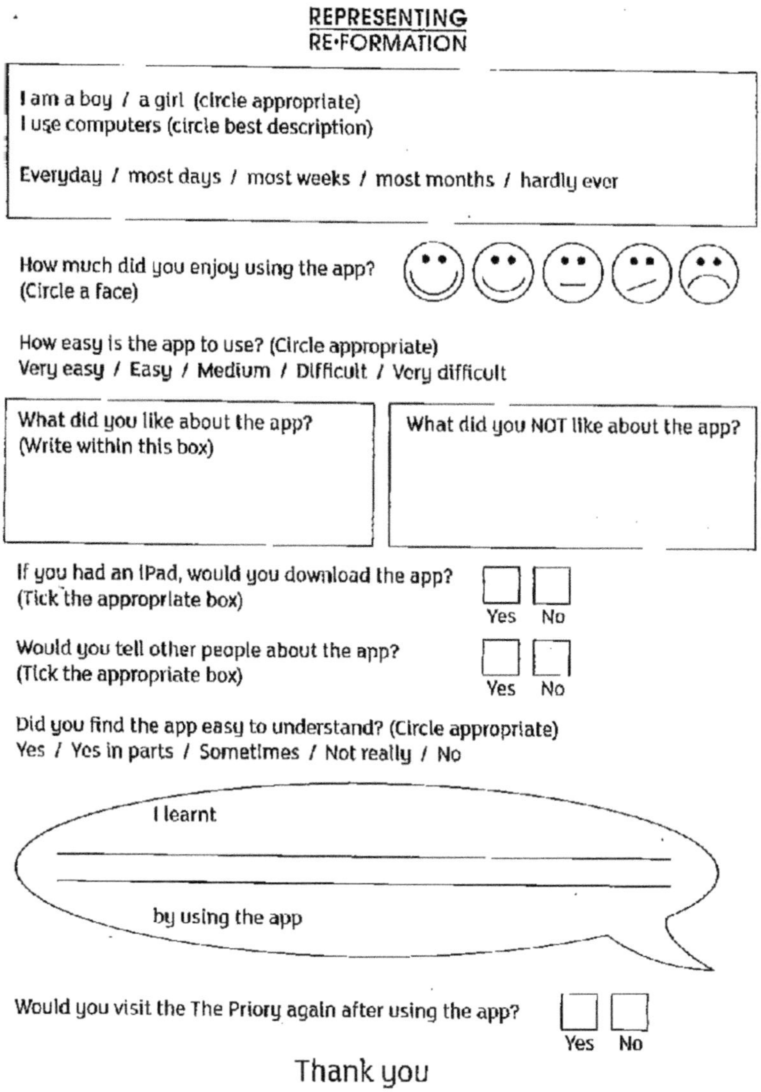

REPRESENTING
RE·FORMATION

I am a boy / a girl (circle appropriate)
I use computers (circle best description)

Everyday / most days / most weeks / most months / hardly ever

How much did you enjoy using the app?
(Circle a face)

How easy is the app to use? (Circle appropriate)
Very easy / Easy / Medium / Difficult / Very difficult

What did you like about the app?
(Write within this box)

What did you NOT like about the app?

If you had an iPad, would you download the app?
(Tick the appropriate box) Yes No

Would you tell other people about the app?
(Tick the appropriate box) Yes No

Did you find the app easy to understand? (Circle appropriate)
Yes / Yes in parts / Sometimes / Not really / No

I learnt

by using the app

Would you visit the The Priory again after using the app? Yes No

Thank you

Fig. 10.5 The evaluation questionnaire for the mobile app

Table 10.2 General demographic data of the participants

School	Total number of children	Gender		Computer usage*				
		Girl	Boy	Everyday	Most days	Most weeks	Most months	Hardly ever
S1	28	17	11	5	19	1	0	2
S2	21	11	10	4	9	5	0	1
S3	50	19	31	10	16	11	1	8
S4	19	9	10	4	11	2	0	2
S5	46	26	20	18	16	8	0	3
Total	**164**	**82**	**82**	**41**	**71**	**27**	**1**	**16**

*Computer usage: Eight children did not respond to this item

10.5 Results and Discussion

Quantitative and qualitative data have been analysed and their respective findings are reported subsequently. The former data focus on five aspects of which three address the participants' perceptions of the quality of the app and two address their behavioural intentions, whereas the latter data focus on specific features of the app that the participants liked and disliked, as well as on what they learned from deploying the app.

10.5.1 Quantitative Findings

In evaluating the five aspects, we explored whether the three variables, namely gender, computer usage and school—had any influence on the findings.

10.5.1.1 Enjoyability

It was measured with a 5-point visual analogue scale (VAS) (Funke and Reips 2012) with the leftmost anchor being most positive and rightmost anchor most negative. In converting the VAS into numeric values with 1 being most positive and 5 being most negative, the average rating was 1.97 (N = 164, SD = 0.88). It implies that the app was generally perceived as rather enjoyable.

- *Gender*: No significant difference in perceived enjoyability of the app between girls (M = 2.04, SD = 0.84) and boys (M = 1.98, SD = 0.93) was detected.
- *Computer usage*: The bivariate correlation between Computer Usage and Enjoyability was very low ($r = 0.04$, $p > 0.05$), indicating that the two variables were independent. The extent to which the participants enjoyed the app was not influenced by how much they had used computing technology before.

- *School*: There were statistically significant differences in perceived enjoyability of the app among the five schools ($F_{4,159} = 2.97$, $p < .05$) (Table 10.3). Results of post hoc Bonferroni test showed that the difference between S1 and S3, which had the highest and lowest average ratings of enjoyability, was highly significant ($t = 3.13$, $df = 76$, $p < .01$).

10.5.1.2 Ease of Use

A 5-point textual scale was used to evaluate this aspect with 'very easy' being the leftmost anchor and 'very difficult' the rightmost anchor. Eleven participants did not respond to this question. In converting the five scale points into corresponding values 1–5, the average rating of ease-of-use is 2.08 (N = 153, SD = 0.95), implying that the participants found it rather easy to use the app.

- *Gender*: No significant difference in perceived Ease of Use of the app between girls (M = 1.96, SD = 0.98) and boys (M = 2.2, SD = 1.00) was detected.
- *Computer usage*: The bivariate correlation between Computer Usage and perceived Ease of Use was positively significant ($r = .182$, $p < .05$). It was a logical finding. The extent to which the participants found the app easy/difficult to use depended much on their previous experience in deploying computing technology.
- *School*: There were statistically significant differences in perceived Ease of Use of the app among the five schools ($F_{4,148} = 3.4$, $p < .05$) (Table 10.4). Results of post hoc Bonferroni test showed that the difference between S3 and S5, which had the highest and lowest average ratings of Ease-of-Use, was highly significant ($t = 3.32$, $df = 86$, $p < .001$).

10.5.1.3 Understandability

While Ease of Use focuses on the tool, Understandability addresses the content delivered in the app. Eight participants did not respond to this item. A 5-point textual scale was used to evaluate this aspect with 'Yes' being the leftmost anchor and 'No' the rightmost anchor, whereas 'Yes in parts', 'Sometimes' and 'Not really' were in between. In converting the five scale points into corresponding values 1–5, the average rating of Understandability is 1.93 (N = 156, SD = 1.04), implying that the participants found parts of the app easy to understand (Sect. 10.5.2).

- *Gender*: No significant difference in perceived ease of use of the app between girls (M = 1.87, SD = 0.98) and boys (M = 199, SD = 1.1) was detected.
- *Computer Usage*: The bivariate correlation between Computer Usage and Understandability was not significant ($r = .158$, $p = .053$). The extent to which the participants found the content understandable seemed independent of their earlier experience in deploying computing technology.

Table 10.3 Results of the influence of the variable School on perceived enjoyability of the app

School (S)	N	Mean	SD	Min	Max
S1	28	2.25	0.645	1	3
S2	21	2.19	0.680	1	3
S3	50	1.66	0.872	1	5
S4	19	1.89	0.994	1	4
S5	46	2.09	0.962	1	4
Total	**164**	**1.98**	**0.879**	**1**	**5**

Table 10.4 Results of the influence of the variable School on perceived Ease-of-Use of the app

School (S)	N	Mean	SD	Min	Max
S1	27	2.04	0.759	1	3
S2	19	2.26	0.933	1	4
S3	44	1.68	0.883	1	5
S4	19	2.21	0.918	1	4
S5	44	2.36	1.036	1	5
Total	**153**	**2.08**	**0.950**	**1**	**5**

Table 10.5 Results of the influence of the variable School on Understandability of the app

School (S)	N	Mean	SD	Min	Max
S1	27	1.81	0.962	1	4
S2	21	2.24	1.044	1	5
S3	45	1.62	0.716	1	3
S4	19	1.74	0.933	1	4
S5	44	2.25	1.296	1	5
Total	**156**	**1.93**	**1.042**	**1**	**5**

- *School*: There were statistically significant differences in perceived Understandability of the app among the five schools ($F_{4,151} = 2.86$, $p < .05$) (Table 10.5). Results of post hoc Bonferroni test showed that the difference between S3 and S5, which had the highest and lowest average ratings of understandability, was highly significant ($t = 2.84$, $df = 87$, $p < .01$).

10.5.1.4 Download

The question was phrased as a hypothetical situation whether the participants intended to download the app if they had the iPad and the app was available. Out of 156 participants who responded to this question, 126 checked ‘Yes’ (81%). This indicated quite a high acceptance rate. Results of Chi-square tests showed that none of the three variables—Gender (75% for Girls vs. 81% for Boys), Computer Usage (the highest of 85% for 'Everyday' versus the lowest of 70% for 'Most days'), and School (the highest of 84% in case of S4 versus the lowest of 67% of S2)—played a significant role in influencing the tendency to download the app.

10.5.1.5 Tell Others

The majority (80%) of the participants responded that they would tell others about the app. Whether they would share the positive or negative experience with the others could not be inferred from their answers. Results of Chi-Square test showed that Computer Usage played a significant role in influencing the tendency of the participants to tell others about the app (χ^2 (3) = 10.68, p < .05). Those who hardly ever used computers had the lowest tendency to do so (50%) as compared with those who used computers 'Most weeks' who had the highest tendency (89%) (cf. 83% and 82% for 'Everyday' and 'Most days', respectively). The former observation is intuitive as those inactive computer users might not be interested in sharing the app. Conversely, results of Chi-Square tests indicated that neither Gender nor School played a significant role in influencing the tendency of the participants to tell others about the app. Furthermore, there was a highly statistically significant association between 'Download' and 'Tell others' (χ^2 (1) = 8.66, $p < .01$). It suggests those who intend to download the app are also very likely to tell others about the app.

In summary, the app was positively perceived by the participants in terms of its Enjoyability, Ease-of-Use, and Understandability. The participants' perceptions of good usability (Ease of Use, Understandability) and positive user experience (Enjoyability) were correlated significantly with their behavioural tendencies to download (reuse) the app and to tell others about it (Table 10.6).

In summary, all statistical tests conducted indicate that gender did not play a significant role in these variables. This can be considered as encouraging observations because both genders have comparable attitudes and behaviours with respect to the use of computing technology. In contrast, Computer Usage played a significant role in Ease of Use and Tell Others, but not in the other variables. Similarly, School played a significant role in the participants' attitudes towards the app but not in their behavioural intention. As no objective data have been collected about five different schools (e.g. quality of teaching, socioeconomic status of children's family), we do not want to speculate the plausible causes for the observed significant differences.

Table 10.6 Correlations between quality perceptions and behavioural tendencies (**p <.001)

Pearson correlation r	Enjoyability	Ease of use	Understandability
Download	0.326**	0.273**	0.288**
Tell others	0.240**	0.220**	0.273**

10.5.2 *Qualitative Findings*

Three open-ended questions aimed to identify what the participants liked and disliked about the app, and what they have learned from using it.

10.5.2.1 Likes of the App

Nine participants did not respond to this item and one response is illegible, leaving 154 valid responses to be analysed. We coded the responses into three categories, namely content-related, technology-related and general feedback. Some responses fall into more than one category, for example, '*clear labelling, different mediums of information, the interactive bits of GPS*'. Table 10.7 displays the distribution with examples. Apparently, the technology-related comments suggest that the location-based app was successful in engaging the participants.

10.5.2.2 Dislikes of the App

Interestingly, the number of blank responses was much higher, 35 as compared with 9 in the case of Likes, two responses were illegible. Another interesting observation is that 23 participants responded to this item with the word 'nothing'. For the remaining responses, we categorised them as either content-related, technology-related, or both. Table 10.8 shows the related results.

Table 10.7 Categories and examples of qualitative responses on the Likes of the app

Category	Frequency	Examples
Content-related	75 (49%)	'I really liked the actors, the funeral music, and moving the grave'; 'it showed old history about the churches'; 'I thought it was really good because you could learn facts about it while visiting' 'I liked the videos and the awesome information' 'that the people told really boring things interestingly'
Technology-related	67 (44%)	'it can detect where you are' 'the app brought the priory to life' 'The walk around GPS' 'sat nav blue dot' 'the way it's a virtual map'
General feedback	18 (7%)	'everything' 'I guessed I like it a lot' 'it was fun' 'I liked the style of it' 'it was good'

Table 10.8 Categories and examples of qualitative responses on Dislikes of the app

Category	Frequency	Examples
Content-related	47 (37%)	'The words were difficult to understand. The videos need to be more interesting. The facts were hard to understand. Maybe a kid version on the app might be nice' 'some of the videos sound were not loud enough and too long' (both) 'the information was not that child friendly' 'They seemed pretty dull talking. They should put more feeling into it'
Technology-related	61 (48%)	'I did not like when you had to press the button to scan because it took a long time to load' 'I think the word font could be bigger and that there should be a pop-up dictionary' 'the blue dot did not tell us where to go' 'it did not scan the barcode' 'it froze a couple of times, hard to restart'

10.5.2.3 Learning from the App

Out of 164 participants, 18 did not respond and seven responses were illegible, leaving 139 responses for further analysis. To analyse individual responses, we adopt the following steps:

(i) Checking their relevance;
(ii) In case of a relevant response, determining whether the learning mentioned is related to the content of the app, technology, or feedback;
(iii) For a content-based response, enumerating how many distinct concepts it covers and assigning one point for each concept.

There was only one case of irrelevance: '*there was a hospital near*'. Several cases are a combination of content-related, technology-related and general feedback. for instance, ('*a lot of history, fun*', '*how to track much more easily and about Thomas Howard*'). Eight cases are technology-related (e.g., 'better map reading') and five cases are general feedback (e.g. '*I liked the app very much*').

From the pedagogical perspective, we are more interested in the content-related responses. As shown in Table 10.9, eight participants scored zero point, either claiming that they did not learn anything (frequency: 4) or failing to specify explicitly what they have learnt (frequency: 4); 59 participants scored 1 point (i.e. named only 1 relevant concept pertaining to the app); two participants scored 5 points. The average score over 139 participants is 1.55 (SD = 1.06). As depicted in Fig. 10.6, the concepts mostly mentioned with the highest frequency of 23 are 'pricry' and 'tomb', followed by 'Howard' (frequency: 17) and Henry VIII (frequency: 14).

Table 10.9 Distribution of the scores earned by the participants on what they have learnt

Scores	Frequency	Examples
0	8	'nothing', 'not really', 'a little bit', 'a lot of things'
1	59	'that there was a tomb', 'about stuff in the priory'; 'some monks lived here'
2	36	'there was a tomb under the church'; 'Duke of Norfolks body wasn't in the vault'
3	21	'I learnt that Thomas Howard was moved from his tomb'; 'about the ghosts that are here and the monks singing'; 'every king like king Henry VIII had a cool coat of arms'
4	3	'I learned that King Henry the VIII destroyed all the monasteries for money'; 'The Duke's body was layed out in the chapel for 1 month';
5	2	'About Henry's tomb and about the priory. Fitzer didn't have a gravestone', 'about Howard's interaction with the churches, the things Thetford, and the history of the Priory, their living'

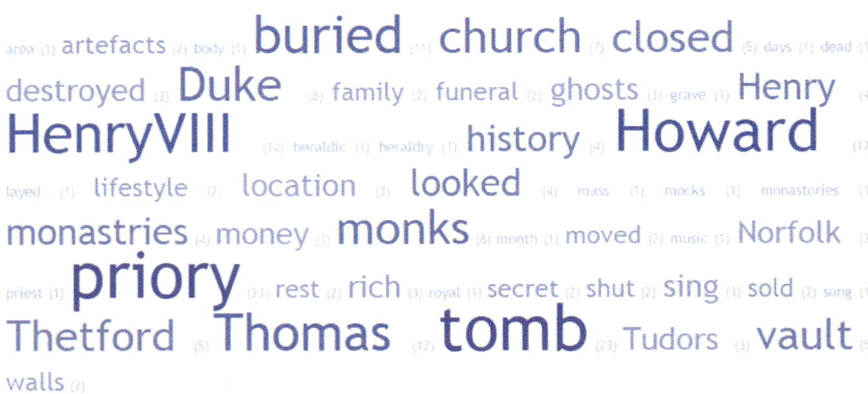

Fig. 10.6 The relative frequencies of learnt concepts (generated with Tagcrowd)

10.5.3 Limitations

There are some limitations to the study. First, given some organisational constraints such as restricted time allotted for visiting both venues, we did not measure the participants' experience in the museum to understand how it could influence their perception and use of the app in the site, especially the two experiences happened close to each other temporally as well as geographically. Second, the background information of the participants could have been richer, for instance, we could have asked about the participants' interest in the subject matter. In cases where the participants were not interested in the historical topic concerned, their overall perception of the app might tend to be lower than those who were already enthusiastic about the topic. Third, due to the time and situational constraints, the questionnaire needed to be short and simple to encourage the participants to complete it. While open-ended questions were included, the qualitative responses would have been richer with interviews where the participants could express their thoughts and feelings in a more elaborate manner.

10.6 Conclusion

Overall, the location-based app was empirically demonstrated to be effective in enabling its users to enjoy the experience of visiting the archaeological site and to acquire the related historical knowledge. Qualitative responses of the survey showed that the technical functions of Augmented Reality (AR), GPS-based navigation, and 3D visualisation are appealing features for children to explore cultural heritage in an engaging way. Nonetheless, the use of videos as a learning medium invited some mixed responses; some children appreciated them whereas some others found them lengthy and boring. Ideally, adaptive content taking users' learning needs, interest and preferences into account and presenting accordingly will be the optimal way of learning content delivery (e.g. Karran et al. 2015; Jailani et al. 2015). Future work can further tap into the power of gamification (Jailani et al. 2015; Mortara et al. 2014). All in all, the main implication we can infer from the research study is that new mobile and interaction technology, when carefully designed, can be a powerful tool in enhancing and disseminating the value of cultural heritage and in utilising the complementarity of museums and their associated archaeological sites nearby.

Acknowledgements The author would like to thank the support of the Arts and Humanities Research Council, UK, and for the project team members of the project *Representing Re-Formation*[5] for co-designing the mobile geo-based AR app and collecting the evaluation data. Thanks also go to participating school children for their kind co-operation and sharing their experiences and ideas.

References

Brown E (ed) (2010) Education in the wild: contextual and location-based mobile learning in action. A report from the STELLAR ARV workshop series

Funke F, Reips UD (2012) Why semantic differentials in web-based research should be made from visual analogue scales and not from 5-point scales. Field Methods 24(3):310–327

Hagen P, Robertson T, Kan M, Sadler K (2005). Emerging research methods for understanding mobile technology use. In: Proceedings of the 17th Australia conference on computer-human interaction: citizens online: considerations for today and the future. Computer-Human interaction special interest group (CHISIG) of Australia, pp 1–10

[5]http://representingreformation.net/the-team/.

Healey M (2005) Linking research and teaching exploring disciplinary spaces and the role of inquiry-based learning. In: Reshaping the university: new relationships between research, scholarship and teaching, pp 67–78

Jailani AK, Kusakabe S, Araki K (2015) Adaptive context-awareness model for cultural heritage information based on user needs. In: 2015 IIAI 4th International Congress on Advanced Applied Informatics (IIAI-AAI). IEEE, pp 339–342

Karran AJ, Fairclough SH, Gilleade K (2015) A framework for psychophysiological classification within a cultural heritage context using interest. ACM Trans Comput-Hum Interact (TOCHI) 21(6):34

Law ELC, Abrahao S (2014) Interplay between user experience and system development (special issue editorial). Int J Hum Comput Stud

Law ELC, Bedall-Hill NL, Parry R, Richards A, Hawker M (2013) Representing and interpreting reformation in the wild. In: Proceedings of the 15th international conference on human-computer interaction with mobile devices and services. ACM, pp 570–575

Mortara M, Catalano CE, Bellotti F, Fiucci G, Houry-Panchetti, M, Petridis P (2014) Learning cultural heritage by serious games. J Cult Herit 15(3):318–325

Sharples M, Kukuluska-Hulme A (2010) Learning using mobile and hand-held devices in ALT Wiki. http://wiki.alt.ac.uk/index.php/Learning_using_mobile_and_handheld_devices

Vavoula G, Sharples M (2009) Meeting the challenges in evaluating mobile learning: a 3-level evaluation framework. Int J Mob Blended Learn 1(2):54–75

Vavoula G, Sharples M, Rudman P, Meek J, Lonsdale P (2009) Myartspace: design and evaluation of support for learning with multimedia phones between classrooms and museums. Comput Educ 53(2):286–299

Wishart J, Triggs P (2010) MuseumScouts: exploring how schools, museums and interactive technologies can work together to support learning. Comput Educ 54(3):669–678. Elsevier

Author Biography

Effie Lai-Chong Law is a full professor in Human-Computer Interaction (HCI) in the Department of Informatics University of Leicester, UK. She earned her PhD degree in psychology at the University of Munich. She has engaged in researching usability and user experience (UX) methodologies, applying them to a range of domains such as technology-enhanced learning, serious games, cultural heritage, health, and e-commerce. Effie chaired two HCI-related COST Actions - MAUSE and TwinTide, and has been actively involved in a number of EU and national projects. Her recent research focus is on automatic emotion analysis with multiple sensors.

Chapter 11
Interactive and Social Technology: Challenges and Opportunities for Museums and Heritage Institutions in Latin America

Letícia Verona, Adriana S Vivacqua and Maria Luiza M Campos

Abstract Cultural institutions, such as museums and heritage sites, face particular challenges when dealing with technology and innovation adoption in developing countries. Social and economic instability, low priority attribution, usually leads to lack of funding and insufficient investment in technological infrastructure to appropriately support innovative projects and interactive visitor participation. These difficulties often mean institutions fall back to traditional, static, one-size-fits-all displays, which frequently fail to meet the interest of modern audiences. Additionally, content generation is slow, usually not adapted to digital media, and teams are limited in what they can do, compromising technology adoption and content evolution. In parallel, in many of these societies, there has been a visible increase in mobile technology dissemination and social media interaction. We believe that this creates an opportunity to engage museum visitors and to approach challenges with novel strategies without requiring a large technological investment on the part of the institution. In this chapter, we explore the challenges faced by cultural institutions in Brazil, based on interviews with local museum directors and curators. We also point out the opportunities to tackle these challenges that arise from the widespread adoption of personal and mobile technology in Brazilian society. Real-life examples from Brazilian museums, art schools, and heritage sites are used to illustrate typical situations.

11.1 Introduction

Technology has a big potential to bring the public closer to museums and heritage institutions and to enrich audience experiences. Besides enabling a wide dissemination of their cultural program and providing pre-visit information for those who intend to visit the institution, websites, mobile apps, and social media can enrich the

L. Verona (✉) · A. S. Vivacqua · M. L. M. Campos
PPGI, Universidade Federal do Rio de Janeiro, Rio de Janeiro, Brazil
e-mail: leticiaverona@ufrj.br

A. Vermeeren et al. (eds.), *Museum Experience Design*, Springer Series on Cultural Computing, https://doi.org/10.1007/978-3-319-58550-5_11

depth and understanding of these visits. As informal learning environments, these institutions can facilitate access to information in different ways and enable an adaptive approach, focused on each visitor's previous background that is currently not possible in schools or universities, given the strict curricula and current teaching practices (Hawkey 2009).

Digital content presentation has the power to show permanent exhibitions through a new perspective, enabling curators and museum interpretation teams to rearrange the objects and display pieces that usually would not be seen together because of time, space, or accessibility limitations. Online educational resources allow teachers and school groups to plan their visits and perform preliminary classroom activities, making the group more prepared for what they are about to see. Interest in artwork and science can be previously awakened making room for more in-depth investigations, reflections, and research during a visit, by presenting educational and provocative materials to the public before the visit. Virtual visiting tools and interactive activities invert the traditional perspective and bring the museum to the classroom, turning it into a school ally in educating children and young people, regardless of distance, time, and access limitations.

Brazil is a big and heterogeneous country and virtual visits to inaccessible museums are indeed a strong democratization tool. Moreover, the Internet can be the ideal vehicle for dissemination and conservation of material produced by museums in symposia, workshops, roundtable discussions, researches, and debates.

Such potentialities, however, face difficulties that emerge from the Brazilian reality, from both schools and museums perspectives. The technology has potential to bring huge benefits for both the visitors and the institution: an enormous research material available online; content exchange between schools and museums all over the world; students and citizens in different countries that could discuss without any intermediaries how their lives are affected by their history, economy, or geography; and visits to foreign libraries and museums. However, the problems are also big: there are few or poor equipment and infrastructure available in Brazilian museums; museums have reduced human resources and/or budget allocated to technology projects; students and employees have language constraints; and museum staff and teachers have very often little knowledge to guide the students in the use of technology.

In Brazil, the majority of cultural and patrimonial institutions are managed and funded by the government. This strong characteristic has benefits: the institutions are not guided by the art market and therefore have the power to present new and/or unknown artists and run experimental curatorial projects without profit-oriented constraints. However, they face the fluctuations of political changes, bureaucracy, and budget limitations. Museum directors are appointed positions and may be dismissed at any time according to authorities' political negotiations. It is not unusual for a previous management initiative to be interrupted, even if its costs are not a problem. Besides, most human resources are civil servants, and hiring a new employee is a long-term process. All these factors create a heavy administration context, where personnel staff is very conservative and bureaucracy prevents the institution to allocate funds for experimental and innovative projects with all the inherent risks, creating a gap between a highly connected public and low-tech adopting museums.

On the other hand, digital media enables the "viral" dissemination of events such as debates and openings, reaching a number of people formerly unthinkable by Brazilian museums. As an example, a Facebook post inviting to the opening of the exhibition "Orixás" at Casa França Brasil[1] was shared by thousands of people, resulting in an audience ten times bigger than the average for the institution. The promotion event on Facebook became a digital place for discussion about Afro-Brazilian culture, involving spontaneous manifestations that happily overwhelmed the museum educators and directors. Unexpected situations like this show that the road is still to be paved and many opportunities can naturally arise from the audience. This theme is also explored in Chap. 6 ("Crowd mining applied to preservation of digital cultural heritage") of this book. To point out what the main challenges and potentialities for the use of interactive, innovative experimental projects involving technology resources by museums, heritage sites, and other cultural institutions are, we have collected opinions and thoughts from four experienced managers and directors of museums, art school, and heritage sites in a qualitative study. The remaining of this chapter is organized as follows: Sect. 11.2 discusses the main challenges faced by museums and other cultural institutions in Brazil, based on a set of interviews we conducted and regarding technology adoption. Section 11.3 presents some guidelines for overcoming these barriers. Section 11.4 includes our final considerations, summarizing risks and benefits of technology support for on-site visitor experiences.

11.2 Interviews with Museum Professionals

11.2.1 Method

To elaborate further on this study, we have interviewed museums, heritage sites, and art schools professionals to find out what they see as the major challenges and opportunities when implementing technology projects in Brazilian museums. We looked for respondents who fulfill all the following criteria: (a) director or management positions in museums with relevance in the Brazilian context; (b) previous experience implementing innovation and technology projects in cultural institutions; and (c) experience with institutions funded by the government. We successfully interviewed four people with high-level positions in museums, heritage sites, and art schools located in Rio de Janeiro and São Paulo. In their career, they have been working at every public level (municipality, state government, and federal government). This is important because each of these levels has its own

[1]Casa França Brasil is a museum located in Rio de Janeiro. The exhibition "Orixás," about Afro-Brazilian religions and culture, was showed in September 2016.

aspects and challenges: a manager with only a "municipality experience" can be very biased and with a limited vision on the state of innovation in Brazilian museums. We were also careful to avoid respondents that are connected to political fluctuations: because the directors of these institutions are frequently appointed positions, it is not rare to find a manager that gets positions when a specific party is in power. Our respondents were selected because of their consistent, technical, independent career.

- Respondent 1: Director of the education division of Moreira Salles Institute in Rio de Janeiro (private museum), former director of Lasar Segall Museum in São Paulo (federal government managed museum), and educational curator of the 27th São Paulo Biennial (the biggest art fair in Latin America);
- Respondent 2: Former director of Escola de Artes Visuais do Parque Lage (School of Visual Arts, managed by Rio de Janeiro State government), former curator of Museum of Contemporary Art from Niterói (managed by the municipality), and current director of Paço Imperial (federal government managed museum), in Rio de Janeiro;
- Respondent 3: Coordinator of Casa França Brasil (Rio de Janeiro state government managed museum) and former coordinator of the education division at Escola de Artes Visuais do Parque Lage (School of Visual Arts); and
- Respondent 4: Manager of the research department in Museu da Casa Brasileira (São Paulo State government managed museum) in São Paulo.

The interviews were semi-structured and conducted in two phases: first, a questionnaire with preliminary questions about their experience with technology was sent to them by e-mail after which a personal interview followed. The questions asked via e-mail were as follows: (a) "What are the challenges faced when implementing innovative technology projects in museums?"; (b) "What management and project strategies do you think would cope with these challenges?"; and (c) "On the other hand, what are the major potentialities to enrich user experience using technology?." Their answers were used as a guide for the personal interviews, performed in a semi-structured way: the respondents were asked to illustrate each challenge they highlighted with previous experiences and testimonies with technology projects.

11.2.2 Results

The e-mail answers are summarized in Table 11.1.

From these results and the testimonies, we could identify three major challenges in the Brazilian museum and heritage institution scenery: the constant demand for maintenance and for content generation and also the resistance from museum managers and personnel to innovate.

Table 11.1 Summarized results

Challenge (respondent's number)	Aspects highlighted (respondent's number)
Maintenance/upkeep of existing systems (4)	Lack of permanent funding (4)
	Lack of interest from museum personnel (2)
	Forced interruption from government (2)
	Technology has relatively high costs (2)
	Resources' need of constant updates (1)
Content generation (3)	Lack of knowledge/resources to generate digital
	Content from museum personnel (3)
	Lack of personnel resources (2)
	High costs to convert from paper/analog to digital (3)
	Changes in digital formats (files, images, etc.) (3)
	Permanent needs for content (2)
Conceptual resistance to use technology (3)	The public should see the artwork with no filters or digital interference (1)
	Resistance from museum personnel to learn and use new technology (2)

11.2.2.1 Maintenance/Upkeep of Existing Systems

Cultural institutions' practices are deeply rooted in the analogic era and are typically project-based. When assembling an exhibition or publishing a book, the institution frequently makes a concentrated effort, allocates staff and resources, and demobilizes them as soon as the project ends. This is reinforced by typical characteristics of institutions funding in Brazil: it is easier to raise funds through sponsors and grants than obtaining a constant and permanent budgetary endowment. But unlike a book or an exhibition, which, once finished, will not generate further costs and needs, technology projects require constant maintenance. "The challenge is to pre-allocate resources for future equipment maintenance that will indeed be necessary.[2] In most cases, to obtain results with a good quality, the cost is much too high. There is a need for permanent maintenance, which many museums cannot afford."[3] In fact, this concern was mentioned by all managers we interviewed, showing us how the constant allocation of funds is a major issue. As a concrete example, we can mention Portfolio magazine, a digital publication of the Escola de Artes Visuais do Parque Lage (EAV). The magazine was created in 2013 as an iOS and Android app and used many multimedia and interactive resources, with content created specifically for digital publishing. Three editions were published. "The digital magazine contributed to the innovation of language, offered research resources, promoted exhibitions that take place in Rio and other cities, as well as disseminated the EAV artistic and intellectual production. Portfolio was a

[2]Testimony given to the authors, January 2017.

[3]Testimony given to the authors, January 2017.

dialogue platform with the city and the national and international art circuit."[4] Unfortunately, despite having been well received by the public, when the governing authorities of Rio de Janeiro changed, the EAV School board also changed and the project was interrupted. Previously published issues are no longer available online due to technological outdating, since the device operating systems updates made them incompatible with the published version of the magazine. With no further interest and budget from the cultural institution for technological updating, the editorial effort vanished. Another kind of obsolescence can be found in São Paulo, at Museu da Casa Brasileira with The Ernani Silva Bruno Archive.[5] The archive holds more than 20,000 cataloged records and objects of Brazilian daily life. It is a rich source for research on Brazilian daily life, with excerpts of texts from chroniclers and travelers, inventories and family wills, and official archive reports from the fifteenth to the nineteenth centuries. There, the maintenance is kept in its simplest form, to avoid discontinuity. Despite the museum remarkable effort in keeping the system online, it was conceived more than 10 years ago and is therefore no longer compatible with smartphones and other mobile devices and does not take advantage of current browsing resources. In this case, the public loses interest because the graphic and functional language has become old and tablets or smartphones cannot be used. This problem is not exclusive to Brazil: the challenge of "Maintaining Progress in Technology, Workflows, and Infrastructure" was considered a "Wicked Challenge" by The New Media Consortium in their 2015 Horizon Report (Johnson et al. 2015), especially regarding long-term maintenance. An important mission for a museum is to protect its collections for future generations. This includes metadata, its relation to physical collection items or digitized material, exhibition catalogs, and digital records, all subject to risks stemming from technology obsolescence. In museums where the collections themselves are made of multimedia records (e.g., sound and video), this issue is particularly serious. When technology is involved, "to protect" means to keep the data, the hardware and software to manipulate these data, as well as trained people who can operate the system. Funding and infrastructure seem to be recurring problems in other Latin American countries (Arjona et al. 1982). In Pitarque and Guardia (1982), for example, the authors also describe how museums in Ecuador and Venezuela are affected by these shortcomings and what steps might be taken to deal with the issue.

11.2.2.2 Content Generation

Technology applications often involve the creation of new content or some degree of adaptation of preexistent content to the new media. Although institutions hold information in many formats about the collection items, in most cases, some treatment is still necessary (e.g., scanning photographs or texts from older books).

[4]Testimony given to the authors, January 2017.

[5]Online Database. http://ernani.mcb.org.br/ernMain.asp. Accessed 10 Jan 2017.

The use of social media requires the constant generation of new content in a very specific manner. All these demand qualified personnel, which is frequently not available. Many projects are held in the content generation phase for many months, simply because the institution cannot allocate people to execute the task. This was already a problem for digital technology projects in museums in the '90s. But after the arrival and huge acceptance of the Internet and, furthermore, social networks, the problem gained dramatic contours.

Not only the constant generation of new content is necessary, but its format and language are also immersed in a changing environment. "The production of content and its presentation to the public demand a discerning look for new (and always changing) technologies and permanent research about the proper language of such technologies."[6]

11.2.2.3 Resistance to Innovation and Change

As discussed in the previous section, the constant demand for new formats and content is a major barrier in the Brazilian context. And this constant need must be fulfilled by the institution staff because the funds raised for the project usually cannot be used for long-term maintenance. This brings the issue of human resources. The museum staff is often a permanent group of civil servants, and the admission of new, young people is a long and bureaucratic process, which does not occur very often. "The major issue is the engagement of the staff of public museums with new platforms and technologies that can publicize the content held by the institution. Any novelty finds cultural resistance about technology usage."[7] But there is also a conceptual issue addressed by our respondents: if the technology is applied during the visitor's experience with the collection objects, it may bring cognitive noise, bias, and overload. This special moment, when the visitor should have the focus on object interpretation and sensing, is to be considered with attention. There must be a joint effort between curators and technology engineers to promote an experience that will leverage and not diminish the impact of this moment on visitors.

"We have diagnosed cases where the rush to insert technological gadgets was not based on actual needs, but on market trends thus not resulting in real benefits for the museum."[8] Managers also mentioned that technology engineers are also very fond of novelty, and sometimes this novelty does not last. As an example, two of them have experienced projects where the programming language used for software development became obsolete just after the project ending, and the effort and costs to maintain the software running turned to be prohibitive. "Museum projects must

---

[6]Testimony given to the authors, January 2017.

[7]Testimony given to the authors, January 2017.

[8]Testimony given to the authors, January 2017.

last decades, but the IT guys always want to use the newest and trending tool, before the market stabilizes to guarantee this tool will survive."[9]

11.3 Discussion: From Challenges to Opportunities

A part of these problems is intrinsic to the Brazilian government structure and quite difficult to address, like the allocation of resources for technology or of proper training to museum staff. However, some attempts can be done to address the challenges in a creative way. In this section, we present some ideas that can guide future research and project development.

Visitor interaction in museum spaces is normally standardized, through information panels presenting static text and images, which present themselves the same way for every visitor, every time in a very traditional communication scheme. Traditional (or mass) means of communication base their structure on the classic paradigm of sender-channel-receiver, granting considerable power to the sender and the channel owner. The Internet structure, based on a network of associations and interactivity, instead allows the receiver to shape the context of the information, and therefore its meaning. The individual obtains what they want, when they want it, and how they want it. The former "receiver" has gained power and control over the communication.

The museum public is no longer formed by passive spectators. As all other knowledge spaces, museums are also routinely visited by a heterogeneous public: museums, galleries, historic places, zoos, and parks usually have a very diverse range of visitors, like school groups, families, artists, curators, and so on. "Visitor diversity may lead to different interpretations of the same content, or to seeing things with distinct perspectives, depending on personal experiences. These differences also mean that diverse visitors may desire to obtain more information on different aspects of what they are seeing. In particular, young people are used to publishing their text, videos, photos at astonishing speed. They really want to interact!"[10]

Interactive experiences can create a two-way street between visitors and organizations, not only providing more information upon request but also enabling visitors to add their impressions or associate new information to the information displayed. Interaction with information becomes tailored to the individual and has the potential to improve the learning experience.

It is the museum's responsibility to explore this interactivity promoting more immersive presentations in the context of artworks. By migrating the visitor from the position of a passive observer to an active agent (that makes choices, writes, asks, creates), the museum establishes a dialogue channel, creating therefore a new

[9]Testimony given to the authors, January 2017.

[10]Testimony given to the authors, January 2017.

model of relationships with the society, in which collaboration and participation are highlighted.

As a knowledge place, a museum is a huge repository of information. This information takes form in books, photographs, handwritten notes, collection databases with metadata, printed programs from previous exhibitions, sound and video records, and so on. We want to take advantage of this repository in technology applications without overloading the museum staff, using the public as our workforce. Already used to interact and publish in social media, the visitors may enrich and adapt this content to fit the technology application, if tasks are properly organized. The use of crowdsourced voluntary resources to help with translation, photomasking, and interpretation of handwritten documents is already a reality in some museum environments, and the British Museum, with its Micropasts Projects, is a shiny example[11] (Bonacchi et al. 2014). The British National Library[12] and the National Library of Israel[13] continuously ask the public to perform tasks (e.g., translating from dialects to English, catalog handwritten notes). Even smaller institutions are also taking advantage of the public's workforce (Hallinan 2014).

The integration and organization of such open repositories of museum knowledge have, however, major challenges (Henry and Brown 2012): information management, especially as related to its organization, correlation, and editing; human–computer interaction, particularly tailoring the experience to the user and the settings, enabling easy access to the museum body of knowledge.

The first issue is information management and, more specifically, information integration. Structures that organize information must be clearly defined and known, so that new information can be incorporated in and properly linked to existing information. When multiple organizations are involved, they might each have its own underlying structures, and the same concepts might appear more than once. Finding points of connection to interlink these structures is one challenge. Navigating both of them together is another one.

One technology that has potential to help in this solution space is Linked Open Data (Berners-Lee et al. 2001). There has been growing adoption of Linked Open Data strategies in libraries, archives, and museums (LODLAM[14]), as evidenced by a number of existent workshops and conferences (for instance, see the MW2016 conference[15] and LODLAM-based tutorials). The British Museum is one institution that has released its collection using semantic technologies (Oomen and Aroyo 2011). Semantic tags, descriptors, and ontologies could help interlink information

[11]Micropasts Project Website, UK. http://micropasts.org.

[12]National Library Crowdsourcing Website, UK. https://www.libcrowds.com/. Accessed 15 Jan 2017.

[13]Israelian National Library Crowdsourcing Website, IL. http://nlics.org/. Accessed 15 Jan 2017.

[14]Linked Open Data in Libraries, Archives, and Museums Website. http://lodlam.net/ Accessed 15 Jan 2017.

[15]Museums and the Web 2016 conference website. http://mw2016.museumsandtheweb.com/ Accessed 15 Jan 2017.

from the museum collection to information found "in the wild," or between institutions.

On the other end of the spectrum, users could be encouraged to contribute with photos, videos, or comments based on their daily experience. This turns them into more active participants in the construction of a museum body of knowledge. When the visitors leave a museum, feelings and memories of the visit are still present. While walking out in the street, something (an object or an event) reminds them of something they saw during the visit. Through an interface, the visitors could send the museum a photo, video, or textual description of the element that reminded them of an exhibit, and link it with the appropriate museum elements. In this situation, visitors are the ones making the connections between information elements, and sending them back to the heritage institutions. Naturally, this also means curators' jobs would change: from handling museum content, they would now have to look through visitor-generated content to decide what should and should not be incorporated in the exhibits. Crowdsourcing is explored in more detail in Chaps. 7, 8, and 9 of this book.

Were a user to visit two different sites, where both had their collections semantically enhanced, it would be easy to create links between them using linked data technology. Thus, when visiting a heritage site (e.g., a castle), objects from the museum (e.g., tapestries) could be inserted (virtually) into the experience, providing additional information and contextualizing the objects in their original space. Some initiatives on outdoor activities are already being undertaken (Wecker et al. 2015), and we believe these have the potential to add to the museum experience. Chapter 14 adds more to this subject as well.

Another issue is how to tailor this experience to different users. The interests and visit dynamics may be different depending on the visitor's age, interests, or previous knowledge. User profiling and modeling techniques can be applied to elicit preferences and interests of a user. Beyond that, any integration with the world outside the museum walls would need to understand not only the location but also the context in which the information is to be presented. Just as there are many opportunities for presenting information, there is also the risk of doing so at an inappropriate moment. Chapters 15 and 16 also deal with personalization and tailoring of information.

A visitor might be struck with a question, be reminded of something or make a mental correlation while visiting an exhibit. He/she should be able to attach this question or comment to the display. He/she should also be able to interactively search for answers, either through the installations or through his/her own devices, and attach these answers to the exhibit at hand. Examples of these interactive applications are mostly extracted from North American and European institution. The application of such solutions in Brazil only lacks a small impulse: technology scientists working together with cultural institutions, two separate worlds, each one with its own vocabulary and problems, especially funding for joint projects. On the good news side, we can count on visitors: Brazil is always placed among the top when it comes to social network usage and mobile adoption. The crowd is ready to collaborate.

11.4 Final Considerations

Several proposals have been made in this chapter to create new forms of engagement with heritage institutions and museums. Previously defined strategies for research (Wecker 2014) provide guidelines for future engagement. However, we feel there are many possibilities still open, even considering the restrictions faced by developing countries like Brazil.

Thus, we would like to explore how museums could become more integrated into their public day-to-day reality and become more of an educational experience than an "archival" space. This involves defining useful technological platforms (cell phone usage is very high in the country, so it would be interesting to take advantage of that), finding new forms of interaction with the audience, leading them to question their knowledge and assumptions, and inspiring them to contribute.

Issues of context and information filtering become very important in this case: how could information overload be avoided when providing museum information? Moreover, how could personal and non-mediated art experience be protected? One of the respondents was very emphatic about this concern: "I am against the excessive use of technology in the museum, because the quality of the experience when you face a technology gadget is not different from what you have in daily life." The respondent meant that the museum should be a place where the contact with the art pieces should not be flattened to what we experience everyday with all the images we see. And continues: "I think the museum is the place to oppose the information overload we experience. It is the place to see without filters, without a screen as intermediary, because the principle of the museum experience is the contact with the primary source, the object that assumes multiple meanings depending on the context it is immersed in."[16]

On the other hand, engaging visitors is not always an easy task. Modern audiences seem to have a short attention span: younger visitors are easily distracted by calls from life outside the museum walls delivered by smartphones and other modern gadgets. Thus, it is important not only to provide the information virtually but also to connect it to its physical embodiment, which is experienced in a visit to the site. Thus, a partial visit to a site would allow the user to collect some information, but not all. Its correlation to the external world would, hopefully, entice the user to come back for another visit. "The use of technology is always welcome because it amplifies the institution's reach, in the scope of education, dissemination of the museum program and events and knowledge management. The audience is more present, is closer and responds positively to museum content."[17]

This chapter presented challenges and opportunities for technology adoption in the cultural scenery in Brazil with a dialectical approach: without listening to the individuals who deal with these limitations and strategies in the real world,

[16]Testimony given to the authors, January 2017.

[17]Testimony given to the authors, January 2017.

technology researchers tend to simplify the existing barriers to any proposed solution. Our main contributions can be summarized as follows:

(a) We have contextualized problems already presented more generally elsewhere to the particularities of a developing country like Brazil;
(b) We have discussed these with some managers and directors of Brazilian institutions, collecting their testimonies and comparing some findings in the literature with real situations;
(c) We have explored in more detail some of the challenges observed and some possibilities brought about by the adoption of new technologies; and
(d) We have proposed some actions that may contribute to reach a larger audience and to captivate the public, taking advantage of participation and interaction through the large use of social networks and other mechanisms available in virtual environments and new communication applications and equipment.

We believe that an interdisciplinary dialogue is necessary and that it can leverage the benefits of technology adoption. Besides, there is no doubt that museums should face the technology challenge to reach their contemporary public, but with a continuous effort to increase interest and participation. Researchers have noted there are special requirements in information systems development in developing countries (Mursu et al. 2000). This also translates to museums: being aware of and catering to these challenges allow designers to create better, self-sustaining solutions that will be applicable to a larger range of situations.

"Technology allows us to be in connection with the contemporary world and to keep up with its transitory aspects—this plural world that moves and organizes itself in fluxes, flows of information and images, where there is no truth anymore. The eye, used to lights, to numbers, to superficiality of data does not stop, does not linger. The pertinent use of technology can bring the visitor to the observation place. With the interest awaken in this way, the visitor becomes a spectator. And I am referring here to the spectator that physically enters the exhibition space. On the other hand, technology allows access to remote places, textual productions, virtual visits, simulations of diverse nature. A new *place* is created—that one inside a computer, a public display, a wall projection. Distance and time are reconfigured there. And this is certainly very good!"[18]

Acknowledgements We gratefully acknowledge Claudia Saldanha, Denise Grinspum, Tania Queiroz, and Wilton Guerra for their testimonies and interviews without which the present study could not have been completed. The authors were supported by Grants from CNPq and FAPERJ during this research. We also thank the kind reviews and comments from the book editors.

[18]Testimony given to the authors, January 2017.

References

Arjona M, Brinkley FK, Camargo Moro F, Ebaks RC, Espinoza M, Lacouture F, Lumbreras LG, Magalhaes A, Mostny G (1982) Museum development and cultural policy: aims, prospects and challenges. Museum 34(2):72–81 (UNESCO, Paris)

Berners-Lee T, Hendler J, Lassila, O (2001) The semantic web. Scientific American (May)

Bonacchi C, Bevan A, Pett D, Keinan-Schoonbaert A, Sparks R, Wexler J, Wilkin N (2014) Crowd-sourced archaeological research: the MicroPasts project. Archaeol Int, 17:61–68

Hallinan ME (2014) Illuminating masterpieces: the Martin museum of art collections crowdsourcing project, Baylor University https://baylor-ir.tdl.org/baylor-ir/handle/2104/9069. Accessed 15 Jan 2017

Hawkey R (2009) Learning with digital technologies in museums, science centers and galleries. J Distance Educ 3:14

Henry D, Brown E (2012) Using an RDF data pipeline to implement cross-collection search. Museums and the web 2012, San Diego, CA

Johnson L, Adams Becker S, Estrada V, Freeman A (2015) NMC horizon report: 2015 museum edition. The New Media Consortium, Austin

Mursu A, Soriyan HA, Olufokuninbi K, Korpela M (2000) Information systems development in a developing country: theoretical analysis of special requirements in Nigeria and Africa. In: Proceedings of the 33rd Hawaii international conference on system sciences (HICSS), IEEE

Oomen J, Aroyo L (2011) Crowdsourcing in the cultural heritage domain: opportunities and challenges. In: Proceedings of the 5th international conference on communities and technologies, Brisbane, Australia, June 2011. ACM, pp 138–149

Pitarque SD, Guardia BR (1982) Museum financing: taking up the challenge. Museum 34(2) (UNESCO, Paris)

Wecker AJ (2014) Personalized cultural heritage experience outside the museum: connecting the museum experience to the outside world. In: International conference on user modeling, adaptation, and personalization, pp 496–501

Wecker AJ, Kuflik T, Stock O (2015) AMuse–an initial plan to associate museum visits to outdoor cultural heritage activities. In: Proceedings of the 8th international conference on personalized access to cultural heritage, vol 1352. CEUR-WS, pp 14–18

Author Biographies

Leticia Verona is a Master's degree student in Information Systems at PPGI-UFRJ and an entrepreneur. Her company is well known for developing technology solutions for Brazilian museums, individual artists and cultural institutions for almost two decades. Her research interests includes how pervasive technology impact user experience during museum visits and afterwards and how museum visitor's attention can be positively focused.

Adriana S. Vivacqua is a professor at the Computer Science Department at the Federal University of Rio de Janeiro. Her main area of interest is context-sensitive technology, and she has supervised students at the graduate and undergraduate levels and written extensively on the subject. She currently holds a Young Researcher Award from FAPERJ and a Productivity Award from CNPq.

Maria Luiza M. Campos is a professor at the Computer Science Department at the Federal University of Rio de Janeiro, with more than 30 years of experience in data and information management. Her main research interests are conceptual modeling and information integration, specially focusing on ontologies and metadata based strategies applied to the semantic web and the e-government and e-Science domains. She has previously worked as a data administrator at the Brazilian Statistical Agency (IBGE) and has, for many years, been engaged in open data initiatives in Brazil.

Chapter 12
Using Mobile Technologies to Capture the Visitor Experience

Marco C. Rozendaal, Arnold P. O. S. Vermeeren and Diana C. Issidorides

Abstract Museums give much consideration to how visitors experience their exhibits. Mobile technologies, such as apps on mobile phones and tablets can capture the visitor experience in an automated, on-the-spot manner. Two apps were designed and used to capture visitors' experiences of interactive exhibits at a science museum. Based on our observations, we discuss (a) the appeal of the technology, (b) the integration of this technology in the overall museum visit and (c) the processing of the collected experience data. Based on our observations, we recommend that museums and science centres critically evaluate the above-mentioned points when considering implementing mobile technologies to capture the visitor experience. Furthermore, we advise institutions to approach mobile technologies as *product service systems* and take into account the infrastructure that is required to make mobile technologies work.

12.1 Introduction

Rather than merely displaying artefacts as objects, museums nowadays tell stories and provide audiences with a rich historical, cultural and scientific context to their artefacts. Furthermore, museums—and science centres in particular—often rely on interactivity as a means to tell these stories in an engaging and playful manner. When institutions instal interactive exhibits in their museums and science centres, how can these institutions assess whether the exhibits are well received by the public and whether the interactive exhibits bring across the visitor experience they

---

M. C. Rozendaal · A. P. O. S. Vermeeren (✉)
TU Delft - Industrial Design Engineering, Landbergstraat 15, 2628 CE Delft, The Netherlands
e-mail: a.p.o.s.vermeeren@tudelft.nl

M. C. Rozendaal
e-mail: m.c.rozendaal@tudelft.nl

D. C. Issidorides
NEMO Science Museum, P.O. Box 421, 1000 AK Amsterdam, The Netherlands

A. Vermeeren et al. (eds.), *Museum Experience Design*, Springer Series on Cultural Computing, https://doi.org/10.1007/978-3-319-58550-5_12

were designed for? Which means of measurement and quality control can be implemented, and how can mobile technologies be utilised towards this purpose?

In this chapter, we discuss how mobile technologies can be applied to capture visitor experiences with interactive exhibits, as well as how institutions can learn from this knowledge. We base our findings on two studies conducted at NEMO Science Museum in Amsterdam, in which we used two apps to capture visitor experiences in two different ways. With the first app, called the *photo*-app, visitors could take pictures of interesting moments while experiencing the exhibits and could then report their experiences using text. With the second app, called the *mirror*-app, visitors were asked to match their experiences of exhibits with a set of predefined experiences that were visualised in the app using animations (i.e. reporting the extent to which a visualised experience mirrored the visitor's experience).

We will first discuss the concept of experience, as well as issues of how to capture visitor experiences and of using mobile technologies in doing so. We then introduce NEMO Science Museum and the two mobile apps in more detail: how they are used and what data they provide. Subsequently, we discuss the findings of the exploratory field studies we conducted in the science museum, and reflect on critical issues in developing and implementing mobile technologies in a museum setting. Specifically, we reflect on the *appeal* of the technology, the *integration* of this technology in the overall museum visit and the *processing* of the resulting experience data. The chapter concludes by providing *recommendations* for museum institutions on how to best implement mobile technologies for assessing visitor experiences.

12.1.1 Experiences

What exactly do we mean by *experience* and how does this relate to the experience of interactive exhibits? In layman's terms, experiences are the things we see, feel and think about; the things we are consciously aware of and that are worthwhile mentioning in either positive or negative terms. In this section, we present some of the theories and models of experience as they are applied in the fields of industrial design, interaction design and heritage studies.

In their work on product experience, Hekkert and Schifferstein (2008) looked into how a design generates an experience. For them, experiences arise from the interaction between a person and a product. In trying to pinpoint the specific factors that influence the experience of an interaction, Locher et al. (2010) found that factors such as personality traits, skills and personal values play a role, as well as the embodiment of a design and the circumstances in which a design is used.

In the field of industrial design, Desmet and Hekkert (2007) have broken down the complexity of subjective experiences into three levels. The first level involves experiences stemming from our direct sensory impressions of the environment and is labelled *aesthetic experience*. The second, called *experience of meaning*, involves interpretations of our direct sensory impressions. The third involves emotional reactions to our environment and is labelled *emotional experience*. When we interact with artefacts, these levels are at work simultaneously; we have an aesthetic impression of a design, we interpret it in terms of its use and cultural significance, and a design elicits emotions in us based on our needs and concerns.

To illustrate the various levels of experience described above, we reflect on one of the interactive exhibits at NEMO Science Museum named 'Mirror Drawing' (Fig. 12.1, left-hand side). In this exhibit, visitors are invited to move a pencil to trace the diagram of a star while looking at their hand as it is reflected in a mirror. The visual feedback of the actions while drawing is mirrored and confronts us with our dependence on visual feedback in motor control. The aesthetic experience of this installation is formed by the formal sensory qualities of the exhibit: its pink colour, glossiness and rounded surfaces. The experience of meaning relates to the associations triggered by the exhibit; for instance, 'fairy tales' 'and 'magic mirror'. The emotional experience relates to, for example, the challenging task of trying to trace the star with a pen only via the star's reflection in the mirror, or the good or bad memories one may have about 'fairy tales' or 'magic'.

In the field of interaction design, the term *user* experience is used. Based on a large survey among experts in the field of user experience design and research, Law et al. (2009) found that although it proved to be difficult for these experts to agree on a shared definition of user experience, they agreed on the fact that user experiences are highly *context-dependent*, *subjective* and *dynamic*. *Context* was found to refer to, for example, the social, physical and activity context of a user.

Fig. 12.1 Mirror Drawing: installation at the NEMO Science Museum. © NEMO Science

User experience is considered *subjective* because the way in which something is experienced is highly dependent on characteristics of the individual who experiences it. It is seen as *dynamic* because experiences continuously change during an interaction.

Within the field of heritage, Pekarik et al. (2014) proposed an experience approach for exhibit design called IPOP that describes the different ways visitors can be attracted to exhibits. The name IPOP stands for Ideas (conceptual, abstract thinking), People (emotional connections), Object(s) (visual language and aesthetics) and Physical (somatic sensations). According to the model, different people have different preferences among these (which is in line with Law et al.'s finding that user experiences are seen as very subjective, or individually different).

Finally, in much of the literature on experience design, human needs are addressed in relation to what makes experiences pleasant and meaningful. For example, Hassenzahl (2010) states that the relation between actions and needs (or motives, values) is believed to colour experiences and to set their emotional tone. According to Hassenzahl (2010), 'understanding actions in terms of motives fulfilled is crucial to an experiential approach to design' (p. 45). He argues that needs categories can provide categories of experiences, which can be used to describe and classify many experiences with interactive products. For capturing experiences, this can be advantageous because the concept of needs as categories is grounded in sound and extensive psychological research (Hassenzahl 2010).

In sum, for assessing experiences, it is important to realise that experiencing something relies on interacting with it, that the way something is experienced is very context-dependent, subjective and dynamic, and that categories of human needs can be used for categorising pleasurable and meaningful experiences.

12.1.2 Capturing Visitor Experiences

How do museums and science centres assess visitor experience and how do institutions apply this information in their practice? As Beghetto (2014) mentions, the way exhibits are intended to be experienced is often not the same as they are actually experienced by the public. Thus, for museums and science centres, it is useful to gain insights into the *actual* visitor experience in order to improve their exhibits.

Different techniques are available to measure visitor experiences in museums and science centres. Sterry and Beaumont (2006) provide an overview of methods for studying families in art museums from both experimental and naturalistic approaches. Some of the techniques she mentions are surveys, focus groups, observations and interviews. An example of an experimental technique is the 'servqual' method (Nowacki 2005), while a naturalistic technique is presented by Coffee (2007).

In the field of experience design and research, Vermeeren et al. (2010) provided an overview of user experience evaluation methods and characterised the many methods that they found based on various features, one of which is *period of experience*. They highlight that in assessing experiences one can focus on conducting the assessment *before* actual interactions (e.g. noticing something before using it, anticipations of experiences), *while* interacting (as experiences are considered to be dynamic, see before), *immediately after* an interaction or *after having used something multiple times*. Another characteristic they highlight is the *location* where the assessment takes place (e.g. lab, field or online). Increasingly, mobile technologies can be and are being used for assessing experiences by having users self-report about their experiences at the location where the experience happens, at moments close to the actual moment of experiencing, thus potentially improving the validity of measurements.

In many cases, devices such as smartphones are used for sampling experiences by asking users to self-report their experiences. For example, Intille et al. (2003) explored the use of experience sampling on smart devices that allow different experience assessment strategies (e.g. multiple choice and multiple response questions). As mobile devices usually offer a wide range of functionalities, self-reports are often complemented by additional data for better understanding what was experienced. For example, in Ståhl et al.'s (2009) Affective Diary, measurements from body sensors and mobile media complement the self-reports. Li et al. (2013) developed an app for assessing emotional experiences of individuals in festival crowds. In their study, an app prompted festival visitors about the feeling they had at that time. The data were then related to their location at the festival. Based on this, crowd maps could be constructed that said something about the physical crowd dynamics as well as about experiences within the crowd.

12.2 Field Studies at NEMO Science Museum

NEMO Science Museum—ranked fifth on the list of best visited Dutch museums in 2015—lies in Amsterdam's harbour district and welcomes more than 500.000 visitors a year. Renowned architect Renzo Piano designed the green copper-clad building that looks like a ship rising from the waters above Amsterdam's IJ tunnel (Figs. 12.2 and 12.3). A wide range of fascinating topics are brought to life, from natural sciences and social sciences to neurosciences.

NEMO Science Museum consists of five floors full of exhibits that invite visitors of all ages to explore *hands-on* and *brains-on* the wondrous world of science and technology, to become tinkerers in different workshops, and even to become subjects in real scientific experiments. Key ingredients of NEMO's mission are to nurture curiosity, critical thinking and a questioning mind. To this end, NEMO has a strong focus on interactivity (for example, see Figs. 12.1 and 12.3).

One of NEMO's innovative research programmes is *Science Live*, which opens up the museum floor to scientific research with NEMO visitors participating as experimental subjects. NEMO Science Museum feels that science centres and museums should not only be about displaying science but also about encouraging

Fig. 12.2 The building of NEMO Science Museum. Designed by Renzo Piano. Picture by DigiDaan © NEMO Science Museum

Fig. 12.3 Impression of an exhibit floor at NEMO Science Museum. Picture by DigiDaan © NEMO Science Museum

its visitors to be part of the scientific process itself, enabling visitors, young and old, to experience how scientific knowledge is acquired and how the scientific method works. We explored the use of two apps for collecting visitor experiences in the NEMO Science Museum, as part of the Science Live programme.

12.2.1 Photo-App Field Study

In the photo-app field study, an app was used to evaluate a total of 12 interactive exhibits. The photo-app was installed on a small handheld device that visitors could take along with them while walking through NEMO Science Museum. The procedure for reporting their experiences via the app involved several steps: visitors first took a picture of the activity they were involved in at the exhibit, were then asked to type in a keyword that expressed the feeling they had during the activity, and were then prompted to use a visual ring for highlighting in the picture the area which produced this feeling. Moreover, visitors were asked to describe their engagement using four word pairs: *pleasant* versus *unpleasant*, *mind* versus *body*, *doing* versus *undergoing* and *alone* versus *together*. The process ended by rating the activity on a five-point scale according to how motivating they found it. The app could be used five times in a row in order to obtain feedback on a *series of experiences* while interacting with an exhibit. Figure 12.4 provides a visual overview of the reporting process.

A total of 255 visitors participated in this field study. Participants included a younger group of range 6–19 years (mean age 11, standard deviation 1.3) and an older group between the ages of 20 and 74 (mean age 43, SD 9.5). Visitors mostly arrived in groups. One group member was asked to be a participant in our study. Researchers assigned participants to a specific interactive exhibit and asked them to report on their experience five times while interacting with that exhibit. Participants could choose these moments freely.

Examples of the result of the capturing process are shown in Fig. 12.5. As can be seen, the data captured from a participant included a series of images of an interactive exhibit. These pictures are diverse: showing the exhibit as a whole or showing only a detail; showing the app user in action or showing someone else engaged with the exhibit. As an overlay on the image, a ring is placed that further highlights one's area of interest. Keywords entered by participants were describing their experience of the exhibit. These keywords ranged from affective comments to more factual ones. Below that, labels were placed that describe the engagement, as a result of how the four switches were set. For example, for the top-left photo, the engagement was described as 'unpleasant-mind-doing-alone'. At the bottom, a number is shown indicating the participant's level of motivation while engaging with the exhibit.

By combining all the experience keywords that participants expressed for an exhibit, a *word cloud* could be constructed that provided a visual overview: the higher the frequency of a word as compared to the other words, the larger the size of

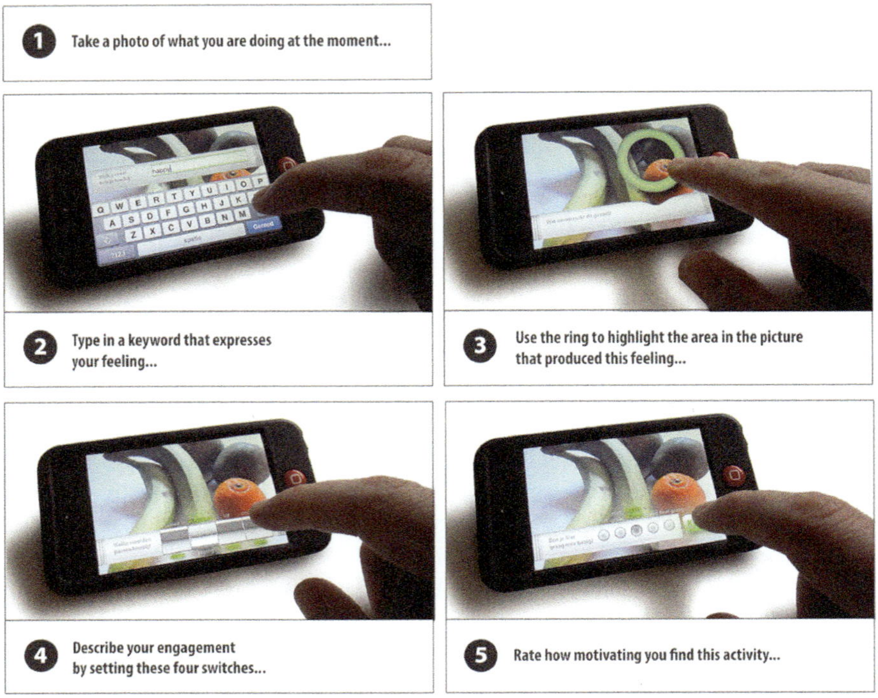

Fig. 12.4 Storyboard explaining the experience-capturing process of the photo-app

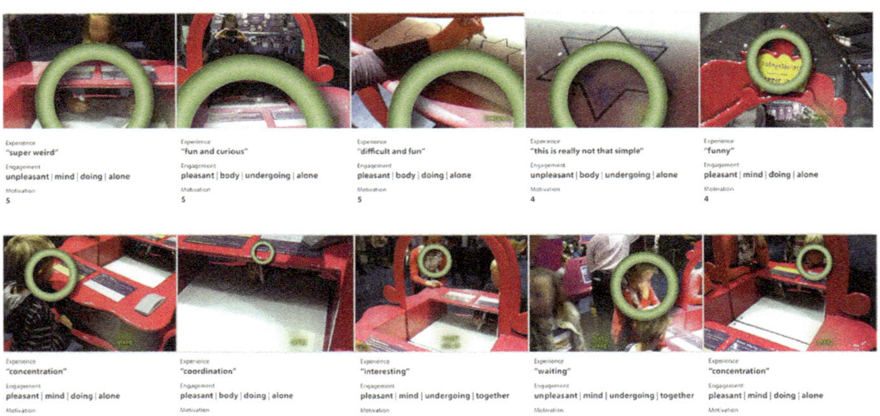

Fig. 12.5 Presentation of the combined output gathered by the photo-app for two participants

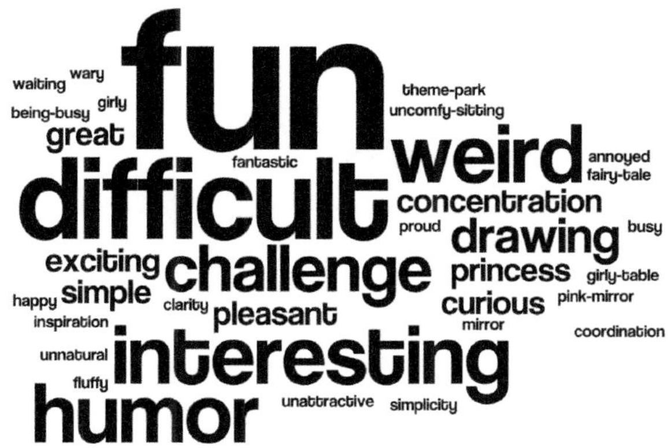

Fig. 12.6 Word cloud presentation of the keywords expressed by participants, based on 77 entries. The higher the frequency of a word as compared to the other words, the larger the size of that word in the word cloud. Translated from expressions in Dutch

that word in the word cloud (Fig. 12.6). The experience keywords for this study were categorised, considering spelling errors and different ways the same concept could be phrased in the simplest form. For example, the category 'Weird' included keywords like 'weird', 'weird feeling', 'super weird' and 'freaky'. These word clouds provide an intuitive description of how the interactive exhibit was experienced. One of the exhibits that visitors reported on was 'Mirror Drawing' (see Fig. 12.1). As indicated by the size of the words in this specific word cloud, many participants considered the exhibit to be about 'drawing' and found it enjoyable (see keywords 'fun', 'interesting' and 'humoristic'), but also 'weird' and 'difficult'.

The engagement labels can be summarised for each interactive exhibit. Figure 12.7 shows the engagement profiles of the 12 exhibits, which are constructed based on how participants set the engagement switches. The position on the vertical axis of the graph shows the *ratio between two positions of a switch*. When one position of a switch was chosen more often, its position on the vertical axis moves up or down depending on the direction the switch is set to. When both positions of the switch were selected equally often, its score moves towards the middle of the vertical axis (as indicated in the graph by the dotted line). Results are shown for each of the four switches separately (this is indicated by different colours in the graph). When looking at 'Mirror Drawing', results showed that participants felt *pleasantly* and *actively* engaged and that they were engaging *alone* and with their *minds*.

The rich data captured by the photo-app allow researchers to explore visitors' experiences of the exhibits in several different ways. For example, by combining the images and highlights with the experience keywords, a map can be created as shown in Fig. 12.8. Visitor experience can thus be mapped onto specific aspects of the exhibit, and thus reveal how different features stand out. The engagement mode switches can be used as additional filters. In order, for example, to selectively show experiences that relate to *social interaction* only, or to filter out the *negative experiences*, etc.

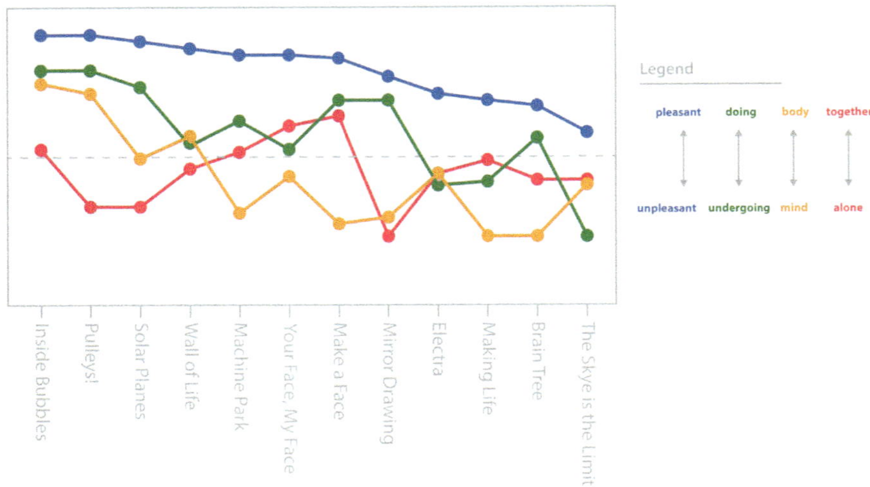

Fig. 12.7 Graph representing the 'engagement profile' of exhibits along four dimensions: pleasant/unpleasant, doing/undergoing, body/mind and together/alone

Fig. 12.8 Impression of an experience map of an interactive exhibit (Mirror Drawing) based on the captured data of the photo-app by combining keywords and highlight data

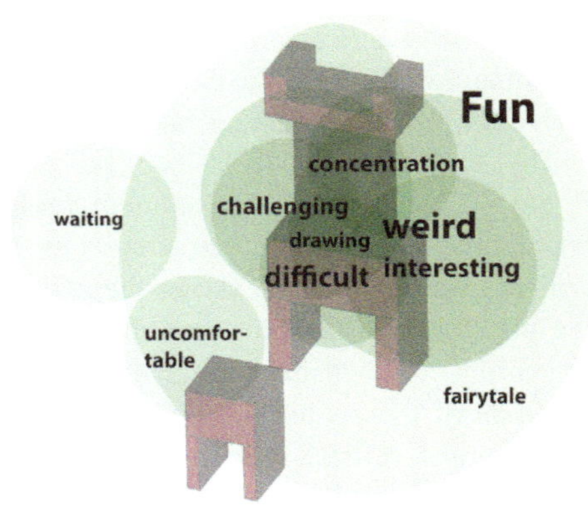

12.2.2 Mirror-App Field Study

In the mirror-app field study, a different app was used to evaluate 12 interactive exhibits. These exhibits were the same as the ones evaluated by the photo-app field study. The mirror-app was installed on a tablet computer, thus a somewhat larger device compared to the handheld device used for the photo-app. With the mirror-app, visitors could match their experience of an exhibit with the experiences depicted by an animated virtual puppet. The starting point and inspiration for developing the mirror-app was that designers of installations may have designed the installation with specific target experiences in mind. The app then was intended to serve as a tool to measure the extent to which the targeted experiences have been realised. To this end, the app had many puppet animations to choose from, each expressing a different experience. For example, when experiencing an exhibit as socially pleasurable, a visitor could select the puppet that displays socially pleasurable behaviour. The focus in the animations was on how the puppet interacts and what it feels like while interacting, *without using words*.

In total, 24 animations were created that communicated different experiences, relying solely on the puppet's movements and non-verbal vocal sounds (i.e. grunts, cries, laughter, etc.). The animations took about 3 seconds each and were looped, i.e. the animation ended where it started, thus allowing a never-ending cycle. Animations were grouped in six themes, inspired by psychological needs theory (Deci and Ryan 2000; Sheldon et al. 2001), and each theme consisted of four animations. For the theme 'physical effort', for example, the animations could be positioned in a quadrant involving *high* or *low* level of physical effort and be interpreted in a *positive* or a *negative* sense. Thus, each animation in the theme 'physical effort' had a specific interaction experience associated with it, namely, either 'relaxing' (*low-pos*), or 'apathetic' (*low-neg*), or 'energetic' (*high-pos*) or 'exhausting' (*high-neg*). A key requirement for developing the animations was that they had to express the four versions of a need in an abstracted way, only showing a puppet and an abstract object, so that they could be easily related to all kinds of different situations. For designing the animations, we explored the desired bodily behaviour of the depicted puppet, by first role playing the experiences ourselves, using a big cardboard box as an object, while making sounds that we felt fitted the experience. The role plays were video-recorded, after which requirements for the animated behaviour and sounds were described and forwarded to the agencies that developed the app. A visual style was proposed to the design agency, and several iterations of styles, animations and sounds were discussed and evaluated until the final version was decided upon. See Fig. 12.9 for an overview of all the themes used in the mirror-app.

The mirror-app was used in the following manner. Participants were asked to report their experience by using the app after they had interacted with an exhibit. In the app, all themes were presented to the participants in random order. The four animations within a theme could be selected by touching one of the four corners on the tablet screen. This would then play the corresponding animation. Therefore, participants could explore the four animations of a theme by moving towards each of the corners until they had identified the animation that best mirrored their own experience. Furthermore, touching the arrows on the left or right side allowed participants to move through the different themes, and numbers 1–6 on top of the screen allowed them to go directly to one of the themes they wished to report on. Headphones were used with the app to allow participants to better hear the sounds and to concentrate on the animations. Figure 12.10 provides a visual overview of the user interface.

A total of 122 visitors of the science museum used the mirror-app and shared their experiences of the exhibits. The same 12 interactive exhibits as in the photo-app field study were chosen for this study. Participants were children between 6 and 13 years of age (mean age 9, standard deviation 1.6). Before going

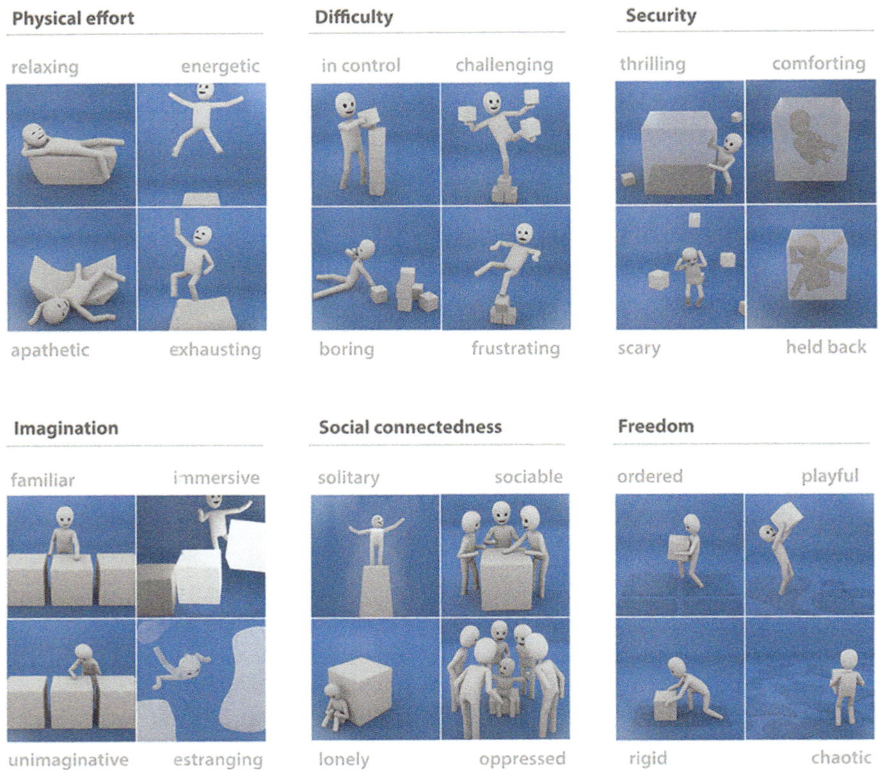

Fig. 12.9 Figure showing 24 experiences for six themes for a high or low level of a different theme (left and right side of a quadrant) and positive or negative affect (top and bottom side of a quadrant)

out to assess the exhibits, they were instructed about the use of the app, going through it once. We asked them to report their experience after they had familiarised themselves with an installation. This took them about 5–10 min. Similar to the photo-app field study, visitors came in groups. Thus, a participant experienced the exhibits in pairs or in small groups. One child in the group was asked to use the app. While using the app, the researchers asked the children to motivate their choices in order to examine their matching strategies (the reasoning for why they linked specific animations to their experiences of the exhibit). This was done to learn about the use and design of the app itself, rather than for learning about the installations.

The data collected by the app consist of frequency data, i.e. the number of times specific animations were chosen. The data can be presented in graphs to show how an interactive exhibit scores across the six themes. Figure 12.11 shows the data collected for 'Mirror Drawing'. The frequency data are presented in quadrants in which the positive experiences are green and the negative ones are red. The larger the quadrant, the more that animation was chosen compared to the other ones.

Fig. 12.10 Visual overview of the mirror-app user interface

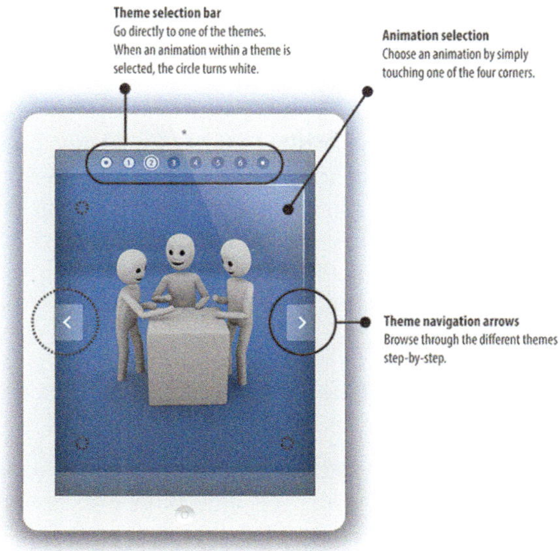

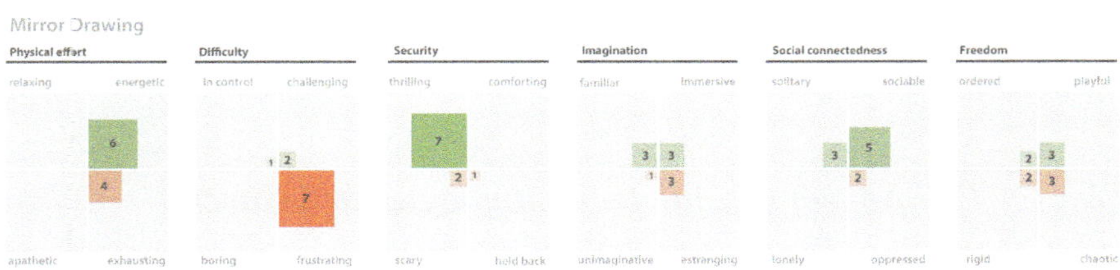

Fig. 12.11 Data visualisation of the results for 'Mirror Drawing' on six experience themes, based on data gathered from 10 participants

For example, when looking at the data gathered for 'Mirror Drawing', with respect to difficulty, this was rated as difficult in a negative sense (i.e. 'frustrating'). As for security, this was low but positive (i.e. 'thrilling'). With respect to physical effort, this was rated as high with about an equal division between positive and negative affect ('energetic' and 'exhausting', respectively). Apparently, tracing the star via its reflection in a mirror was a very difficult task to perform; nevertheless, it brought participants in a thrilling and energetic state. Visualisations like this can also be used to at the same time visualise the targeted experiences (e.g. in the form of outlined boxes) as well as the reported experiences for comparison purposes.

In sum, two apps have been designed for allowing people to self-report their experiences on location, during or immediately after an experience. The photo-app was developed mainly as a tool to gain a detailed and rich understanding of an interactive experience (through free text and 'switches'), also relating the experience to elements of the installation that had contributed to the experience (through the pictures and rings). Insights from using the photo-app are mainly for determining how to improve a specific experience (as in formative evaluations; e.g. see Roto et al. 2015), rather than for objectively determining whether a targeted experience has been achieved (as in summative evaluation). The mirror-app focuses on the latter. The measured data from the mirror-app are less rich, but can be used to quantify the extent to which a targeted experience has been achieved. It does so by disentangling the experience into various predefined experiential aspects and asking participants to score those.

12.3 Observations and Implications for Design

Based on the two conceptually different app designs and the way they were applied in NEMO, we can discuss how mobile technologies can be applied to capture visitor experiences. Our reflections concern (a) the *appeal* of the mobile technology to visitors, (b) the *integration* of the mobile technology in the overall visitor experience and (c) the *processing* of the mobile technology data. Based on our studies, we see these three aspects as critical for effectively implementing mobile technologies for assessing visitor experiences in museum settings.

12.3.1 The Appeal of Mobile Technologies to Visitors

We found that it is critical to design the mobile technology in a way that motivates visitors to share their experiences during their museum visit. Mobile technologies such as smartphones and tablet computers are commonplace nowadays; so many people are familiar with them and have no problem using them. However, design quality can be decisive for the extent to which visitors will be motivated to use these mobile technologies during their visit. The app design is critical for the aesthetic appreciation and usability of computing devices (Hassenzahl 2004).

During our field studies, we noticed that mobile technologies had a strong appeal to visitors, especially children. The user interfaces of both apps were designed to be intuitive, and visitors (young and old) learned to use the apps quickly. The functionality of the apps was based on moving through the questions step by step via simple swiping actions. Moreover, the emphasis was given to the appearance of the user interface: a sleek metallic look for the photo-app and a friendly white-blue look for the mirror-app. Furthermore, user interfaces that incorporated sound in their design have been shown to increase usability as well as the level of immersion one experiences during use (Nees and Walker 2009).

12.3.2 *Integrating the Use of Mobile Technologies in the Overall Visitor Experience*

We found that it is important that the mobile technology blends in with the overall visitor experience in the museum. We will reflect on the implementation of mobile technology with groups of visitors and the interplay between experiencing an interactive exhibit and reporting on that experience through mobile technology.

12.3.2.1 Social Use of Mobile Technology

Our studies in the science museum indicate that mobile technologies should be designed in such a way that their use does not disrupt the social interactions in a group. When an app is given to one of the people in a group, it soon becomes the focus of everyone in the group–*the mobile technology becomes shared.* We observed a mother helping her child type keywords, a child asking his father to take a picture of him with the interactive exhibit, but we also observed the impatience of people when the reporting process took too much time or when the apps could not be shared readily enough. In terms of the actual experience assessment, we observed people negotiating with each other, or discussing their views about an interactive exhibit.

The photo-app could be shared more easily than the mirror-app. The photo-app was smaller in size and did not make use of headphones and could, therefore, be more easily passed around in the group. Further, reporting with the photo-app could be easily done standing up while the mirror-app required one to sit down, hereby physically restricting one's freedom of movement. Moreover, the headphones isolated a person from environmental sounds and conversations. These observations clearly indicate a preference for the photo-app compared to the mirror-app concerning sharing.

12.3.2.2 Balancing the Interplay Between Experiencing an Interactive Exhibit and Reporting on that Experience

When developing experience-capturing techniques in the field, care should be given to ensure that the technique provides a *reflection time-out*, yet does not *distract people too much* from engaging with the interactive exhibits. When the required response is too fleeting, visitors might not take the time to take a step back to reflect on what was most important to them in the experience. When using the tool asks too much attention by itself, the experience of the tool dominates the experience of the interactive exhibit, and results might be skewed. Both apps imposed new experiences while interacting with an exhibit, albeit in different ways. With the photo-app, visitors were asked to *create content* (i.e. take a picture, provide a verbal response, etc.), while the mirror-app involved a *matching task*. In this respect, the mirror-app required less *cognitive effort* than the photo-app. However, we discovered that the long attention span required by the latter was difficult to maintain in a busy environment like NEMO, with the result that some visitors become annoyed, which may therefore have led to less accurate responses.

Another factor is the *media richness* of the mobile technology. Since the mirror-app involves animation with sound, it is more of a sensory experience compared to the photo-app. Rich media, in terms of sensory vividness, have the power to captivate (Steuer 1992). This was evident in the children liking and focusing on the animations so much that they forgot about the aim of the assessment. Although this made the app highly motivating to use, the data captured can be less valid as a result of this, as the experience of the app might have overshadowed the experience of the exhibit.

Furthermore, the *number of interruptions* can affect the balance between visitor engagement with the interactive exhibit, on the one hand, and the distraction factor due to the reflection time-out, on the other hand. The photo-app required participants to report on their experience five times in a row. This can be considered more intrusive, compared to only one report at the end of an interactive experience, as required by the mirror-app.

12.3.3 Processing the Collected Data

Our studies show that it is critical to obtain experience data in a way that is not only *insightful in general but also caters to the specific needs of the institution*. Do museums and science centres want to know about visitor experience for benchmarking or do they want to gain in-depth insights into how the interactive exhibits are experienced?

The two apps provided data about the visitor experience in different ways. The photo-app collected *qualitative* data (photos with highlights and keywords) as well as *quantitative* data (engagement mode and motivation scale). The mirror-app collected *quantitative* data only (number of times animations were selected). Assessing the visitor experience to gain *insight into visitors' motivations* favours a qualitative data approach, in which visitors (creatively) share their experience via rich media. This technique allows one to explore the individual experiences of visitors in detail. Assessing the visitor experience for *benchmarking* favours a quantitative approach, since different exhibits can then be easily compared on their performance using a set of predefined criteria. Due to their complexity, qualitative data are more difficult to use for benchmarking purposes.

When asking visitors to report on their experience of exhibits by typing in keywords (as with the photo-app) or by selecting animations (as with the mirror-app), they responded differently. In both studies, we observed many types of responses, ranging from mentioning *concrete* aspects of the experience, the *activity* one was engaged in, the *emotions* felt, the *ambience* of the experience, to a *judgment* of the experience. This variety was considered a strength in the photo-app since these descriptions together provided a holistic representation of the experience (as depicted in the word clouds). However, for the mirror-app, the different interpretations of the shown animations were problematic since this assessment technique assumed a common understanding of them.

Developments in data analysis techniques provide opportunities for processing both qualitative and quantitative data. Examples are analytical tools such as text sentiment and opinion analysers (Pang and Lee 2008). Such techniques allow keywords given by visitors to be monitored in real time, hereby automatically assessing the *affective tone* of an exhibit or overall museum setting. Another exciting development is 'photosynth' by Microsoft. With this technique, the researchers demonstrated how the 'Notre Dame' in Paris, France can be automatically constructed as a virtual model based upon the numerous pictures taken by tourists and uploaded on the Internet, a technique explained in detail by Snavely et al. (2008). Such technologies allow data mining of large amounts of user-generated content (i.e. texts and photos) and provide new opportunities for assessing the visitor experience in the future.

12.4 Recommendations for Museum Institutions

The insights gained through the design and evaluation of the photo-app and mirror-app led to several recommendations regarding the design and implementation of mobile technologies for capturing visitor experience in museums and science centres. After first summarising our findings, we will elaborate on mobile technologies as *product service systems*. Recommendations will be given on different levels of implementation.

In designing mobile technologies, the *appeal* of the technology is important in order to stimulate visitors to share their experiences. We recommend that emphasis be given to the design in terms of *usability* and *aesthetics*: mobile technologies should be intuitive in use, and their aesthetics should be appealing to the museum's audience. Furthermore, since the mobile technology may be *used in groups*, it should enable sharing. We recommend keeping the mobile technology compact, so that it can be *passed around* in the group, allowing freedom of movement, and so that it does not create a *sensory disconnection* from group members, something that the use of headphones can create. For the mobile technology not to disrupt the museum visit, we recommend to keep the capturing process *simple*, to keep the experience provided by the mobile technology *within boundaries* so that it does not overshadow the experiences that are provided by the exhibits proper, and to *limit* the number of interruptions to a minimum. In terms of data collection and processing, there should be a match between the needs of the institution and the type of data that are collected by the mobile technology. In general, collecting visitor insight favours a qualitative data approach whereas benchmarking favours a quantitative one.

For museums, it is important to realise that the two mobile technologies that we have designed should not be considered as stand-alone products, but rather as *product service systems*. Product service systems are aggregations of products and services organised around a specific functionality (Baines et al. 2007). With respect to the mobile technologies used in the current study, the app (as explained in detail in this chapter) is just one element of this system. Setting up this complete system requires an *infrastructure*, *database* and *visualisation software*. For example, a communication infrastructure required Wi-Fi hotspots to be installed in the museum floors for data to come through. A database had to be installed to store the collected data with the appropriate means for data protection. Specific consideration needs to be given to how the collected data can be meaningfully presented to museum institutions, so that they can make sense of it. Issues such as these may easily be overlooked by museums, but they are critical to the actual implementation and success of the product service system.

12.5 Conclusions

In this chapter, we presented two experience assessment apps that were used to evaluate 12 interactive exhibits at NEMO Science Museum. We discussed the application of the two apps with respect to the *appeal* of the mobile technology to visitors, the *integration* of the mobile technology in the overall visitor experience and the *processing* of the collected visitor data. Based on our observations, we recommend that museums and science centres critically evaluate the above-mentioned points when considering implementing mobile technologies to capture the visitor experience. Furthermore, we advise institutions to approach mobile technologies as *product service systems* and take into account the infrastructure that is required to make mobile technologies work.

Acknowledgements This research was part of *Science Live*, the innovative research programme of NEMO Science Museum that enables scientists to carry out real, publishable, peer-reviewed research using NEMO visitors as volunteers. This study has further been made possible by the Dutch Creative Industries and Scientific Program (CRISP). The authors would further like to thank: Alt-N, Shapers and KlevR Audio Design in producing the apps, and many thanks go to the Industrial Design students that have helped in conducting both experiments.

References

Baines TS, Lightfoot HW, Evans S, Neely A, Greenough R, Peppard J, Wilson H (2007) State-of-the-art in product-service systems. In: Proc Inst Mech Eng Part B J Eng Manuf 221 (10):1543–1552. https://doi.org/10.1243/09544054JEM858

Beghetto RA (2014) The exhibit as planned versus the exhibit as experienced. Curator Mus J 57(1):1–4. https://doi.org/10.1111/cura.12047

Coffee K (2007) Audience research and the museum experience as social practice. Mus Manag Curatorship 22(4):377–389. https://doi.org/10.1080/09647770701757732

Deci EL, Ryan RM (2000) The "what" and "why" of goal pursuits: Human needs and the self-determination of behavior. Psychol Inq 11(4):227–268

Desmet PM, Hekkert P (2007) Framework of product experience. Int J Des 1(1):57–66

Hassenzahl M (2004) The interplay of beauty, goodness, and usability in interactive products. Hum Comput Interact 19(4):319–349. https://doi.org/10.1207/s15327051hci1904_2

Hassenzahl M (2010) Experience design: technology for all the right reasons. Morgan and Claypool. https://doi.org/10.2200/S00261ED1V01Y201003HCI008

Hekkert P, Schifferstein HNJ (2008) Introducing Product Experience. In: Schifferstein H, Hekkert P (eds) Product experience. Elsevier Press, Amsterdam, the Netherlands, pp 1–8

Intille SS, Rondoni J, Kukla C, Ancona I, Bao L (2003) A context-aware experience sampling tool. In: CHI'03 extended abstracts on Human factors in computing systems. ACM, Ft. Lauderdale, Florida, USA, pp 972–973

Law EL-C, Roto V, Vermeeren APOS, Kort J, Hassenzahl M (2009) Understanding, scoping and defining user experience: a survey approach. In Proceedings of CHI 2009, the 27th annual CHI conference on human factors in computing systems. ACM, New York

Li J, Erkin Z, de Ridder H, Vermeeren A (2013) A field study on real-time self-reported emotions in crowds. In: Proceedings of the ICT open. Eindhoven, The Netherlands, pp 80–84

Locher P, Overbeeke K, Wensveen S (2010) Aesthetic interaction: a framework. Des Issues 26(2):70–79

Nees MA, Walker BN (2009) Auditory interfaces and sonification. In: Stephanidis C (ed) The universal access handbook. CRC Press, Boca Raton, Florida, USA, pp 507–521

Nowacki MM (2005) Evaluating a museum as a tourist product using the servqual method. Mus Manag Curatorship 20(3):235–250

Pang B, Lee L (2008) Opinion mining and sentiment analysis. Found Trends Inf Retr 2(1–2): 1–135

Pekarik AJ, Schreiber JB, Hanemann N, Richmond K, Mogel B (2014) IPOP: A theory of experience preference. Curator Mus J 57(1):5–27

Roto V, Vermeeren APOS, Law EL-C, Väänänen-Vainio-Mattila K, Obrist M (2015) User experience evaluation; which method to choose (Notes of a course given at the conferences SAICSIT 2010, NordiCHI 2010, INTERACT 2011, CHI 2012 and CHI 2013). Accessed from: http://www.allaboutux.org/files/UX-evaluation-methods-CourseMaterial.pdf

Sheldon KM, Elliot AJ, Kim Y, Kasser T (2001) What is satisfying about satisfying events? Testing 10 candidate psychological needs. J Pers Soc Psychol 80(2):325–339

Snavely N, Seitz SM, Szeliski R (2008) Modeling the world from internet photo collections. Int J Comput Vis 80(2):189–210

Ståhl A, Höök K, Svensson M, Taylor AS, Combetto M (2009) Experiencing the affective diary. Pers Ubiquitous Comput 13(5):365–378

Sterry P, Beaumont E (2006) Methods for studying family visitors in art museums: a cross-disciplinary review of current research. Mus Manag Curatorship. 21 (3):222–239

Steuer J (1992) Defining virtual reality: dimensions determining telepresence. J Commun 42(4): 73–93

Vermeeren APOS, Law E, Roto V, Obrist M, Hoonhout J, Väänänen-Vainio-Mattila K (2010) User experience evaluation methods: current state and development needs. In: Proceedings of the 6th nordic conference on human-computer interaction: extending boundaries. ACM, New York, NY, USA, pp 521–530

Author Biographies

Marco Rozendaal is an assistant professor of interaction design at Delft University of Technology. He has a background in media technology and the arts. In his work, he explores new interaction design paradigms engendered by emerging technologies to understand their social opportunities and ethical implications.

Arnold P. O. S. Vermeeren is Assistant Professor at TU Delft, Faculty of Industrial Design Engineering and Director of the Faculty's MuseumFutures Lab. He was educated as an industrial designer and has been involved in various EU-funded projects on User Experience (UX) as well as a large variety of museum experience-related projects. His current focus is on designing museum experiences for long term engagement, using novel technologies, and making connections to the world outside the museum.

Diana Issidorides holds a PhD in cognitive psychology from the Free University in Amsterdam (NL) and is Senior Scientist and Senior Exhibition Developer at NEMO Science Museum.

Chapter 13
A Critical Reflection on Three Paradigms in Museum Experience Design

Amalia Sabiescu

Abstract This chapter identifies and describes three technological paradigms in museum experience design, all positioned within an overarching visitor-centredness frame: (1) User-centred experience design, which emphasises modelling experience design in response to visitor views and interests, through methods adapted from or inspired by user-centred approaches in Human–Computer Interaction; (2) Participatory experience design, which shifts the emphasis from the product to the process of design and invites the visitor to become partner in the design of experiences; and (3) Agile experience design, in which the main preoccupation is with being constantly responsive to evolving visitor aims and needs, and innovating the experiential offer on an ongoing basis. In the context of museum experience design, each of these paradigms represents a systematic way of delivering value to the public through meaningfully designed experiences. The chapter contributes a critical reflection on the importance of acknowledging the existence and endorsement of these paradigms, which can impact museum practice beyond single design projects. In particular, I will discuss to what extent working within a certain paradigm can be transformative for the way museums function, how they are organised and how they engage with their public.

13.1 Introduction

Two influential articles, written at about the same time, approach from different angles the question of paradigmatic shifts in the field of Human–Computer Interaction (HCI). In her 2006 paper 'When second wave HCI meets third wave challenges', Susan Bødker argues that the field of HCI was transitioning from a second to a third wave (or paradigmatic model of research and design). She identifies the first wave in HCI as model-driven, informed by cognitive science and concerned with information processing. In first wave approaches, we speak about

A. Sabiescu (✉)
Loughborough University London, London, UK
e-mail: a.g.sabiescu@lboro.ac.uk

A. Vermeeren et al. (eds.), *Museum Experience Design*, Springer Series on Cultural Computing, https://doi.org/10.1007/978-3-319-58550-5_13

'human factors'; the human is a subject whose involvement in the design process is as a tester gauging the quality of interaction. Second wave HCI shifted, as Liam Bannon (1986) evocatively wrote, 'from human factors to human actors', thus placing human experience centre stage and making technology instrumental to people-defined requirements in situated contexts. The centrality of people led to the formulation of methodologies that encouraged user participation in the design process, such as participatory design and contextual inquiry. The third wave broke away with the rationality and instrumentality of HCI, which supported mostly work-related practices, and brought to the foreground experience and subjective meaning making in a sociocultural context. Where the second wave focused on context and situatedness, third wave HCI amplifies the spectrum of human experience considering continuities between work, leisure and daily routines, and puts central stage concepts such as experience, culture and emotions. Bødker (2006) argues that the transition from the second to the third wave surfaced new questions and challenges, as research was confronted with third wave questions, but still inheriting theories, methodologies and techniques from second wave HCI. In the paper 'The three paradigms of HCI' Harrison et al. (2007) aim for a more systematic and consistent treatment of HCI waves into paradigms that frame the research and design of human–machine interaction. Their paper problematises and debates whether we can speak of paradigms in HCI and the implications for future HCI research and design.

There are echoes from the three waves of HCI to be found in museum experience design, an area which has grown and developed under significant influence from HCI work. Starting from similar premises, in this chapter I ask the question: Can we identify as well such paradigmatic design waves, orientations or paradigms in museum experience design? And if so, what are the implications of working within one or another of these design paradigms for museum practice?

As a starting point, the chapter identifies and describes three paradigms in museum experience design, all working within an overarching visitor-centredness frame. I use the notion of *design paradigm* in a sense similar to that of *wave* (Bødker 2006) or *paradigm* in the field of HCI (Harrison et al. 2007) with reference to the families of theories, methodologies and procedures endorsed by a community of researchers and practitioners in a design discipline. A more nuanced understanding of paradigms in social science and design disciplines is provided later in the chapter. The three paradigms described are:

1. User-centred experience design, the first orientation to have historically broken with functional models in museum management and public communication, by bringing together the focus on experience together with the centrality of visitor views, interests and personal meanings.
2. Participatory experience design, which comes up with a new value statement, shifting the stress from the product to the process of design, and emphasising the value of direct user participation in the design process.
3. Agile experience design, characterised by a preoccupation with offering experiences that meet visitor interests and are constantly innovated and improved

through a swift, iterative design process conducted by cross-disciplinary teams with flattened hierarchies. Thus, the visitor is treated like a valued customer with dynamic and evolving tastes and interests to which the museum aims to respond promptly, drawing on Lean and Agile methodologies adapted from software design, business and manufacturing.

These museum experience design paradigms share a common purpose vector in that they are all preoccupied with delivering value to their public and recognise the public itself as the arbiter of quality. In other words, they are all visitor-centred. Yet, there are differences between them concerning the valid ways of going about delivering on that value. The chapter outlines the axiological and epistemological considerations associated with each design paradigm, and the patterns of relations between museums and visitors instantiated in each. On this basis, the second part of the chapter raises some questions with respect to the implications of endorsing a design paradigm over the long term. In particular, it reflects on how enduring work within a certain design paradigm may have ripple effects in changing organisational structures and relations with visitors.

13.2 Delivering Value in the Visitor-Centred Museum: Three Design Paradigms

Visitor-centredness is now an undisputed central aspect of the mission of many museums. As Samis and Michaelson (2017) point out, visitor-centredness is an overarching paradigm within which the curatorial, interpretive, managerial and communicative practices of museums are configured, putting the importance of the visitor on equal footing with that of museum collections. Drawing on this perspective, this chapter examines museum experience design within a visitor-centred overarching frame as a key practice through which museums deliver value to their visitors and to society as a whole. Museum experiences are some of the fundamental means through which museums link to and communicate with their audiences. Their design, thereafter, is the generative space within which such experiences are crafted, attentive to considerations of quality, meaningfulness, relevance and value.

There are countless ways to organise design so as to make such experiences meaningful, but the concern in these pages is to understand which of these approaches are systematic, so that they can be easily understood, employed, transferred, improved and thus inspire future museum practice. I refer to these systematic assemblages of conceptions, understandings and approaches in a field of practice or research discipline as 'paradigm'. The most established meaning of 'paradigm' comes from the sociology of science, and finds expression in Thomas Kuhn's theory about the structure of scientific revolutions and paradigm shifts. For Kuhn (1996), paradigms are models of reality that define the problems and questions to be asked, the methods to go about studying reality and the ways of drawing valid conclusions in a specific scientific discipline. A paradigm shift indicates a turnaround where the base model of reality is questioned and a new model comes to replace it. The classical example is the shift from Newtonian mechanics to Einstein's relativism in physics, within which the traditional questions, theories and methods for studying physical phenomena fundamentally changed.

However, Kuhn's assertions are focused on natural sciences, and some scholars (Kuhn included) argue that in the social sciences the same understanding of paradigms does not apply (Dogan 2001). Parallel concepts in the social sciences are worldviews, research traditions (Laudan 1977) or social paradigms (Handa 1986), where the primary principles or assumptions cannot ultimately be proven right or disproved by scientific experiments. The criteria for validity and recognition rather lie in the degree to which sets of assumptions about the nature of being, knowledge or social life enjoy acceptance by communities of researchers in a social science discipline.

In this chapter, I focus on *design* paradigms, referring to the sets of assumptions, theories, perspectives and established methods and procedures that are adhered to by design communities, and from which criteria for design validity are sourced. The approach aligns with two of Kuhn's arguments. First, that paradigms are specific to a certain discipline, they are 'what the members of a scientific community, and they alone, share' (Kuhn 1977: 294). Second, that a paradigm contains accepted theories, methodologies and tried out practices that 'define the *legitimate* problems and methods of a research field for succeeding generations of practitioners'. (Kuhn 1996: 10, my *emphasis*). Thus, the nature of design paradigms in museum experience design is dictated by concerns and aims that are specific for the community of museum experience design practitioners and researchers, and their legitimacy is as well sanctioned by the same community. While museum experience design cannot be considered a discipline in its own right, we can nonetheless define it as an interdisciplinary area at the crossroads between museum studies, visitor studies and design. Its boundaries, though porous and flexible, are defined by the central preoccupation of field professionals and researchers who take a central interest in the design and development of experiences for museum stakeholders.

The central preoccupation of museum experience design regards the nature of the museum experience, and the valid ways of going about designing museum experiences. A design paradigm is characterised by a range of considerations that systematise the design process towards this goal:

- Value statement: Values and aims that validate the design process and generate criteria for assessing the quality of the designed product or service
- Knowledge production: The valid ways of producing knowledge to inform the design process and enhance the quality of the experience delivered
- Relation with beneficiaries in the design process: how are the views of beneficiaries (museum patrons, users or visitors) integrated in the process of design, and what patterns of relatedness between designers and beneficiaries are instantiated
- Methodologies and procedures for designing and assessing experiences.

Table 13.1 Characteristic features of three paradigms in museum experience design

Design paradigm	Value statement	Knowledge production	Relation with beneficiaries in design	Design methodologies
User-centred experience design	Satisfactory user experience, usefulness in context	Designer-led, user-informed knowledge production	Visitor as user and informant involved in key design stages as consultant (mediated design involvement)	Forms of user-centred design
Participatory experience design	Visitor participation in design has intrinsic value	Participatory knowledge production; designers and users co-create knowledge	Visitor as design partner (direct design involvement)	Participatory design, contextual inquiry, some forms of crowd sourcing
Agile experience design	Fast responsiveness to change and to evolution of visitor tastes and interests; maximum value with efficient investment of resources and minimum waste	Designer-led, user-informed knowledge production in continuous cycles	Visitor as customer and informant, involved in continuous cyclic design processes (continuous mediated design involvement)	Agile and Lean methodologies such as Scrum

Further in this section, these considerations are outlined for each of the three design paradigms introduced—user-centred experience design, participatory experience design and Agile experience design (also summed up in Table 13.1).

13.2.1 User-Centred Experience Design

User-centred design (UCD) refers to a framework and underlying design philosophy which emphasises the importance of users and of creating meaningful products and services for them, by considering their needs and interests during the design and development process. In museum experience design, user-centred approaches started emerging at a moment when museums were transitioning from functional models focused on collection management and preservation to an increased attention to visitor views, voices and interests. This shift is well-documented in museum and visitor studies. For example, a decade ago, Hooper-Greenhill called attention to the emergence of the 'interpretative paradigm', which implied a transition from 'thinking about visitors as an undifferentiated mass public to beginning to accept visitors as active interpreters and performers of meaning-making practices within complex cultural sites' (2006, p. 362). This shift is about acknowledging the active role of visitors in constructing personal meanings, understandings and experiences. It follows upon a transactional view of the museum visit, based on transfer of information from museum experts as authoritative sources to visitors, seen as passive recipients. Thus, in this first design orientation the quality of an experience is assessed on virtue of its capacity to engage visitors and support attainment of context-specific goals, from learning to entertainment.

Value statement UCD approaches to museum experience design emphasise the centrality of visitor views and the importance of offering experiences that are judged meaningful from their own point of view. This is an important point for understanding why UCD approaches in museum experience design mark a break from earlier stances in exhibition design and museum communication. Exhibition design in the 1970s and the 1980s were also concerned with visitors, but within a different framework, influenced by models in communication sciences cherished at the time: museum experts created messages to be transmitted to visitors, and their effectiveness was judged according to the degree to which visitors were able to decipher, understand and retain these messages (Hooper-Greenhill 1994). Foregrounding the concept of *experience* breaks away with this model, by acknowledging visitors' own interpretive capacities and their abilities to build understandings and construct meanings from museum experiences from their own point of view (Ibid.).

Knowledge production In UCD, the visitor is the ultimate arbiter of the quality of the experience designed for them. Thus, knowledge about the visitor has crucial importance in this space: What are their interests and preferences? How do they tend to behave in museums? What are they looking for? How much do they know and what approaches are best to engage them? How likely are they to prefer some over other modalities of engagement? And so on. Knowledge about or views from visitors are fed within the design space through various means: tools such as surveys and interviews can be employed in the preliminary phases of design, midway early prototypes are tested with users, and the quality of fully-fledged experiences can be assessed through observation of interaction, interviews and surveys.

Relation with beneficiaries in design Users' involvement in the design process can be described as mediated design involvement: UCD gathers users' views and feedbacks, interprets them in design teams and consequently shapes the design to fit their needs and interests. Users, thereafter, fill the role of testers and informants. This role is nonetheless important and can be considered a form of user participation. Drawing on Nina Simon's typology of public participation patterns in cultural institutions,[1] user involvement in UCD is akin to the category of

[1]Nina Simon (2010) proposes a typology of forms of public participation in cultural institutions which spans: (1) contributory projects, in which visitors input ideas, comments or objects in processes ideated and controlled by the institutions; (2) collaborative projects, which invite visitors to take part in the ideation and creation of projects, which are thereafter developed and managed by institutions; (3) co-creative projects, in which members of institutions work side by side with the public or community members to ideate, design and run programmes that are aligned to the interests of the latter; and (4) hosted projects, in which ideas and design come from the public and are hosted in cultural institutions, which offer spaces and resources.

contributory projects, in which ideas, content or comments are sourced from the public and integrated in programmes, thereafter managed by institutions.

Methodologies There are manifold methodologies that can be used convergently in user-centred museum experience design, from visitor surveys and interviews before or in early stages of design to observation of users in galleries and tests of early prototypes. Methods follow the design continuum, which is often iterative, with appropriate user tests and consultation at each point and can, for instance, include: personas and scenarios sketching for illustrating model users and experiential pathways; qualitative and quantitative research to gauge user tastes and interests in early design stages; mock-ups and prototypes for user tests during design, and final evaluation through, for example, observation, interviews or surveys when experiences are deployed.

13.2.2 Participatory Experience Design

The beginnings of participatory design (PD) are found in Scandinavia in the 1970s, and represent the pinnacle of a fundamental rethinking of values and processes in the design and development of products and services, from top-down to bottom-up approaches with the direct involvement of end users. Perhaps one of the most significant shifts associated with participatory and cooperative forms of design is an increased concern with the *process* of design itself (Gronbaek et al. 1993). Whereas earlier HCI work was rather concerned with the end product, PD reconsiders these premises and claims that to design better fitted products and services, we need to focus attention on the design process: How is the work process defined? Who participates? What criteria are adopted for linking features of end products with desirability and usefulness from the viewpoint of end users?

Given this process (over product) focus, the appropriation of participatory design approaches in museums represent a quality change from user-centred approaches. As Taxén (2004, 2005) argues: UCD approaches in museum experience design emphasise the importance of incorporating user views and feedbacks in the design process and for the evaluation of the final outcome, without however inviting them to become part of the design team. A step further from UCD, many of the PD initiatives in museums are explicitly concerned with enabling visitors to bring their own views and interpretations in the design process and to forge more enduring, horizontal relationships of exchange and cooperation between museums and visitors (Taxén 2004).

Value statement The focus on the process of design (Gronbaek et al. 1993) generates a first principle of values and quality criteria for PD, namely that user participation in design increases efficiency and quality of products and services. Apart from this, PD is also a democratic practice, and in some contexts user participation in design is a value in and of itself. As Suchman (1993) states, the two sets of considerations are interrelated: PD enables users to become part of the design and development process, which enables horizontal relationships and exchanges and enhances a more thorough understanding of user needs and usage scenarios. This, in turn, will lead to designing products and services that are more relevant and appropriate for users. In original Scandinavian approaches, the democratic value of PD went even further, and contributed in some cases to rethinking practices and processes in the workplace (Gronbaek et al. 1993).

Knowledge production The criteria for producing valid knowledge to inform design give weight to involving the users in the design process. Visitor knowledge is validated and brought to equal status with that of designers, wherefrom it follows that visitor views are to be incorporated all throughout the design process in an unmediated way. Thus, PD brings with it the democratisation of knowledge production in museum experience design. Even further, visitor views matter not only as a means to an end but also in and of themselves. For example, in some museum contexts participatory approaches are used not only to make experience design more efficient but also to give voice to visitors in the museum space. Watkins (2007) reports on a participatory social media experiment at the Australian Museum which was specifically set up to enable 'the Museum to act as a social media hub for external communities of interest to co-create their own narrative-based interpretations of the Museum's content' (p. 161).

Relation with beneficiaries in design The production of valid knowledge and visitor engagement in design are closely connected in PD. It is not only that visitors' knowledge and views matter but also that their value comes forth when they are the ones to express them by direct involvement in the design process. Thus, in PD visitors are brought inside the design space, on equal footing with content experts and designers. From casual informant, in participatory design approaches the visitor becomes design partner. Reflecting again on Nina Simon's (2010) typology of public participation in cultural institutions, user involvement in PD can fall into collaborative or co-creative patterns, depending on the share of control and decision-making that is conferred upon users.

Methodologies Whilst there is a rich array of PD approaches, methods and techniques (see Muller 2003; Muller et al. 1993), the understanding in many contexts is that the value of user participation overrides ready-made participation procedures to be followed. The involvement of certain groups such as children, or communities in diverse sociocultural contexts asks for the delineation of new methods, often defined in interaction between designers and the beneficiary user groups (Sabiescu et al. 2014). Thus, several methodological approaches are documented in museum experience design projects, many of them adapted to context and to user categories. For example, the project KidStory aimed to adapt PD approaches from the HCI to the museum field, and with this to seek ways to foster higher engagement of museum visitors (Taxén 2004). This project also placed under scrutiny the question of methods in museum PD, and argued that established HCI methods could not be merely adopted but had to be reconfigured for engaging museum visitors. Hall and Bannon (2005) report on a cooperative design project at the Hunt Museum,

Limerick, Ireland within the European project SHAPE. One of the aims was to understand how cooperative design could spur interaction, but also enhance children's interpretive experiences and abilities in museums, which asked for participatory methods to be crafted in context.

13.2.3 Agile Experience Design

The origins of Agile and Lean methodologies are found in work done in the 70s and 80s in software development on the one hand, and management and organisation studies on the other. In 1970, Winston Royce's article 'Managing the Development of Large Software Systems' put forth a critique of sequential development models in software development. He argued that these were flawed due to lack of communication between teams responsible with each phase and inability to define all requirements in advance. Similar considerations were advanced in management studies by Hirotaka Takeuchi and Ikujiro Nonaka, in their (1986) article 'The New New Product Development Game'. The article criticises the traditional model of product development, where specialised teams complete a portion of the product and then hand it over to the next team of specialists in the chain. The model was based on specialisation and segmentation, and each team was only aware of their limited part in the overall process to be completed. They proposed a new approach, based on iterative experimentation conducted by cross-disciplinary teams, all being involved together in the development process from beginning till the end. Museums have been experimenting with Agile at least since 2008 (see Ellis et al. 2008), and since then it has been adopted both for experience design (e.g. Mannion et al. 2015; Sabiescu and Charatzopoulou, this volume) as well as for rethinking organisational practices (e.g. Hegley et al. 2016).

Value statement Agile approaches embrace values related to responsiveness to change, fast innovation, and delivering maximum value with efficient investment of resources and minimum waste. Similar to participatory design, they also stress values related to the work process, such as collaboration in cross-disciplinary teams, autonomy and accountability over hierarchical structures controlled from the top-down. However, different from PD, these decentralised and hierarchical structures do not include the user directly in design processes and decisions, thereafter in most instances the user steps back in the role of informant, as in UCD.

Knowledge production The central tenet of Takeuchi and Nonaka's (1986) theory is that the new products developed by organisations are direct reflections of new knowledge produced or converted in organisation teams, through their interaction during the work process. Thus, product development teams can be configured to best afford the creation of new knowledge, and this is further reflected in the design and development of novel products and services. For example, cross-disciplinary teams afford a type of interaction which can lead to new ideas, concepts and designs that would not come out in teams specialised in an area.

Like in PD, the focus is on the design process, and attention is on how the design space is configured to afford production of new knowledge and innovation.

Relation with beneficiaries in design In Agile approaches, the visitor steps back to a position of sporadic informant in the design process, in ways similar to UCD. Here as well, the visitor is the arbiter of the quality of the experience designed for them, their views are gathered and information about their preferences and behaviour is tracked and interpreted by design teams to inform new iterations of design. However, in reality there are some subtle differences. Agile has a central concern with delivering quality in a continuous fashion and with efficient investment of resources, in response to a changing context and to evolving visitor tastes and interests (some of which the museum itself may help to evolve). Each iteration/sprint/phase/step releases an advanced prototype of a potentially future and perfected offer. The keyword differentiator here is continuity: in a sense design never stops, it continues as ready to experience but somehow always unfinished products and services hit the market—in this case on site or digital museum spaces. And whilst experiences are staged, they continue to be tested and inform new design processes from which new experiences will come forth. The experience in use is an event but also a test bed. And the visitor who experiences it is at the same time a tester. Thus, in time, we are witnessing the development of a continuous relationship in which the museum is interested in the evolution of visitor tastes, innovates accordingly and helps to develop these tastes.

Methodologies When it comes to methodology, for many Agile is rather a movement or a broad framework of principles, and does not come with ready-to-use design and development methods. The Agile manifesto (2001) is widely cited, however it does not provide concrete steps but rather a series of principles, such as the importance of interaction in teams, delivering working products rather than thoroughly documenting them, and responsiveness to change over keeping tied to a predefined plan. Several Agile methodologies were developed that put these principles in practice, the most well-known of these being Scrum. In their 1986 article, Nonaka and Takeuchi sketched key methodological principles that were later disseminated as Scrum by Sutherland and Schwaber (see Schwaber 1997; Sutherland 2001; Sutherland et al. 2007): iterative design and development, cross-disciplinary teams working together all throughout the development process, collaboration during work doubled by autonomy and a sense of purpose by each and all team members.

As a sum, Agile methodologies advocate designing in incremental and iterative stages, punctuated by user feedback. Work is done in teams dedicated to advancing the project through collaborative but autonomous work. Rather than being controlled, the Agile team is led by a manager, but is also autonomous and goal-driven: each member is accountable for their part and for the success of the whole project. Each stage in the iteration leads to producing a minimum viable product (MVP—a product that meets the minimum requests/needs of customers, but released to gather user feedback for future improvement), or a product increment. In a sense, a product is always perfectible, this is why users are fundamental for gauging quality and relevance, and their feedback can push a marketed product back to the design stage where a new product increment is planned.

The thin literature on Agile practices in museums reveals a concern with adapting methodologies and making the Agile work process fit for the museum context. Adaptation is often times done ad hoc, borrowing from methods and approaches used in business, manufacturing and software development to serve the needs of a particular project. In the long run, and as museums gain experience in running Agile projects, new, field-specific methods are emerging. The key methodological aspects emphasised in existing literature include cross-disciplinary team work, decentralisation, iterative design process and continuous testing with users (Hegley et al. 2016; Sabiescu and Charatzopoulou 2015; Mannion et al. 2015).

13.3 Critical Reflection

After having reviewed the three experience design paradigms, in this section, I look at the implications of thinking of and embracing these families of approaches and methodologies as paradigms for museum practice, drawing attention to four consequential aspects. The first is a reflection on purpose and means in visitor-centred design approaches, and the relations established between the design paradigms introduced. The next two have to do with the implications of embracing a certain design paradigm for museum practice, and discuss links to change—in organisational structures and in relations with visitors. The fourth calls for more awareness to the premises underpinning our design choices, and particularly the question of epistemology and knowledge production.

13.3.1 Nested Paradigms in a Visitor-Centredness Frame

The three design paradigms described are closely interconnected. In particular, they all share a unique purpose, in that the end aim and value that underpins valid design is the quality of the museum experience. They also agree on the ultimate criterion for quality assessment, which stands in visitor satisfaction. This central value is already well-represented in UCD, and we speak about being user-centred or visitor-centred when it comes to describing the overall orientation to experience design embraced by a museum that places visitor interests at the centre. Historically, it was also UCD that broke with a tradition of design that separated rigidly between experts (who controlled the design process) and users (for whom the product or service was intended, but whose ideas were hardly considered during design). Thus, in a way PD and Agile approaches can be considered nested within, variations of, or building upon user-centred design. Despite this common vector, there are reasons for positioning UCD, PD and Agile as distinctive experience design paradigms, chiefly because they approach differently questions of knowledge production, methods and relations with users in design. Furthermore, and as I argue further in this section, these reasons have to do as well with the ripple effects that consistent long-term adoption of a certain design paradigm is likely to cause. The next two sections examine the kind of changes that are likely triggered by systematic adoption of a design paradigm.

13.3.2 Design Paradigms and Organisational Change

Museum activities—from curatorial to communicative—are interlinked, and a concern with delivering public value (Falk and Dierking 2013) permeates them, asking for concerted efforts that are often at odds with traditional, hierarchical and rigid organisational structures. Thus, many museums that are transitioning towards visitor-centred practices come to realise that this transition may require deep organisational change (Samis and Michaelson 2017). As this chapter is being written, there are already published studies that associate models of museum functioning with a certain design paradigm. The most well-known is Nina Simon's *The participatory museum* (2010). A more recent paper for the Museums and the Web conference titled *The Agile museum* (Hegley et al. 2016) describes how Agile-inspired practices and models can completely reconfigure the way museums are organised and how they deliver value to their public. But to what extent can we speak of the user-centred museum, the participatory museum, or the Agile museum? In practice, many museums are selective and opportunistic in employing a certain design approach and often there is not a perfect fit between an orientation embraced at institutional level, and that adopted in design projects. Several design approaches can be encountered in the same museum at the same time, and they can be applied opportunistically to long-term programmes, short-term exhibit environments or (in some cases) come to characterise the work approach of a department. Thus, rather than pure forms, I suggest that at the moment what we are seeing in practice are *interweaving design orientations* guided by experimental approaches. For instance, the British Museum launched in 2014 a new user-centred digital strategy, but within, it has since been experimenting with Lean and Agile methodologies for the redesign of its multimedia guide (Mannion et al. 2015) and for its digital learning programmes (Sabiescu and Charatzopoulou 2015 and this volume).

Significant and enduring organisational change is rather associated with long-term and museum-wide endorsement of principles and practices that converge in visitor-centredness. The UCD, PD or Agile work of a digital media or education department for single projects is less likely to reverberate in wider organisational change on its own. In themselves, those processes may ask for certain expertise and disciplinary orientations to be covered in a team, or the enactment of values and attitudes with respect to public participation that will leave a trace—such as patterns for cross-disciplinary team configurations for delivering on certain types of projects.

But for wider organisational change to occur, there needs to surface an understanding of how visitor-centred principles and approaches enable a museum to deliver better on its mission, and the kind of work configurations and practices these may require.

Samis and Michaelson (2017) point to different ways that museum organisational structures may change in relation to embracing a visitor-centred approach: the emergence of new, cross-disciplinary teams, often within altered hierarchies with more horizontal orientations; emergence of new roles such as experience designers; team leadership positions filled by diverse roles—educators, interpretive specialists or experience designers; and streamlined and simplified work processes crossing disciplinary areas. Some of these changes are effected top-down, by visionary museum directors; some others are the result of long-term work in a participatory vein, moving from ad hoc project-focused configurations to formalisation of new structures.

Going back to the design paradigms introduced, the aspect to bear in mind is, to what extent does the type of paradigm embraced reverberate in diverse vectors of change? The examples above can all be associated broadly with visitor-centredness, but on close inspection we can think about nuanced impacts associated with endorsement of principles and practices within a design paradigm. For instance, UCD puts emphasis on understanding and meeting visitor interests, by gathering information and then interpreting it in design teams. This sits well with the idea of cross-disciplinary teams where curators, educators, experience designers and interpretive specialists bring together their expertise for the creation of meaningful experiences for visitors. Co-creation and participatory design paradigms, with their array of methodologies that allow the visitor to step inside the creative process, may lead up to changes in relation to decentralisation of work and decision-making. Quite paradoxically, even if Agile does not adhere to participatory principles such as those embraced in PD, it does contribute to the same shift nurtured by PD practices: more decentralised structures. Given its focus on collaborative, yet autonomous work in iterative cycles, Agile engenders a move away from top-down and hierarchical to horizontal, decentralised and fluid workflows and structures. In time, this may reverberate in decentralisation and flattened hierarchies at institutional level.

13.3.3 Changing Relations with Visitors

Each design philosophy and methodology endorses and enacts (implicitly or explicitly) a certain philosophy of how knowledge is or should be produced to benefit the primary aim of design. It further unpacks this philosophy in a family of methodologies and methods to materialise this knowledge in the products and services delivered. This is visible in the way the design space is instantiated, who participates and how this influences the shape of the product or service designed. For example, a museum that embraces a position as the unique holder of knowledge and authority over its production will design spaces and artefacts based on expert curatorial knowledge, and give very little weight if at all to asking visitors' opinions. By way of contrast, museums that embrace visitor-centred value propositions will go to great lengths to find ways to constantly elicit user views, interests and appreciation of museum engagements, so that they can make their future experiences more user-relevant.

Thus, there is a very powerful relation between what are considered valid ways of knowledge production and the instantiation of the design space. In here, the relation between museum staff, designers and patrons is of particular importance, and also who is involved in the design process, to what extent, and how. Each of the three paradigms introduced above approaches differently the definition of the design space and the involvement of design beneficiaries in this space. Whilst all paradigms are visitor-centred, in UCD approaches the visitor is rather an informant, in a consultative role. In PD approaches, it becomes a partner, on equal grounds and sharing authority with museum staff and designers. In Agile approaches, the visitor falls back to being an informant, but as different from UCD, their involvement in the design process is less fragmented and more continuous, as in a sense a museum experience never ceases to be work in progress. Thus, by encouraging practices inspired or driven by these paradigms, in the long term there is the possibility for museums to plant the seeds of changing relationships with their audiences.

13.3.4 The Question of Epistemology

I have, thus far argued that embracing a certain design paradigm has the potential to trigger or ask for organisational change in museums, and changing patterns of relationships with visitors. Further, I suggested that at least to some extent, these changes can be traced back to the question of knowledge production, in particular the recognition of which knowledge is valid and useful for informing design. The additional aspect I want to emphasise is that it is important for museum staff to cultivate awareness about their position regarding knowledge production, ways of producing and sharing it, and its links to experience design. As Nina Simon (2010) suggests, the difference between traditional and participatory design approaches is simply in the way information flows between users and a cultural institution. Underpinning this claim is an acknowledgement of how knowledge and information are pivotal in museum functionings and activities. Museums are places for knowledge production, circulation and exchange. Some of this knowledge is explicit, and makes its way in varied forms and representations to audiences, for example, through interpretive panels, audio guide content and exhibition guides. Some of it is implicit, and embedded in the museum staff, workflows, artefacts and processes that characterise the day-to-day functioning of the museum. A cross-section of this knowledge stands at the basis of the new products and services that the museum offers. The design of new products, services, and visitor experiences, are all materialisations of this implicit and explicit knowledge that covers a broad range of areas, from collection-related to visitor behaviour and appropriate technologies. What are considered valid ways of knowledge production and how they are infused in design are matters that reverberate more broadly in the internal workings of museum, and further affect the relations with audiences.

In sum, epistemological aspects—what can be known and how we can go about knowing it—can prove to be fundamental for the way museums develop as institutions. In the three paradigms described, epistemological aspects can be inferred, but are rarely directly treated in museum literatures. For example, because UCD advocates user-focused design, but not direct user involvement in affecting design decisions, it can be inferred that knowledge is something that can be elicited in a context (such as a user test) and transmitted in another context (an iteration of the design process, where it is interpreted by design specialists), maintaining a kind of validity and substantiality that evoke positivistic undertones. The often times implicit rather than explicit epistemological premises of PD are that knowledge is a product of interaction, it comes out in processes and practices through the communication and exchange of different parties. Thus, to produce new products and services that are useful for end users, it is not sufficient to merely collect their views, and then test products with users at different stages, as was the case in UCD. Rather, to make certain that the products designed meet user needs, it is necessary for user views to be included directly and in an unmediated manner in the design process. This is similar to the epistemological premises of Agile approaches sketched by Nonaka, Takeuchi, Konno and colleagues in several articles, by which knowledge creation is a participatory process, it is not produced in individual minds but stems from collective interplay and interaction, thereafter it can be enhanced by specific team configurations (see for instance Nonaka and Konno 1998, p. 40).

What these examples show is that there is a strong relation between the underlying assumptions about knowledge creation and the way a design space is configured—who can participate, whose views are valid, whose views do not matter or whose views may matter but need to be interpreted to make them valid. The more we are aware of these underlying assumptions, the more we become aware as well of the implications of our design choices, as each design choice is not neutral, but value-laden. Even more importantly, awareness can enable us to give fruitful directions to these choices. For instance, a museum that started working with PD in small projects may be more inclined to expand participatory approaches to broader museum activities if the assumptions regarding visitor involvement in PD are explicated, and their value acknowledged and disseminated across the museum.

13.4 Concluding Thoughts

Samis and Michaelson (2017) argue that 'an audience-centered paradigm is here to stay'. The three design paradigms introduced thus far can be considered three facets of visitor-centredness as a major frame that characterises museum functioning in the contemporary era. They are all, in a sense, answers to the *How* question, when it comes to delivering satisfactory, meaningful experiences to visitors. Yet, the main argument put forth in this chapter is that embracing one or another of these paradigms has implications that go beyond the type and quality of the experience designed and developed through a certain methodological approach. Serious and long-term engagement with a certain way of working has the potential to spur and sustain deeper change in museum practice. I have suggested that two changes are fundamental: First, endorsing a design paradigm over the long term and allowing it to reverberate in wider museum operations may bring about changes in the organisational structure: in how departments work together, leadership patterns or the addition of new roles and departments. This depends on whether a paradigm is embraced as a philosophy to guide long-term museum practice, or just as a methodology in stand-alone design projects. Second, working within one paradigm can contribute to changing relations with visitors. In here as well, the potential for change depends on the extent to which design approaches are embraced as philosophies guiding museum practice, or merely as methods in projects of limited scale. The most telling example is that of PD and participatory approaches. A small-scale PD project will not change relations with visitors in the long term. But enduring participatory practices, such as those described by Nina Simon in *The Art of Relevance* (2016) and *The participatory museum* (2010), will.

This is why in the latter part of the chapter, I drew attention to the question of epistemology. Being aware of the epistemological premises of our design engagements in museums, of how we produce and circulate knowledge and who has the right to be involved is fundamental for understanding (and ultimately better guiding) design processes and the consequences of our design choices for broader museum practice.

References

Bannon L (1986) From human factors to human actors: the role of psychology and human-computer interaction studies in system design. In: Greenbaum J, Kyng M (eds) Design at work: cooperative design of computer systems. Erlbaum, pp 25–44

Bødker S (2006) When second wave HCI meets third wave challenges. In: Proceedings of the 4th nordic conference on human-computer interaction: changing roles. ACM, New York, pp 1–8. https://doi.org/10.1145/1182475.1182476

Dogan M (2001) Smelser NJ, Baltes B (eds) International encyclopedia of the social and behavioral sciences. pp 16–11023

Ellis D et al (2008) Agile methods for project management. In: Trant J, Bearman D (eds) Museums and the web 2008: proceedings, Toronto: archives and museum informatics. Published March 31, 2008. Consulted January 19, 2017. http://www.archimuse.com/mw2008/papers/jenkins/jenkins.html

Falk JH, Dierking LD (2013) The museum experience revisited. Routledge

Gronbaek K, Grudin J, Bodker S, Bannon L (1993) Achieving cooperative system design: shifting from a product to a process focus. Schuler D, Namioka A (eds) Participatory design: principles and practices. Lawrence Erlbaum Associates, Hillsdale, NJ, pp 79–97

Hall T, Bannon L (2005) Co-operative design of children'sinteraction in museums: a case studyin the Hunt Museum. CoDesign 1(3):187–218
Handa ML (1986) Peace paradigm: transcending liberal and marxian paradigms paper presented in international symposium on science, technology and development, New Delhi, India, March 20–25, 1987, Mimeographed at O.I.S.E., University of Toronto, Canada (1986)
Harrison S, Tatar D, Sengers P (2007) The three paradigms of HCI. In: Alt. Chi. Session at the SIGCHI conference on human factors in computing systems San Jose, California, USA
Hegley D, Tongen M, David A (2016) The Agile museum. In: MW2016: Museums and the web 2016. Published January 15, 2016. Consulted January 19, 2017. http://mw2016.museumsandtheweb.com/paper/the-agile-museum/
Hooper-Greenhill E (1994) Education, communication and interpretation: towards a critical pedagogy in museums. In: Hooper-Greenhill (ed.) The educational role of the museum. 2nd edn. Routledge, London, pp 3–27
Kuhn T (1977) The essential tension: selected studies in scientific tradition and change
Kuhn T (1996) The structure of scientific revolutions, 3d edn. University of Chicago Press, Chicago. (1st ed., 1962)
Laudan L (1977) Progress and Its problems: towards a theory of scientific growth. University of California Press, Berkeley
Mannion S, Sabiescu A, Robinson W (2015) An audio state of mind: understanding behaviour around audio guides and visitor media. In: MW2015: museums and the web 2015. Published February 1, 2015. Consulted December 19, 2016. http://mw2015.museumsandtheweb.com/paper/an-audio-state-of-mind-understanding-behviour-around-audio-guides-and-visitor-media/
Muller MJ (2003) Participatory design: the third space in HCI. Hum Comput Interaction Dev Process 4235:165–185
Muller MJ, Wildman DM, White EA (1993) Taxonomy of PD practices: a brief practitioner's guide. Commun ACM 36(6):26–28
Nonaka I, Konno N (1998) The concept of "ba": Building a foundation for knowledge creation. Calif Manag Rev 40(3):40–54
Sabiescu AG, David S, van Zyl I, Cantoni L (2014) Emerging spaces in community-based participatory design: reflections from two case studies. In: Proceedings of the 13th participatory design conference: research papers, vol 1. ACM, New York, pp 1–10
Sabiescu A, Charatzopoulou K (2015) Shaping a culture of lifelong learning for young audiences: a case study on the samsung digital discovery centre at the British museum. RICHES EU project deliverable
Samis P, Michaelson M (2017) The visitor-centred museum. Routledge, New York and London
Schwaber K (1997) Scrum development process. In: Business object design and implementation. Springer London, pp 117–134
Simon N (2010) The participatory museum. Museum 2.0
Simon N (2016) The art of relevance. Museum 2.0, Santa Cruz, CA
Suchman L (1993) Foreword. In: Schuler D, Namioka A (eds) Participatory design: principles and practices. Lawrence Erlbaum Associates, Hillsdale, NJ, pp vii–ix
Sutherland J (2001) Inventing and reinventing SCRUM in five companies. sur le site officiel de l'alliance agile
Sutherland J, Viktorov A, Blount J, Puntikov N (2007) Distributed scrum: Agile project management with outsourced development teams. In: 40th annual Hawaii international conference on system sciences, 2007. HICSS 2007. IEEE, Waikoloa, 274a p
Takeuchi H, Nonaka I (1986) The new product development game. Harvard Business Review
Taxén G (2004) Introducing participatory design in museums. In: Proceedings of the eighth conference on Participatory design: artful integration: interweaving media, materials and practices, vol 1. ACM, New York, pp 204–213

Taxén G (2005) Participatory design in museums. Visitor-oriented perspectives on exhibition design. Unpublished doctoral dissertation. Royal Institute of Technology, Stockholm, Sweden

Watkins J (2007) Social media, participatory design and cultural engagement. In: Proceedings of the 19th Australasian conference on Computer-Human Interaction: Entertaining User Interfaces. ACM, New York, pp 161–166

Author Biography

Amalia Sabiescu is a communication scientist with an interdisciplinary research track at the interface between information and communication technology (ICT), culture and development studies. Her research explores the integration, use and impact of ICT in cultural and creative practice, community contexts, and intersections with issues of citizen voice, participation, and social inclusion. She is affiliated with the Institute for Media and Creative Industries at Loughborough University London.

Part IV
Museums as Part of an Ecosystem

In this section, we look at the design opportunities and implications opened up by conceiving of museums not as isolated cultural entities, but as part of interconnected ecosystems. There are diverse ways to employ an ecosystem metaphor for situating museums, which can be inspirational for design: the metaphor can refer to systems of connected institutions—other museums and cultural institutions, but also diverse institutional stakeholders that partake in the design and delivery of cultural and educational experiences (such as community centres, schools and technology companies). Or, it can point to even more diverse categories of stakeholders, spaces and relations in an environment such as a city, all of which impact upon the way museums relate and connect to their audiences. Even more broadly, it may imply acknowledging the sociocultural, economic and institutional embeddedness of the museum. Inevitably, employing an ecosystem metaphor implies accounting for complexity and multiple layers of significance that can hardly be considered together in situated design initiatives. Thus, the chapters in this section cut through this complexity and illustrate, each, specific frameworks that use ecological or ecosystem approaches and structures to situate and drive design.

Calvi and Hover introduce *Becoming Vincent*, an emblematic example of designing cultural experiences across multiple cultural sites. Their chapter illustrates the design process for creating a digital system that integrates storytelling and Virtual Reality to provide a coherent and meaningful engagement with various Vincent van Gogh heritage sites in North-Brabant, the Netherlands. Their analysis singles out and provides reflections on the challenges raised by designing for museum ecosystems, ranging from having to meet diverse institutional aims and goals, blending and drawing on diverse instances of disciplinary knowledge, and selecting content to appeal to tourists while, at the same time, meeting the requirements of cultural heritage experts.

Vermeeren, Shih, van der Laan, Calvi, Yoon and Keller make a case for the design of trajectories of experiences across multiple cultural sites. The authors exemplify this idea with the design of a treasure hunt game for the museum

Mauritshuis in The Hague, which sought to provide a *holistic* experience for travellers, by suggesting and supporting cultural engagement beyond the museum visit. This design approach opens up opportunities for engaging visitors with a richer set of experiences, and a more coherent, inter-linked cultural landscape in a city context. At the same time, it raises numerous challenges for design, from deciding on content focus to technical solutions and financial coverage, which are examined in the chapter.

Sabiescu and Charatzopoulou propose an ecological perspective for designing digital learning experiences for museums at the intersection of two ecosystems: the museum ecosystem, including museum spaces, collections, staff and audiences; and the broader education ecosystem made of diverse institutions, learning spaces, teachers, learners and educational stakeholders that shape education trends. They introduce the case study of the Samsung Digital Discovery Centre at the British Museum, and examine the Centre's approach to designing digital learning experiences from an ecological perspective. On this basis, the authors flesh out the interrelated concepts of *learning ecology* and *interpretive ecology*, and illustrate how they can be used to inspire and drive the design of digital learning experiences in museums.

Each of these chapters takes a unique perspective to what it means to design museum experiences whilst thinking of museums as elements of an ecosystem. They all converge, however, in pointing to the importance of embedding museum experience design within a holistic and relational perspective. Holistically, insofar as design is positioned within and needs to account for a complex array of elements beyond the linear relation between single museums and their audiences. And relationally, as these elements are all connected in meaningful ways, and often at various levels, for instance physically (same or nearby location), in their mission (such as museums and schools linked by their educational mission), in touristic or city routes, or content-wise (depending on how museum cultural artefacts travelled and the contexts they draw their meaning from). Thus, each of these relations can be explored in the design process when working in an ecological perspective.

Chapter 14
Becoming Vincent: A Multifaceted Story in a Multifaceted Ecosystem

Licia Calvi and Moniek Hover

Abstract This chapter presents the process that led to the development of a virtual experience for the church in Etten-Leur, which is part of the heritage related to Vincent van Gogh and which hosts a permanent exhibition related to the artist's life in the area. As such, it is one of the elements in the *Becoming Vincent* project. This chapter highlights the complexity of the heritage ecosystem underlying the project, consisting of various stakeholders with diverse, sometimes diverging or even incompatible, interests and goals. In this chapter, we discuss how we coped with this diversity and we draw some of the lessons we learnt from this process for future use. The most important lesson is the need to involve all stakeholders from the start of the process and to treat them equally, despite visible differences in their relative interest in the outcome of the project, in order to give them the feeling to have ownership on the expected outcome, and therefore to enhance the chances that they will still support the project after its completion. At the same time, it is important to keep the network structure simple and clear in order to avoid unnecessary or redundant passages in the knowledge transmission within this web of relations. While not specific for museums but prone to be applied to any complex networked situation, this approach has helped us cope with a complex cultural ecosystem.

14.1 Introduction

In the *Becoming Vincent* project (Calvi et al. 2014), a team of experts from NHTV University of Applied Sciences in Breda was asked to develop a narrative concept and matching storylines that would link and upgrade the various Vincent van Gogh

L. Calvi (✉)
Academy for Digital Entertainment, NHTV—Breda University of Applied Sciences, Hopmansstraat 1, 4800, DX Breda, The Netherlands
e-mail: Calvi.L@nhtv.nl

M. Hover
Academy for Leisure, NHTV—Breda University of Applied Sciences, Archimedesstraat 17, 4816 Breda, The Netherlands

A. Vermeeren et al. (eds.), *Museum Experience Design*, Springer Series on Cultural Computing, https://doi.org/10.1007/978-3-319-58550-5_14

heritage sites in Brabant, the Netherlands, in order to eventually attract more international tourists to this province. These sites include institutions like museums and information centers, but also locations and authentic places where Van Gogh lived and spent the longest part of his life. All these places are characterized by their intrinsic diversity and yet genuine authenticity, which makes them unique in the relatively scattered landscape of Van Gogh's heritage in the Netherlands.

A narrative concept, that we called *Becoming Vincent,* and that is based on a storytelling model (Calvi and Hover 2015), was developed (Calvi et al. 2014). This has been translated into a couple of digital products, both using the Oculus Rift. The first one was a quick-and-dirty prototype developed to test the acceptability of the device (Calvi et al. 2015). The second one, a creative game, was a full-fledged experience in virtual reality (VR) developed around one of the locations from the original narrative concept (see in Fig. 14.1). In this chapter, we discuss the genesis of this VR experience, focusing in particular on the several dilemmas and problems that we had to face in an attempt to connect diverse stakeholders, locations, and stories with their sometimes conflicting interests and heterogeneous expectations and expertise of a multifaceted ecosystem (including institutionally recognized heritage sites, professionals, and volunteers) that needed to be combined into coherent and meaningful visitor experiences. This would result in a journey along Van Gogh's life outside the constrained space of physical museums. These dilemmas included

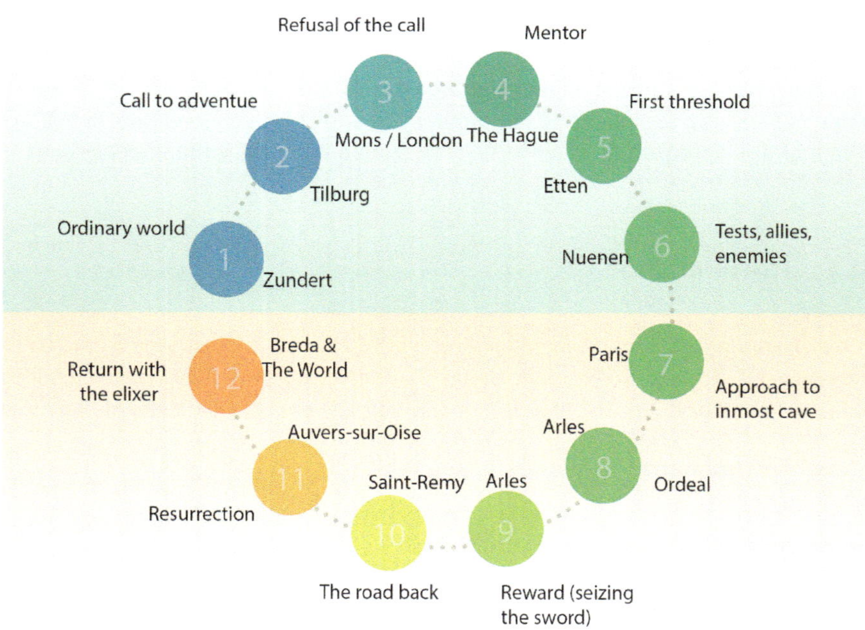

Fig. 14.1 The hero's journey (*external circle*) and Vincent's journey (*internal circle*)

combining authentic heritage sites with a VR encounter with Vincent van Gogh that would not lock tourists away from the real physical locations but that, on the contrary, would represent a trigger for them to explore and visit more of them. We faced storytelling dilemmas in the choice of the most memorable and significant events in Van Gogh's life to appeal to an internationally diverse audience in a way that would touch them emotionally. Additionally, there were dilemmas on how to accommodate the expertise of an art historian who was the curator of one of the museums, and who was very much concerned about the traceability of the facts portrayed in the virtual experience, for instance via the letters Vincent wrote to his brother. Here, the principles of script writing and of compelling storytelling sometimes came into conflict with the focus on factual information and details only. Thus, all in all, it was an exercise in balancing and compromising.

14.1.1 The **Becoming Vincent** *Project*

Becoming Vincent (Calvi et al. 2014) was started in view of the 125th commemoration of Vincent van Gogh's death in 2015.

The project consisted of connecting all original locations related to Van Gogh's life and heritage, in the Netherlands and abroad (mainly in France and in Belgium), by means of a narrative concept. This concept uses a storytelling tool, i.e., the hero's journey (Bouma 2010), to match each of the 12 steps in this journey to a different period in Van Gogh's life (Fig. 14.1). Such periods follow each other chronologically according to Vincent's life. It is amazing to see how well they match this storytelling model (for a full description of the model, see Calvi and Hover 2015).

Each step/location in Fig. 14.1 is given a specific theme. This theme has emerged as conspicuous by studying Van Gogh's life, through for instance more than 800 letters he has written to his brother Theo. The theme is used as the lens to tell the story of Vincent in that specific location. For example, for Etten-Leur ("Etten" in Fig. 14.1), the theme is "making choices". From his biography we know that, at that time, Vincent had decided to go against his father and chose to become an artist. In a well-known episode which took place around the Christmas period in 1881, and which is documented in the letters and reported in all his biographies, he had a violent fight on this with his parents and, as a consequence, he left home (see below).

The structure in Fig. 14.1 is also divided into two halves: the upper half (light green) corresponds to the period in which Vincent van Gogh spent most of his time in the Dutch Southern region of Brabant and spans most of his life. This is the time when he was still struggling to find himself and his role in life. This is why we called it *Becoming Vincent*. The lower half (light orange), which corresponds to the last 5–6 years of his life, which he spent in France, are the years when he was known for the genius that he was. We, therefore, called this part *Being Vincent*: this is the Vincent van Gogh we all know.

Becoming Vincent, in fact, has a double meaning: on the one hand, it means getting to know the process Vincent had gone through from child to young man in order to become the painter Van Gogh, whose genius is recognized worldwide. On the other hand, it also means that anybody who gets to know his story told according to the model depicted in Fig. 14.1 can empathize with him and feel like "becoming" Vincent themselves, through identification.

This is why we chose to tell Vincent's story using virtual reality: it provides an immersive experience that facilitates identification with the protagonist and allows for an emotional connection with him.

14.2 Design Case

14.2.1 Genesis of the Virtual Experience

Back in 2014, we developed a quick-and-dirty prototype of a virtual experience with the Oculus Rift (Calvi et al. 2015) to visualize the narrative concept presented in the previous section for potential stakeholders and future follow-up projects. This very brief experience portrayed the young child Vincent in the garden of his house in Zundert (Fig. 14.2), where he was born and had spent his childhood. Many of the

Fig. 14.2 The Oculus Rift experience of the garden in Zundert presented at the V & A exhibit in London in 2014 Photos source: Moniek Hover

Fig. 14.3 The church in Etten-Leur as it is today (*left*). Credits: Yhoitink (Own work) [CC BY-SA 3.0 nl (http://creativecommons.org/licenses/bysa/3.0/nl/deed.en)], via Wikimedia Commons. And in a drawing by Vincent van Gogh (*right*) Credits: Van Gogh Museum, Amsterdam (Vincent van Gogh Stichting)

letters he has written to his brother Theo contain sweet memories of this garden and the nature around Zundert.

The garden itself had been rebuilt a couple of years earlier using letters from the Van Gogh family members as a reference. Having a virtual experience taking place next to that same (rebuilt) garden was a way, we believed, to reactualize it and to offer visitors of the house in Zundert the possibility to live both a physical and a virtual experience augmented with an encounter with the child Vincent.

This encounter could in itself open up unforeseen scenarios for the visitors in that they could, through the storytelling device of identification (see further), sympathize and empathize with the young Vincent. This was, in fact, one of the two objectives set forth by *Becoming Vincent* as already mentioned above (Calvi and Hover 2015). This experience was very well received.

As a consequence, in 2015, the municipality of Etten-Leur commissioned us to develop a similar experience for the church where Vincent's father had been a vicar (Fig. 14.3) and where Vincent lived as a young man.

14.2.2 Stakeholders Involved

For the development of this new virtual experience, four different stakeholders were involved: one was an art historian and the curator of a museum which has some of Van Gogh's artwork. Having an expert knowledge on Van Gogh's life and art, her role and objective in this project was to check that the story that would be told in the virtual experience precisely matched the events that took place during Vincent's life in Etten-Leur. Another stakeholder, the actual commissioner, was a representative of several local governments in West Brabant, who had commissioned the overall Van Gogh project since its beginning, back in 2014. As such, he knew precisely what approach had been followed thus far and, in a way, what could be expected from this additional follow-up project (see however further in Sect. 14.3 for a discussion on the stakeholders' actual expectations). He has layman knowledge of Van Gogh's art and life, and no experience whatsoever with virtual reality and video games *tout court*. His main interest and concern was to have a final product that could put West Brabant, as the cradle of Van Gogh's genius, on the map, internationally. A third stakeholder was the actual client, who would personally use the final product in his role as guide and volunteer in the church in Etten-Leur. He has an expert but non-professional knowledge of Van Gogh's life and art, and therefore very much relied on the art historian's expertise on this. His interest and purpose in this project was to make sure that this heritage site could get more visibility thanks to this new application and could also bring Van Gogh closer to many more tourists. He had also almost no experience with virtual reality and video games. The last stakeholder was one of the game developers. He started as last year Bachelor's student working on this project as part of his education, in a team of about 10 other (2nd year) students. He later took on the lead of the project and remained involved alone as a freelance developer until the end, making sure that the final product could be delivered as a full-fledged experience. As a game programmer, he had experience developing other games (although this one may not be called a game at all), although more the sort of shooter-kind of games, and as such was rather inexperienced with the type of content and approach that this project required. His main focus during most of the project was on development and his main interest and goal were delivering a high-quality product.

14.2.3 Issues Related to Designing for a Variety of Stakeholders

Becoming Vincent represents an example of an ecosystem in which diverse stakeholders are involved. Designing for such a complex environment, first, implies a recognition of whom the stakeholders affected by the design are, and second, to identify their respective goals and interests (Boutelle 2004). Their goals may differ when not being openly in conflict (Boutelle 2004): this is where design comes into play and takes up the fundamental role of addressing and resolving such conflicts. Stakeholder analysis (Freeman 1984) allows designers to identify the specific stakeholders' interests, and to anticipate their possible reactions to the project ("Will they still support it, when their interests are not properly addressed? To what extent will they be eager to compromise?"). This is achieved by prioritizing their individual interest in the project outcome and their real influence in its deployment.

In our case, conflicts among stakeholders' interests and goals were clearly identifiable in the mismatch between what the art historian wanted (i.e., a verifiable and factual account of an important and life-changing event in Van Gogh's, the painter, life), and what the client wanted (i.e., a memorable experience through an emotional encounter with Vincent, the young man). The commissioner and the designers of the VR experience, who mainly wanted to tell an engaging story, also shared the client's perspective.

In the end, the art historian felt that her goals had not been properly taken into consideration, that the compromise we had sought to achieve was not adequately addressing her concerns (see Sect. 14.3 for the script that was ultimately approved by all stakeholders involved). For this reason, she ultimately decided to distance herself from this project (i.e., to not be affiliated with it).

What we did here as part of our design choices was in fact not to identify each stakeholder's interest and importance in the process and, by way of matching them, decide which stakeholder's perspective had to be given priority, as suggested by Boutelle (2004). On the contrary, we sided with the client because we could better identify with his view on and ideas of this project. As a matter of fact, he had a high interest in the project, as he would have to personally and directly support it in his function as guide inside the church in Etten, and was very influential as he would have been the primary person to promote and support this product (what he actually also did, see for the details the discussion in Sect. 14.3.1).

Jung (2011) defines museums as ecosystems, adopting an ecological perspective that originates from Bateson's ecology of mind, in which all elements, both "human and non-human (…), are interconnected and independent". Although *Becoming Vincent* is not a museum and is not limited to one single institution, it concerns all authentic locations (therefore going beyond mere museums) where Vincent van Gogh has lived, as depicted in Fig. 14.1. Thus, it can also be seen as "a web of relationships" (Jung 2011), that act as communicating vessels: if one does not function properly, the complete ecosystem suffers. In the specific instance of the *Becoming Vincent* project described in this chapter, we could witness this in the need and difficulty to balance the opposite forces and weights playing amongst its stakeholders (see also in Sect. 14.3), a struggle that could only be resolved with one stakeholder, namely the art historian, detaching herself from the project. Differences in the (project) network are actually normal and even vital: what is crucial is to be able to find a common denominator that connects all stakeholders involved in it, one that can make sense of the unbalances among them and that can potentially offer a new perspective where a resolution of such conflicts can be possible (Nevejan 2007). This common denominator is referred to as *the third point,* by borrowing it from Sergei Eisenstein's filmmaking technique: "The third point, this ethical position, is often already part of the variety of relationships in the crucial network but not explicitly formulated" (Nevejan 2007, p. 139). In *Becoming Vincent*, this third point is Van Gogh as a painter, which is essential to one stakeholder (the art historian, again) and important but less central to others (both the client and the commissioner, who rather focused on Vincent as a person. See for the details Table 14.1, Sect. 14.3.3).

Such ecological system thinking (Capra 1996) assumes that knowledge is transmitted circularly, as in a network, with no hierarchy, no predefined order and no unidirectionality (Jung 2011). In order for this to be possible, members not only need to consider each other as peers, while acknowledging their differences in competences, interests, and skills, but they also need to respect and trust one another. In the specific case of *Becoming Vincent*, our stakeholders did have trust in one another, also because they had had previous professional contacts among themselves: the client, for example, relied on and deeply trusted the art historian's expert knowledge, although he was not prepared to completely give up his idea of having an emotional experience, more than a merely historical account, of a turning point in Vincent's life.

14.3 The Stakeholders' Experience with the Design Process

We were interested in understanding how the different stakeholders had experienced the whole design process, what they had learnt from it, whether their expectations had been met and what they would improve were they given the opportunity to design the same experience again.

We interviewed three of the stakeholders (not the curator, as her experience of the process had already emerged during the project), a few months after the project had ended and about 1 month after the virtual experience had formally been announced through the press and launched with an official celebration in the church of Etten-Leur (Fig. 14.4). We did this by means of an open-questions interview and word associations.

Before discussing the interview results, we will illustrate the process the development of this experience went through, to highlight the dilemmas and hurdles we had encountered.

14.3.1 An Illustration of Decision-Making with Stakeholders

We start this illustration with the client giving us an indication of the event that could be portrayed in the virtual experience and that he considered as a turning

Fig. 14.4 The launch of the virtual experience in the church in Etten-Leur in Dec. 2016. Photo source: Chips and Salsa/Van Gogh Kerk Etten-Leur

point (see for a discussion of the 5-phase storytelling approach in Calvi and Hover 2016) in Vincent's life. This event took place just before Christmas in 1881 when Vincent had announced to his parents that he wanted to devote his life to art, going against his father's will who wanted him to follow his footsteps as a vicar. This episode represents a paradigmatic moment in the life and evolution of Vincent, both as a man and as an artist and it is essential for understanding his later growth and the choices, both personal and artistic, he had made.

We, therefore, started to study Vincent's life in depth, by reading his letters and his biography. In this discovery process, the contribution of the art historian has been essential. The first tangible result of this collaboration has been the writing of the script of the story that we wanted to tell in the virtual experience. But this was not without difficulties. Figure 14.5 shows the outcome and the various polishing stages it went through.

As can be noted from Fig. 14.5, the original script depicting a possible dialogue between Vincent and his parents is glossed by the art historian (purple bubble in the figure) noting "this is an interpretation…. But I know that you chose to go for it". Indeed, our goal was to write an engaging story, one that could be further enhanced by the specificity of the virtual medium we wanted to tell it by and that could deepen the viewers' experience. To achieve this, we had to use the art of storytelling and of script writing, we were prepared to dramatize the real events tweaking some of the actual facts that took place in Van Gogh's life to the storyline we had chosen, if we wanted to touch viewers emotionally. And this especially in view of the identification process that lies at the heart of *Becoming Vincent* (see above and further also).

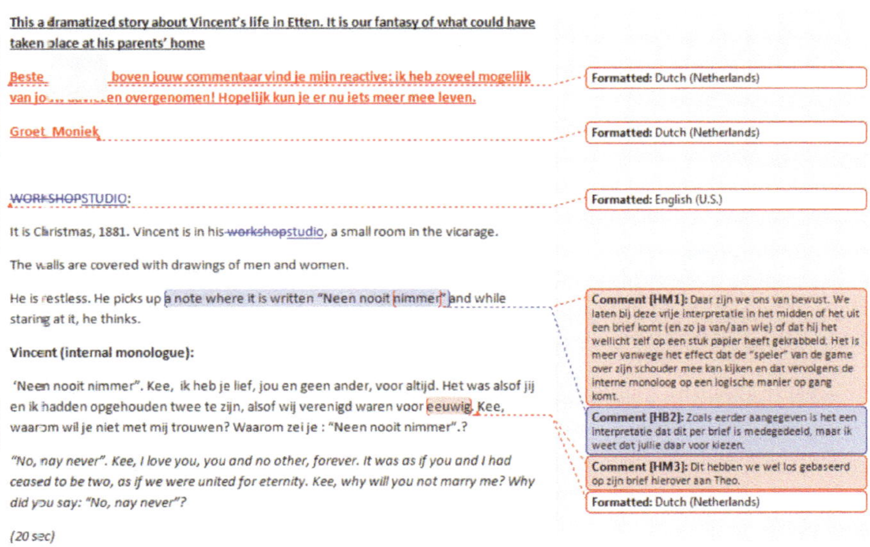
This a dramatized story about Vincent's life in Etten. It is our fantasy of what could have taken place at his parents' home

Beste boven jouw commentaar vind je mijn reactive: ik heb zoveel mogelijk van jo… …en overgenomen! Hopelijk kun je er nu iets meer mee leven.

Groet Moniek

~~WORKSHOP~~STUDIO:

It is Christmas, 1881. Vincent is in his ~~workshop~~studio, a small room in the vicarage.

The walls are covered with drawings of men and women.

He is restless. He picks up a note where it is written "Neen nooit nimmer" and while staring at it, he thinks.

Vincent (internal monologue):

'Neen nooit nimmer". Kee, ik heb je lief, jou en geen ander, voor altijd. Het was alsof jij en ik hadden opgehouden twee te zijn, alsof wij verenigd waren voor eeuwig. Kee, waarom wil je niet met mij trouwen? Waarom zei je : "Neen nooit nimmer".?

"No, nay never". Kee, I love you, you and no other, forever. It was as if you and I had ceased to be two, as if we were united for eternity. Kee, why will you not marry me? Why did you say: "No, nay never"?

(20 sec)

Formatted: Dutch (Netherlands)

Formatted: Dutch (Netherlands)

Formatted: English (U.S.)

Comment [HM1]: Daar zijn we ons van bewust. We laten bij deze vrije interpretatie in het midden of het uit een brief komt (en zo ja van/aan wie) of dat hij het wellicht zelf op een stuk papier heeft gekrabbeld. Het is meer vanwege het effect dat de "speler" van de game over zijn schouder mee kan kijken en dat vervolgens de interne monoloog op een logische manier op gang komt.

Comment [HB2]: Zoals eerder aangegeven is het een interpretatie dat dit per brief is medegedeeld, maar ik weet dat jullie daar voor kiezen.

Comment [HM3]: Dit hebben we wel los gebaseerd op zijn brief hierover aan Theo.

Formatted: Dutch (Netherlands)

Fig. 14.5 The script of the story in the virtual experience

The art historian, however, was much more concerned with the true veracity, accuracy, and traceability of these facts than with the ultimate experience for the viewers. Hence, her remarks in the script. For example, we wanted to end the experience visually, after Vincent had announced to have no interest in becoming a vicar and had been sent away by his father, by having Vincent leaving the house smashing the front door and having the father lock it after him to emphasize this dramatic and irreversible moment in Vincent's life, this fundamental turning point. Alas, there was no trace of the father locking the door in any of the letters written by Vincent, nor in any other documents reporting his life!

This is one of many more examples when our mutual expectations (ours and the art historian's) with respect to the end product ("What is the purpose of this experience?"; "What do we want this experience to be used for?") and expertise collided.

To reach a compromise, we added the following sentence at the beginning of the script "*This is a dramatized story about Vincent's life in Etten. It is our fantasy of what could have taken place at his parents' home.*"

With this disclaimer, the art historian's concerns were put at rest even though she was still not completely convinced of the added value of this experience from a historiographical perspective. Even though this (i.e., historiographical research) had never been the purpose of this project, she thought that, as a curator, she could no longer be further affiliated with this product.

Eventually, this script was converted into a storyboard for the virtual experience with the Oculus Rift (Fig. 14.6).

14.3.2 The Stakeholders' Interviews

Through the stakeholders' interviews we wanted to learn:

- How they had experienced the process of developing this product
- If they felt that their interests, expectations, and expertise had been met
- How they thought the collaboration (with all these diverse expectations) went, by naming as examples of their answer something that was positive and something that did not go well
- How they would improve the process, had they had the opportunity to experience it anew
- If they were happy with the final result.

What follows is a concise discussion of their answers, classified by the categories that had emerged during the analysis of the interview data.

The Process

All three stakeholders reported to have found the process of developing this game a valuable learning experience. Working with students, as this had started as a students' project for 2nd year game design students, was experienced as enriching for

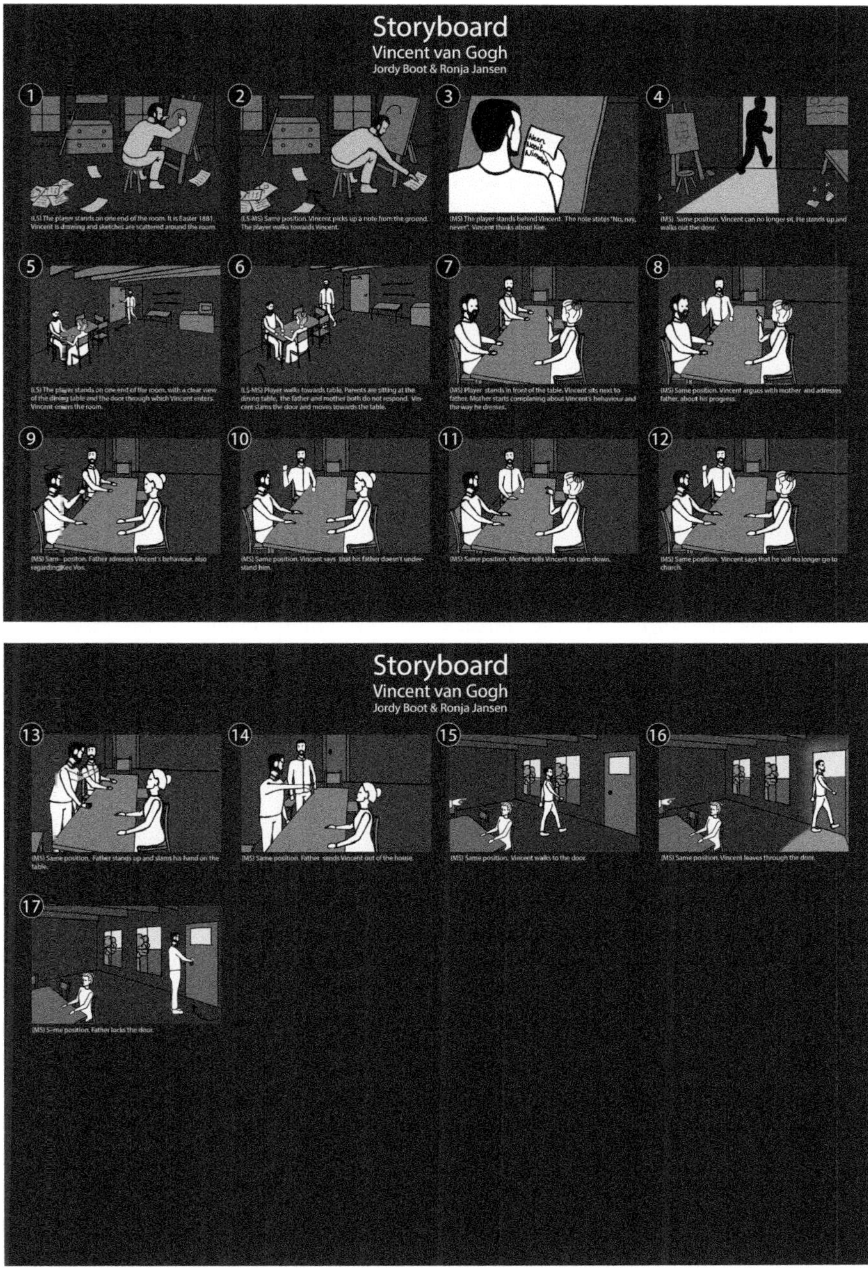

Fig. 14.6 Storyboard of the story in the virtual experience, developed by the game design students the authors were working with

both the commissioner and the client, even though the work had not always been smooth and faultless, and, looking at it from a distance, it looked also a little bit chaotic. The commissioner admits that at both sides, theirs and ours, there had been a bit of searching, every now and then, about how to handle the process. Hence, the feeling of uncertainty and of chaos that was originated.

Also the developer, with the different roles he had taken up along the project (initially "programmer" when he was a student and member of a team, and later, when he had become freelancer, "leader" and ultimately sole responsible for the final delivery of the product) had experienced the process, especially at the beginning, as rather unclear in terms of what was expected. The majority of the students' team could not figure out what the idea behind the project was and what they were expected to build: a game, an experience, or something totally different? For them, this was also the first assignment of this type as an artistic project, which added to their confusion. The situation was chaotic and frustrating also because of some internal miscommunications with the direction of the school about how their work as students would be considered from an educational point of view and their possible remuneration for it. This unclarity resulted in a few interruptions throughout the process.

Further in the process, it had become easier to clearly recognize and identify these various difficulties and the hurdles that had emerged and it was possible to tackle them on a one-to-one basis with the stakeholders involved (sometimes the client and the developer directly, for example) to ensure a faster and more ad hoc and effective solution. Ultimately, this has been such a positive experience, that the client hopes to have more of such collaborations!

The Collaboration

For the client as well as for the commissioner, this was a completely new world they were exploring, not so much for the collaboration with students but rather for what this collaboration was about (that is, the development of a virtual experience). In that, they had to put a lot of trust in us, as lecturers and responsibles of the students' work, but most importantly, in the students. At the beginning, it has been a sort of blind exploration, like sailing in sight, especially for what the technical part of the project might have implied and for what they could expect as a result. They were helpless and had to trust us unconditionally. *"To put Van Gogh in a game environment"*, as the commissioner put it, *"seemed to be a nice idea"*, but he admitted that he had no clue whether this would work and how it would work: it might as well have turned into a boring outcome. What the commissioner recognizes to have learned about this is to look at things from a different perspective than his own, namely that of the various other people involved in the project, such as the students: they might have had a clearer idea of how to carry it out based on their own experience of developing games. Therefore, for him the most important insight from this experience was learning to trust and learning to adopt someone else's perspective on a topic, namely developing a virtual experience, which was not his own expertise.

A point of concern for the commissioner was the size of the team, which was rather large, with 10 students involved in the design of the experience. The team was also very heterogeneous, considering that three different lecturers spread over several departments within the university were involved as coaches. This is also where the chaos the commissioner had been mentioning was coming from. However, he recognized that this diversity has precisely been one of the key elements for the success of this collaboration.

Also, the developer experienced that there were too many people involved, too many "*hands in the pot*", too many layers in the hierarchy, too many steps between them as developers and the client. He admitted that this hindered the communication and was also not a guarantee that the right message could be given to the right person at the right time.

And yet, the collaboration has been a success and still is, with the commissioner still loosely collaborating with some of us on different projects. In particular, collaboration with the developer is still ongoing; he proves to be extremely trustworthy and professional. Also, the client recognizes that the collaboration with the other stakeholders was very pleasant and valuable. He confesses to have been particularly impressed by the enthusiasm and commitment of all those involved, in particular of the developer: everybody wanted to succeed and worked hard to achieve this outcome.

A final positive remark about the collaboration was mentioned by the developer: he has appreciated the fact that for such an important project client and commissioner have come to our institution and have accepted this to be a students' project. This shows trust in the students. And this gave them the opportunity to have a serious work experience and to build an impressive portfolio.

The Communication

Communication, as the most visible part of collaboration, could have been better and more straightforward, as reported by all stakeholders interviewed. The developer reported for example on how, once all intermediate steps had been removed, he could communicate directly with both the client and the commissioner. This resulted in a more satisfying workflow and in the feeling of having ownership of the final product for all of them, because in this way both client and commissioner could immediately give feedback and instantly see if and how their feedback was processed and integrated by the developer. Only then could this really be an iterative creative process! All three agreed that communication must also be in person as much as possible and not mediated by technology, to be really effective.

Expectations Management

Each stakeholder had different expectations at the beginning of the project: the commissioner, for example, expected a 360° experience about Van Gogh but had no clue of what the storyline could be and how this could be visualized and ultimately experienced by the viewers. The client just wanted an immersive and impressive experience. The developer had no clear expectations and was unsure but curious at the same time of how working for such a heterogeneous consortium would be and how this might affect the end result. At the beginning of the project, it seemed that these expectations might have been difficult to meet precisely because of the chaotic, unstructured, and unclear situation discussed earlier (see under "The collaboration").

Each of the stakeholders, however, stated they found that this project was a success not only because, ultimately, their expectations have been met, but also because they have even been exceeded to some extent. The client reported for example, that his observations of the visitors' behavior one month after the experience has been installed in the church is that most visitors are "captured" by it and can feel completely immersed in the original parsonage in Etten, the location where the experience takes place. As one of the volunteers on this site, he is fascinated by and grateful to this experience, because it allows the visitors to get to know the original Van Gogh family's house that does not exist anymore. He also noted how the story told in the experience is complementary to the one that he tells visitors in the church during his guided tours: thanks to this, he finds that also his oral story becomes an experience. This is precisely one of the goals that we had in mind with this development: not to lock visitors away from the authentic physical location, but precisely to offer them an additional lens to experience it.

Most importantly though, with respect to expectations management, is the fact that all three stakeholders confess to feel proud of the game: this is the best outcome we could expect to achieve! The commissioner for instance, who had to convince the alderman and 19 local governments to invest in this project, could see how enthusiastic and impressed these decision-makers were when experiencing this game. And this, despite the challenge he admits to have faced to get the alderman and the other policy-makers along and to keep them interested during the process, since they were not directly participating in the several phases the project went through. Because this project has taken longer than expected, it has not been an easy task to accomplish: it has been a struggle almost. However, the commissioner genuinely confesses that their enthusiasm when they saw the end product, repays him for all his efforts. What is most remarkable is that now that all local governments see the end product, they have started to develop ideas on their own about how to use it, about other contexts for which something like this could also be developed or about how to extend it further. For the local governments of West Brabant, this project was indeed meant as a pilot: not so much in the sense that they were thinking of having many more virtual experiences around Van Gogh, but instead in that they wanted to experiment with this technology, with games and experiences, and verify the possibilities that it offers, for further developments.

Based on what the visitors tell him, the client very much appreciates that the virtual experience can give them the feeling of being in the parsonage themselves, and next to Vincent. However, he is critical of how this has been rendered, visually. He believes that the historical research could have been done better, not so much in terms of verification of factual events as the art historian was concerned about, but historiographically, to check the veracity of the environment. For example, the parsonage that is depicted in the game is only barely representative of what parsonages in the nineteenth century in Holland used to look like. In fact, he admits that this is rather an imaginative one: for example, he knows that in reality, Vincent's workshop was much smaller than it is in the game. According to him, this does not help the total immersion into a truly nineteenth century atmosphere. A more thorough historiographical research could have prevented these shortcomings.

Another critical point he reported relates to the characters themselves: their movements are rather clumsy, rigid. "*Wooden*" is the term he uses, and he states that they do not speak the right dialect. The mother's voice does not correspond to her real age for instance as, in the game, she sounds far too young.

14.3.3 The Stakeholders' Word Associations

We asked the stakeholders to react to a set of opposite terms that could be used to describe this project, dichotomies that have emerged during the process as problematic if at all reconcilable, and to report aloud all that came to mind. These words were presented in pairs (see below), without further explaining them, unless asked for by the interviewees, with the only instruction to mention aloud anything they could think of, with no fear of saying something wrong, because there was no right or wrong answer associated to them. Word-pairs included:

Facts—Storytelling

Museum—Experience

Physical—Virtual

Van Gogh the painter—Vincent the man.

Table 14.1 reports the term they chose from these dichotomies and the explanation they gave to justify it.

Table 14.1 Word chosen by the stakeholders from the opposite associations given and the explanation they gave to justify their choice

Stakeholder	Facts—Storytelling	Museum—Experience	Physical—Virtual	Van Gogh the painter—Vincent the man
The commissioner	Storytelling: "*you need it to take people into the story, to attract a broader audience to a specific topic (like it was with Van Gogh). For this reason, the way the story is told is more important to them than pure factual information.*"	A combination of both, depending on how experience is defined. The Etten-Leur experience may not be ideal for a virtual experience in a museum. But it is for the Etten church in that it is well integrated into its physical context. So, they enrich one another.	Also, a combination of both would do best in relation to this project (as explained for the previous association).	Vincent the man, for his life story which he did not know before this project. He knew the paintings but they were not very telling to him. Now he feels connected to the man and can understand him and his art better. This does add much to him and to his appreciation of Van Gogh the painter also.
The client	Facts: the story is well reported in the experience but in a somehow simple and superficial way.	Experience: the visitors experience the virtual game with the Oculus Rift as an experience and in this way the (physical) church also becomes part of this experience.	Virtual: visitors are lost in the game, in the sense that they feel totally immersed in the past and forget the "here and now". Meeting Vincent Van Gogh is very special.	This dichotomy should have been explored more in depth during the earlier phases of the project, when the narrative concept has been developed, even though the current virtual experience gives a first impression of how this relationship might have been and how it entices viewers to learn more. This "need" to get to know more about it might even take the form of a follow-up project.

(continued)

Table 14.1 (continued)

Stakeholder	Facts—Storytelling	Museum—Experience	Physical—Virtual	Van Gogh the painter—Vincent the man
The developer	Storytelling: "*it is more exciting and facts are usually boring.*"	Experience: "*When you go to a museum and you have an experience there, then they are the same. Nowadays museums tend to combine the two, I find museums without experience boring.*"	Virtual: because VR offers more possibilities to do, to act than one can get in a physical, real environment (like in an escape room) without endangering a person. When the virtual becomes more real, it is better.	Van Gogh the painter: He did not know Vincent the man but only Van Gogh the painter. This project has helped him discover a part of Vincent the man, but a part does not make the man. The virtual experience shows a phase of Vincent's life but it is not enough to get to know the full man. More is needed: more details, more story, more facts also.

14.4 Discussion

14.4.1 Dilemmas

From Table 14.1, various dilemmas that hampered our project and that reflect its multifaceted ecosystem could be derived. These dilemmas have to do with the difficulty of harmonizing conflicting interests, heterogeneous expectations, and different expertise and may be recognized in similar projects.

Physical Versus Digital
This dichotomy, i.e., physical versus digital, expresses the fear that a digital experience might lock visitors away from its physical counterpart. In this project, it was a very sensitive matter as the ultimate goal of the virtual experience was precisely to entice viewers to visit the physical location portrayed in the virtual game. This fear reflects the two emerging social behaviors, both parallel and yet irreconcilable: one toward hyper-connectedness, and one toward escapism from anything digital and online.

In this respect, it is good to see that both the commissioner and the client considered the virtual experience as well harmonized inside the church. Both reported that they think the two reinforce one another and add a different *tessera* to the complex mosaic that is the total experience of visitors, that none of them taken in isolation would be able to offer. Therefore, this was a perfect match!

Novelty Versus Content

A concern that we had to face with the adoption of virtual reality as the medium to convey this experience was whether this technology would distract viewers from the story.

Our own studies (Syrrett, Calvi and van Gisbergen 2016) relative to a 360° movie viewed with the Oculus Rift, in fact precisely express this concern. The subjects who participated in our experiments had in most cases no experience with the device (i.e., the Oculus). Many mentioned that as this was their first encounter with the Oculus Rift, they were more interested in the features of the display than in what was actually being shown. They admitted that being distracted was mainly due to the newness of the device and of the experience with that device, assuming that this could eventually wear off by use, when they would have seen more 360° movies. The participants were trying to experience all of the possible features in the Oculus and were, therefore, less interested in following the actual storyline. It is to be expected that when the device becomes more accessible and no longer unfamiliar, the viewers will no longer be distracted by it, to the point that this will have become invisible to them, and they will pay more attention to the content instead of to the technology and environment context. The same can be said for any new technology.

We did not do any experiments to measure the visitors' experience with the virtual game in the Etten church yet. But the accidental observations reported by the client reassure us on the added value of virtual reality.

Craftsmanship and Authenticity

The importance of and attention to content is related to another emerging trend in society, that is the increasing value associated with craftsmanship, in the belief that this will provide a real, genuine, and authentic experience. Even more: experiences should be *slow,* to be able to fully appreciate them, and should be unique (van der Laan 2017).

Uniqueness and authenticity is what we have tried to achieve with this virtual experience: its uniqueness lies in the possibility for visitors to be immersed into an old parsonage and next to Vincent van Gogh; its authenticity is due to the fact that an authentic location is reproduced, authentic is the church where it is placed (along with all other locations in the *Becoming Vincent* model, see again in Fig. 14.1) and authentic is also the importance that both the church and the parsonage had in Vincent's life. However, authenticity was a difficult issue to tackle in this project, in various ways: in the design itself, as the client reported the difficulty in reproducing exactly a real parsonage; and more in general, in a cultural-historical sense, as well represented by the art historian's plea for a facts check.

Storytelling Versus Facts

Storytelling techniques apply to all kinds of stories, both fictional and factual. This is why storytelling can help turn any experience into a memorable and meaningful experience, by unlocking values that would otherwise be not so immediately recognizable by the listeners (or readers/viewers).

As a matter of fact, telling stories does not only serve to inform others about something (this would be the factual stories): stories can also be told to engage people (Gabriel 2000); to help people attach meaning to places, images, or objects (Chronis 2012); to transmit emotional and symbolic values; to teach something about the world and oneself (Hover and Vugts 2013; Zipes 1997).

Stories can be so powerful thanks to the process of identification: this happens when the readers (or the listeners) can identify themselves with the (struggles and dilemmas of the) main character of the story that is being told (McKee 1998). This is what we have tried to achieve using storytelling to tell an episode in Vincent van Gogh's life. For us, it was less important to only report factual information. We rather wanted the viewers to identify with Vincent as in the true spirit of the *Becoming Vincent* project. This is why we had to give the story a more dramatic twist by introducing a few fictional elements.

This process can be further enhanced by the use of images or of authentic objects belonging to this main character. In our case, this authentic element was the location, i.e., the church itself, whose role has been strengthened by the virtual medium, as also reported by the client after observing the visitors having the virtual experience.

The added value of this approach was shared by the client and the commissioner also, as reported in the discussion above.

14.4.2 Lessons Learned

From our discussion above, three main lessons can be drawn when handling within such a complex ecosystem of stakeholders:

- Identify the relevant stakeholders and involve them all in all phases of the process, from the start: this will give them the feeling that no decision is imposed on them top-down but that, if not fully in charge, they are at least co-responsible for the choices that are made. This bottom-up approach is what Boutelle (2004) suggests through prioritizing stakeholders based on their interest and importance in the project (see in Sect. 14.2.3). In this way, all stakeholders feel they co-own the results and they will be eager to support the project further.
- Streamline the process workflow and structure, set a procedure, a tight planning and schedule with clear milestones and good communication. Although this may be difficult with a lot of stakeholders, a problem-resilient approach and a clear task division usually help. This may imply implementing a simple hierarchical structure to facilitate communication with no unnecessary and redundant intermediate steps. It also implies allowing for frequent and direct

communication (such as in our case, between client and developer): this makes the process smoother, faster and ensures better results not only in terms of product but also in terms of the personal satisfaction and fulfillment of those involved. Nevejan suggests to use *boundary objects* to facilitate communication and to avoid incommensurability (2007). A boundary object *"is meant to provoke discussion and in so doing it reveals flaws and misunderstandings between the different perceptions of the various contributors and their understanding of their contribution to the end product."* (Nevejan 2007, p. 142). In our project, the script represented in Fig. 14.5 served as a boundary object and in line with this quote precisely helped to highlight the different aspirations with the end product. This is important to avoid that "common sense" will dominate and regulate the collaboration (Nevejan 2007).

- Ensure that the project is always somehow visible to the people who are behind the scenes, those who have invested money in it for example but are not in the direct line of communication and involvement.

14.5 Conclusion

This chapter presents a case on how to design for various stakeholders in the cultural heritage sector. Not so much an ecosystem in the sense of "museum(s) as ecosystems" or as "museum(s) in socio-cultural ecosystems" (Sabiescu and Charatzopoulou 2018), since the project discussed in this chapter does not correspond to one single museum, nor is it limited to museums as such. However, it spans beyond mere museums to include various cultural institutions and all authentic locations where Van Gogh has lived, and whose center is not a museum but what Nevejan calls a *common ground* (2007), in the figure of Vincent van Gogh, both as a man and as an artist. In particular, in this chapter we have analyzed the issues surfacing when "orchestrat(ing) uncommon ground" (Nevejan 2007), when diverse stakeholders, all connected to one of the authentic locations mentioned earlier, have to negotiate on how to express a common interest but from different perspectives and having dissimilar priorities and expectations. The lessons we have learned apply to any situation, practice or business where people from different disciplines have to collaborate.

Acknowledgements We would like to thank the stakeholders who were involved in this phase of the *Becoming Vincent* project: Nico Sommen, Pierre van Damme, Oliver Engels, and the art historian. Our gratitude also goes to Fernando Cabello, game design lecturer, who has guided the student team working on the virtual experience, and all students involved, in particular, Margit Meesters as the initial project leader.

References

Bouma, M (2010) Storytelling in 12 stappen, op reis met de held. Uitgeverij Augustus

Boutelle J (2004) Understanding organizational stakeholders for design success. Accessed from: http://boxesandarrows.com/understanding-organizational-stakeholders-for-design-success/

Calvi L, Bouwknegt H, Hover M, Ouwens F, van Waalwijk J. van Schendel A (2014) Experiencing Van Gogh's heritage: a case study. In: Proceedings of the electronic visualisation and the arts conference (EVA London), 2014, London, 8–10 July 2014, pp 71–72

Calvi L, Hover M (2015) 'Becoming Vincent': a case study on the narrative concept linking Vincent van Gogh's heritage sites. In: Vaugeois NL, Parker P, Weighill A (eds) Innovative leisure practices: cases as conduits between theory and practice, vol 1. Vancouver Island University, World Leisure Centre of Excellence, pp 49–60

Calvi L, Hover M, Ouwens F, van Waalwijk J (2015) Visualising Vincent's life: an engaging experience into Van Gogh's heritage. In: DeSForM 2015, aesthetics of interaction: dynamic, multisensory, wise. 9th international conference on design and semantics of form and movement. Milano, 13–17 October 2015, pp 312–315

Calvi L, Hover M (2016) Crossroads. Life changing stories from the second world war: a (transmedia) storytelling approach to world war II heritage. VIEW J Eur Telev Hist Cult Vol. 5, No. 10, pp. 52–66. http://www.viewjournal.eu

Capra F (1996) The web of life: a new scientific understanding of living systems. Anchor Books, New York

Chronis A (2012) Tourists as story-builders: narrative construction at a heriatige museum. J Travel Tourism Mark pp 444–459

Freeman RE (1984) Strategic management: a stakeholder approach. Pittman, Boston

Gabriel Y (2000) Storytelling in organizations: facts, fictions, and fantasies. OUP Oxford

Hover M, Vugts O (2013) Efteling en Sprookjesboom. Storytelling tussen traditie en vernieuwing. In: NRIT, Trendrapport toerisme, recreatie en vrijetijd. Nieuwegein: NRIT Media, pp 272–275

Jung Y (2011) The art museum ecosystem: a new alternative model. Mus Manag Curatorship 26 (4) 321–338

McKee R (1998) Story. substance, structure, style, and the principles of screenwriting. York, Methuen

Nevejan C (2007) Orchestrating uncommon ground. In: Brickwood C, Ferran B, Garcia D, Putnam T (eds) (Un)common ground – creative encounters between sectors and disciplines. BIS Publishers, Amsterdam, pp 136–143

Sabiescu A, Charatzopoulou K (2018) The museum as ecosystem and museums in learning ecosystems. In: Vermeeren A, Calvi L, Sabiescu A (eds) Museum experience design – crowds, ecosystems and novel technologies. Springer, pp 325–345

Syrett H, Calvi L, van Gisbergen M (2016) The oculus rift film experience: a case study on understanding films in a head mounted display. In: Poppe R et al. (eds) INTETAIN 2016. LNCS, vol 178, pp 1–12, 2017

Van der Laan R (2017) The hidden gems project, putting small local museums on the map. Master's thesis, TUDelft

Zipes J (1997) Happily ever after. fairy tales, children and the culture industry. Routledge, New York

Author Biographies

Licia Calvi is a Senior Lecturer and Researcher at the Academy for Digital Entertainment at NHTV University of Applied Sciences (Breda, the Netherlands), where she teaches courses in Interactivity and in Media Theory within the Master of Media Innovation. An interaction designer by education, she has been designing interactive systems for various purposes and different domains.

Moniek Hover is Professor in Storytelling at NHTV University of Applied Sciences (Breda, the Netherlands), where she teaches in the applied and the academic bachelor's and master's programs in the field of leisure and tourism. At NHTV, she leads the research program line of storytelling and consumer experience. With multidisciplinary NHTV teams, she provides (storytelling-based) research and development projects in the field of leisure and tourism.

Chapter 15
Designing Trajectories of Experiences: In Museums, Around Museums, or Including Museums

Arnold P. O. S. Vermeeren, Hung-Chu Shih, Rik van der Laan, Licia Calvi, JungKyoon Yoon and Ianus Keller

Abstract Recently, museums have increasingly become parts of ecosystems of people and organizations in their functioning. As a consequence, museum experience designers are stimulated to think in a holistic way, about experiences of people that engage with networks including the museum, as well as about the role of individual museums within such ecosystems (Vermeeren et al in Museum experience design – crowds, ecosystems and novel technologies, 2018a). This raises the questions of: What are ways in which a museum experience relates to experiencing its embedding context? And, what does this imply for the process of designing the museum experiences? In two design case studies, four ideas for museum experiences have been developed based on different ways in which museums relate to their embedded network. The ideas illustrate how the focus of the design may be different depending on the role the museum plays in the overall experience, and how the design process is complicated by having to deal with a larger group of stakeholders when designing. Finally, all ideas came forth from taking a broader view of the potential museum target group than seeing them solely as visitors to the museum. This was seen as crucial for inspiring solutions to museum experiences beyond more traditional museum visiting experiences.

A. P. O. S. Vermeeren (✉) · H.-C. Shih · R. van der Laan · J. Yoon · I. Keller
TU Delft - Industrial Design Engineering, Landbergstraat 15, 2628 CE Delft, The Netherlands
e-mail: a.p.o.s.vermeeren@tudelft.nl

L. Calvi
NHTV - Breda University of Applied Sciences - Academy for Digital Entertainment, Hopmansstraat 1, 4800 DX Breda, The Netherlands

J. Yoon
University of Liverpool—School of Engineering, Harrison-Hughes Building, L69 3GH Liverpool, UK

A. Vermeeren et al. (eds.), *Museum Experience Design*, Springer Series on Cultural Computing, https://doi.org/10.1007/978-3-319-58550-5_15

15.1 Introduction

One of the current trends in the functioning of museums is the change from a focus on single museums to one on connected museums (Vermeeren et al. 2018a), museums as parts of networks of people and organizations. In terms of designing for experiences this trend implies that one no longer only designs for visitors' experiences before, during, and after museum visits, but that one thinks in a more holistic way, about experiences of people that engage with the system of connected people and organizations as a whole, as well as about the role of individual museums within such ecosystems (Vermeeren et al. 2018a).

The above raises the questions of: What are ways in which a museum experience relates to experiencing its embedding context? And: Will the museum experience be central in an arrangement of surrounding smaller experiences? Will the museum experience be one of many elements in a trail of experiences? What does this imply for the process of designing the museum experiences?

In this chapter, we explore such issues, based on two design cases. First, we discuss the case of the Mauritshuis, a Dutch museum famous for its rich collections of Dutch Golden Age paintings. We discuss the design of a mobile application (an app) for the Mauritshuis aimed at providing young adult visitors of the Mauritshuis with a more engaging way of appreciating its paintings, at the same time raising interest for and connecting them to modern Dutch culture outside of the Mauritshuis. We will briefly summarize how the app is designed to fulfill the above promise.

The second case concerns the search for a way of connecting small, local heritage museums (we named them Hidden Gems) to an audience of young adults, aged 18–30, by addressing thresholds that were identified to be limiting the likeliness of young adults visiting these museums. Solutions were sought in connecting small museums to the world outside the museums themselves. Three conceptual designs were developed: a label for branding the group of small museums as a whole, a platform for connecting performing artists to the small museums, and a pop-up hostel for solo-travelers, designed for multi-day travels along multiple cultural heritage locations.

We will discuss, and reflect on, challenges we encountered, as well as on implications of designing museum experiences that extend to beyond the individual museum visiting experience.

15.2 Design Case 1: The Mauritshuis

The Mauritshuis study was conducted as the second author's Master Graduation project at the Faculty of Industrial Design Engineering (TU Delft) in collaboration with The Mauritshuis[1] and museum design agency Kiss the Frog[2] (Shih 2015).

[1]http://www.mauritshuis.nl.

[2]http://www.kissthefrog.nl.

The Mauritshuis is a Dutch art museum, in the center of The Hague, mainly exhibiting paintings from the Dutch Golden Age period (seventeenth century), including Rembrandt and Vermeer. Many of its visitors not only visit the museum for its paintings, but also for its historic building, and its elegant, romantic, and cozy atmosphere. According to a Needscope study conducted by TNS-NIPO[3] for the Mauritshuis, the museum fulfills visitors' needs for *enrichment* (providing visitors with in-depth information about the Golden Age paintings) and *reflection* (stimulated by its relaxing atmosphere).

A study by the Dutch Museum Association in 2010 showed that the museum sector in the Netherlands would meet at least three challenges in the near future: cuts in subsidies, an increase of the number of international tourists, and the rise of the digital generation (Museumvereniging 2010). These challenges motivated the Mauritshuis to look for new potential visitors. One of these is the group of *young adult travelers*. The starting point for the new design became: *create a conceptual design for the Mauritshuis that will improve the art appreciation of young adult travelers, and at the same time motivates them to explore the local culture outside the museum.*

15.2.1 Designing an App for the Mauritshuis

An experience design approach was taken consisting of three main phases (see Shih et al. 2016 for more details): (1) identifying the needs of the young adult travelers, through interviews and *contextmapping* sessions (Sleeswijk-Visser et al. 2005); (2) developing a variety of design ideas and converging toward one conceptual solution (this included two types of brainstorm sessions); (3) developing the solution in more detail and evaluating it with users in the Mauritshuis. Figure 15.1 presents an overview of the design process.

15.2.1.1 Identifying the Needs of Young Adult Travelers

In line with the signaled trend of seeing museums as parts of networks of organizations and people, the starting point for this project was to design a museum experience embedded in a more comprehensive travel experience. Thus, from the start, a broad perspective had been taken for identifying the needs of young adult travelers, a perspective broader than that of visiting the Mauritshuis. Needs of young adult travelers and visitors to the Mauritshuis were identified in two different studies. In the first study, 16 young adults from various cultural backgrounds visiting the Mauritshuis were interviewed, to learn what aspects of the museum lead to positive experiences, and to observe and discuss how they behaved as individuals as well as in groups when going through the Mauritshuis.

[3]http://www.tns-nipo.com/.

Identifying needs of young adults travellers

Interviews

Contextmapping
(sensitizing booklet + follow-up interviews)

Outcomes: 4 personas; 2 museum journeys; more specific design brief

Designing design ideas: towards two concepts

Brainstorms (outcome: 7 design ideas)

Concept development (outcome: 2 conceptual design ideas)

Concept evaluation session

Outcomes: 1 conceptual design; 5 key design intentions

Developing and evaluating a detailed design

Detailing the design

Evaluating the design

Outcomes: 1 design proposal; suggestions for further development

Fig. 15.1 Phases in the Mauritshuis project design process

A contextmapping study (Sleeswijk-Visser et al. 2005) was conducted as the second study involving young adult travelers (non-visitors of the Mauritshuis). The contextmapping study consisted of two phases: *sensitizing booklet* and *follow-up interview session*. The aim of this study was to learn about the values and interests of young adult travelers when traveling abroad, as well as understanding how these values and interests influence museum experiences. For the contextmapping study, seven participants (young adults: three Taiwanese, one Chinese, one German, one Spanish, and one Turkish) were asked to use a sensitizing booklet for a few days, to bring back memories of travel experiences of a trip they had made in their recent past. The booklet was aimed at making them reflect on the topic before having an interview. It helped them remember their travel purposes, their interests, their travel schedules, their social interactions, and how they explored local life during their trips. This was done by providing them with tasks such as mapping a timeline of a day on their trip, mapping their social network during the trip, asking them to describe their best or most impressive moments, their personal way of exploring local life, as well as thinking of an imaginary, desired way of exploring the local culture.

In the follow-up interview session, participants shared, explained, and discussed the information in the booklets, and were then asked to elaborate on the timeline of their travel, as represented in their booklet by making a visual collage of it. The collages were shared and discussed among participants.

The combined results of the two studies led to four personas (i.e., *high art seekers*, *hipsters*, *famous attraction seekers*, and *outgoers*), who could be clustered around two typical museum journeys (*individual foreign explorers*: high art seekers and hipsters; *foreign experience seekers in groups*: famous attraction seekers and outgoers). One of the conclusions was also that all personas would like to *talk to locals to learn more about the country*, and to get specific information that would be useful for traveling, while hipsters, high art seekers, and outgoers would even be willing to travel along with locals. Things all personas would like to explore are *local food, local events, local places undiscovered by the majority of the tourists, local scenic views, common history, and unique attractions*. These insights, derived from the study with young adults as non-Mauritshuis visitors, proved to be of crucial importance for inspiring the way in which the designed museum visiting experience would be connected to modern culture outside the museum.

15.2.1.2 Designing the App: Generating Ideas, Converging Toward a Solution

Based on the needs of the young adult travelers, ideas were generated through two brainstorm sessions. These sessions led to seven ideas, which were then merged into two conceptual designs that were evaluated by role-playing the use of the conceptual designs in a simulated museum environment with paper prototypes (see Fig. 15.2).

It was concluded that the final design would be based on a combination of two conceptual designs and that it would need to have the following characteristics (formulated as design intentions); it should *(1) motivate the young adult travelers to look into the details of the paintings; (2) awaken young adult travelers' interests in the paintings; (3) make the young adult traveler's museum experience joyful and fun; (4) evoke the young adult travelers' interests in the Dutch local culture by connecting the traditional culture depicted in paintings to the current culture;* and *(5) motivate the young adult travelers to explore the local culture after leaving the museum.*

15.2.1.3 Detailed Design: The Treasure Hunt App

The final design proposal was a treasure hunting museum app that also contains the function of giving travel tips to the young adult travelers for exploring The Hague. The treasures to be found are elements in famous as well as less famous paintings that connect to stories that are interesting for the young adult travelers.

When starting the app, a short movie briefly introduces the treasure hunting game. Visitors should then select a room to go to. When entering the room they would engage in a *"find the painting"* game based on hints. For example, a hint such as "light and shadow" could refer to Ruben's painting "Old Woman and Boy with Candles"[4]. Having found the painting, the app depicts it, but in the depicted painting a few details would be different from the real painting. The player of the game indicates in the app the location of the difference and is then provided with the opportunity of listening to an audio fragment about or related to that detail, narrated by a young adult, local to the city of The Hague. Typically in the audio fragment,

[4]https://www.mauritshuis.nl/en/explore/the-collection/artworks/old-woman-and-boy-with-candles-1150/.

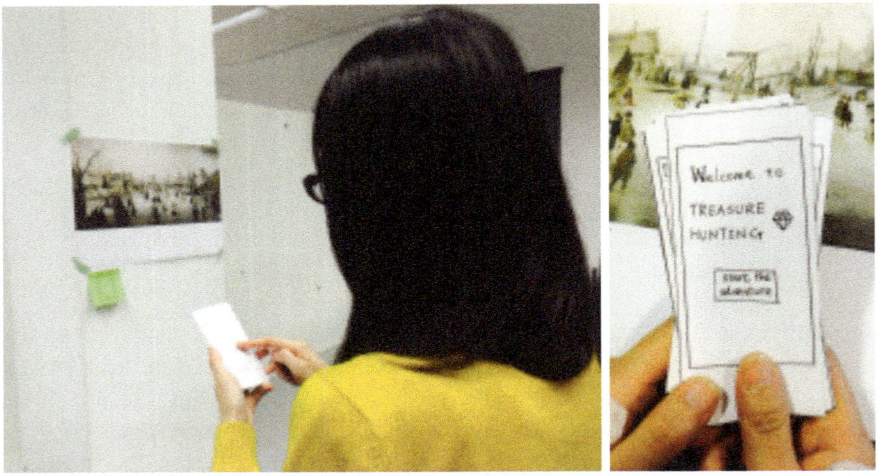

Fig. 15.2 Stills from a video taken of role-playing the conceptual designs in a simulated museum environment with paper prototypes

the story would start by explaining the painting and the depicted aspects of traditional Dutch culture, and would then connect the story to modern Dutch culture. After having identified five "treasures" (stories related to identified differences), travel tips related to the modern Dutch culture topics would be unlocked. For example, in the app version of the painting *Still Life with Cheeses, Almonds and Pretzels*[5] the color of the beer bottle would be changed from brown to green, referring to the color of the modern Dutch beer brand Heineken, and one of the breads would be changed into a bread roll with a Dutch "kroket" (popular meat snack) with the travel tip explaining where to get such a snack.

Thus, the app not only serves as an engaging museum visiting app, but through its collected travel tips also serves as a guide for further exploring modern Dutch culture outside the museum (see Fig. 15.3).

15.2.1.4 Evaluating the Design

The app was tested with nine visitors to the Mauritshuis (age 18–34 years old) from various countries. Participants matched the profiles of the personas of "hipsters" and "popular attraction seekers'. The aim of the test was to evaluate the extent to which the design would fulfill the five design intentions. For the test a partly functional prototype of the app was used, which allowed playing the game, but was limited to just a few treasures, and participants had to search for them in a predefined order.

---

[5]https://www.mauritshuis.nl/en/explore/the-collection/artworks/still-life-with-cheeses-almonds-and-pretzels-1203/.

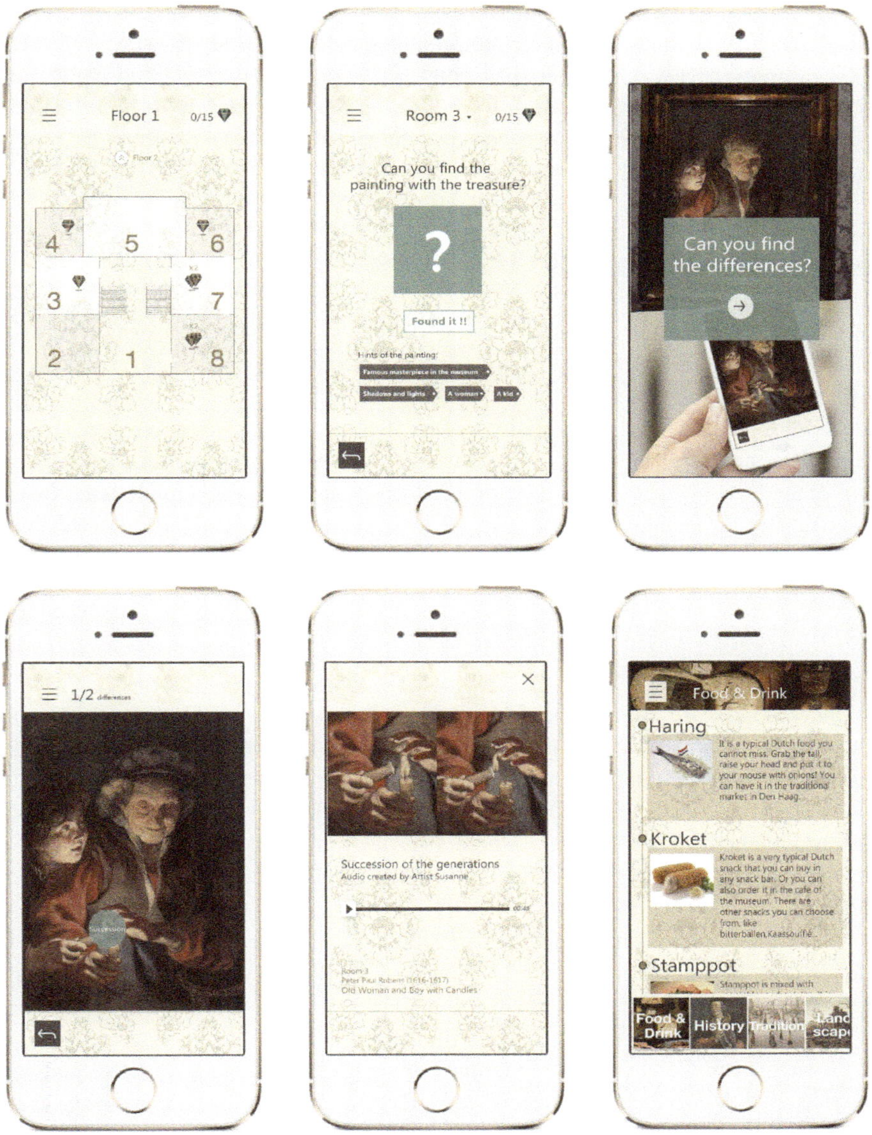

Fig. 15.3 Example screens from the app. From left to right: (top row) select room to visit, find the painting with the treasure, explanation of finding a treasure, (bottom row) treasure found in painting, audio fragment after finding treasure, travel tips

The test results showed that the treasure hunting game triggered participants to interact with the paintings, and had increased their interests to explore the paintings and listen to the audio stories. Participants very much liked the idea of introducing the local culture through the visit to the Mauritshuis, and then further exploring it in the city. They appreciated the audio stories about the local culture, but would also have liked to get some more information about the artwork themselves. The travel tips, categorized by different topics (such as Food and Drink, Landscapes, and History) were considered very useful for filtering what they would want to do in the city of The Hague. They emphasized that the travel tips indeed should be unique and recommended by the locals.

15.2.1.5 Interim Conclusion

In sum, in this design case, the starting point was to inspire the design through placing a museum visit in a larger encompassing context of experiencing local culture. This required a study on the needs of the potential visitors in relation to this embedding experience specifically, rather than to the museum visit per se. It resulted in an app that enhanced the museum visit experience and that in a playful way linked the objects in the museum to places that the young adults could visit in their further traveling.

15.3 Design Case 2: Hidden Gems Museums

In the second case study—the Hidden Gems study—we explored ways of connecting small local museums to young adults. This study was conducted as the third author's Master Graduation project at the Faculty of Industrial Design Engineering (TU Delft). It was done in collaboration with the Academy for Digital Entertainment of NHTV Breda University of Applied Sciences and two Dutch provincial heritage institutes: Erfgoedhuis-ZH and ErfgoedBrabant (van der Laan 2017).

The Hidden Gems project focuses on small, local museums that tell the story of the territory they are in through the objects they display. Their collections of objects are usually very specific and specialized: they are often about local history, or about a way of life that does not exist anymore (for example, craftsmanship—see in (Vermeeren and Calvi 2018b). Examples of such museums in the Netherlands are the museums Molenaar Old Tractors[6] in Berkel and museum De Timmerwerf in De Lier.[7] Molenaars Old Tractors is a small museum with a collection of 85 tractors of a specific brand (McGormick). It was founded by the father of the current owner, who was the first in the village to own a tractor in 1939. The current owner, 4 years old at that time, and his wife tell the stories of the quality of the brand and of how the tractor was used. The tractors are shown in the shed of an eighteenth century museum farm where the current owners live. Also about the farm, they have

[6]http://www.molenaarsoudetractoren.nl/.

[7]http://www.detimmerwerf.nl/.

interesting stories to share. Museum De Timmerwerf is a museum of carpentry. In a preserved carpenter's workshop volunteers demonstrate how the objects that are exhibited can be used, and tell stories about what the life of a carpenter looked like in the old days. The type of small museums we focus on in this study typically has an authentic feel. It is because of this authentic feel, and because one often finds these museums in small villages in rural areas, that we refer to these museums as Hidden Gems. In the Hidden Gems project, the young adults of age 18–30 years old have been identified as a potential target group of visitors.

15.3.1 Overview of the Design Approach

The initial brief for the project was *to develop a number of conceptual designs that can motivate young adults to get and stay engaged with small museums*. Thus, the challenge was to identify opportunities for aligning the needs and interests of young adults to those of the small museums, and to turn those opportunities into conceptual designs. Hence, the project started with studying the typical characteristics, needs, strengths (etcetera) of small museums, as well as gaining a better understanding of the young adults' needs and interests and their current barriers in engaging with the small museums (phase one). In the second phase, design criteria were formulated and seven conceptual design directions were envisioned. The design directions were then evaluated using the design criteria, and three ideas were selected to be further developed in the conceptual design phase. These three ideas were evaluated with museum volunteers, young adults and the provincial heritage institutes (phase three). Figure 15.4 presents an overview of the process.

15.3.1.1 Analysis of Small Museums' and Young Adults' Interests

In search for possible ways of relating small museums to young adults, the project started with a study on the characteristics, strengths, possibilities, and organization of the small museums.

Small Museums Together with the provincial Heritage Institute Erfgoedhuis-ZH, a list of museums was compiled as cases to start this phase with. It consisted of 16 museums, 13 of which fell in the category of museums we targeted, and three were bigger, but were still included to better be able to identify what is specific for small museums. Observations were done in these museums, focusing on staff, visitors, location, subject matter, and presentation of the subject matter. There were informal conversations with 20 museum staff members and semi-structured interviews with 6 staff members. Additionally, during the period of observations, conversations, and interviews, the 13 small museums were sent an extensive survey about their staff, visitors, income, goals, problems, needs, and wishes. Nine of the museum staff members responded, of which two from the same museum. The authenticity of the

Fig. 15.4 Overview of the Hidden Gems design process

ANALYSIS: IDENTIFYING NEEDS OF YOUNG ADULTS AND CHARACTERISTICS AND STRENGTHS OF SMALL MUSEUMS

- Observations in museums
- Interviews, conversations, surveys with museum volunteers
- Surveys with young adults
- Interviews/conversations with solo-travelers and hostel staff members

Outcomes: characteristics of small museums, interests and needs of young adults, thresholds for visiting small museums

DESIGN: DEVELOPING DESIGN DIRECTIONS

- Formulating design criteria
- Searching for connections between young adults and small museums
- Brainstorming and creating design directions
- Evaluating design directions and selecting conceptual designs

Outcomes: design criteria, 3 conceptual designs

EVALUATION: CONCEPTUAL DESIGN EVALUATION

- Detailing the conceptual designs
- Evaluating the conceptual design with museums and young adults

Outcomes: promotional leaflets, evaluation results, recommendations.

experience in the small museums and of their locations was observed as an important asset of the small museums. The staff of these museums has a passion for the museum and found preservation of the heritage much more important than making money through additional visitors. However, they were also aware of the need for digitization and digital presence (via websites and social media). For realizing that need the skills of the staff formed a problem though, as these volunteers generally are not so familiar with the digital world. Further, the location of the museums is usually a given. They are bound to the location they are in, as this often forms part of their heritage. A problem with that is that in many cases these locations do not have optimal connections to public transport or main roads. Additionally, because these museums run on volunteers and visitor numbers are very small, many small museums have very limited opening hours (for example, only on Saturday or Sunday afternoons). Figure 15.5 shows an overview of the main conclusions about the small museums.

Young Adults (Aged 18–30) To gain a better understanding of the world of the young adults, initially a survey was sent out focusing on young adults in relation to museums (50 respondents). As in the Mauritshuis case, there proved to be a need for taking a broader perspective on the needs of young adults. Thus, another survey was sent out focusing on young adults in relation to their activities (52 respondents). From the surveys, it became clear that within the group of young adults it is mainly the solo-travelers that visit museums. However, the surveys also showed that solo-travelers usually do not visit *small* museums (which is confirmed by the observations in the small museums, where no solo-travelers were seen). After the surveys, 25 conversations with solo-travelers and 10 hostel staff members were held

- Small museums would like to have more visitors
  - Opening hours are a threshold
  - Location is a threshold
- The specificity of the museum subject could be a threshold for visitors
  - Presentation of the subject is very standard (no interactivity)
  - Not much variation in exhibitions
- Small museums have too little volunteers to maintain more opening hours
  - Volunteers are nearly all 45+
  - Volunteers are enthusiastic and involved with the subject
- Small museums are not very well known
  - Budget for advertisement is too low
  - Advertisement is done at the wrong places

Fig. 15.5 Main conclusions from the study on small museums

Solo-travelers…

- Look for fun
  - Fun activities
  - Fun social experiences
- Look for new experiences (something different)
  - Interest in culture
  - Interest in authentic experiences
- Choose their activities based on word-of-mouth
- Are sensitive for 'must-see' activities
- Are interested in meeting people
  - Fellow travelers
  - Locals
- Are restricted by their budget
  - They choose well-established activities
  - More specific activities are based on personal preferences (affinity to the subject)
- Duration of their stay differs a lot
  - Some stay days
  - Others stay for months

Fig. 15.6 Main conclusions from the study on solo-travelers

at 5 different hostels. Additionally, an online analysis was done about travelers' trends in relation to this target group to find out what drives them. Figure 15.6 provides an overview of some of the important findings on the solo-travelers.

The study made clear that solo-travelers would potentially be very interested in the Hidden Gems museums. These museums possess a set of characteristics that provide an "authentic" experience and solo-travelers are very interested in authenticity and in experiencing something unique. Thus, instead of changing the Hidden Gems museums themselves and running the risk of destroying their authenticity, the choice was made to deal with the thresholds that keep the solo-travelers from visiting them.

Three main thresholds were identified as follows:

1. *Visibility*: solo-travelers are not aware of the existence of Hidden Gems museums

2. *Location*: the museums are mostly in villages and it takes considerable time to visit them, especially in relation to the time that currently can be spent on visiting the museum.
3. *Lack of social experiences*: solo-travelers pick their activities largely based on the chance to meet new people, especially of their own age. Currently, however, young adults do not visit these museums, so there will be no such social experiences.

Note that the choice of dealing with these thresholds implies that opportunities were sought in the context in which the museums function, and in their relationship to the outside world, rather than in improving exhibits per se.

15.3.1.2 Developing Design Directions

Based on the findings of the analysis phase, a set of design criteria in the form of requirements and wishes were formulated. Requirements included for example: *keeping the authenticity of the location; appealing to millennial solo-travelers; the potential for drawing in new visitors for the museums; and facilitating positive word-of-mouth advertisement.*

In the initial design phase, seven design directions were developed, which were then further developed into three conceptual designs, focusing on different levels of detail in terms of segments of potential visitors.

15.3.2 Three Conceptual Designs

Three conceptual designs were developed: a Hidden Gems label (targeted at a general audience for small museums), Amuse-um (targeted at young adults), and a pop-up hostel (targeted at solo-travelers as a subgroup of young adults).

15.3.2.1 Conceptual Design 1: Hidden Gems Label and Platform

The first conceptual design consists of a shared platform for Hidden Gems museums. It basically is a label assigned to museums that possess the Hidden Gems characteristics mentioned in Fig. 15.5. An accompanying website would make these museums visible on the Internet.

The rationale behind the label is as follows. The specificity of the subject, the size of the collection, and the time needed to reach the locations make return visits, from anybody other than locals unlikely (even if visitors had a very pleasant experience). However when the "experience" is labeled "Hidden Gems", and when many other museums with that label can be found in the Netherlands, visitors may be inclined to visit another "Hidden Gems" museum somewhere else. Thus, instead

Fig. 15.7 Proposed logo for the Hidden Gems network

of inciting return visits to a specific museum, these museums could incite "return" visits to other "Hidden Gems" museums and vice versa. With a network of these "Hidden Gems" all over the Netherlands (or even beyond), the number of potential visitors could increase substantially.

Thus, this conceptual design proposes a solution for the *visibility* threshold, by making use of creating a network of similar museums that as a whole has a better chance of making itself visible (Fig. 15.7).

15.3.2.2 Conceptual Design 2: Amuse-Um: Location-Based Performance Community

The second Hidden Gems design idea consists of an Internet platform for bringing together Hidden Gems museums and location-based performance artists. The platform hosts communities of performers and of small museums that are interested in connecting the two. Through this platform, performers can find places with a specific authentic or otherwise interesting atmosphere that would match their preferred kind of performances. Museums, in turn, can offer their spaces as a place for such performances and through which they can reach a new audience. Their visit could leave performance visitors with a good memory of the museum as a location, leading to positive ratings on the platform and making the museum more visible. Moreover, the platform would allow for expanding the museum experience, by adding performances to the museum visit, as well as allowing for the social experience of meeting other visitors with similar interests afterward. A museum visit, in this case, could, prior to the performances, consist of short explanations about the traditional, local culture the museum represents, and the visit could be concluded by a social activity such as having a drink together. This expansion of the museum experience can make undertaking the relatively long trip to the museum more worthwhile to the young adults.

Fig. 15.8 A fictional website illustrating a platform where museums and performers meet

Thus, this design deals with the three identified thresholds by connecting the world of small museums to a largely unrelated world outside of the museum context, namely that of location-based performers (Fig. 15.8).

15.3.2.3 Conceptual Design 3: Pop-up Hostel

The third Hidden Gems idea consists of a mobile, pop-up hostel. This idea focuses on a subgroup of the young adults, namely the solo-travelers. Nowadays, many of these solo-travelers visit hostels in the bigger cities, for shorter or longer periods. For them also, the aspects of visibility, remote location, and lack of social activities are often thresholds for visiting the Hidden Gems. A pop-up hostel that travels through the countryside visiting Hidden Gems would make the travel an inherent part of their holidays (instead of a time-consuming but necessary activity for reaching the museum) and would turn the museum visit into a social experience.

The pop-up hostel consists of a van or recreational vehicle with a trailer, containing all necessities for a sleepover. From the museum's perspective, one of the strengths of this idea could be the word-of-mouth advertising through this initiative. Solo-travelers typically select their destinations based on word-of-mouth recommendations, also through social media. The more interesting the travels and the museum visits, the more it will lead to positive reviews and new visits. The initiative for pop-up hostels visiting specific museums would largely be at the organization exploiting the pop-up hostel, whilst the role of the museum could be limited to just making themselves visible to such organizations. Museums themselves can decide on the extent to which they want or do not want to expand the experience around the museum visit. This ranges from just opening the doors for

Fig. 15.9 Storyboard illustrating a day in the trip of a pop-up hostel. Traveling from the Nationaal Sleepvaart museum in Maassluis, then visiting the picturesque village of Hellevoetsluis, and staying overnight near Hidden Gem museum ship Lichtschip 12 in Hellevoetsluis

the travelers to visit the museum, through museums opening their doors and arranging a campsite nearby the museum, to hosting the hostel at the location of the museum and organizing extra activities during the visit (Fig. 15.9).

Thus, this design concept builds upon the idea of connecting a small museum to the world of hostel visiting solo-travelers, as well as to other activities in the countryside around the small museum.

15.3.3 Evaluation

The three conceptual ideas were evaluated by checking them with the design criteria formulated at the start of phase 2 and by getting feedback from small museums, provincial heritage institute Erfgoedhuis-ZH, and young adults.

For each of the three conceptual design ideas a promotional leaflet was produced, in a style that would present the initiative as if it already existed (Fig. 15.10). These leaflets were sent to four small museums and the provincial Heritage Institute Erfgoedhuis-ZH for evaluating them in interviews.

For evaluating the ideas with the young adults, 20 travelers were interviewed in 2 hostels. They were presented with collages showing them the conceptual designs visually (Fig. 15.11). To them, the Hidden Gems platform was not presented as a separate idea, but as an umbrella platform for the other two initiatives.

To the museum volunteers, the Hidden Gems label and platform proved to be easy to understand. They were well appreciated by them. They spontaneously linked the label to other museums with similar characteristics. However, they emphasized that the label and platform should be low maintenance and preferably free or low cost to them. Therefore, an overarching organization managing this, or subsidies would be required for creating and maintaining the website. In general, the museums were most enthusiastic about:

Fig. 15.10 Leaflets presenting the three conceptual ideas for evaluating them with museums and the provincial Heritage Institute Erfgoedhuis-ZH

- the promotion and visibility the platform would provide
- the opportunity that the platform provides for finding museum-subject-related expertise or volunteers that may be shared among museums or with the outside world
- the easy and natural way of allowing communication between similar museums.

With respect to the Amuse-um idea, the museums showed an open attitude, but they also indicated they would not want to actively engage in organizing performances. However, they liked that the platform would facilitate activities that can take place in the museums. In general, the museums felt they needed to have more concrete, practical information about the initiative, before taking more interest in it. The young adults indicated that performances would indeed make it more worthwhile to travel the distance to the museums. They would prefer music performances. However, they also indicated there would be a considerable chance that they would look for music performances in the cities they are in, unless (for the travelers) hostels would organize trips to the museum performances.

For the pop-up hostel, museums showed more enthusiasm than for the Amuse-um idea. Two of them in particular very much welcomed the idea. During the interview, they spontaneously started showing places where the pop-up hostel could be placed, and they started brainstorming about extra possibilities for activities. For instance, Museum Bescherming Bevolking (a museum about civil protection in times of war) talked about providing army bunk beds, opening existing outdoor toilet facilities and was open to ideas such as showing movies or having campfires at night. Molenaars Old Tractors indicated to be willing to provide access to a canteen (which could also be used to sleep in), and the toilet in the

Fig. 15.11 Collages of the conceptual ideas, for evaluating them with travelers

farmhouse. A few days after the interview the museum even sent an email with the idea of organizing a beer-tasting event during a potential pop-up hostel visit.

In conclusion, it seemed that these museums would not only want to host the pop-up hostel, but would actually be willing to put some extra effort in accommodating the guests. They perceived the pop-up hostel as a fun experience for themselves as well as for their regular guests.

By the travelers, the pop-up hostel was indeed perceived as fulfilling a need and as resolving the most prevalent thresholds travelers may experience, namely distance and lack of social contacts. A very important issue about this design would be its cost. It should not be over 30 euros per night in order to be a realistic option for most solo-travelers. In terms of realization of the pop-up hostel, travelers clearly mentioned to be not very demanding. They need facilities such as sleeping accommodation, toilet, shower, place to cook, and a common area (living "room"/ "chill" space) but indicated that they would not require much from most facilities. The common area, however, would need to have a certain, specific atmosphere. This common area in combination with the museums and villages around them would be what these solo-travelers would base their choice on. The travelers also made clear that besides museums, other "Hidden Gems"-like activities should be included in their trips, in order to provide more variation. These activities should be specific to the visited locations and preferably have a typical Dutch character.

15.4 Discussion

In the Introduction section, we mentioned the current trend of designing for museums as parts of networks of people and organizations, instead of for individual museums (Vermeeren et al. 2017). We noted that for museum experience design this would imply that one no longer only designs for visitors' experiences before, during and after a museum visit, but that one thinks in a more holistic way about experiences of people that engage with the network as a whole, as well as about a museum's role within such network. Four design ideas from two design cases have been described illustrating different ways in which museums can be embedded in networks.

All four design ideas are based on connecting the museums to the outside world, though in different ways (see Table 15.1 for an overview).

The Mauritshuis app was designed with the content of paintings in the museum as the starting point. An experience was created around visiting multiple paintings in a playful way, with audio stories connecting the content to current local culture. After the museum visit, the visitor would get further travel tips based on the audio fragments that discussed the local culture. In other words the app focuses on the Mauritshuis, and then stimulates visitors to visit local, current cultural places.

In the Hidden Gems project, the Hidden Gems label and platform were based on a network of similar museums. This platform provides museums of a specific kind with a branding label and a website that connects them. It can thus stimulate return visits not to individual museums but to museums of a similar kind.

Amuse-um, the platform for location-based performances in museums, is yet another kind of network. Where the Hidden Gems platform is a platform on which museums only present themselves to potential visitors, Amuse-um is a platform for

Table 15.1 The various ways in which design ideas in the two design cases create a relation between the museum and the outside world

Case	Treasure hunt app (Mauritshuis case)	Hidden Gems label and platform	Amuse-um (Hidden Gems case)	Mobile hostel (Hidden Gems case)
Design focus	Content depicted on paintings in the museum	Authentic character of the museum	Museum as an interesting location. Performers in need of a location	Solo-travelers on tour
Mechanism of connecting the museum to the outside world	Suggest other places to visit, based on museum content	Make museums with a similar character visible and findable	Create a shared marketplace and communication platform	Make museums an interesting place to make a stopover

bringing together networks of performers and of museums. It serves as a kind of marketplace, where performers can offer their services to museums, and vice versa.

In the pop-up hostel idea, the museum plays yet another role. The design focuses largely on travelers, and incorporates the museums in the travels. The museums themselves can decide in agreement with the organization running the mobile hostel, what role it wants them to play: just being one of the places the hostel stops at for a regular visit, or being a place where special events are organized for the travelers that come by, or even organizing a place for the hostel to stay overnight, either at the location of the museum itself or in the neighborhood. In this network, the museum forms one of the experiences that are embedded in the larger trip of visiting multiple Hidden Gems across a certain region.

In all presented cases, lessons were learned, specifically related to designing experiences for situations in which a museum is not considered as a standalone place to visit, but as related to the outside world: as embedded in networks of institutions and people. These lessons relate to needs' identification at the outset of a project, to decisions with regard to what the central focus is in the design process, as well as to issues of ownership and networks of stakeholders involved in realizing the design idea.

15.4.1 Identifying Needs from a Broader Perspective

Experience design usually starts with identifying the needs, values (etc.) of the users one will design for (e.g., see Hassenzahl 2010 and Hassenzahl et al. 2010). This is very much in line with what Falk and Dierking suggest about museum visitor experiences, namely that the public seeks leisure experiences that meet specific identity-related needs and values (Falk and Dierking 2013). Thus, when designing for museum visitor experiences one should focus on museum visitors' identity-related needs and values, for which Falk and Dierking identified seven categories of motivations for visiting the museum. In our design cases we took a broader perspective: not only focusing on motivations for visiting a museum, but also on more general motivations and interests, such as those related to the travel in which a museum visit can be embedded. Based on this wider focus, personas can, for example, be developed as a complement to the museum visit role categories that Falk and Dierking (2013) suggest. Indeed, for connecting the Mauritshuis museum experience to the local, modern culture, the contextmapping study that focused on travel rather than on a visit to the Mauritshuis provided us with more inspiration than the interviews about actual visits to the Mauritshuis, enabling us to envision how the museum experience could contribute to enriching the travel experiences. In the Hidden Gems project, the inspiration for Amuse-um and the pop-up hostel came largely from conversations and surveys about young adults and their activities, rather than from discussing their museum visits.

We conclude that for a more holistic design that views a museum as being embedded in networks of people and organizations, the focus of a need identification study at the start of a design process should take a broader perspective on the needs of the visitors, for example: looking into their day-to-day activities and interests; for example, viewing them as travelers, rather than as museum visitors only.

15.4.2 Balancing the Focus

One of the challenges we experienced when designing for museums as part of connected people and institutions, was that of balancing what the focus of the design should be. In the Mauritshuis case, when visiting a museum of classical art, much of the visitor's focus of attention should be on experiencing that art. On the other hand, the aim was to also raise interest in the local culture around the museum, and to later provide concrete help in exploring that local culture. Gradually raising that interest during the visit requires drawing attention to it, and thus getting away from the artworks themselves. The answers of the participants in the final user tests indicated how difficult it is to deal with this challenge. We recorded answers such as: "The information about the local culture takes me a bit away from the museum, maybe it should be less, but the intention of it is good" and "I did not expect to get information not directly related to the painting. The information is good, but not what I expected". On the other hand, one participant said: "I really found the story about how tall the Dutch are, interesting because I found it myself on the street that the people here are really, really tall … It is really interesting information" and "It is a good way to start exploring the city. […] Usually when you visit a different country, you don't have that. It is quite difficult sometimes to find a local when you travel".

In the Hidden Gems project, it is also clear that the conceptual design ideas varied much in their focus. While in the Mauritshuis project the main focus was on the artworks themselves, in the Hidden Gems project all ideas focused on other things than the objects on display. The Hidden Gems platform focused on finding the museum based on its character, the idea of Amuse-um focused on the atmosphere of the museum as a location, and the focus for the pop-up hostel was on the museum affordances for providing a stopover travel.

We conclude that when designing experiences for the museum in networks of people and other organizations, carefully and creatively considering the design focus opens up the space for developing unconventional solutions.

15.4.3 Ownership and Networks of Stakeholders

In the Mauritshuis project, the second author had initiated the idea of the design assignment herself, only after which collaboration with the Mauritshuis started. From that point on, the Mauritshuis was seen as the client, hence the focus was on the Mauritshuis as having future ownership over exploiting the app. One could argue that for a truly holistic experience design approach one should start from the local culture (in this case in The Hague) instead of from the Mauritshuis. An interesting experiment would be to re-do the design project using that as a starting point. How would the design be different? Most likely, it would have focused on a "The Hague travel experience". We imagine that such a design would start from overviews of possible experiences in The Hague. However, such overviews would then lead to people visiting places to have the desired experiences, and it is very likely that specific designs would be designed for those as well.

Building such networks of designs not only requires that participating institutions (organizations, etc.) are networked digitally through their offerings, but also that they continuously keep each other up to date about their offerings, actively looking for how their offerings can be connected to other offerings in the network. We imagine this would require much collaboration between partners in The Hague network, probably including also technological and procedural standardization or an overarching organization.

In the Hidden Gems project, the three design ideas led to different models in terms of which stakeholders should be owners of the initiatives. While in the Mauritshuis the prime initiative would be at the museum, in case of the Hidden Gems platform an umbrella organization bringing together the museums would have to be found; one that could justify spending effort and time on setting up and maintaining the platform. The Amuse-um idea would be something that could grow from groups of volunteers in the world of performances (as the museums had already indicated that they would welcome it, but would not put effort in initiating it). In case of the pop-up hostel, probably a start-up company would be needed to organize such travels. That organization would then need to have close contacts with the museums to arrange interesting travels.

We conclude that when designing experiences for the museum in networks of people and other organizations, ownership of the design is not necessarily at the museum. New parties next to the museum will have to be involved in the process of developing as well as of exploiting the designed experiences.

15.5 Conclusion

We conducted two design case studies in which various ideas were developed for experiences in, around, or including museums that are part of networks of people and organizations. We learned that broadening the perspective that lies at the basis of the design brief may lead to new design opportunities. However, taking such an approach also implies that museums may not always be central to the design idea, and that ownership of the resulting initiatives or products may be either in or outside the museum itself. This can lead to new types of business models for running them.

Acknowledgements We would like to thank Geert-Jan Borgstein of The Mauritshuis, Ronald Theunissen of Kiss the Frog, Evelien Masselink of Erfgoedhuis-ZH, and all museum volunteers for providing us with the opportunity to conduct these studies. We thank all participants in the studies for their participation.

References

Falk JH, Dierking LD (2013) The museum experience revisited. Left Coast Press, Walnut Creek (CA)

Hassenzahl M (2010) Experience design: technology for all the right reasons. (Carroll JM ed). Morgan and Claypool

Hassenzahl M, Diefenbach S, Göritz A (2010) Needs, affect, and interactive products – Facets of user experience. Interact Comput 22(5):353–362

Museumvereniging (2010) Agenda 2026: study on the future of the Dutch Museum sector http://www.museumvereniging.nl/Portals/0/6-Publicaties/Bestanden/Agenda%202026%20PDF%20v4%2035231%20eng%20hi-res.pdf

Shih H-C (2015) Treasure hunt in the mauritshuis (Master of science graduation report) Delft University of Technology, Faculty of Industrial Design Engineering

Shih H-C, Yoon Y, Vermeeren APOS (2016) Positive emotions for inciting behaviour - playing with paintings to enhance museum experience. In: Proceedings of design and emotion conference 2016, Amsterdam, 28–30 September 2016

Sleeswijk Visser F, Stappers PJ, van der Lugt R, Sanders EB (2005) Contextmapping: experiences from practice. CoDesign 1(2):119–149

Vermeeren APOS, Calvi L, Sabiescu A, Trocchianesi R, Stuedahl D, Giaccardi E, Radice S (2018a) Future museum experience design: crowds, ecosystems and novel technologies. In: Vermeeren A, Calvi L, Sabiescu A (eds) Museum experience design – crowds, ecosystems and novel technologies (this book)

Vermeeren APOS, Calvi L (2018b) How to get small museums involved in digital innovation: a design-inclusive research approach. In: Ciolfi L, Damala A, Hornecker E, Lechner M, Maye L (eds) Cultural heritage communities: technologies and challenges. Routledge

van der Laan R (2017) The Hidden Gems project – putting small local museums on the map (Master of science graduation report) Delft University of Technology, Faculty of Industrial Design Engineering

Author Biographies

Arnold P. O. S. Vermeeren is Assistant Professor at TU Delft, Faculty of Industrial Design Engineering and Director of the Faculty's MuseumFutures Lab. He was educated as an industrial designer and has been involved in various EU-funded projects on User Experience (UX) as well as a large variety of museum experience-related projects. His current focus is on designing museum experiences for long term engagement, using novel technologies, and making connections to the world outside the museum.

Hung-Chu Shih graduated from Industrial Design Engineering of TU Delft in 2015. She is an UX researcher who helps companies toward user-centered design with qualitative research and workshops. Her research focuses on bringing customer's loyalty to an emotional level and building strong relationships between companies and customers.

Rik van der Laan graduated from the faculty of Industrial Design Engineering at the Delft University of Technology in 2017 with a Master of Science in Design for Interaction. Driven by a combination of intuition and results his works reside in-between the arts and design. Rik is currently expanding his portfolio to visualize the common features in his diverse interests within design.

Licia Calvi is a Senior Lecturer and Researcher at the Academy for Digital Entertainment at NHTV University of Applied Sciences (Breda, the Netherlands), where she teaches courses in Interactivity and in Media Theory within the Master of Media Innovation. An interaction designer by education, she has been designing interactive systems for various purposes and different domains.

JungKyoon Yoon is a PhD candidate at the Faculty of Industrial Design Engineering of Delft University of Technology. His research focuses on emotion-driven design, mainly concerning how designers can be supported to work with a nuanced understanding of positive emotions. He previously worked as an interaction designer at Naver where he supported the development of an internet search service, social media, and product simulations.

Ianus Keller is a teacher of practice at TU Delft, Faculty of Industrial Design Engineering and designer at For Inspiration Only. He was educated as an industrial designer and finished his PhD Cum Laude on how designers collect and organize visual material for inspiration.

Chapter 16
The Museum as Ecosystem and Museums in Learning Ecosystems

Amalia Sabiescu and Katerina Charatzopoulou

Abstract In this chapter, we suggest that ecological thinking can inform the design of audience-centred and society-relevant learning experiences in museums, with a focus on digital learning. We draw attention to two interrelated perspectives for positioning museum learning experiences: First, their embedding in the museum ecosystem, which includes the collections and spaces, but also museum staff, audiences and the intricate webs of interactions and relationships that underpin the everyday life of the museum. Second, the place of the museum in a broader education ecosystem, which includes formal and informal education providers, learners, as well as other social and institutional actors that shape educational practice. We illustrate this perspective through a case study of a successful long-term partnership between a museum and a technology company for innovating the learning offer for young audiences: The Samsung Digital Discovery Centre at the British Museum. We use a communicative ecologies framework to examine the context and determinants of the Samsung Centre digital learning design approach, how this evolved, and its impacts on the variety of digital interaction patterns that are offered and constantly refined by the Centre. On this basis, we discuss implications for the design of digital learning experiences in museums in increasingly interconnected ecosystems, within and outside museum walls.

16.1 Introduction

Significant attention has been placed lately on the educational value of museums and their growing importance as informal education providers. The premises upon which the educational mission of museums resides have been brought to shape from the 1980s, and include: the rise of the concept of 'experience' and tailored

---

A. Sabiescu (✉)
Loughborough University London, London, UK
e-mail: a.g.sabiescu@lboro.ac.uk

K. Charatzopoulou
Independent Researcher, Berlin, Germany

A. Vermeeren et al. (eds.), *Museum Experience Design*, Springer Series on Cultural Computing, https://doi.org/10.1007/978-3-319-58550-5_16

approaches to designing museum-specific learning experiences; keeping a focus on collections and contextual knowledge around them as the centrepiece of museum learning content (Cannon-Brookes 1992, p. 501); and the importance of audiences and audience-centred approaches to the museum and learning experience design (Roberts 1997; Samis and Michaelson 2017).

Apart from developments in the museum and cultural sector, the role of the museum as an educational actor of growing significance was leveraged by societal shifts happening throughout the past decades. Our societies are now changing at an accelerated pace, so that the knowledge and skills for the exercise of citizenship and employability need to be adapted to a rapidly evolving socio-economic context. These developments question and challenge previously widely accepted assumptions about the separation between learning, work and everyday life (Charatzopoulou et al. 2016). These notions are replaced by the idea that learning is a lifelong endeavour, not restricted to formal education but pursued by an individual all throughout their lifetime, for their personal growth and fulfilment and to keep up with a changing society and economy (Sharples 2000).

In this context, museums can play a significant role as education providers and as agents shaping the future of education (Center for the Future of Museums 2014:10). But how can museums embrace their educational mission, be aligned to societal trends and dynamically evolving learner needs, whilst continuing to deliver on their mission to preserve and curate collections representing a particular area of scientific or cultural knowledge? In this chapter, we suggest that ecological thinking can inform the design of museum learning experiences that are both aligned to museums' mission of preservation and curation and society-relevant. We expand on two interrelated perspectives for employing ecological thinking in learning design: First, the embedding of learning experiences in the museum ecosystem, which includes the collections, spaces, as well as museum staff, audiences and the interactions and relationships that underpin the everyday life of the museum inside and outside the galleries. Second, the place of the museum in a broader education ecosystem, which includes formal and informal education providers (from schools to other museums and community centres), learners, as well as agencies, policy-makers, companies and other actors that shape educational practice in a social context.

An ecological analysis dwelling on these two vantage points enables an in-depth look at how the design of learning experiences can balance complex sets of requirements associated on the one hand with the broader education ecosystem in which a museum is situated, and on the other with the museum mission, agenda and principles that unify its approach to visitor experience design. We illustrate this perspective through a case study of a successful long-term partnership between a museum and a technology company for innovating the learning offer for young audiences. The Samsung Digital Discovery Centre (SDDC)[1] was opened in 2009 as the result of a partnership between the British Museum and Samsung Electronics.

[1]www.britishmuseum.org/learning/samsung_centre.aspx.

The Centre aims to be an innovative provider of educational opportunities for schools and young audiences both integrated in and occupying a distinctive place in a broad ecosystem of learning provision, encompassing the UK legal and institutional infrastructure for education, schools, learners and other agencies that ensure good quality education at national and local level. At the same time, the learning offer is collection-centred and aligned to the mission and the principles for experience design endorsed by the British Museum. A versatile approach to learning experience design is used to deliver a learning offer that is relevant for both the museum mission and its audiences.

This chapter offers an analysis of the SDDC case, drawing on qualitative research conducted within the European project RICHES[2] (2014–2016), which examined the design of digital learning experiences at the Centre and their social relevance within a lifelong learning paradigm (Sabiescu and Charatzopoulou 2015). In this chapter, we use a communicative ecologies framework (Hearn and Foth 2007; Tacchi 2006), to examine the context and determinants of the SDDC digital learning design approach, how this evolved, and its impacts on the digital interaction patterns that are offered and constantly refined by the Centre.

In the remainder of the chapter, we will first outline what an ecological perspective means in socio-cultural environments, and then zoom in on museum ecologies. We then apply a communicative ecologies analysis to the SDDC case, mapping ecological elements and processes, and relating these to the SDDC digital learning design strategy. Finally, we discuss the implications of our analysis for designing digital learning experiences in museums. We will look at diverse understandings of the concept *learning ecology* (e.g. Jackson 2013, 2016; Lemke 1997) and critically examine the role of museums in these ecologies. We flesh out the concept of *interpretive ecology* (Mannion et al. 2016), which captures the meanings and interpretations invested in museum exhibits, spatial design and digital media, and how visitors interact with and make sense of these in personalised learning experiences.

16.2 Ecological Perspectives on Museums

This section lays the theoretical basis for thinking of museums as ecologies, and of them being embedded in an ecology, or multiple ecologies. After tracing some key features of ecological thinking applied to socio-cultural environments, we will discuss different approaches to analysing the museum in ecological terms. We will thereafter introduce the analytical framework used in this chapter, drawing on communicative ecologies (Hearn and Foth 2007; Tacchi 2006).

[2]www.riches-project.eu.

16.2.1 Ecology and Ecosystems in Socio-Cultural Environments

Ecological frameworks have been used in the social sciences and humanities as paradigms, metaphors or analytical frames that draw attention to the interrelatedness and interdependency between social actors, processes and their socio-cultural and physical environments (Lugan 1993). Ecological frameworks draw on a parallelism between the natural world and the human and social world: In the natural sciences, an ecosystem refers to a community of organisms interacting with other organisms and the physical environment. By analogy, we can conceive of social and cultural ecosystems in which human life, social processes and interactions and socio-cultural change and development occur. Ecological frameworks have been advanced in several social science and humanities disciplines, to name just a few:

- In anthropology, sociology and cultural studies: cultural ecology,[3] cultural ecosystems and ecologies of knowledge (Finke 2013); ecology of mind (Bateson 1973); ecosocial systems and social ecologies (Lemke 1997);
- In communication and media studies: communicative ecologies (Hearn and Foth 2007; Slater 2013; Tacchi 2006); ecology of communication (Altheide 1994); information ecologies (Nardi and O'Day 1999);
- In education studies: learning ecologies (Jackson 2013; 2016; Barron 2006) and learning ecosystems (Center for the Future of Museums 2014).

There is significant variation across ecological concepts and frameworks, not least influenced by the specific requirements and constraints of the disciplines and objects of study within which they have been developed. We can, nonetheless, abstract a series of underlying principles that are generally present in ecological frameworks:

Holism: Ecological frameworks take a holistic analytical stance, which focuses on the examination of phenomena and processes in context. This differs from the analysis of discrete entities extracted from their context (such as technology assessed as a stand-alone artefact) and their causal relationships (such as the way technology as stand-alone artefact may influence certain human behaviours).

Systems thinking: This implies looking at human society, communities and contexts of life in terms of many dynamic, nested systems that embed interacting entities, and are themselves interacting in larger systems (Latham and Simmons 2014). Human activities and cognitive and emotional behaviours occur in specific contexts, and derive their meaning in relation to these (Jackson 2013).

Interrelatedness and interdependency: In a social system, social acts and semiotic (meaning-making) activities occur in relation to other social actors and the

[3]The term 'cultural ecology' has been used earlier in anthropology to capture how cultural change is influenced or induced by the need to adapt to the environment (see Steward 1972). The frameworks we review here, by contrast, use ecology as an overarching conceptual and analytical frame for studying socio-cultural processes and systems.

environment. Moreover, the features that we may attribute to a certain agent are manifested and made possible in interaction with or on virtue of relating to other processes and agents (Slater 2013). For example, the skills of reading and writing in a certain language and using a specific alphabet are not individual properties of an agent, but are embedded in a socio-cultural system. Within this system, the agent shares and accepts conventions about the meaning of written signs and their associations with sounds and words, which are meaningful only insofar as the broader community agrees on their meaning.

Interdependent change and co-evolution: Because they are interrelated in an interactional system, change in any of the entities in an ecosystem is at the same time conditioned by and impacts upon the other entities that coexist in the ecosystem (Nardi and O'Day 1999). Development and evolution are likewise connected, and many of the issues in socio-cultural systems are caused by fragmented change, whose impacts have not been fully absorbed, causing disruption and confusion. An example is the need to change copyright laws to keep up with developments related to new forms of ownership and understandings of intellectual property associated with the advent of digital media in the publishing sector.

Another key characteristic of socio-cultural ecologies, and one which distinguishes them from natural world ecologies, regards the dimensions of knowledge production and exchange, meaning-making and interpretation. Whilst interaction and exchange in natural ecosystems can be described as well in terms of communicative exchange, it is only in socio-cultural ecosystems involving human interaction that communication is endowed with layers of subjective meaning-making and interpretation.

What is so special about ecosocial systems among all other possible ecosystems is not that they contain us and our things, but that our behavior within the system, and so the overall dynamics of the system as a whole, depends not just on the principles that govern the flow of matter and energy in all ecosystems, but also on what those flows mean for us. (Lemke 1997, p. 40).

16.2.2 Museums as Ecosystems

The analysis of museums in ecological terms proposed in this chapter focuses on two perspectives relevant to our study: first, on museums as ecosystems, by analogy to any kind of socio-cultural institution, with its interrelated institutional actors, spaces, processes and mediating technologies; and second, on museums as part of broader socio-cultural ecosystems, which underpin different kinds of relations, exchanges and activities between museums and other socio-cultural actors and institutions. Beyond just a scholarly or analytical exercise, it is sensible to acknowledge that thinking of museums in ecological terms is also historically embedded, it relates to evolving perceptions about the role of museums in our societies, as well as the evolution of organisational and exhibition practices inside the museum. On the one hand, the design of museum spaces, exhibitions and experiences has evolved from a single focus on exhibits to an increased acknowledgement of the context—spatial, cultural and interpretive—in which they are entrenched (Vermeeren et al. 2016). This perspective is enhanced by thinking of museums as ecosystems that embed collections, installations, as well as the agents (museum staff, visitors) and their exchanges, messages and activities. From another viewpoint, in the past few decades, the social role of the museum became the object of study and debate. As Falk and Dierking (2013) argue, whilst museums have been projects for the public good ever since being first founded, the notion of 'public value' has been used more recently to rethink and reframe the role of the museum. This value is something that is determined by the aspirations and needs of different kinds of audiences, and can be attained by maintaining a constant dialogue between museums and communities (Scott, Dodd and Sandell 2015). In short, museums are part of the fabric of societies and communities, and their value is both acknowledged and enhanced by seeking and strengthening relations, exchanges and activities within these nested ecosystems.

Several frames have been conceptualised in the museum studies literature that focus on one or unify the two perspectives. Bell (2002) uses the notion of 'cultural ecology' to capture the museum space and the museum experience within this space. Her framework focuses on the interactional affordances offered in the museum, where every visit is a ritual performed by interacting with objects and people, accessing information and deriving personal meanings and understandings.

A dual frame, uniting the two perspectives outlined above, is proposed by Latham and Simmons (2014) who introduce the notion of a 'holistic museum ecosystem', composed of:

- The internal system, which comprises the inner museum (collections and people who manage and study them) and the outer museum (the devices and programmes that enable the translation of this knowledge into information for public outreach); and
- The external system, which stands for the local and global context that influences the museum functioning.

Some other approaches give a more central position to the interpretive layers in social ecologies and museum ecologies, such as the knowledge produced, the communicative exchanges and the myriad of meanings generated by any one interpretive agent, but also values and standards (see for example Wakkary and Evernden 2005). For Gay and Hembrooke (2004), museum ecologies are developed around museum visit experiences and relate to visitors' acts of interpretation, subjective experiencing and interaction. They identify three keystone museum ecologies that describe visitor experiences:

- Sacred-space ecology, where the museum is a somewhat distant, authoritarian place of knowledge, but also of spiritual recollection, set aside from the outside world;
- Social and recreational ecology, which sees museums as sites of sociality, interaction and engagement, rather associated with having fun, taking a break from everyday routines and spending some leisure time;
- Learning ecology, where visitors see museums as places of learning.

16.2.3 In Search of an Analytical Framework: Communicative Ecologies

The examples introduced above showcase the diverse ways in which we can use ecological thinking to make sense of museums. In the remainder of this chapter, we want to draw attention to the processes of meaning-making, interpretation, knowledge production and communication that underpin museum learning. Thus, we will use as analytical tool an ecological framework that can help us interpret the complexity of museum-related processes and practices from a communicative viewpoint. 'Communicative ecologies' refers to 'The whole structure of communication and information flows in the people's ways of life, and the complete ensemble of (symbolic and material) resources for communication in a locality, and the social networks which organize and mediate them'. (Slater 2013, p. 42).

The communicative ecologies framework affords an analytical modelling of social worlds by singling out the information and communication flows and their relations with social networks, media and communication resources and practices. Hearn and Foth (2007) suggest focusing the analysis on three layers of the communicative ecology: social, discursive and technological. Whilst these are separated for analytical purposes, the processes in there are interrelated and mutually influencing. Below, we interpret these layers in relation to museums and museum learning:

The social layer refers to people and the networks they are associated to, including the informal ones (such as personal networks) and the formal ones such as institutional networks. In our analysis, we use this dimension to examine social agents in interaction: the people (individuals or groups) that interact with, exchange information and derive meaning from engaging with a museum at any one moment. We also draw attention to the networks—spontaneous or enduring—that they cultivate through repeated interactions and communication exchanges, and the formalised processes within these networks. In an institution such as a museum, communication and interaction processes are formalised, and provide patterns that often times create expectations to be followed up on (looking for a museum map at the entrance, or asking for a guided tour are examples of such expectations).

The discursive layer refers to information, content knowledge, meanings and interpretations that can take a variety of forms: they can be produced individually or collectively and shared, stored and modified; they may be represented and manipulated through different media, such as the account of a historical event communicated orally, in writing, or through computer animation.

The technological layer refers to the tools and infrastructures that mediate human activity and meaning-making, and the affordances they offer. This includes traditional and digital media for producing information, sharing it, communicating and providing feedback. In our analysis, we look at the mediational qualities and the affordances of artefacts or constellations of artefacts. For instance, a fixed digital station in a museum offers a different range of interaction affordances from a mobile device on which a visitor has downloaded an app. A multimedia environment, computers in a digital learning lounge and mobile devices together with informative panels and labels interconnected in the museum space can create an infrastructure that affords an even broader variety of experiential and learning engagements.

16.3 Case Study: The Samsung Digital Discovery Centre

16.3.1 About the Samsung Centre

Opened in 2009, the Samsung Digital Discovery Centre (SDDC) was the result of a partnership between the British Museum and Samsung Electronics, which aimed to provide a new, experimental digital learning platform for young audiences. The partnership was initially signed for 5 years, within which time the SDDC welcomed more than 51,000 visitors from 3 to 18 years old, and around 5,000 schools every year. The partnership was renewed in 2013 for another 5 years, along with a sponsorship for updating and improving the Centre's digital technologies equipment to support experimentation with new types of programmes (Sabiescu and Charatzopoulou 2015).

SDDC offers digital learning sessions free of charge for schools, families and teenagers. The sessions focus on one or more cultural areas covered by the museum collections, including Ancient Egypt, Asia, Ancient Rome, Ancient Greece, pre-Columbian civilisations in the Americas and Africa.

School sessions are designed following the curricular areas of the English national curriculum, organised according to class levels or Key Stages (KS)[4]. For example, SDDC sessions can be linked to curricular subjects such as History, Religious Education, Geography, Music and Computing. Each session has a support sheet made available on the SDDC website, which describes the aims and outline of the session, links to curricular areas, key topics covered, as well as ideas for activities that teachers can propose to their students before or after the session.

Family sessions take place during weekends, and can be conducted in the SDDC digital studio, in the museum galleries or distributing activities across both. They are designed to be playful and engage family groups (rather than children alone). Some of these are experimental, such as the *Innovation Labs*—spaces where families are invited to engage with new modalities of interaction, creative concepts or technologies. *Teen sessions,* offered as well during weekends, are designed to

[4]The British national curriculum is organised around key stages (KS), as follows: Early years (3–5 years old); KS1 (School years 1–2; 5–7 y.o.); KS2 (School years 3–6; 7–11 y.o.); KS3 (School years 7–9; 11–14 y.o.); KS4 (School years 10–11; 14–16 y.o.).

appeal to teens and their interests. The themes approached range from 3D printing to game design and animation.

Learning sessions are designed in relation to specific learning goals, and seek to cultivate knowledge and skill areas that are relevant to society, or which link to and complement curricular subjects in schools. The range of skills and competences targeted is varied, constantly updated and includes for instance:

- Applied creative skills such as drawing, object design or playing a musical instrument;
- Digital and information literacy competences, ranging from applied skills such as video production, video editing, 3D animation to more generic information literacy competences, for instance, capacity to review critically, select and employ information for the desired purpose;
- Citizenship, personal and social competences such as creativity and collaborative work, social interaction and group work abilities (Sabiescu and Charatzopoulou 2015).

At the same time, all learning activities are collection-focused and designed to enable participants to engage and interact in new, meaningful ways with the museum objects. Most sessions focus on a specific cultural area or period, while some take a comparative perspective to examine objects, events or customs in different historical periods or geographical areas. For example, in the session *Around the world in a day,* students explore objects created at the same moment in time in five different ancient cultures, then create a multimedia broadcast about one of the objects. The range of activities offered is revised and renewed periodically for all audiences. In addition, special programmes and activities are run which can focus on a temporary exhibition, be organised in the frame of a creative partnership or for trying out a new technology.

16.3.2 An Ecological Perspective on the Samsung Digital Discovery Centre

As a museum learning lab that has innovation and experimentation with digital media within its core tenets, the Samsung Centre can be seen to function within the constraints and opportunities of two ecosystems: the museum ecosystem and the learning ecosystem. Each of these ecosystems provides resources, infrastructures and affordances that both constrain and open up opportunities for the Samsung Centre and its learning mission. This section examines these aspects following the analytical elements introduced in Sect. 16.2.3 on the communicative ecologies analytical framework.

16.3.2.1 The Samsung Centre in the Museum Ecosystem

Social Layer The most important agents that shape the digital learning activities are the SDDC team, the other museum staff that supports their activity, as well as the various learning audiences: teachers and students, families and teens. Within the museum, the SDDC is part of the Schools and Young Audiences department, which forms part of the museum's broader education department, called Learning, Volunteers and Audiences. The Centre is run by a small team, responsible for designing, managing and evaluating learning sessions and works mostly independently. However, it embraces the principles and works as well in close cooperation with the Schools and Young Audiences and the Learning departments for developing special programmes and activities.

The target audiences—families, schools and teens—each have their own background knowledge and interests, which are important attributes when making decisions on the design of digital learning sessions. For instance, families seek a pleasurable, light experience, which nonetheless affords building knowledge, skills and attitudes for kids. Families may prefer to be engaged as a whole (parents and children together) in activities. Schools, on the other hand, have more complex requirements. They visit in seemingly homogenous units: classes of students accompanied by an instructor, all students sharing a certain level of education, a common curriculum in schools and formalised interaction patterns among teachers and students. Nonetheless, and beneath the apparent homogeneity, individual students have different aptitudes, learning styles, interests and personal skills. Examining audience features at these two levels (collective and individual) will generate diverse sets of requirements and insights to inform the design of digital learning experiences that respond to their needs, interests and aptitudes.

Discursive Layer As a digital learning lab, the SDDC designs and delivers learning experiences optimised for digital delivery. Learning content is shaped by attention to a complex range of factors, out of which two stand out: the centrality of the museum collection and responsiveness to audience needs, or in other words—collection-centeredness and audience-centeredness. The main source of information for learning content is the pool of knowledge and information surrounding the museum collection, as well as the artefacts themselves. Despite this common pool, a wide variety of learning sessions can be organised when considering diverse audience needs. Content can be created, co-created or delivered using different repertoires and storylines, as the same information can be shaped and delivered differently for a high school student, a very young child or a visiting family. Thus, we draw attention to how an audience-centred approach will influence the types of content and discourses produced and delivered through learning experiences, despite them all being focused on the museum collection and contextual information around it.

Technological Layer The technological infrastructure and tools are fit for supporting both studio-based work and gallery explorations. In the galleries, technologies are used for media capture, close examination of objects or mobile-guided gallery trails punctuated by games and quizzes. The supporting devices are mobile phones, tablets, audio and video recorders and digital cameras. Activities in the digital studio are, on the other hand, focused on content editing and composition using laptops, mobile phones or tablets, or content visualisation on the smartboard or 3D television. The studio also includes a green screen, which is used in some sessions to produce digital photographs and videos in which participants are featured in imagery displayed on museum objects. It is important to note as well the learning and interaction affordances of these media tools. For instance, mobile devices afford gallery exploration, easy sharing and combinations of individual and group work; whilst engaging small groups with creative work on a shared computer will require group members to each take (and eventually rotate) tasks in the creative process. These are important elements to consider when balancing the learning goals of a session against technology affordances, during its design.

16.3.2.2 The Samsung Centre Within a Wider Learning Ecosystem

Social Layer At this level of analysis, we zoom out to consider the manifold social agents that shape the activities of the Samsung centre, not only when they are physically present in the museum, but also as they act and connect in social networks during their daily (study, professional and personal) lives. We focus on education and learning as a lens for identifying the most influential of these agents and networks, which can be seen at local (London), national (the UK) or even global level. The most important of these agents are at local level: key audiences such as schools and learners, community centres and informal learning providers, but also other museums and cultural institutions. Apart from the key audiences, there are other actors on the educational scene, which shape education and the skills needed in society, for instance, the UK Department for Education, and the Department for Culture, Media and Sport.

The social layer can be analysed, as suggested above, at collective or at individual level. It can also be examined by focusing on individual agents or on the agents embedded in an institutional context—such as a school or a cultural organisation. Shifting between these different levels of analysis expands the range of insights and requirements for shaping the design of learning experiences. For example, as an institution, a school can come up with standards, criteria and expectations for the type of learning content that students should be exposed to, in a museum learning centre. Teachers come with their own expectations and requirements for their classes; and individual students have their own learning styles and interests.

Discursive Layer Seen from a learning ecosystem perspective, the learning content needs to be socially relevant, which means it has to respond to the needs of key audiences (families, teens and schools) and align to socially accepted notions regarding the skills, values and knowledge that are to be enhanced through education. The content and skill areas covered by SDDC activities are periodically revised, to keep aligned to social and technological advancements and their impacts on requirements for new skills and competences. For instance, taking guidance from government strategies and the National Endowment for Science, Technology and the Arts (NESTA) on new types of skills to be cultivated by education, SDDC proposed new sessions in fields such as design, making and crafts and big data (Sabiescu and Charatzopoulou 2015). SDDC learning content is aligned as well to the key competences for lifelong learning endorsed by the European Commission, such as digital competences, social, civic and communicative competences (European Parliament 2006). These competences are not reduced to knowledge and skills, but may encompass as well attitudes and values such as awareness of and respect for cultural diversity and intercultural competences that can be shaped in interaction with diverse cultural artefacts in a cultural history museum (Sabiescu and Charatzopoulou 2015).

Technological Layer Digital technologies are widely used in Western societies, especially in vibrant cities such as London. Their usage is permeating personal, professional and study lives, which need to be considered by a learning centre such as the SDDC when they develop their digital learning strategy. For instance, the propensity to use social media, the interest in gaming and playful technologies, but also the kinds of technologies that are used or are absent from (but desirable in) schools. Within this sociotechnical web, the SDDC digital learning offer needs to be both relevant and unique. For instance, digital activities must aim for enhancement of desirable skills (such as cooperation skills, visual thinking and creativity enhanced through group digital creation activities) but also bring novelty with respect to what can be done in schools (where some technologies are absent and many types of interactive and playful sessions are more difficult to organise). Thus, a balance needs to be struck between keeping relevant for and aligned to the way technology is used in society by key audiences, the digital skills that are asked for on job markets and in curricula, and the types of activities that can be afforded in the museum.

16.3.3 Approach to Designing Digital Learning Experiences

Based on our communicative ecologies analysis, we unpack below four design principles elicited from the SDDC approach to the design of digital learning experiences:

1. An object-based learning framework, which stems from the key mission of the British Museum as a cultural institution: providing access to and accessible interpretation of its collections and the knowledge they embody.
2. Learner-centred design, which is about considering the needs of the diverse audiences and the most effective ways of engaging them in learning programmes.
3. Technological mediation, which is about making the best of the qualities of technology for learning, without however allowing it to become the centrepiece of learning programmes.

4. Iterative design and experimentation, which characterise the overall design approach of the SDDC and enables the Centre to constantly innovate and improve their educational offer.

An Object-based Learning Framework Object-based learning refers to focusing learning activities on museum artefacts, as tangible evidence of culture, history, ways of life and events. Sessions involve close examination of objects, access to contextual information surrounding them, but also creative activities which represent, interpret or discuss the meanings of objects and contextual information. Activities of exploration, interpretation and creative production are enhanced by digital media. For example, the family session *Make a mosaic mask* uses imagery inspired by representations of Aztec gods. After examining artefacts, families use tablets to draw mosaic masks, which can then be printed and taken home.

Learner-Centred Design One of the central principles characterising the design approach of the SDDC is that the learning programmes need to be relevant for each audience, which means that not only the content, but also the learning approach and ways of engagement are shaped to fit definite audience profiles. There are three elements underpinning the focus on the learner in the digital learning design process, further unpacked below:

a. A participatory learning framework
b. Audience profiling
c. Responding to different learning styles

Participatory learning, constructivism and inquiry-based learning theories frame the engagement approach of learning activities. All these theories converge in recognising the role of the learner in constructing their own meanings and understandings. Thus, learning is not a mere transfer of information from teacher to student, but a co-creation of knowledge. The educators are there not to teach in an authoritative way, but in a role of facilitators, for creating the conditions for learning to take place, through the active involvement of the learner, in a sense enabling learners to construct their own understandings and creative responses (Sabiescu and Charatzopoulou 2015). Inquiry, exploration and creation are encouraged, rather than memorisation of facts or frontal lecturing.

Audience profiling refers to the way the learning content and ways of engagement are modelled according to the developmental stage and the audiences addressed, considering broad categories such as schools (and key stages within school audiences), families and teens. School sessions are devised as learning activities with well-defined learning goals and outcomes aligned to curricular areas. The design of a school session considers the key stage addressed and the corresponding subjects, and may involve advisory panels including teachers to ensure curricular relevance. Ways of engagement are also tailored according to the developmental stage. For instance, students in Early Stages are engaged in hands-on manipulation and kinaesthetic learning, which comes naturally for this young group. KS1 and KS2 students are inquisitive, like to explore and ask questions, so sessions that blend Q&A and inquiry-based content exploration are devised (Sabiescu and Charatzopoulou 2015). Apart from curricular alignment, sessions are also new or different from what can be taught in schools; they may use technology, content or engagement approaches that are not afforded or are not typical in formal education, such as for instance gallery exploration using mobile apps.

Sessions for families are designed to engage the entire group (rather than children alone) in light, playful interaction that make the museum spaces feel approachable and welcoming. Sessions are conceived to invite families and young children to explore the galleries in game-like activities, create and manipulate digital content or devise their own exploration pathways in the museum galleries. Whilst most activities involve children and adults together, in more complex ones, tasks can be split among children and parents.

Teen sessions offer content and ways of engagement fit for the teenage developmental stage. Sessions are conceived to link to areas of interest for teens and are furthering teenagers' agenda rather than imposing the museum's agenda. Sessions are experiential and avoid authoritarian teacher–student patterns of interaction. Instead, they are modelled on a master-apprentice model which was found to be effective for engaging teens. For example, in *Teens timelapse animation skills workshop,* teens learn to animate clocks in the British Museum's collection by using stop-motion animation software under the guidance of a professional animator.

Accommodating different learning styles The blend of participatory engagement approaches and digital technology affords a wide variety of interactions, which can be tailored for supporting different learning styles. For example, visual learning is enhanced through close examination of objects, multimedia representation and manipulation of imagery created by students. Likewise, kinaesthetic learning, which is rewarding particularly for young students, is supported through hands-on experimentation, craft and making activities. Sessions are periodically reviewed to expand and improve on ways of accommodating different learning styles.

Technological Mediation It is more appropriate to speak of digital mediation, rather than of digital technology per se, as being central to the activities of the Samsung Centre. The focus is placed on the mediational qualities of technology, rather than the mere use of a certain type of technology. When employed skilfully, technology can bring about or support ranges of interaction patterns and engagement modes that in turn facilitate learning. Examples are numerous: media capture in galleries to facilitate close attention to artefacts; exploration of gallery trails through apps that encourage students to examine closely object features, test them through quizzes or challenge them to work and create together as a group; group-based creative activities using imagery captured by students in gallery explorations; and so on. Rewarding qualities of technology come about when used in participatory or inquiry-based learning approaches, in which technology is effectively used as a mediating artefact for experiential learning, and where students are encouraged to become active agents in their own learning pursuit, whilst instructors take the role of facilitators (Sabiescu and Charatzopoulou 2015).

Iterative Design and Experimentation The SDDC design approach is inspired by Agile and Lean methodologies, embracing principles of iteration, responsiveness to evolving needs and constant improvement. In Agile development approaches, the work is organised in short cycles or sprints, with defined goals and outcomes for each sprint. This enables constant assessment of progress in relation to goals, ongoing adaptiveness of process and constantly improved products. Lean methodology advocates a focus on the customer (in the case of the SDDC, the learner), simplicity in work, and maximum value with minimum waste (either in workload or unnecessary product features). In practice, the SDDC perfects its sessions throughout several iterations, with attention to meeting learner needs and be aligned with trends (e.g. on technology and needed competences) in education and society. New types of sessions are constantly proposed, some of these starting experimentally such as the ones delivered in the Innovation Lab, to try out new technologies or interactions patterns. The chapter by Sabiescu on paradigms for museum technology and experience design (Chap. 13, this volume) provides a more in-depth investigation on Lean and Agile methodologies and how they afford flexibility, responsiveness and constant innovation in museum experience design.

16.4 Discussion

We have thus far unpacked an analysis of learning design in a museum digital learning centre, focusing on communicative aspects from an ecological perspective. We underline once again that our endeavour in this study was analytical, and as part of this study we did not engage with ecological frameworks to directly inform design (for this purpose, see for instance Wakkary and Evernden 2005). Rather, we have showed, through retrospective analysis, how by using ecological thinking we can trace back and relate significant features of a digital learning design strategy to important elements of interacting ecosystems—a museum ecosystem and a broader learning ecosystem. We sum up and discuss the main implications of our study along four areas.

16.4.1 Museums in Learning Ecosystems

One argument line that we built in this chapter is that ecological perspectives can be employed to shed light on the role that museums can play in education, and how they can best collaborate with other stakeholders in learning provision. Several conceptualisations of learning ecologies and learning ecosystems have been advanced to cut through the complexity of these systemic relations and better shed light on the role of diverse actors in education. Frameworks take different stances with respect to the elemental components and relations that can be represented, modelled and intervened into, and may include for instance a focus on:

- Spatiality, situatedness and context: Learning ecologies as *'the set of contexts found in physical or virtual spaces that provide opportunities for learning. Each context is comprised of a unique configuration of activities, material resources, relationships and the interactions that emerge from them'* (Barron 2006, p. 195).
- The learner and self-created ecologies: Learning ecologies as *'the process(es) I create in a particular context for a particular purpose that provide me with opportunities, relationships and resources for learning, development and achievement'* (Jackson 2013);
- Provision of resources and opportunities for learning: *'ecology of learning opportunities'* (Erstad and Sefton-Green 2013, p. 5) or *'learning resources'* (Knowles 1981, p. 135–136).

Ecological perspectives can shed light on key developments in learning at social level that can have an influence on the museum learning offer. Two of these developments are particularly relevant for the argument in this chapter. First, the set-up of new pan-institutional structures for learning provision, which link among diverse socio-cultural and economic actors, leveraged by adoption of digital technology for cooperation and communication (Charatzopoulou et al. 2016). Museums can partner with schools, community centres, technology companies, other socio-cultural institutions or actors in the media and creative industries sectors. Joint partnerships between museums and technology companies have led to innovative concepts for delivering cultural and scientific content. Apart from the SDDC case, which we examined in this chapter, there are other successful partnerships such as the *Louvre-DNP Museum Lab,*[5] *The Hermitage Museum Project*[6] which is a long-term partnership between IBM and the State Hermitage Museum and *Google Chrome Web Lab,*[7] in which The Science Museum in London partnered with Google.

A second important trend is the creation of new learning spaces in museums. Whether called digital learning centres, learning labs or learning studios, the specificity of these spaces stand in bringing and enacting specific approaches to learning (such as inquiry-based learning, constructivist approaches and Do-It-Yourself concepts) along with the tools needed to accompany learners in tailored educational journeys. Well-known examples are the Learning Labs in the USA, which enact a learning approach based on the HOMAGO model (standing for Hanging Out, Messing Around and Geeking Out) for engaging youth in learning experiences in ways that connect to their own interests and patterns of media usage (Ito et al. 2009).

[5]www.museumlab.eu/.

[6]www.research.ibm.com/haifa/projects/software/hermitage/.

[7]www.chromeweblab.com/.

16.4.2 Ecological Thinking and Learning Experience Design

We suggest that ecological thinking—which we adopted as a frame for analysing the determinants and context of learning design in a specific context—can be used more directly to inform learning design. Adopting an ecological framework focused on communicative aspects, this implies examining the interconnections and interactions among social agents, mediating technologies and social discourses within two interacting ecosystems—the museum and the learning ecosystem—as a context for learning experiences design. Within this frame, we draw attention as well to the notion of *context* defined from a constructivist perspective, which sees learning as facilitation within a meaningfully designed environment where the learner constructs their own knowledge (Barab and Roth 2006). Thus, the types of experiences designed by the SDDC can be seen as such contexts or spaces that provide affordances and resources for individualised learning experiences to be constructed. This is similar to what Barab and Roth (2006:9) call 'curricular-based ecosystems' in formal education: *The emphasis is on establishing rich contexts and then providing necessary scaffolds to support the learner in successfully enlisting meaningful trajectories through the network* (2006, p. 9).

16.4.3 Employing a Communicative Ecologies Framework

The communicative ecologies framework that we employed in the analysis enabled us to surface and examine the relations between social, discursive and technological spheres, seen as interrelated and mutually influencing. Following the interrelations between these spheres, we showed how elements from the two ecosystems can be linked to the digital learning design strategy of the SDDC. For example, the focus on the collection that is central to the British Museum learning mission is modelled in an object-based learning framework, meaning that each learning scenario integrates some sort of interaction with museum objects—in the gallery, or captured, digitised, manipulated and transformed in new creative acts.

A communicative ecologies framework also allowed us to rethink communication in the museum in relation to learning and interpretation, and the role of museum audiences in communicative acts. Communication is one of the central missions of museums expressed in the definition of ICOM (2007). Yet, as commented by Desvallées and Mairesse (2010), it took a long time for museums to put in practice their communicative function in both strategy and practical approaches: from a mission centred on preservation until well into the first half of the twentieth century, to a gradually growing communication agenda in the second half, and towards a relatively recent shift towards co-creative approaches to communication and interpretation (p. 29–30). The communicative ecologies perspective we employed allowed us to show how very diverse actors will leave their trace over communicative and educational practices in museums, particularly when a learner-centred approach is endorsed. This can be mediated through decisions taken by the design team—for example in considering the needs of specific audience groups when designing learning experiences. And second, from the audience's side, when they interpret and reconstruct their own meanings from interactions with objects and content within a museum exhibition or programme.

The analysis of the two ecosystems through a communicative ecology lens enabled us as well to shed light on the crucial role of museum educators for designing learning experiences that are relevant for audiences and resonant with museum principles and agenda. In the SDDC case, to make learning valuable for diverse learners, educators have to glimpse into their interests and needs, and understand how to design learning experiences that can be both engaging and educational. At the same time, they have to make certain that learning design corresponds to the museum mission and values; and further that the learning content and approach is relevant in a societal context that privileges the acquisition of certain skills, attitudes and competences in educational settings.

16.4.4 Perspective Shift: The Learner's Interpretive Ecologies

There are other aspects that came across as important during our study. We draw attention to what we consider the most important of these: the centrality of the personal context of learners (micro level context) and their subjective interpretation and engagement with learning. Whilst our study was geared towards unpacking design considerations, and did not collect data from learners, it did reveal the concern of the SDDC with modelling learning experiences focusing on audience needs and different ways of engagement and learning styles. It is interesting to shift the perspective from the designers to the learners, and understand how encounters with the spaces and scenarios designed are experienced from different viewpoints.

A concept that embodies the centrality of visitors' subjective interpretation and meaning-making is that of *interpretive ecology* (Mannion et al. 2016), referring to subjective meanings and interpretations that individual visitors construct as they interact with museum exhibits, spatial design and digital media; and how they navigate, in personal ways, the interactional spaces designed for them. These engagements are best described by what Barab and Roth (2006) call *life-worlds*, referring to the environment seen from the subjective viewpoint of an individual learner. From this perspective, any learning situation can be seen as a web centred on the learner and in a sense generating dynamically its own ecology. This view resonates with Jackson's definition of learning ecologies, which is contextualised and learner-centred: each learning situation creates its own ecology, which is focused on the learner (Jackson 2013, 2016). Similarly, Erstad and Sefton-Green (2013) consider that the concepts of 'digital competence' and 'digital *bildung*' in education should be analysed from a holistic viewpoint linking different learning settings and learning practices—in and out-of-school—and reconfiguring their interrelationships focusing on the learner. There is, moreover, something specific to museums as different from formal education environments: visits are one off, intense, but short experiences. Many visitors come only once, but even in the case of repeat visitors, each experience is unique, and the experiential line of continuity is drawn not by the museum, but by the visitors themselves. In these settings, it is, therefore, all the more important to pay attention to personal, interpretive contexts, analysed at the micro level.

16.5 Conclusion

There is always some form of exchange happening in natural world ecosystems: organisms exchange matter and energy with their environment (animate and inanimate), they acquire sensorial information (such as smell, temperature, sound) and respond or adapt to it. These exchanges are a form of communication which takes place constantly between living organisms and the environment. Socio-cultural ecosystems are no different. But there is a fundamental aspect which is only characteristic of humans and human societies. Human beings interpret subjectively the information received, they attribute significance and meaning to events and contexts with which they interact, and produce new information which can be shared, accumulated in time and accessed by current and future generations. In time, knowledge, norms and values are sedimented in communities and societies, giving rise to what we call cultural heritage, and its material and immaterial manifestations.

In this chapter, we drew attention to processes of meaning-making, interpretation, knowledge production and communication that are inherently human activities and also strongly represented in institutions and contexts that are concerned with cultural interpretation and learning, such as museums. We suggested that ecological frameworks, with their holistic approach and analytical focus on interrelatedness and connectivity, can shed light on how diverse actors in multiple ecologies of learning can connect, cooperate and eventually produce insights that can sustain a more effective design of museum learning experiences. Further, we showed how a communicative ecologies perspective (Hearn and Foth 2007) can enhance a holistic view of museum learning activities, seen in the context of interrelated processes of social interaction, discursive acts and technological mediation. A communicative ecology analysis enabled us to reveal and examine the connections between social, discursive and technological spheres and how they can inform the design of digital learning experiences within a museum digital learning centre. We suggest that future research can shed more light on a complementary direction, which shifts the perspective to the learners and reverts to their point of view to understand how they construct their learning pathways (Jackson 2013, 2016) and personal interpretations, which Mannion and colleagues (2016) refer to as 'interpretive ecologies'.

Acknowledgements This chapter draws upon research conducted in the frame of the RICHES project, which was funded under EU 7th Framework Programme for research, technological development and demonstration, grant agreement no. 612789.

References

Altheide DL (1994) An ecology of communication: toward a mapping of the effective environment. Sociol Q 35(4):665–683

Barab SA, Roth WM (2006) Curriculum-based ecosystems: supporting knowing from an ecological perspective. Educ Res 35(5):3–13

Barron B (2006) Interest and self-sustained learning as catalysts of development: a learning ecology perspective. Hum Dev 49:193–224

Bateson G (1973) Steps to an ecology of mind. Paladin, London

Bell G (2002) Making sense of museums: the museum as 'cultural ecology'. Intel Labs

Cannon-Brookes P (1992) The nature of museum collections. In: Thompson JMA (eds) Manual of curatorship. Butterworth-Heinemann, Boston, pp 500–512

Center for the Future of Museums (2014) Building the future of education: museums and the learning ecosystem. American Alliance of Museums, Washington DC

Charatzopoulou et al. (2016) Access, participation, learning: digital strategies for audience engagement with cultural heritage in museums and libraries. RICHES EU project deliverable D6.1., May 2016

Desvallées A, Mairesse F (eds) (2010) Key concepts of museology. Armand Colin

Erstad O, Sefton-Green J (2013) Digital disconnect? The digital learner and the school. In: Erstad O, Sefton-Green J (eds) Identity, community and learning lives in the digital age. Cambridge University Press, Cambridge, pp 87–104

European Parliament (2006) Recommendation 2006/962/EC of the European Parliament and of the Council of 18.12.2006 on key competences for lifelong learning. Official J L 394 of 30.12.2006

Falk JH, Dierking LD (2013) The museum experience revisited. Routledge

Finke P (2013) A brief outline of evolutionary cultural ecology. Tradit Syst Theory Major Figures Contemp Dev 11(2013):293

Gay G, Hembrooke H (2004) Activity-centered design: an ecological approach to designing smart tools and usable systems. MIT Press, Cambridge

Hearn G, Foth M (2007) Communicative ecologies: editorial preface. Electron J Commun 17(1–2)

Ito M, Baumer S, Bittanti M, Cody R, Stephenson BH, Horst HA, Perkel D (2009) Hanging out, messing around, and geeking out: kids living and learning with new media. MIT Press, Boston, MA

Jackson NJ (2016) Exploring learning ecologies. Chalk Mountain

Jackson NJ (2013) The concept of learning ecologies. Lifewide learning, education and personal development. ebook

Knowles MS (1981) The future of lifelong learning. In: Collins Z (ed) Museums. Adults and the Humanities, Washington DC, AAM, pp 131–143

Latham KF, Simmons JE (2014) Foundations of museum studies: evolving systems of knowledge: evolving systems of knowledge. ABC-CLIO

Lemke JL (1997) Cognition, context, and learning: a social semiotic perspective. Situated cognition: social, semiotic, and psychological perspectives, pp 37–56

Lugan JC (1993) La systémique sociale. Presses universitaires de France, Paris

Mannion S, Sabiescu A, Robinson W (2016) Innovate or stagnate: disrupting the conventional audio guide. In: Proceedings, MW2016: museums and the web 2016
Narci BA, O'Day V (1999) Information ecologies: using technology with heart. MIT Press, Cambridge
Roberts L (1997) From knowledge to narrative. educators and the changing museum. Smithsonian Institution Press, Washington
Sabiescu A, Charatzopoulou K (2015) Shaping a culture of lifelong learning for young audiences: a case study on the samsung digital discovery centre at the british museum. RICHES EU project deliverable
Samis P, Michaelson M (2017) The visitor-centred museum. Routledge, New York and London
Scott C, Dodd J, Sandell R (2015) Cultural value - user value of museums and galleries: a critical review of the literature. Arts and Humanities Research Council, Leicester, p 2015
Sharples M (2000) The design of personal mobile technologies for lifelong learning. Comput Educ 34(3):177–193
Slater D (2013) New media, development and globalisation. Making connections in the Global South. Polity Press, Cambridge
Steward JH (1972) Theory of culture change: the methodology of multilinear evolution. University of Illinois Press, Champaign
Tacchi J (2006) Studying communicative ecologies: an ethnographic approach to information and communication technologies. Paper presented at the 56th annual conference of the international communication association
Vermeeren AP, Calvi L, Sabiescu A, Trocchianesi R, Stuedahl D, Giaccardi E (2016) Involving the crowd in future museum experience design. In: Proceedings of the 2016 CHI conference extended abstracts on human factors in computing systems. ACM, New York, pp 3347–3354
Wakkary R, Evernden D (2005) Museum as ecology: a case study analysis of an ambient intelligent museum guide. Museums and web 2005: selected papers from an international conference, pp 151–164

Author Biographies

Amalia Sabiescu is a communication scientist with an interdisciplinary research track at the interface between information and communication technology (ICT), culture and development studies. Her research explores the integration, use and impact of ICT in cultural and creative practice, community contexts, and intersections with issues of citizen voice, participation, and social inclusion. She is affiliated with the Institute for Media and Creative Industries at Loughborough University London.

Katerina Charatzopoulou holds a postgraduate degree in Classical archaeology and an MA in Information and Documentation Science from the University of Paris Ouest. She has extensive experience in digital heritage projects ranging from collections documentation and interpretation to the design and evaluation of multimedia resources for research and education. She works currently as an independent researcher based in Berlin.